D0779536

Staunton Public Library
1 Churchville Avenue
Staunton, VA 24401

Beauty is the Beast ™

Shojo Beat

4

Story & Art by Tomo Matsumoto

Table of Contents

Chapter 18 4

Chapter 19 37

Chapter 20 71

Chapter 21 101

Chapter 22 129

Chapter 23 159

Bonus 190

Glossary 191

BEAUTY IS THE BEAST

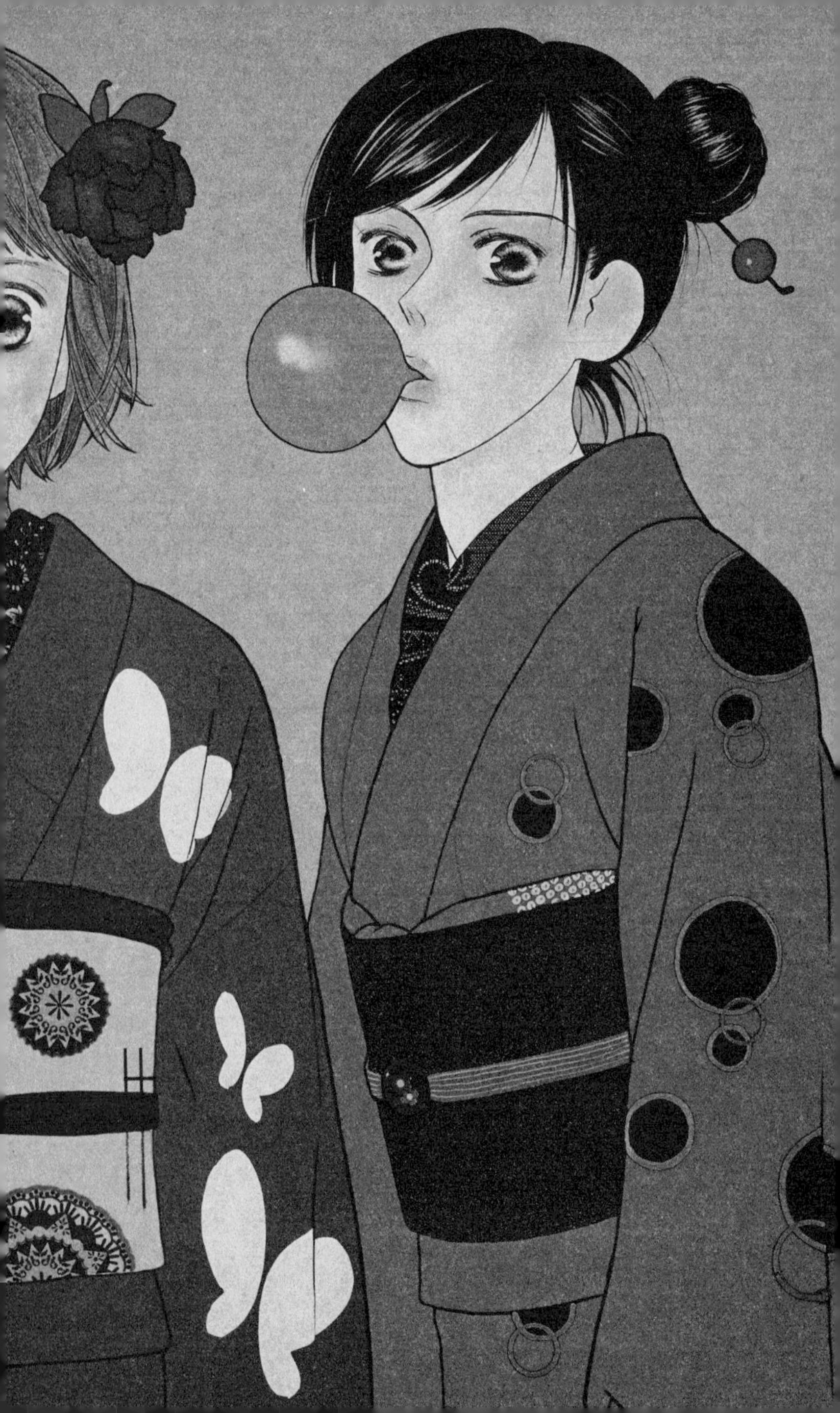

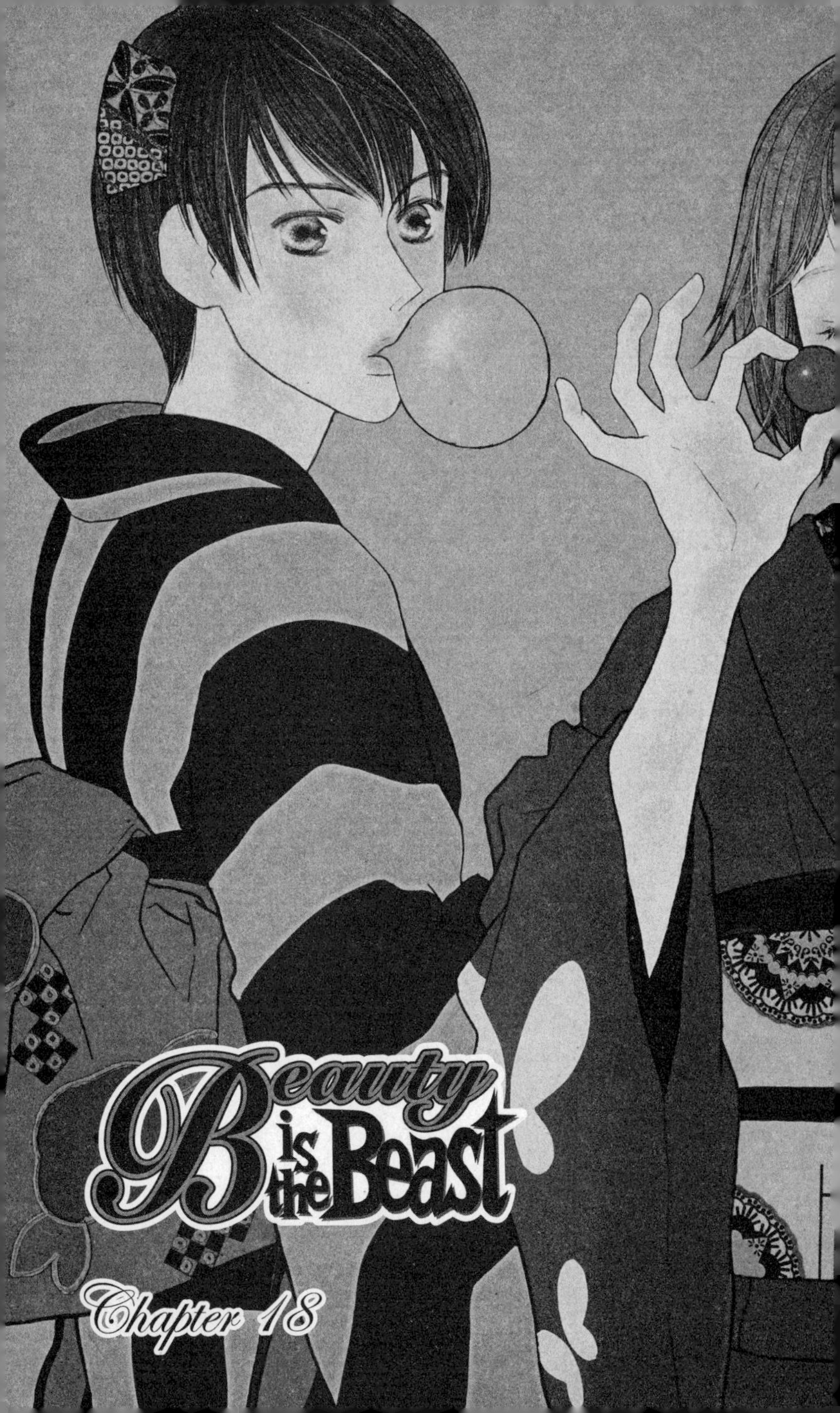
Beauty is the Beast
Chapter 18

HOUYU
GIGA

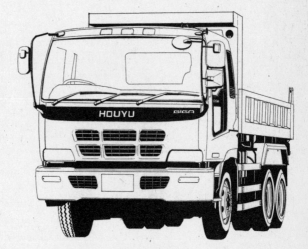

BEAUTY IS THE BEAST

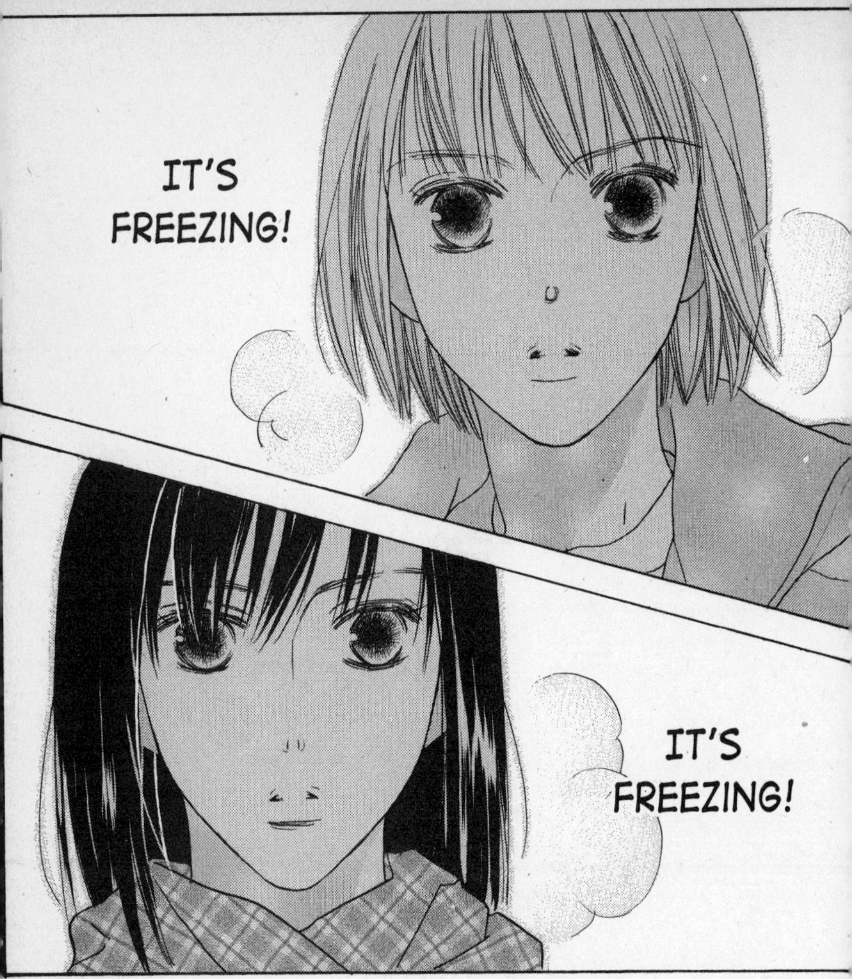
IT'S FREEZING!
IT'S FREEZING!

Hokkaido Stew

Hello. I'm Tomo Matsumoto.
How's everyone doing?
When I wrote that I always have a hard time deciding what to write in these spaces, everyone reacted with, "Well, anything is all right!" (☺)
There might be times when you feel like, "I don't understand what she's talking about." And I'm sorry, but I'll do what I want to do.
So I'll be happy if you'll come with me.
Okay, here we go.

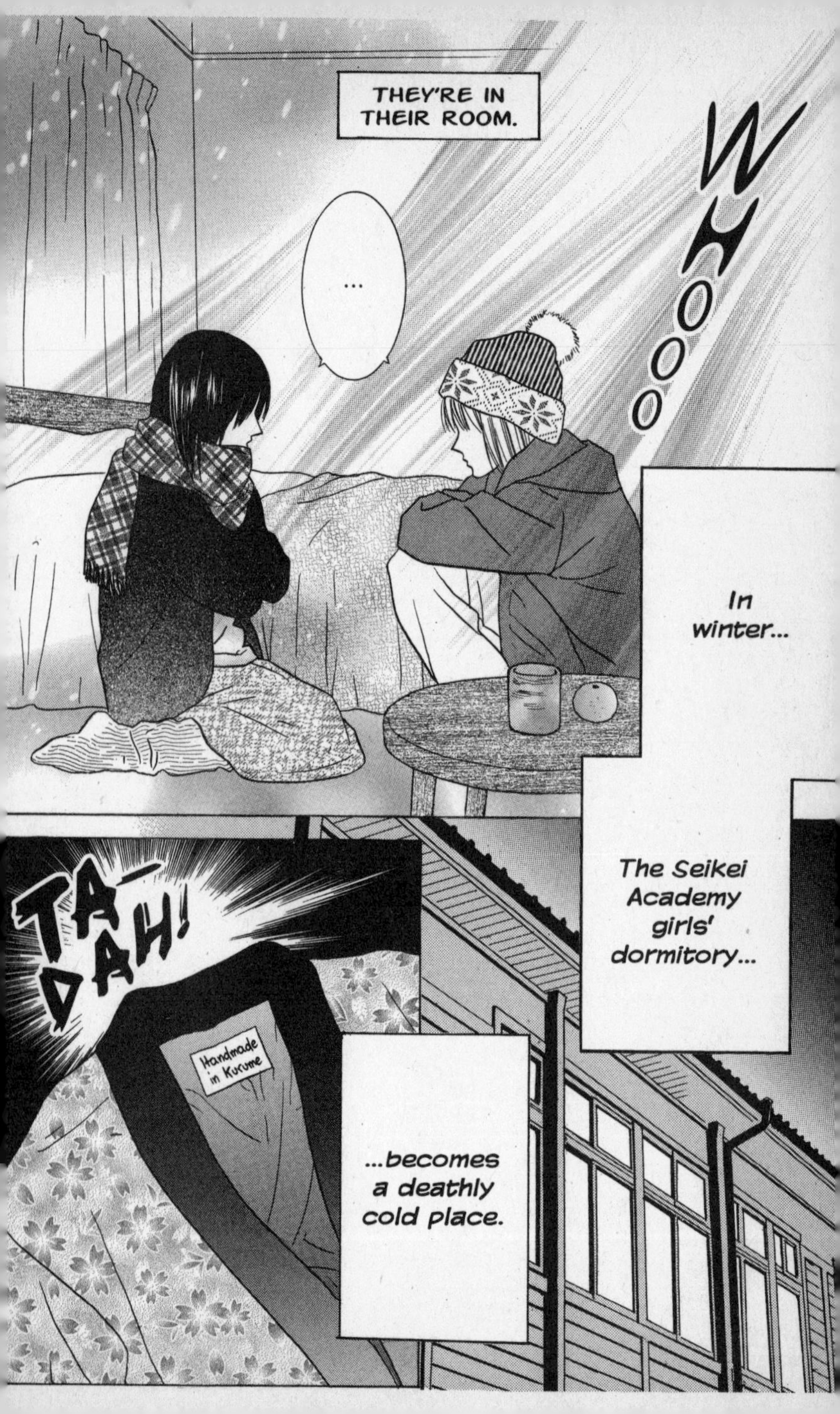

WHOOOOO
THEY'RE IN THEIR ROOM.
...
In winter...
The Seikei Academy girls' dormitory...
...becomes a deathly cold place.
TA-DAH!
Handmade in Kurume

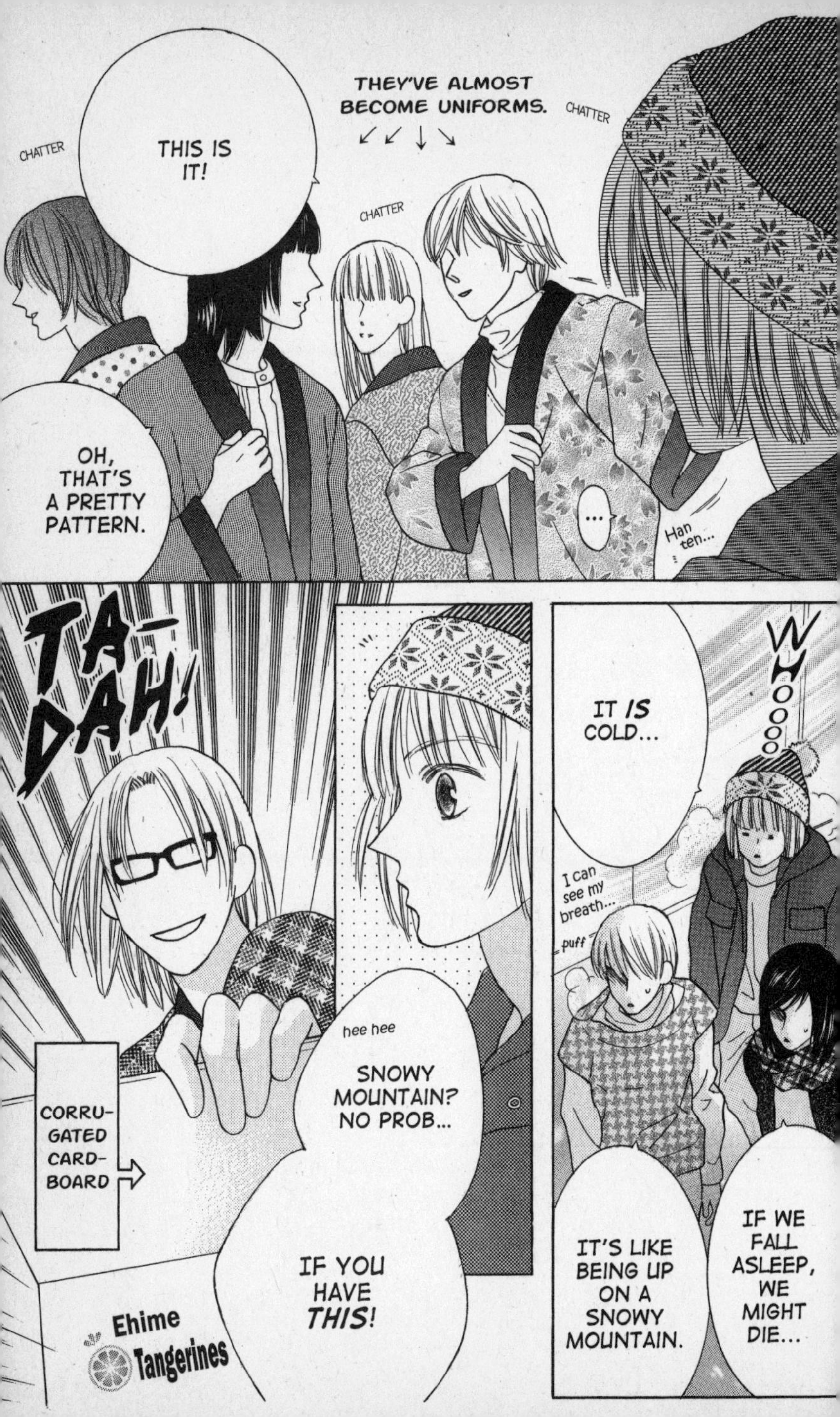
CHATTER
THEY'VE ALMOST BECOME UNIFORMS.
CHATTER
THIS IS IT!
CHATTER
Han ten...
...
OH, THAT'S A PRETTY PATTERN.
WHOOOO
IT *IS* COLD...
I can see my breath...
puff
IF WE FALL ASLEEP, WE MIGHT DIE...
IT'S LIKE BEING UP ON A SNOWY MOUNTAIN.
hee hee
SNOWY MOUNTAIN? NO PROB...
TA-DAH!
IF YOU HAVE *THIS*!
CORRUGATED CARDBOARD
Ehime Tangerines

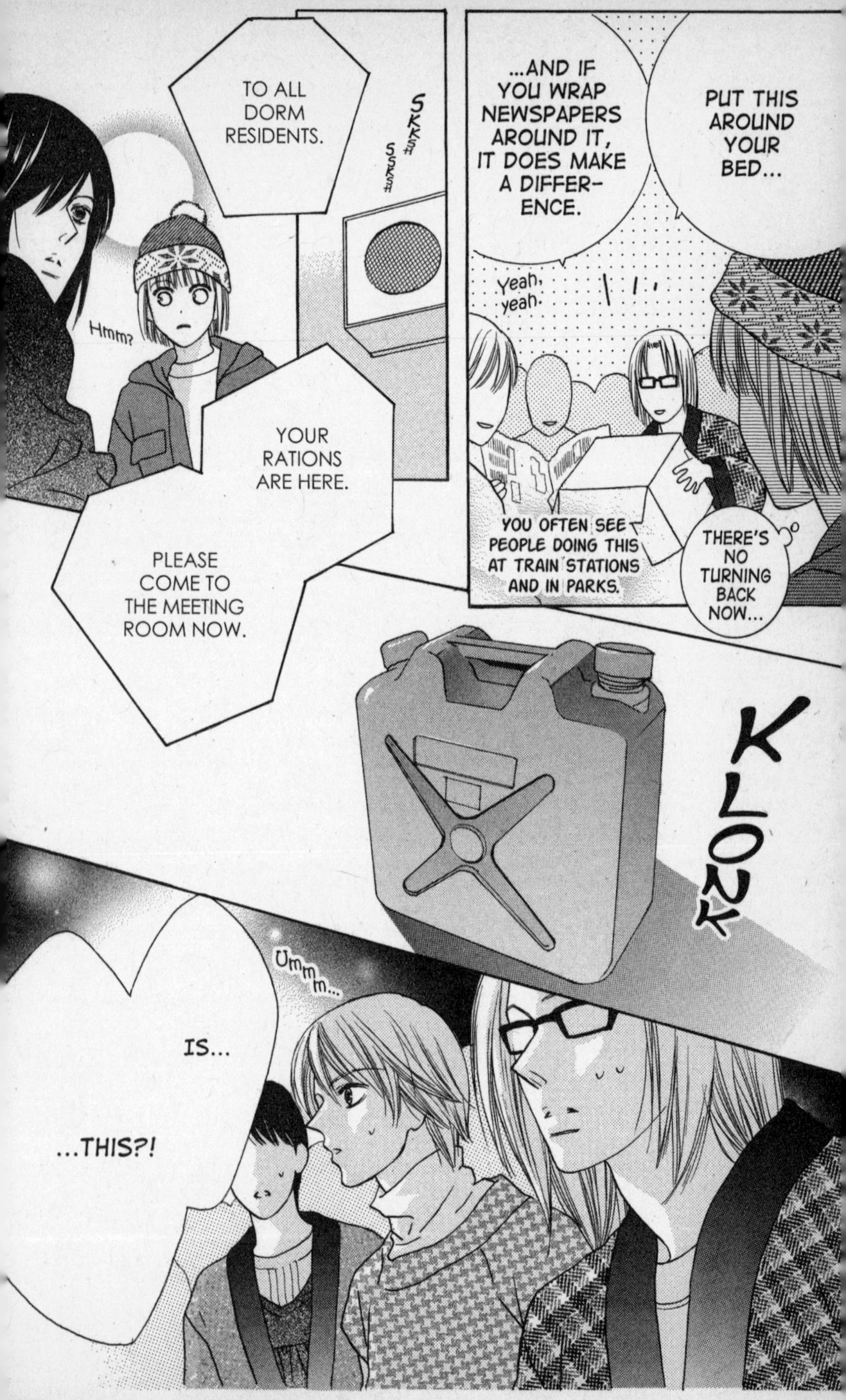

PUT THIS AROUND YOUR BED...
...AND IF YOU WRAP NEWSPAPERS AROUND IT, IT DOES MAKE A DIFFER-ENCE.
Yeah, yeah.
YOU OFTEN SEE PEOPLE DOING THIS AT TRAIN STATIONS AND IN PARKS.
THERE'S NO TURNING BACK NOW...
TO ALL DORM RESIDENTS.
SKKSH SSKSH
Hmm?
YOUR RATIONS ARE HERE.
PLEASE COME TO THE MEETING ROOM NOW.
KLONK
Ummm...
IS...
...THIS?!

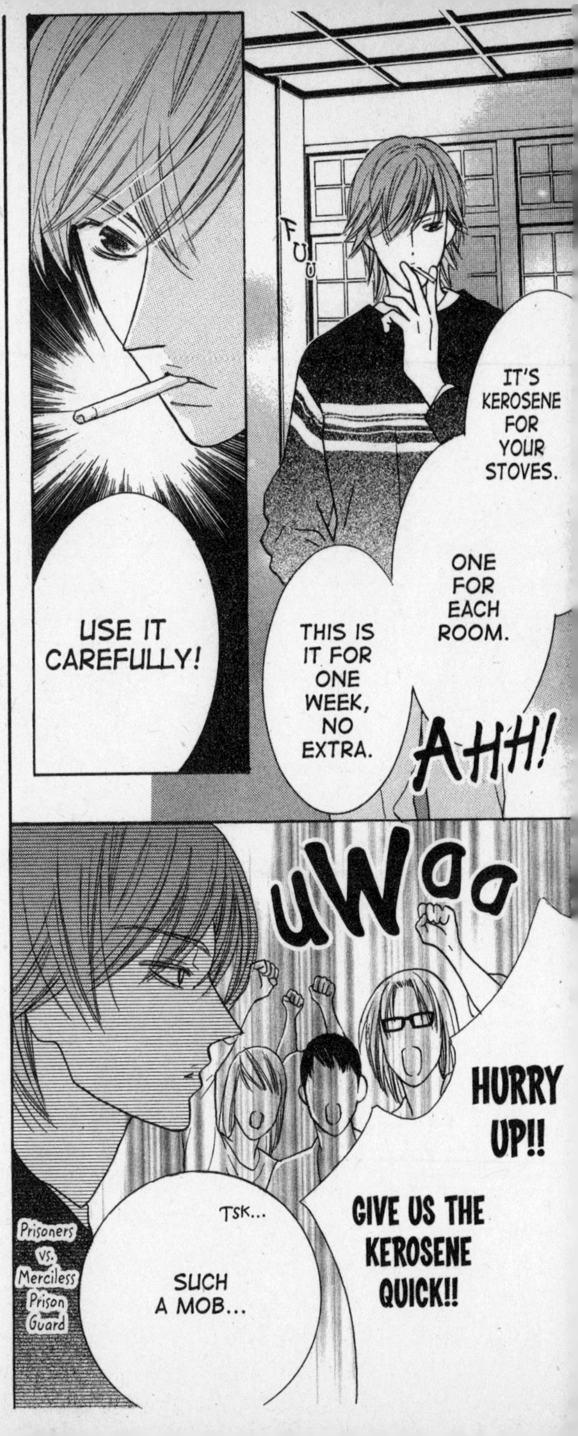
FUU
IT'S KEROSENE FOR YOUR STOVES.
ONE FOR EACH ROOM.
THIS IS IT FOR ONE WEEK, NO EXTRA.
AHH!
USE IT CAREFULLY!
uWaa
HURRY UP!!
GIVE US THE KEROSENE QUICK!!
TSK...
SUCH A MOB...
Prisoners vs. Merciless Prison Guard

1

About Deathly Cold Places

The dorm I lived in was like this. I was surprised! In the pamphlet it said "air conditioning and heating provided" but it wasn't. Everyone complained that they were duped. (☺) But in the winter, kerosene stoves were distributed to each room, so we cooked sweet potatoes like Eimi and company, and made ramen. (Sounds like the Showa era, when it was Heisei...) In the summer, we simply took off our clothes. Electric fans were prohibited, so the dorm was full of nudists. (What the hell?)

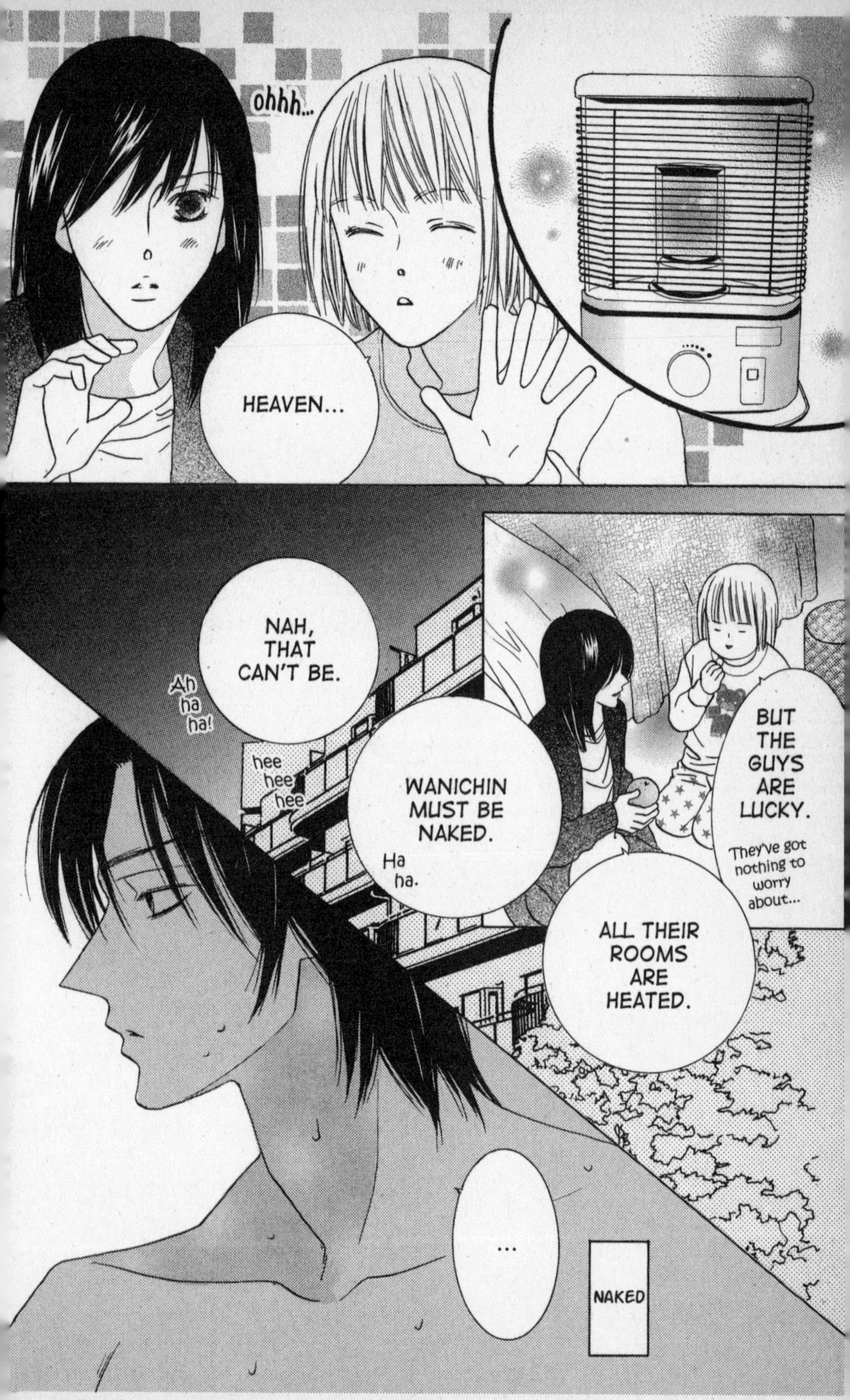

ohhh...
HEAVEN...
BUT THE GUYS ARE LUCKY.
They've got nothing to worry about...
ALL THEIR ROOMS ARE HEATED.
WANICHIN MUST BE NAKED.
Ha ha.
hee hee hee
NAH, THAT CAN'T BE.
Ah ha ha!
...
NAKED

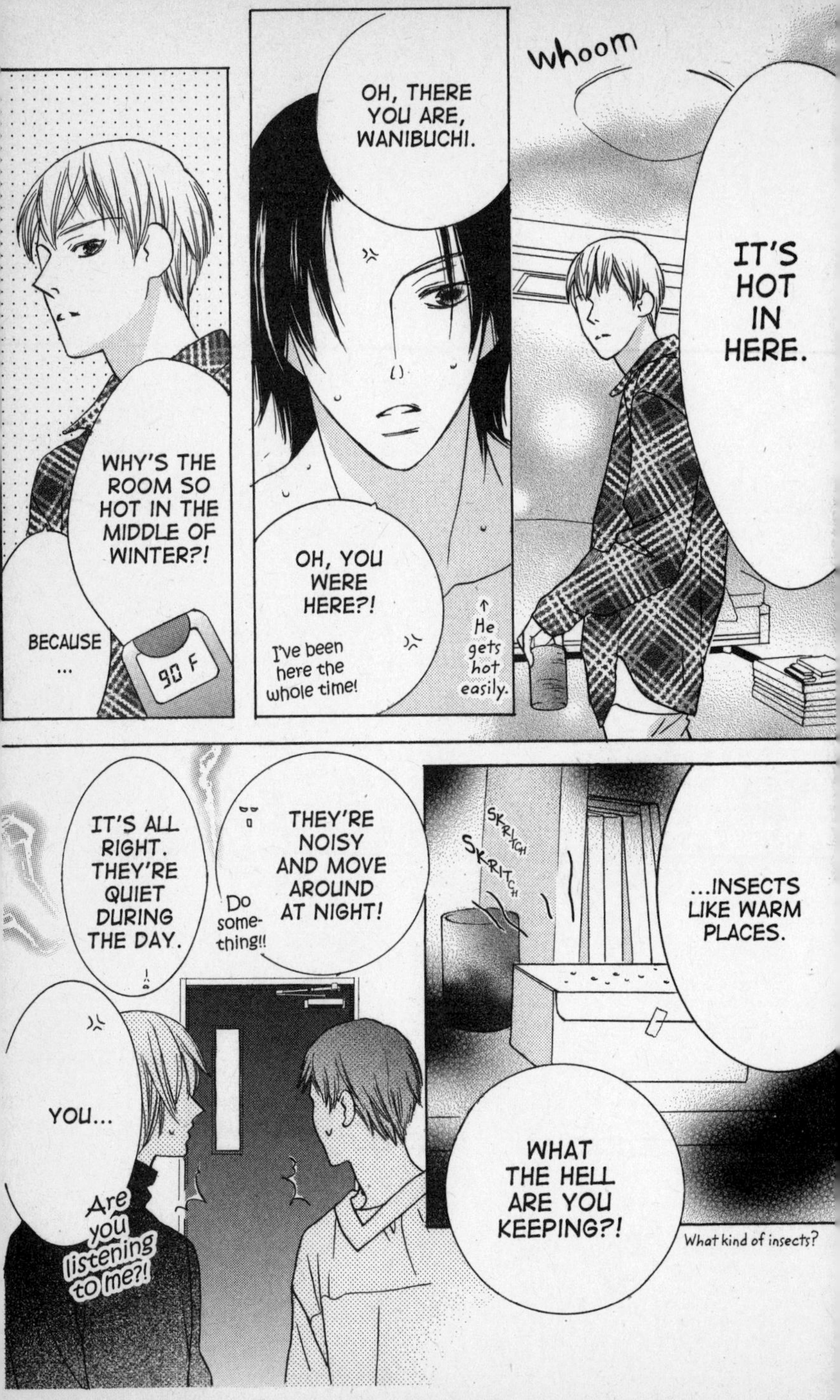
whoom
IT'S HOT IN HERE.
OH, THERE YOU ARE, WANIBUCHI.
OH, YOU WERE HERE?!
I've been here the whole time!
↑ He gets hot easily.
WHY'S THE ROOM SO HOT IN THE MIDDLE OF WINTER?!
BECAUSE ...
90 F
...INSECTS LIKE WARM PLACES.
SKRITCH
SKRITCH
WHAT THE HELL ARE YOU KEEPING?!
What kind of insects?
THEY'RE NOISY AND MOVE AROUND AT NIGHT!
Do some-thing!!
IT'S ALL RIGHT. THEY'RE QUIET DURING THE DAY.
YOU...
Are you listening to me?!

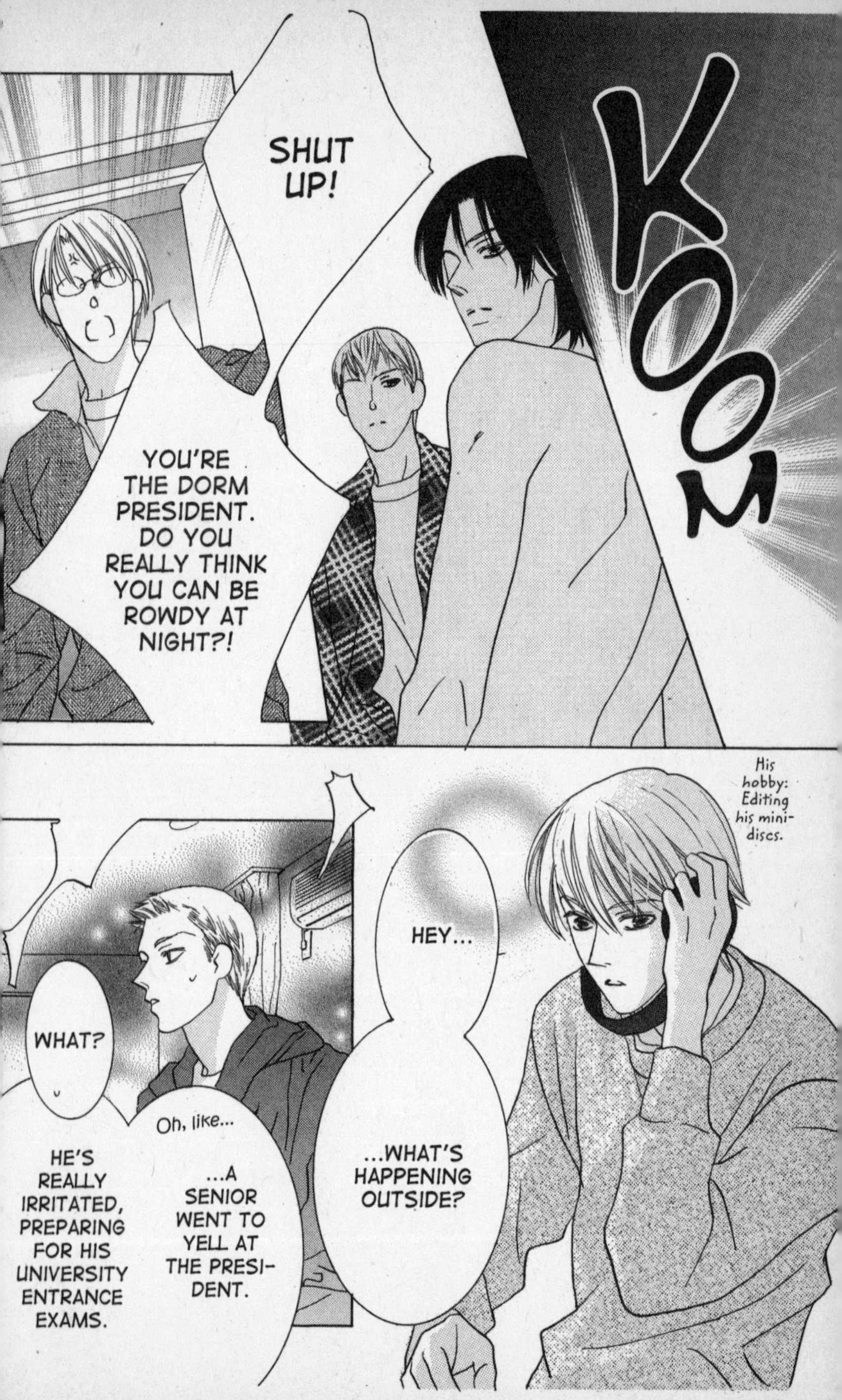
KOOM
SHUT UP!
YOU'RE THE DORM PRESIDENT. DO YOU REALLY THINK YOU CAN BE ROWDY AT NIGHT?!
His hobby: Editing his mini-discs.
HEY...
...WHAT'S HAPPENING OUTSIDE?
WHAT?
Oh, like...
...A SENIOR WENT TO YELL AT THE PRESI-DENT.
HE'S REALLY IRRITATED, PREPARING FOR HIS UNIVERSITY ENTRANCE EXAMS.

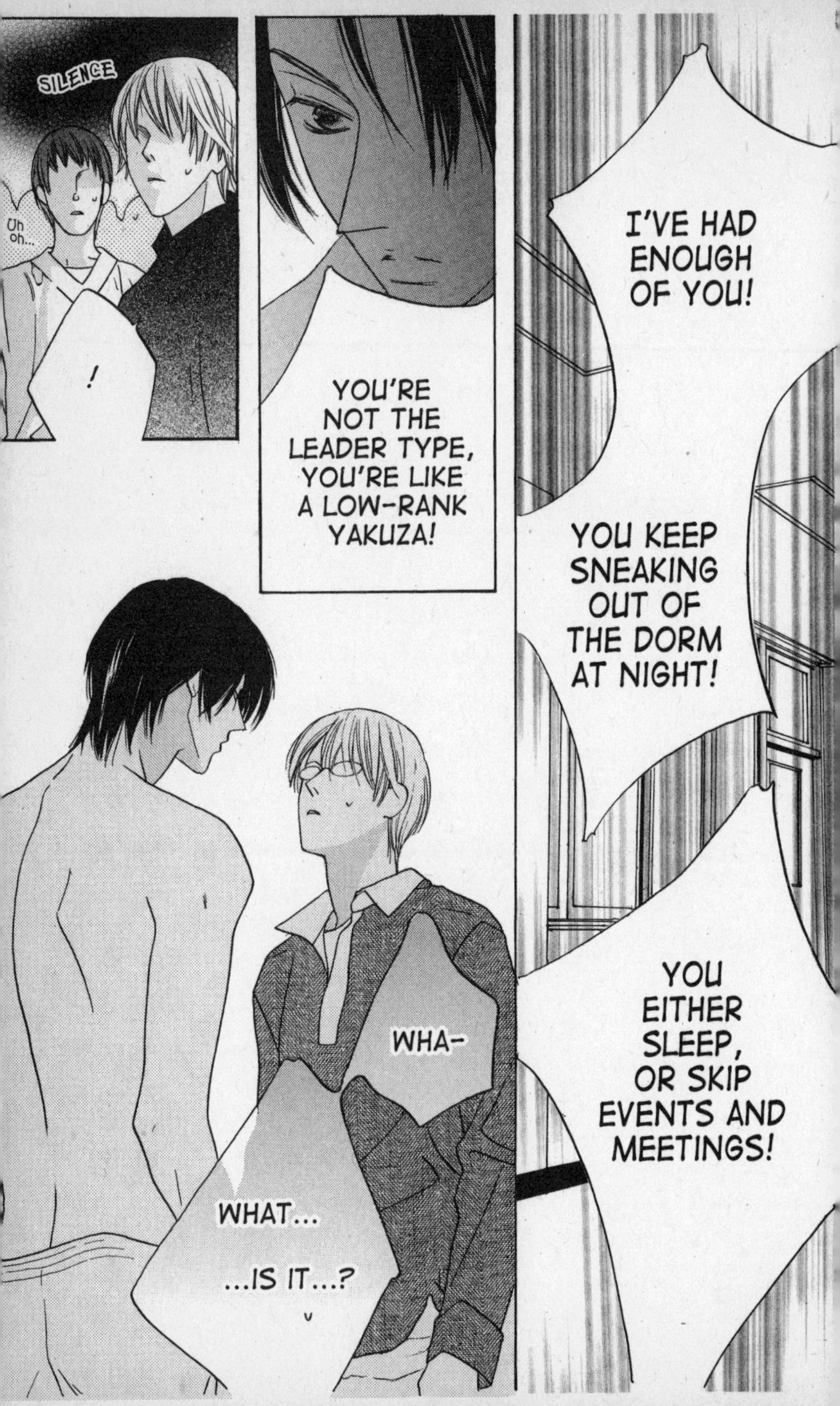
I'VE HAD ENOUGH OF YOU!
YOU KEEP SNEAKING OUT OF THE DORM AT NIGHT!
YOU EITHER SLEEP, OR SKIP EVENTS AND MEETINGS!
YOU'RE NOT THE LEADER TYPE, YOU'RE LIKE A LOW-RANK YAKUZA!
SILENCE
Uh oh...
!
WHA-
WHAT...
...IS IT...?

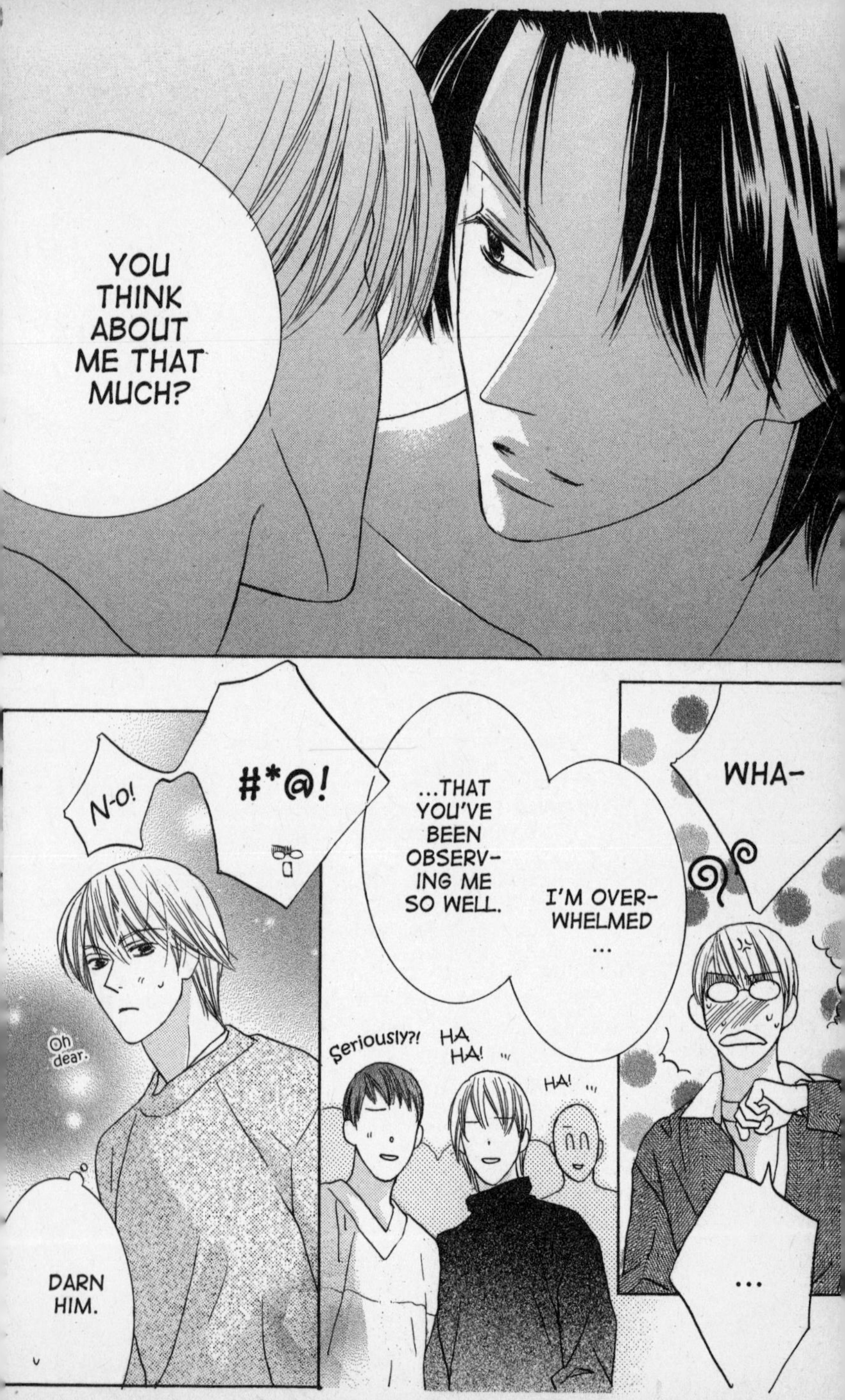
YOU THINK ABOUT ME THAT MUCH?
WHA-
...
I'M OVER-WHELMED ...
...THAT YOU'VE BEEN OBSERV-ING ME SO WELL.
HA!
HA HA!
Seriously?!
#*@!
N-O!
Oh dear.
DARN HIM.

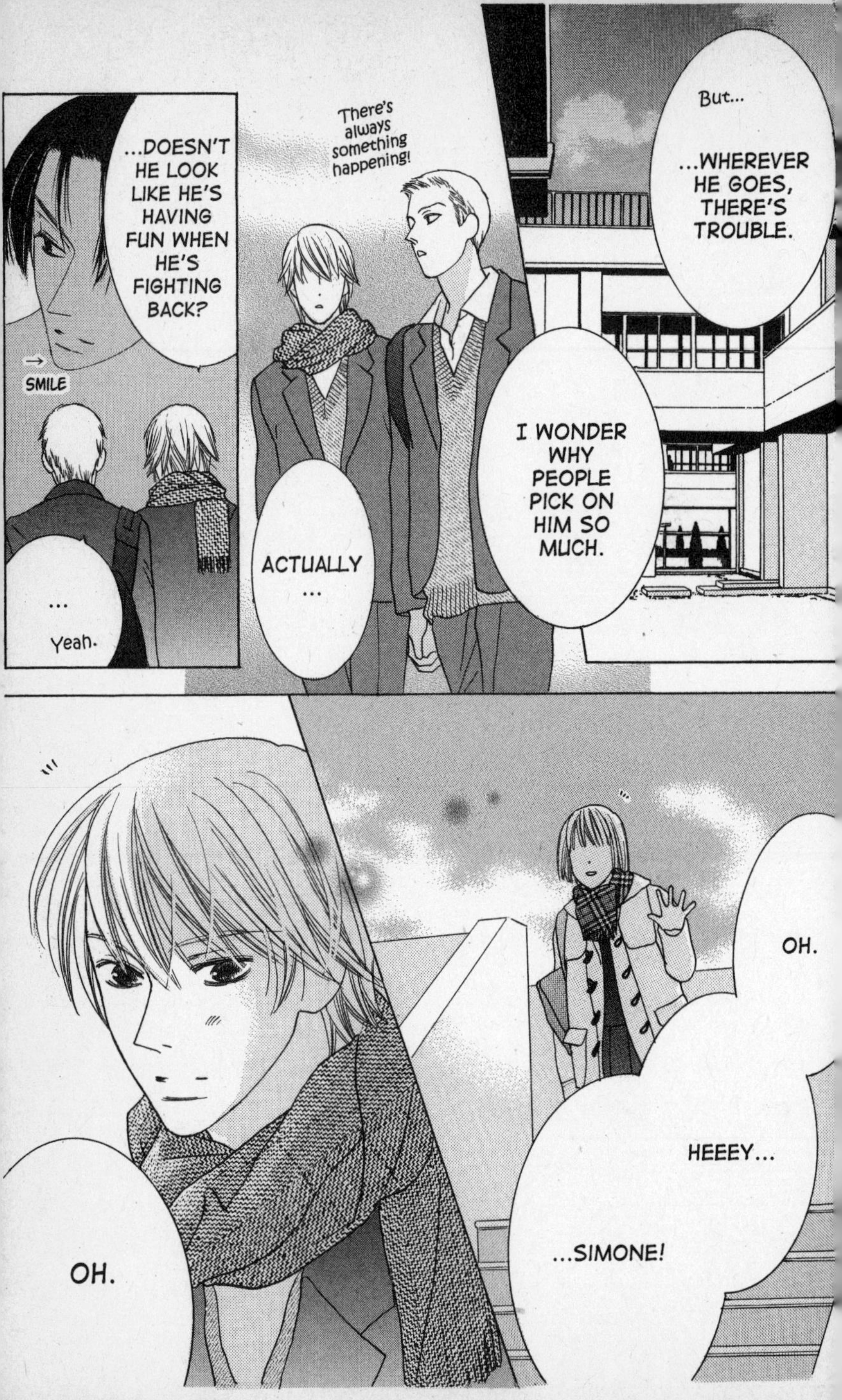
But...
...WHEREVER HE GOES, THERE'S TROUBLE.
I WONDER WHY PEOPLE PICK ON HIM SO MUCH.
There's always something happening!
ACTUALLY ...
...DOESN'T HE LOOK LIKE HE'S HAVING FUN WHEN HE'S FIGHTING BACK?
→ SMILE
... Yeah.
OH.
HEEEY...
...SIMONE!
OH.

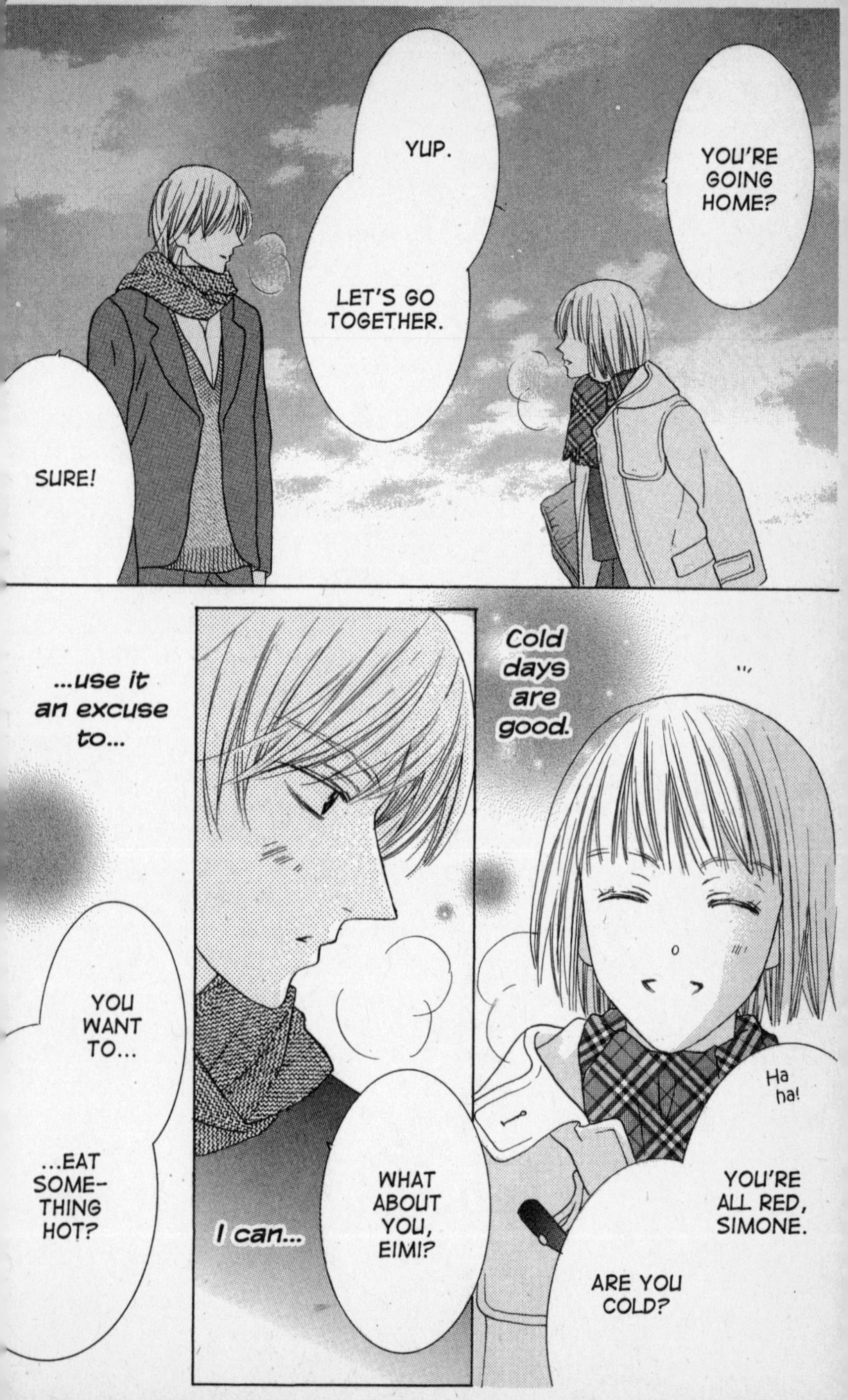
YOU'RE GOING HOME?
YUP.
LET'S GO TOGETHER.
SURE!
Ha ha!
YOU'RE ALL RED, SIMONE.
ARE YOU COLD?
Cold days are good.
WHAT ABOUT YOU, EIMI?
I can...
...use it an excuse to...
YOU WANT TO...
...EAT SOMETHING HOT?

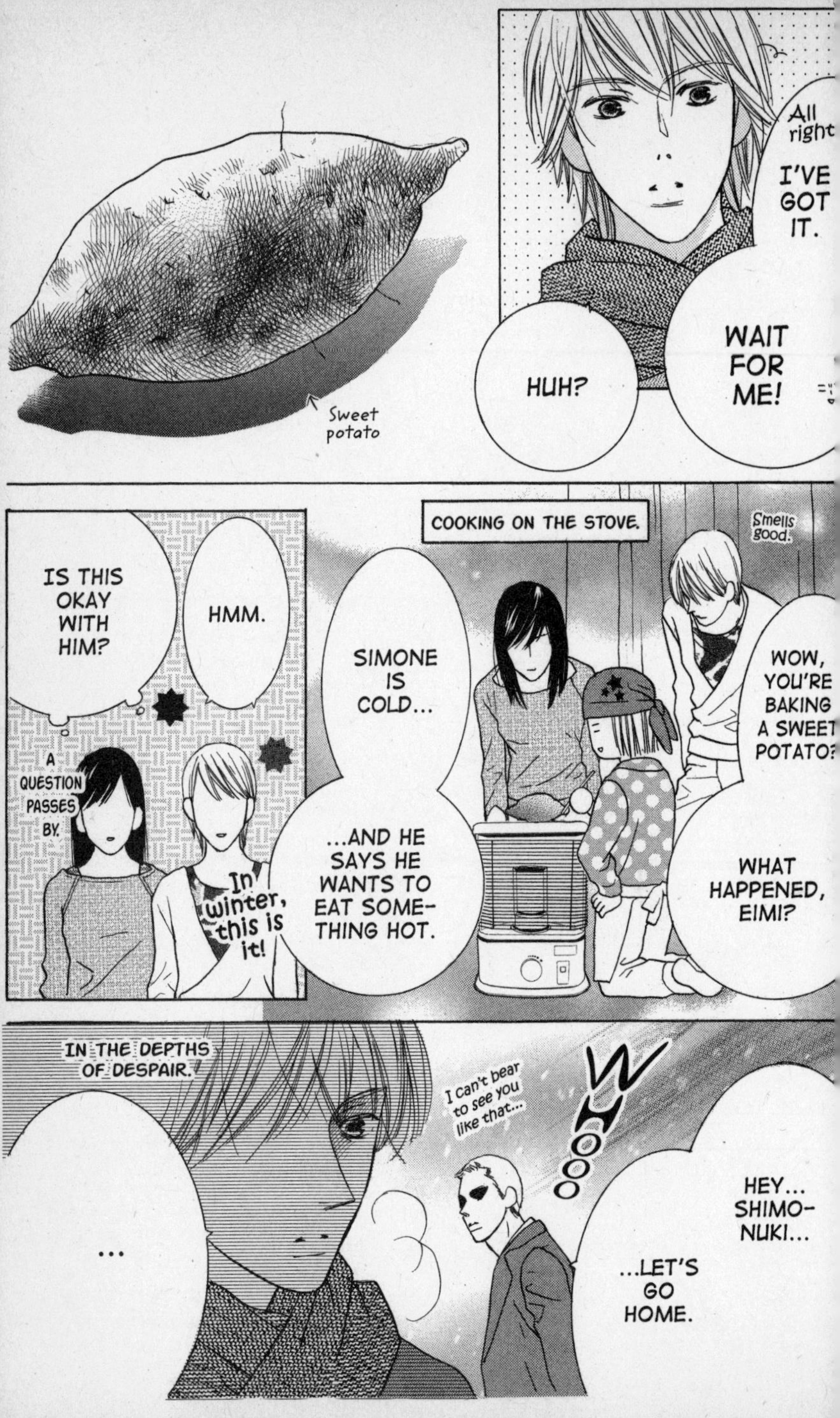
All right
I'VE GOT IT.
WAIT FOR ME!
HUH?
Sweet potato
COOKING ON THE STOVE.
Smells good.
WOW, YOU'RE BAKING A SWEET POTATO?
WHAT HAPPENED, EIMI?
SIMONE IS COLD...
...AND HE SAYS HE WANTS TO EAT SOME-THING HOT.
HMM.
IS THIS OKAY WITH HIM?
A QUESTION PASSES BY.
In winter, this is it!
HEY... SHIMO-NUKI...
...LET'S GO HOME.
WHOOOO
I can't bear to see you like that...
IN THE DEPTHS OF DESPAIR.
...

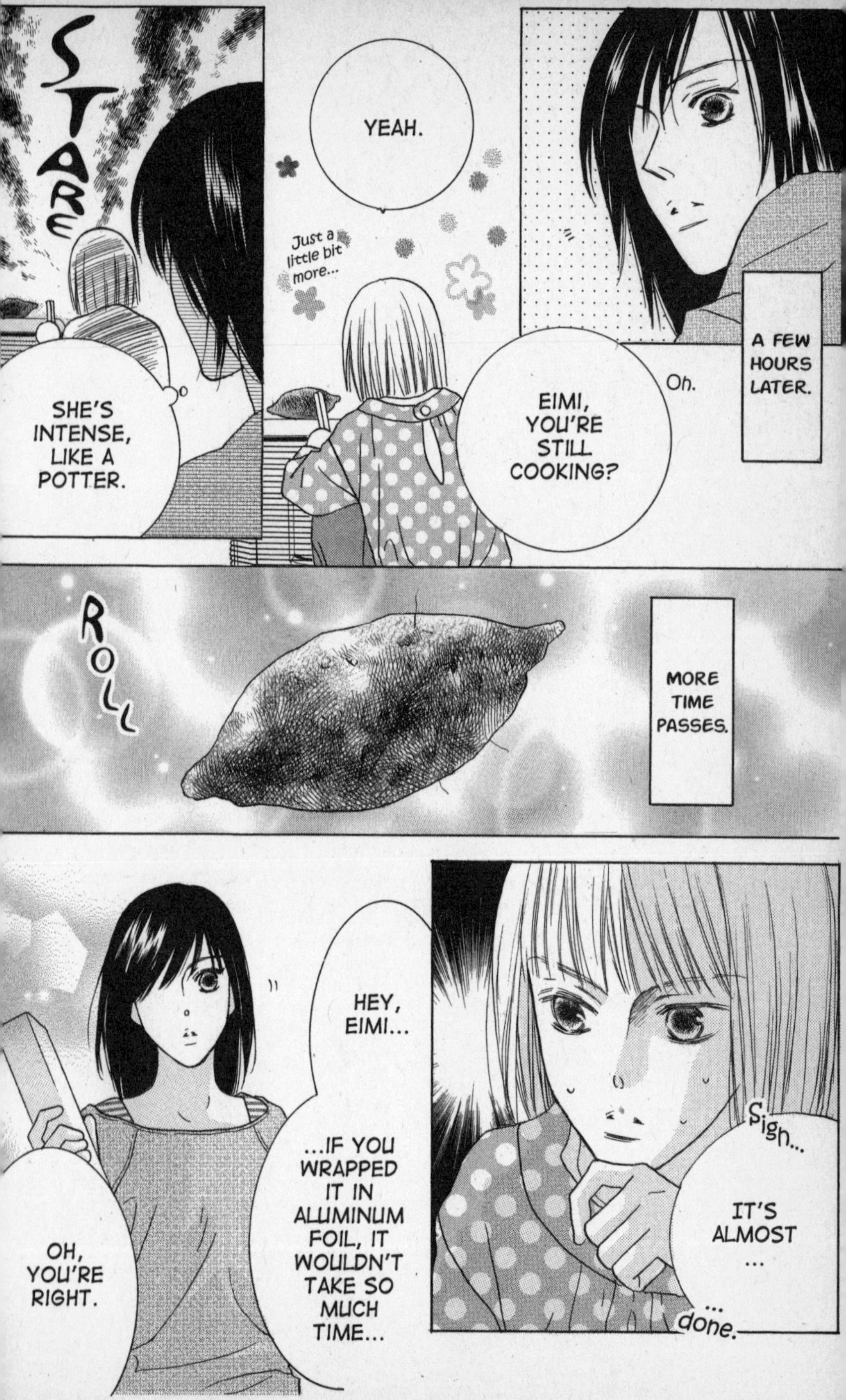
A FEW HOURS LATER.
Oh.
EIMI, YOU'RE STILL COOKING?
YEAH.
Just a little bit more...
STARE
SHE'S INTENSE, LIKE A POTTER.
MORE TIME PASSES.
ROLL
Sigh...
IT'S ALMOST ...
... done.
HEY, EIMI...
...IF YOU WRAPPED IT IN ALUMINUM FOIL, IT WOULDN'T TAKE SO MUCH TIME...
OH, YOU'RE RIGHT.

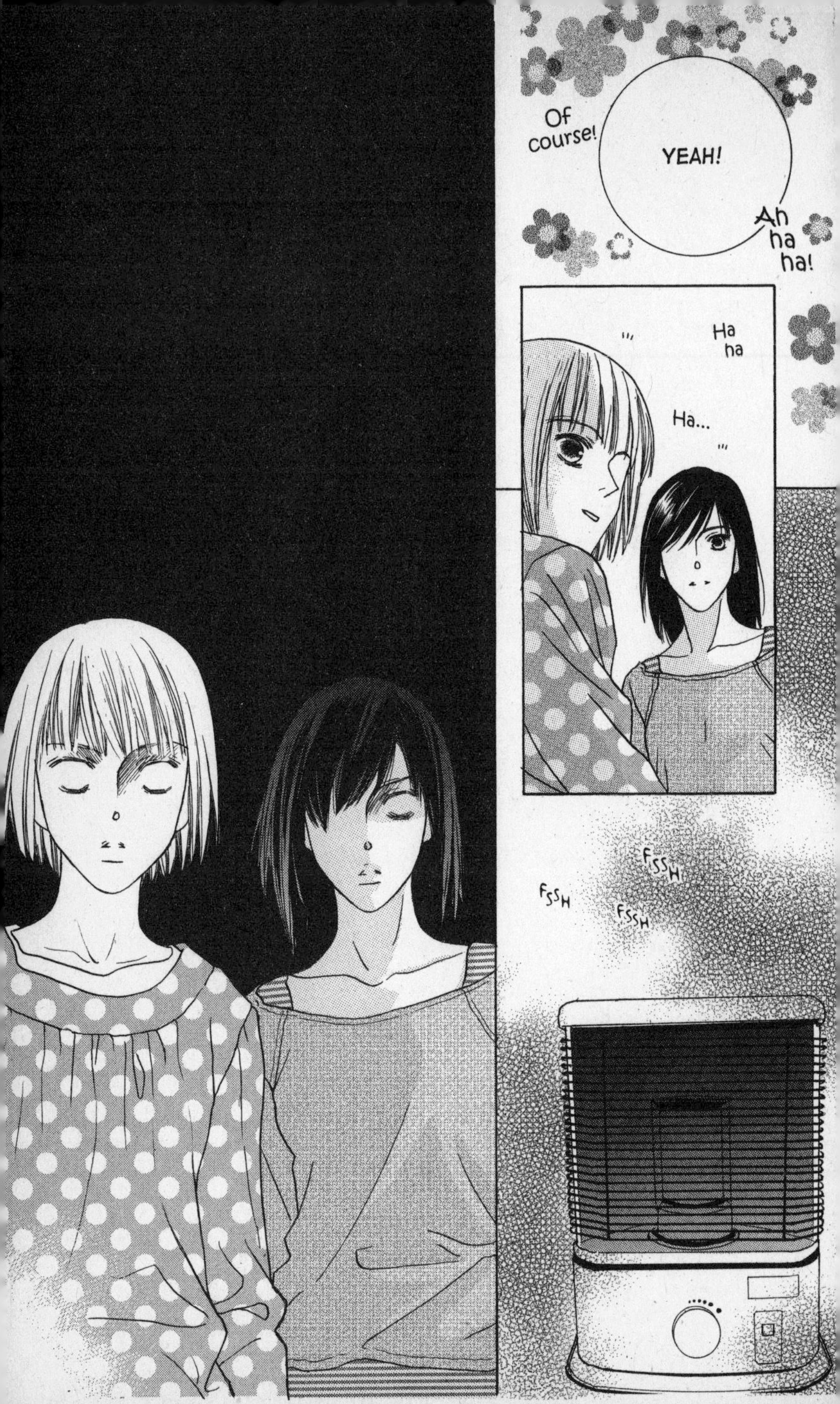
YEAH!
Of course!
Ah ha ha!
Ha ha
Ha...
FSSH
FSSH
FSSH

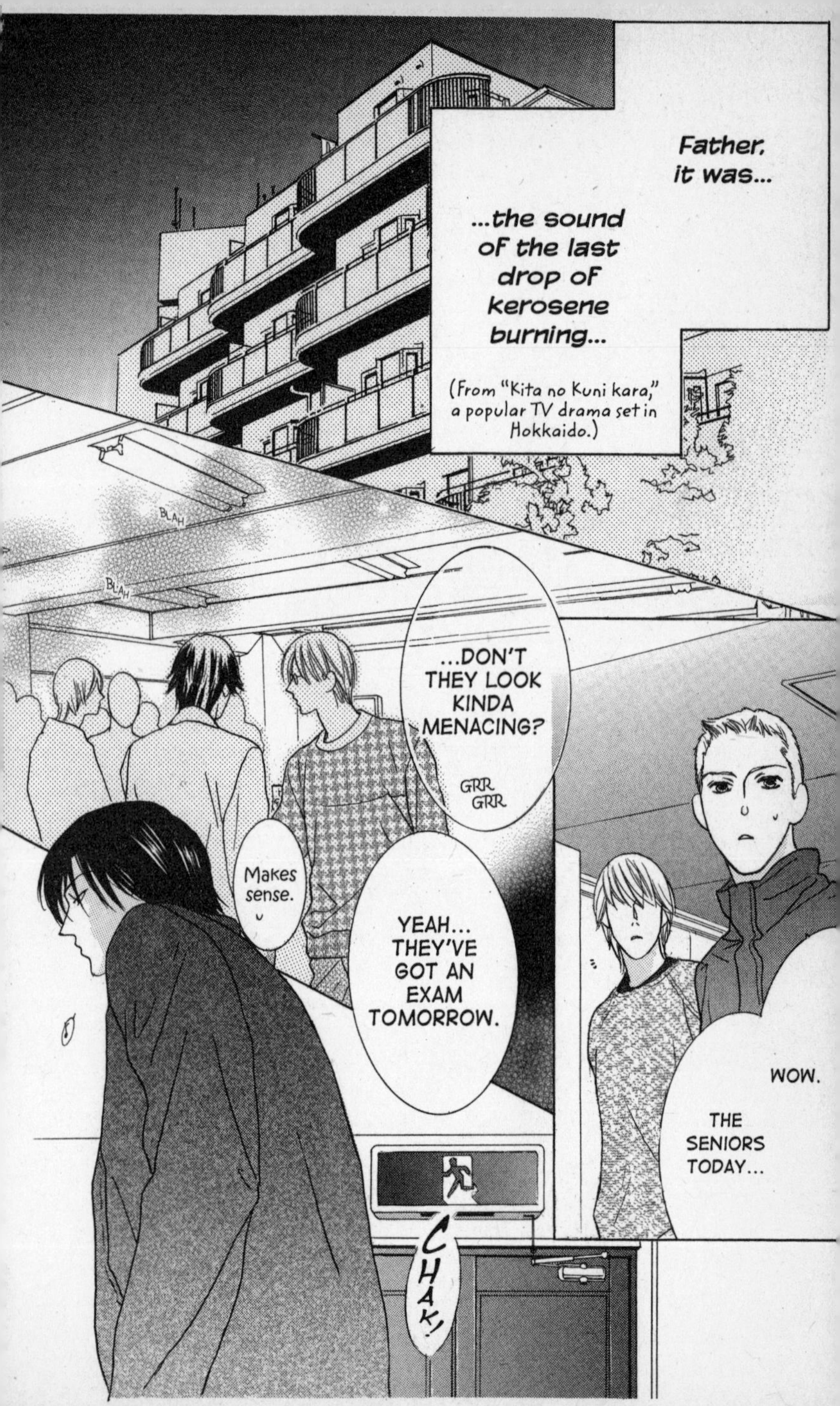
Father, it was...
...the sound of the last drop of kerosene burning...
(From "Kita no Kuni kara," a popular TV drama set in Hokkaido.)
BLAH
BLAH
WOW.
THE SENIORS TODAY...
...DON'T THEY LOOK KINDA MENACING?
GRR GRR
YEAH... THEY'VE GOT AN EXAM TOMORROW.
Makes sense.
CHAK!

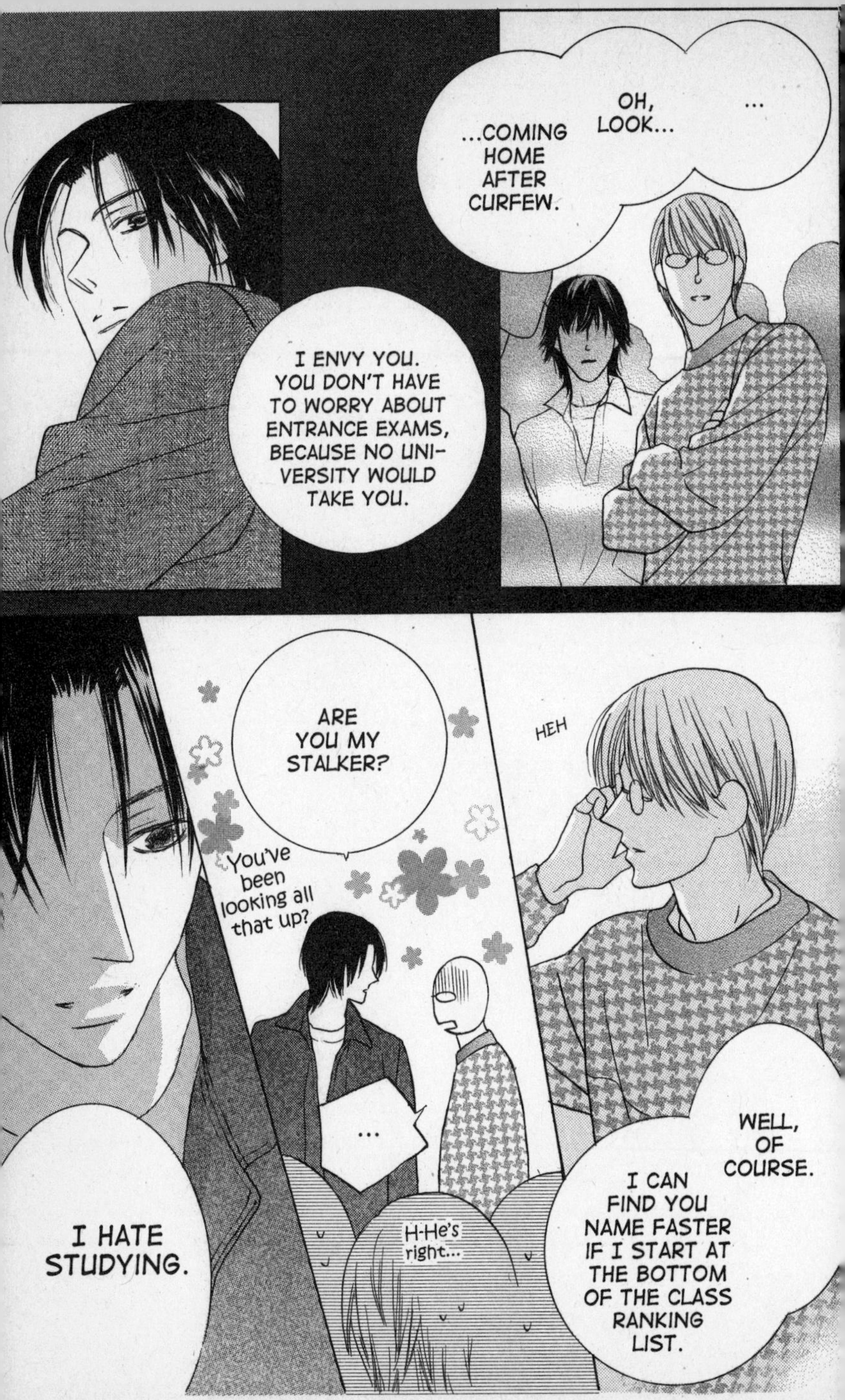
...
OH, LOOK...
...COMING HOME AFTER CURFEW.
I ENVY YOU. YOU DON'T HAVE TO WORRY ABOUT ENTRANCE EXAMS, BECAUSE NO UNI-VERSITY WOULD TAKE YOU.
HEH
WELL, OF COURSE.
I CAN FIND YOU NAME FASTER IF I START AT THE BOTTOM OF THE CLASS RANKING LIST.
ARE YOU MY STALKER?
You've been looking all that up?
...
H-He's right...
I HATE STUDYING.

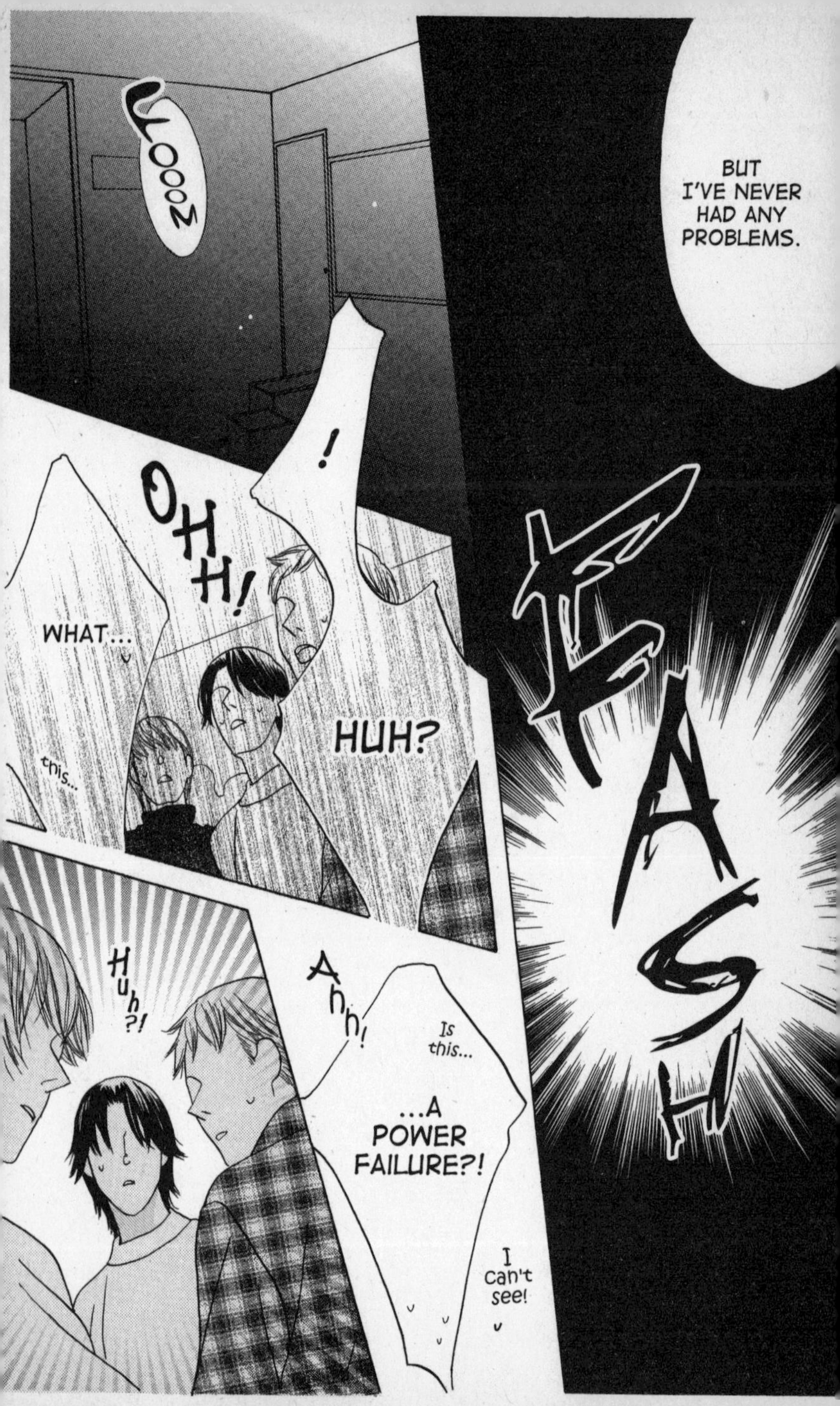
BUT I'VE NEVER HAD ANY PROBLEMS.
FLASH
LOOOM
!
OHH!
HUH?
WHAT...
this...
Ahh!
Is this...
...A POWER FAILURE?!
I can't see!
Huh?!

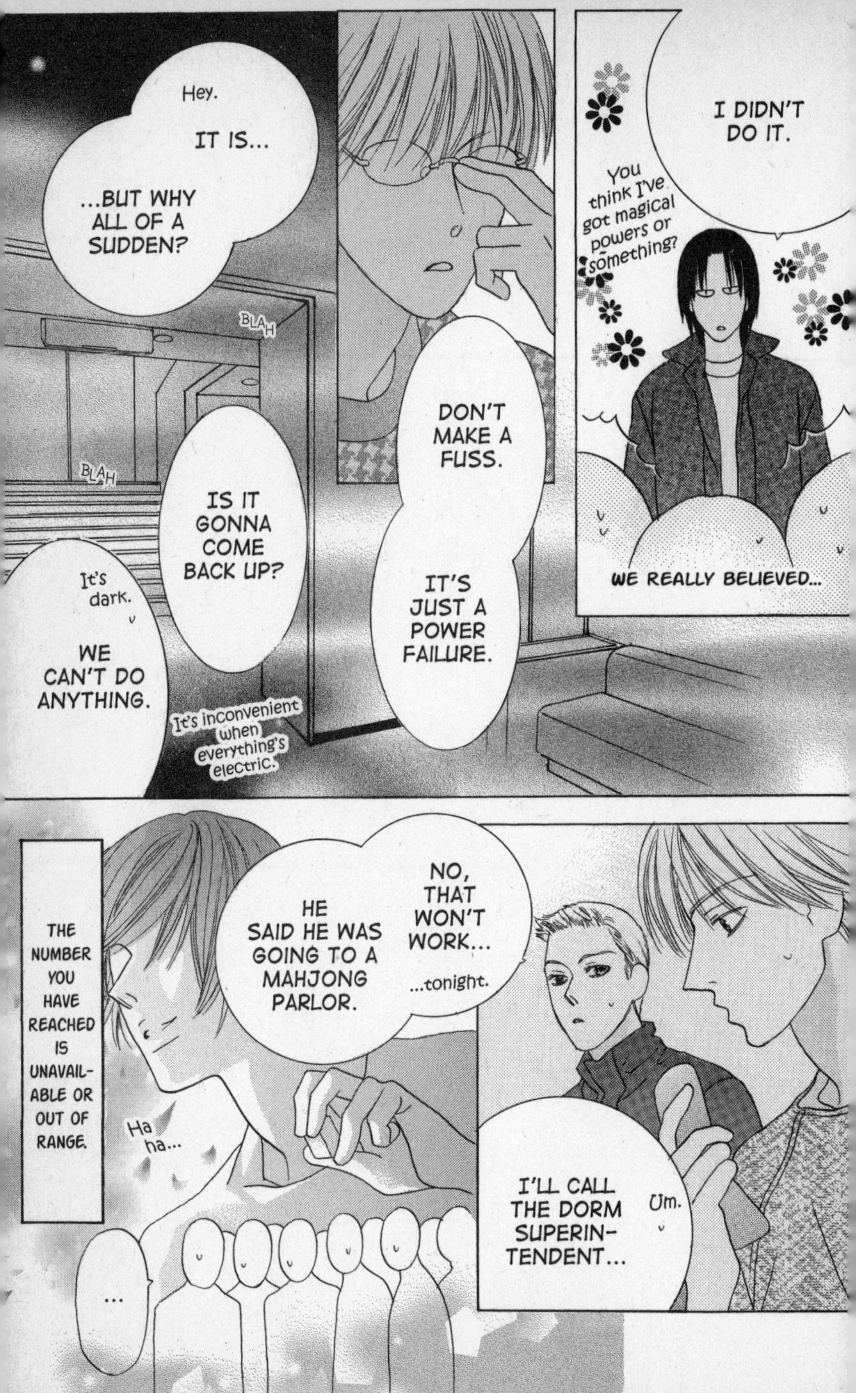
I DIDN'T DO IT.
You think I've got magical powers or something?
WE REALLY BELIEVED...
DON'T MAKE A FUSS.
IT'S JUST A POWER FAILURE.
Hey.
IT IS...
...BUT WHY ALL OF A SUDDEN?
BLAH
BLAH
IS IT GONNA COME BACK UP?
It's dark.
WE CAN'T DO ANYTHING.
It's inconvenient when everything's electric.
I'LL CALL THE DORM SUPERIN-TENDENT...
Um.
NO, THAT WON'T WORK...
...tonight.
HE SAID HE WAS GOING TO A MAHJONG PARLOR.
THE NUMBER YOU HAVE REACHED IS UNAVAIL-ABLE OR OUT OF RANGE.
Ha ha...
...

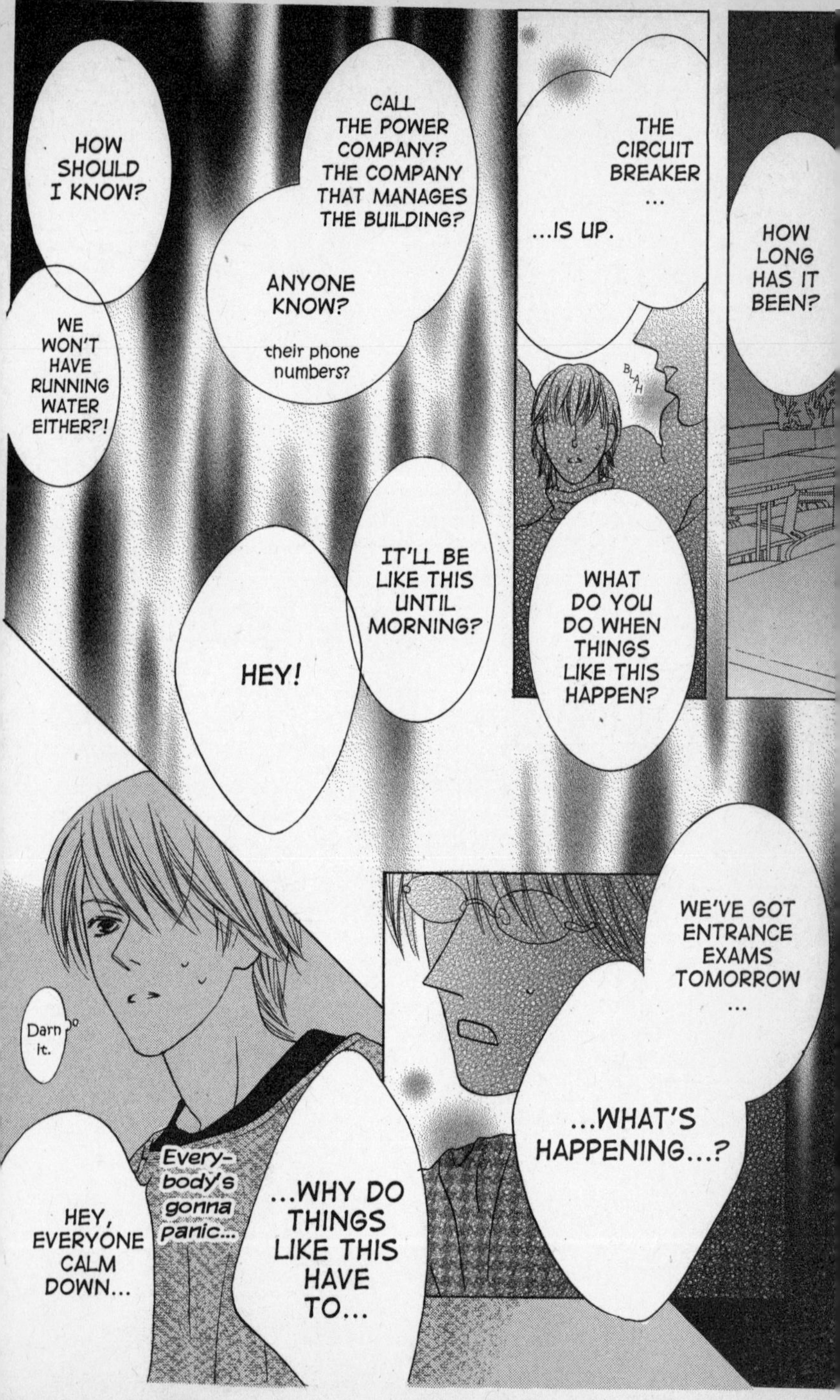
HOW LONG HAS IT BEEN?
THE CIRCUIT BREAKER ...
...IS UP.
BLAH
WHAT DO YOU DO WHEN THINGS LIKE THIS HAPPEN?
CALL THE POWER COMPANY? THE COMPANY THAT MANAGES THE BUILDING?
ANYONE KNOW?
their phone numbers?
HOW SHOULD I KNOW?
WE WON'T HAVE RUNNING WATER EITHER?!
IT'LL BE LIKE THIS UNTIL MORNING?
HEY!
WE'VE GOT ENTRANCE EXAMS TOMORROW ...
...WHAT'S HAPPENING...?
...WHY DO THINGS LIKE THIS HAVE TO...
Darn it.
Every-body's gonna panic...
HEY, EVERYONE CALM DOWN...

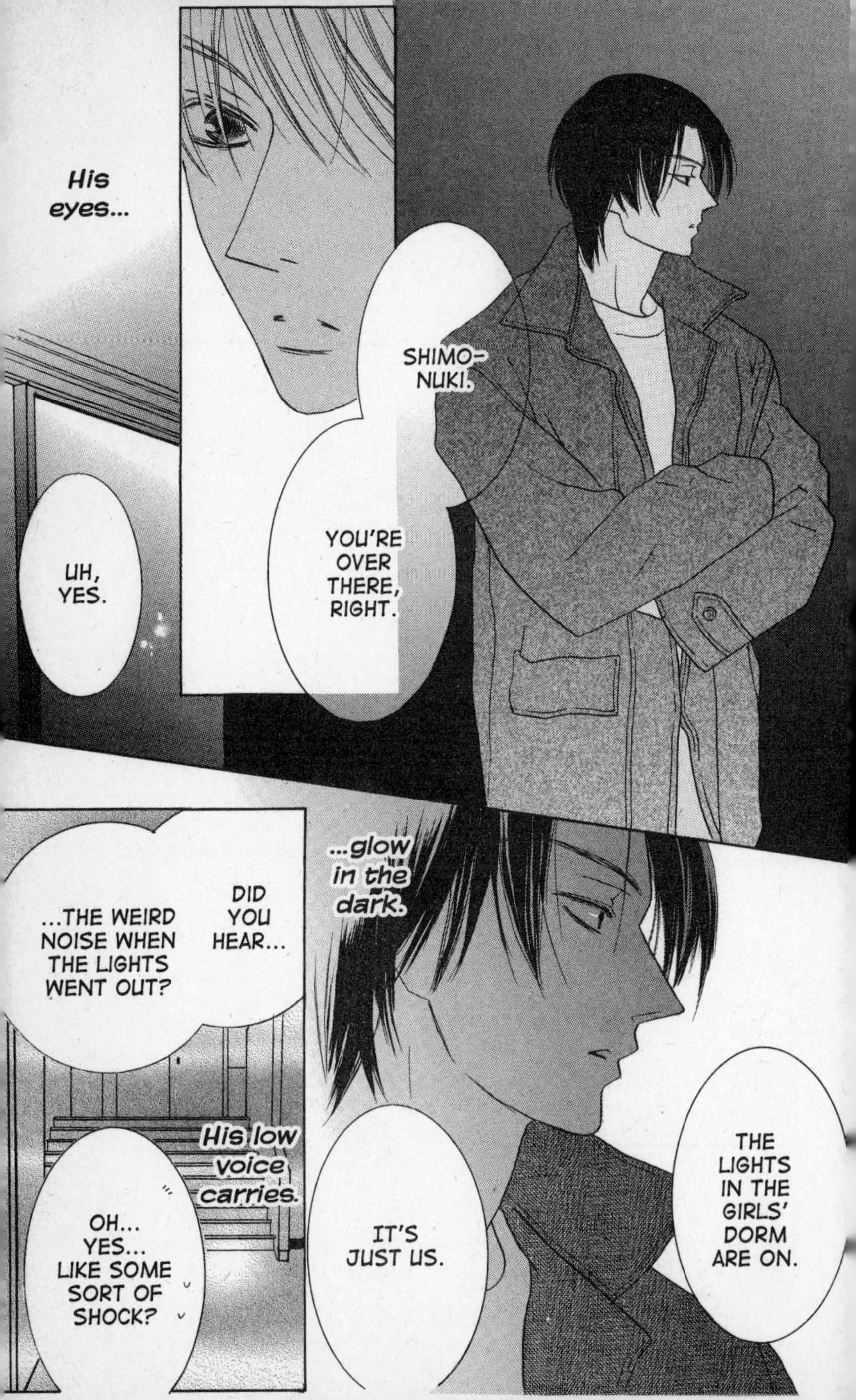
SHIMO-NUKI.
YOU'RE OVER THERE, RIGHT.
His eyes...
UH, YES.
...glow in the dark.
THE LIGHTS IN THE GIRLS' DORM ARE ON.
IT'S JUST US.
His low voice carries.
DID YOU HEAR...
...THE WEIRD NOISE WHEN THE LIGHTS WENT OUT?
OH... YES... LIKE SOME SORT OF SHOCK?

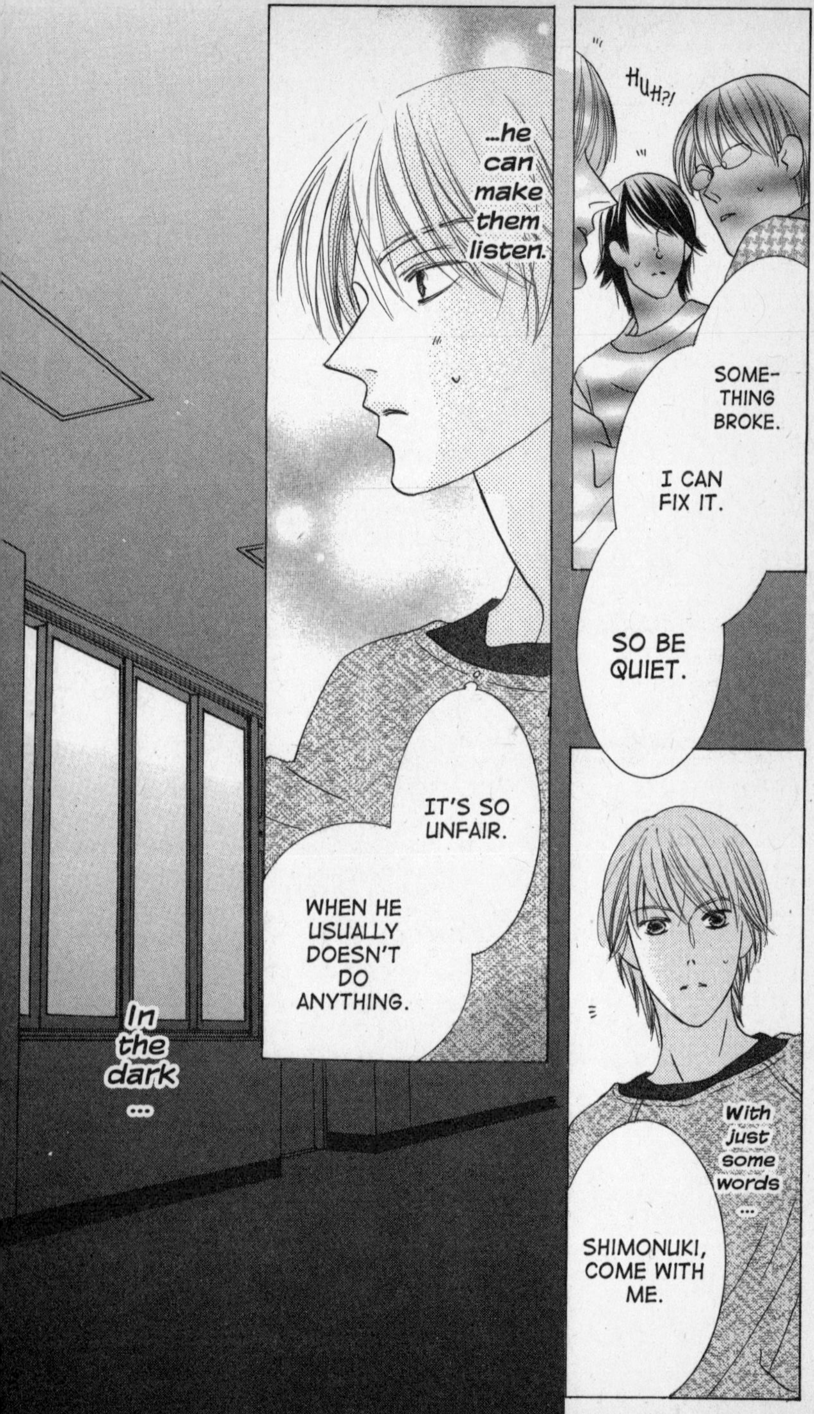
HUH?!
SOMETHING BROKE.
I CAN FIX IT.
SO BE QUIET.
With just some words...
SHIMONUKI, COME WITH ME.
...he can make them listen.
IT'S SO UNFAIR.
WHEN HE USUALLY DOESN'T DO ANYTHING.
In the dark...

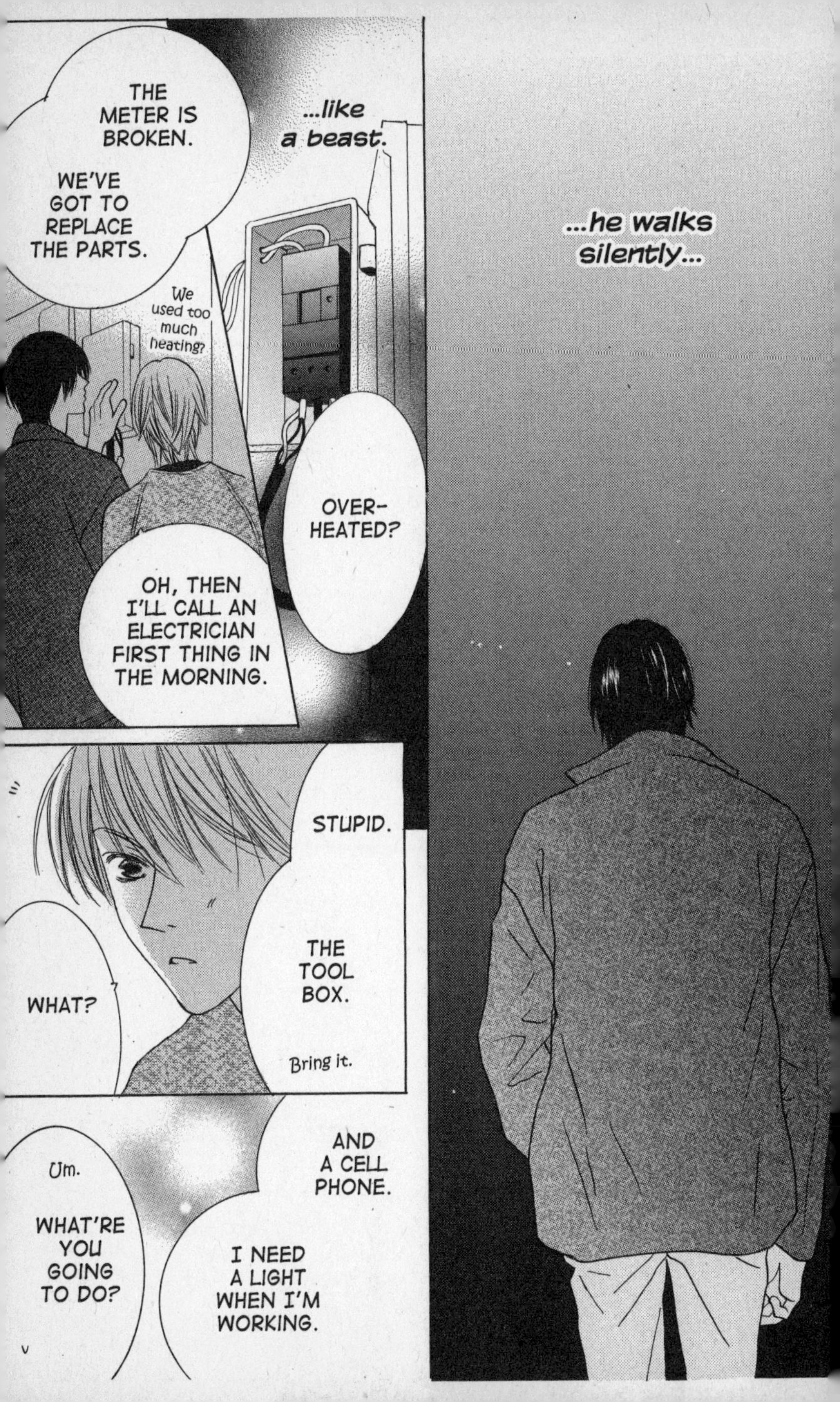

...he walks silently...
...like a beast.
THE METER IS BROKEN.
WE'VE GOT TO REPLACE THE PARTS.
We used too much heating?
OVER-HEATED?
OH, THEN I'LL CALL AN ELECTRICIAN FIRST THING IN THE MORNING.
STUPID.
THE TOOL BOX.
Bring it.
WHAT?
AND A CELL PHONE.
Um.
WHAT'RE YOU GOING TO DO?
I NEED A LIGHT WHEN I'M WORKING.

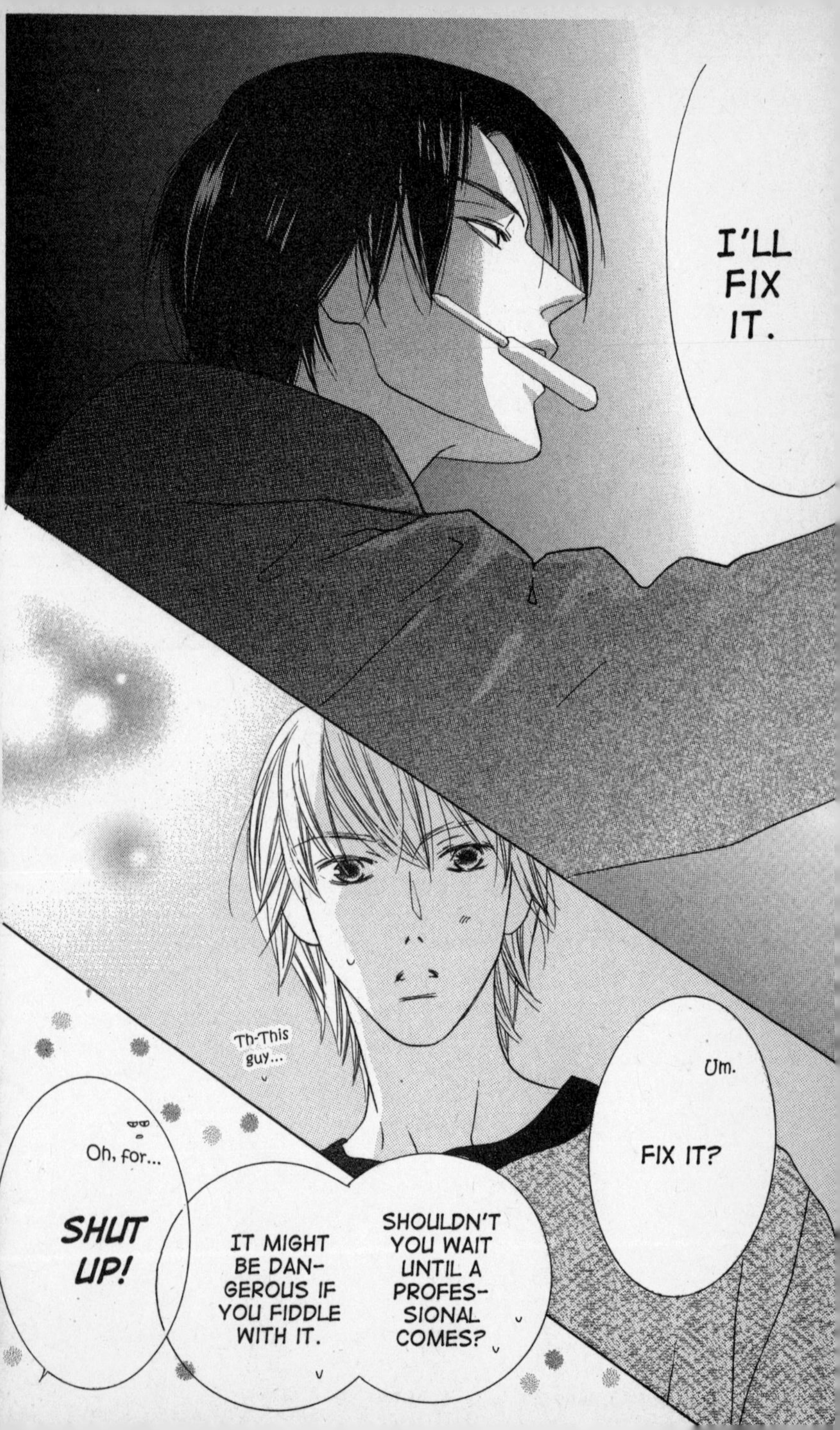
I'LL FIX IT.
Um.
FIX IT?
SHOULDN'T YOU WAIT UNTIL A PROFES-SIONAL COMES?
IT MIGHT BE DAN-GEROUS IF YOU FIDDLE WITH IT.
Th-This guy...
Oh, for...
SHUT UP!

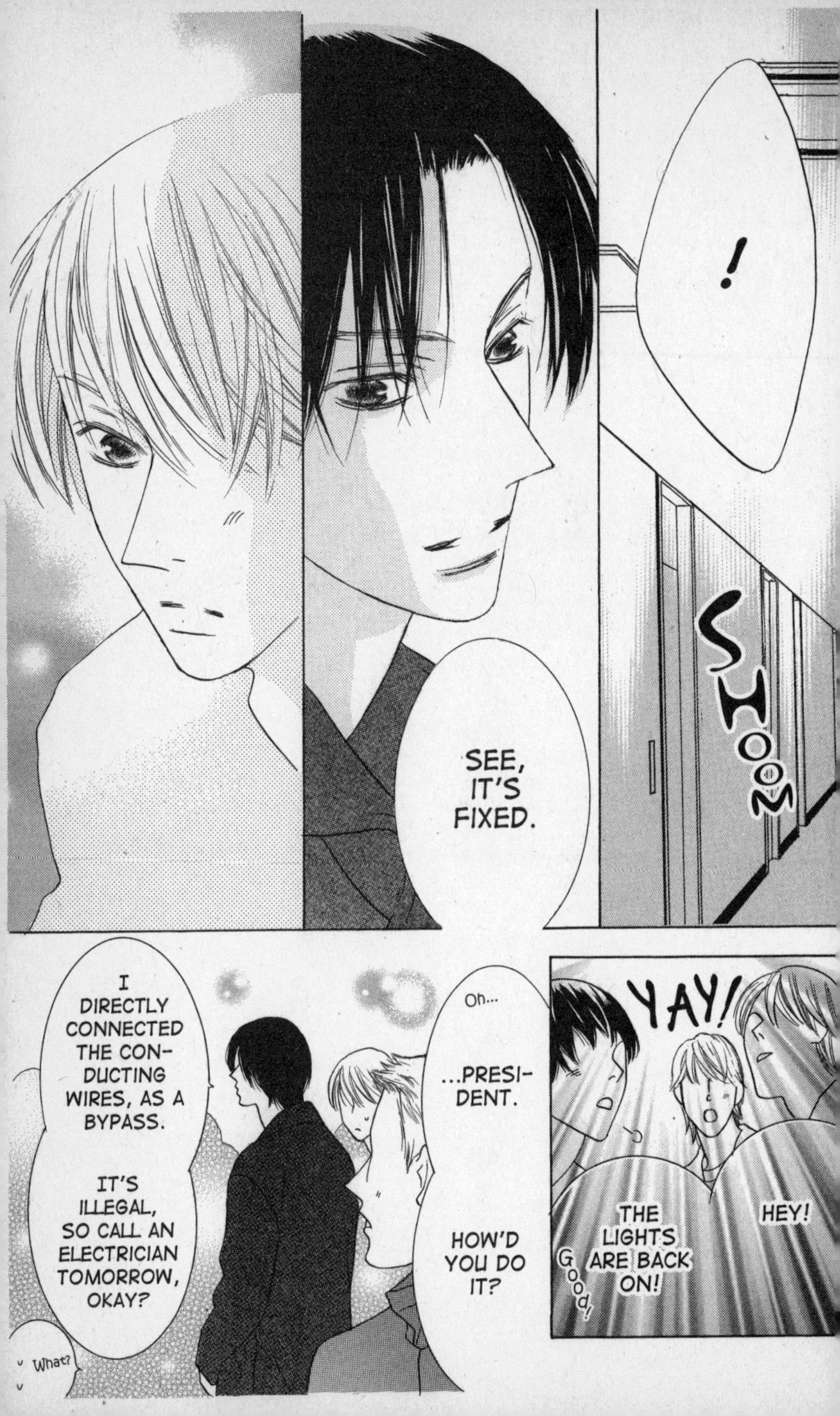
!
SHOOM
SEE, IT'S FIXED.
YAY!
HEY!
THE LIGHTS ARE BACK ON!
Good!
Oh...
...PRESI-DENT.
HOW'D YOU DO IT?
I DIRECTLY CONNECTED THE CON-DUCTING WIRES, AS A BYPASS.
IT'S ILLEGAL, SO CALL AN ELECTRICIAN TOMORROW, OKAY?
What?

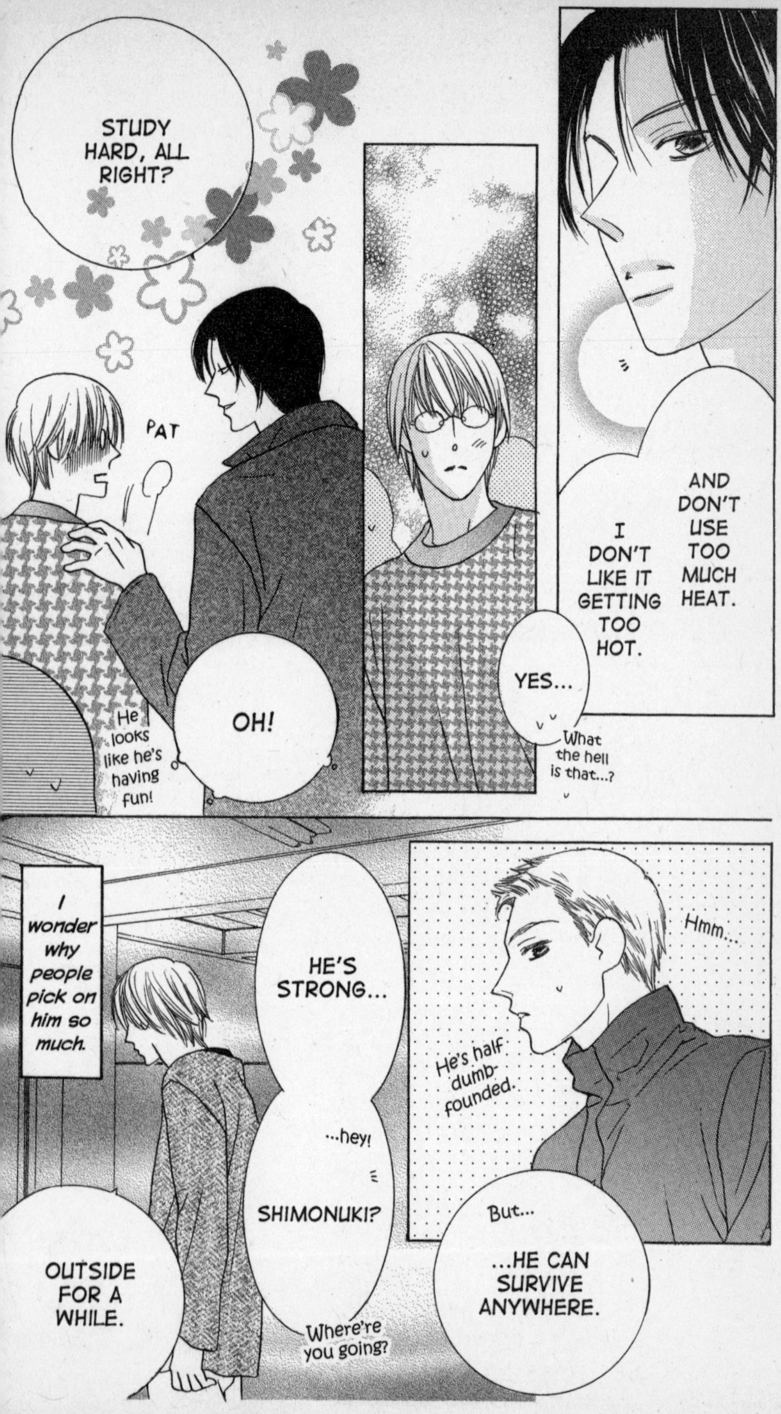
AND DON'T USE TOO MUCH HEAT.
I DON'T LIKE IT GETTING TOO HOT.
YES...
What the hell is that...?
STUDY HARD, ALL RIGHT?
PAT
OH!
He looks like he's having fun!
Hmm...
He's half dumbfounded.
But...
...HE CAN SURVIVE ANYWHERE.
I wonder why people pick on him so much.
HE'S STRONG...
...hey!
SHIMONUKI?
Where're you going?
OUTSIDE FOR A WHILE.

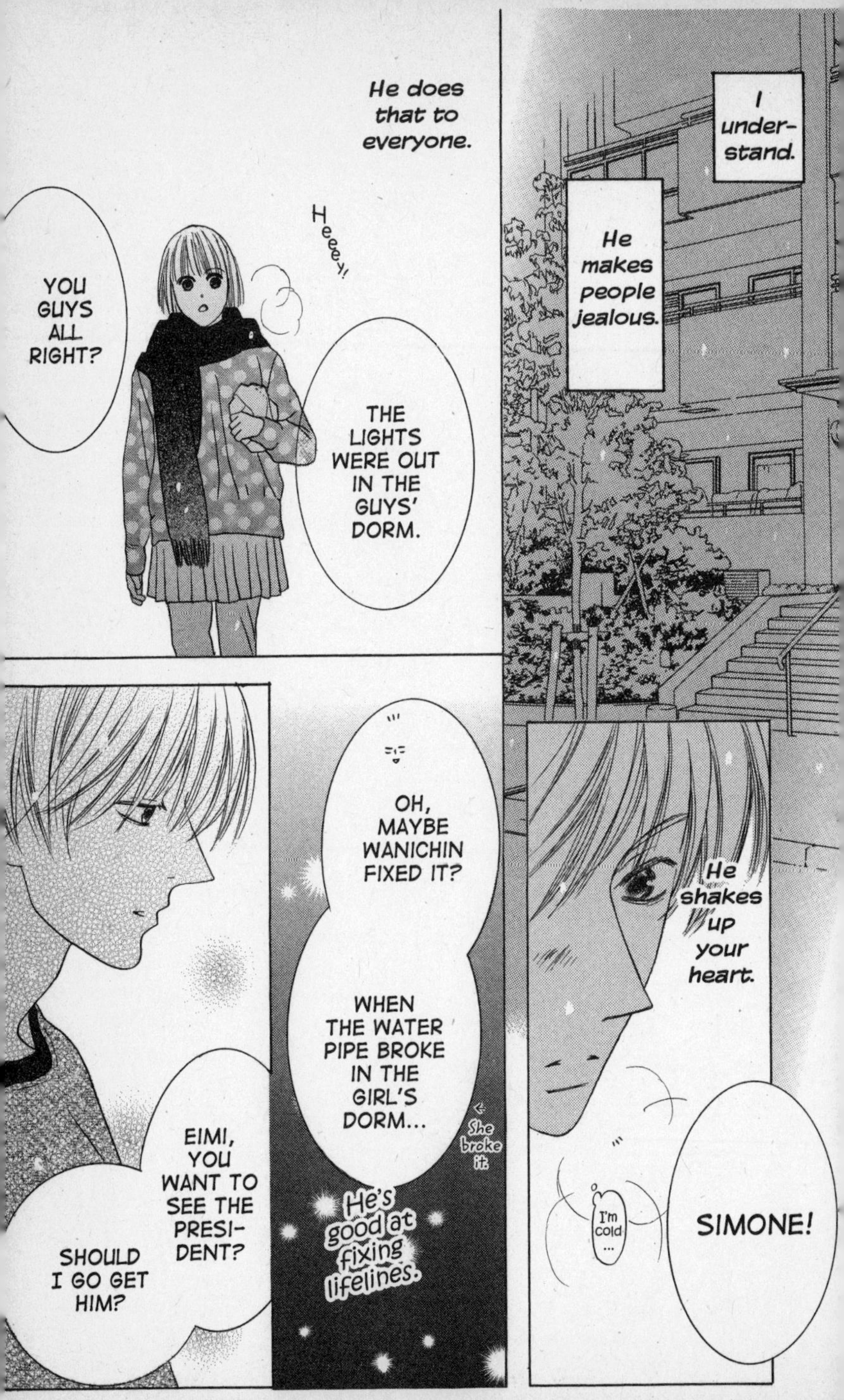
I understand.
He makes people jealous.
He does that to everyone.
Heeey!
THE LIGHTS WERE OUT IN THE GUYS' DORM.
YOU GUYS ALL RIGHT?
He shakes up your heart.
SIMONE!
I'm cold...
OH, MAYBE WANICHIN FIXED IT?
WHEN THE WATER PIPE BROKE IN THE GIRL'S DORM...
She broke it.
He's good at fixing lifelines.
EIMI, YOU WANT TO SEE THE PRESIDENT?
SHOULD I GO GET HIM?

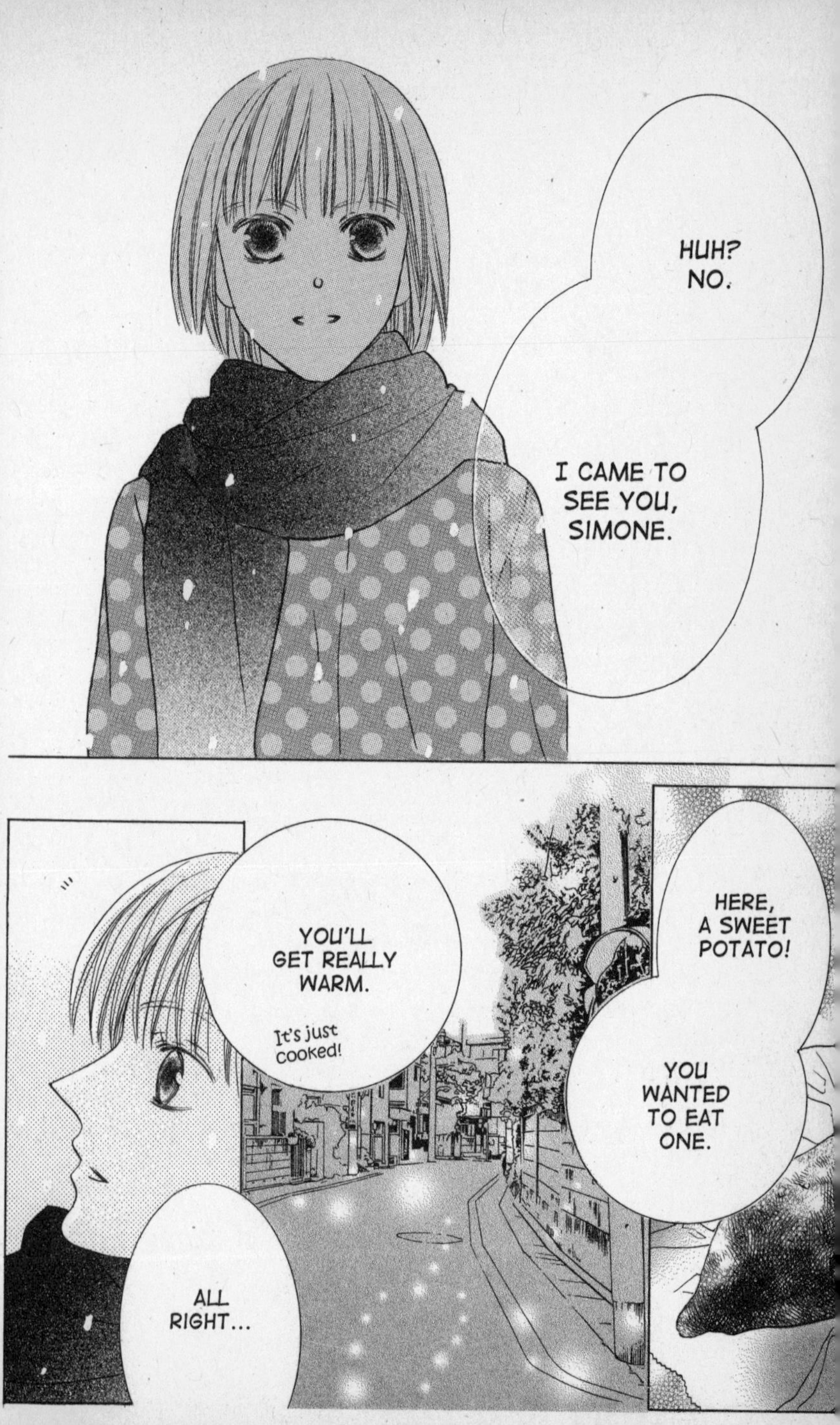
HUH? NO.
I CAME TO SEE YOU, SIMONE.
HERE, A SWEET POTATO!
YOU WANTED TO EAT ONE.
YOU'LL GET REALLY WARM.
It's just cooked!
ALL RIGHT...

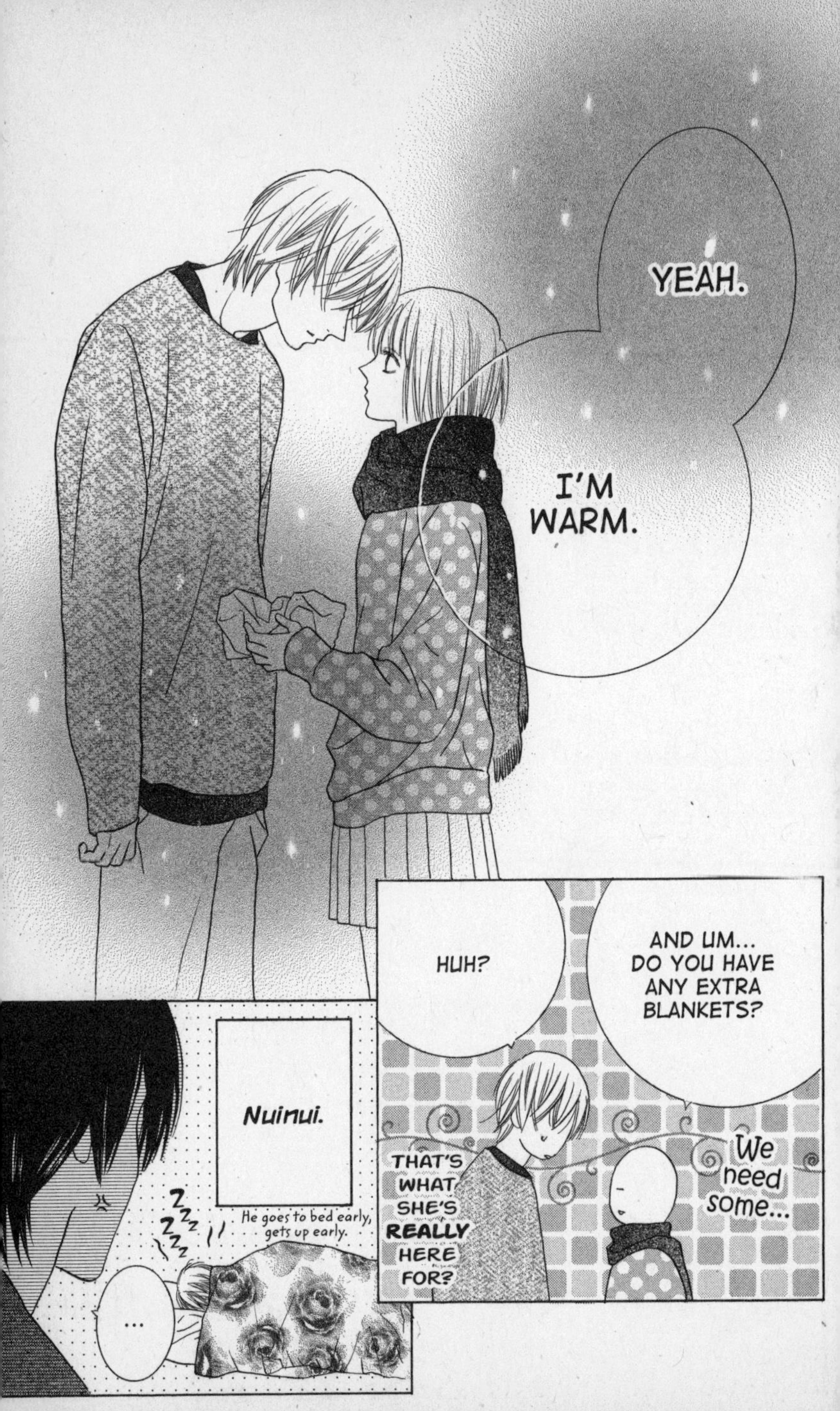
YEAH.
I'M WARM.
AND UM... DO YOU HAVE ANY EXTRA BLANKETS?
HUH?
We need some...
THAT'S WHAT SHE'S REALLY HERE FOR?
Nuinui.
He goes to bed early, gets up early.
ZZZZ
...

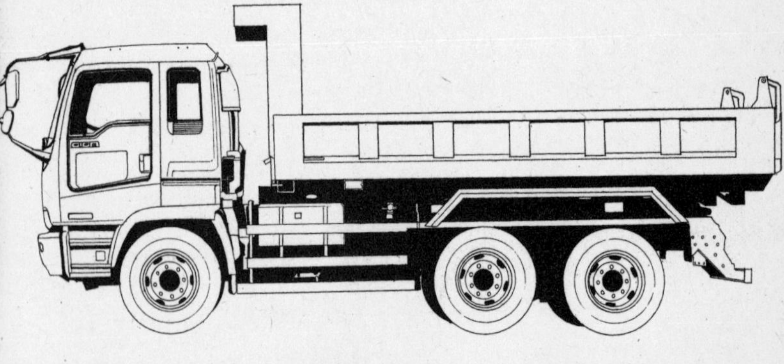

BEAUTY IS THE BEAST

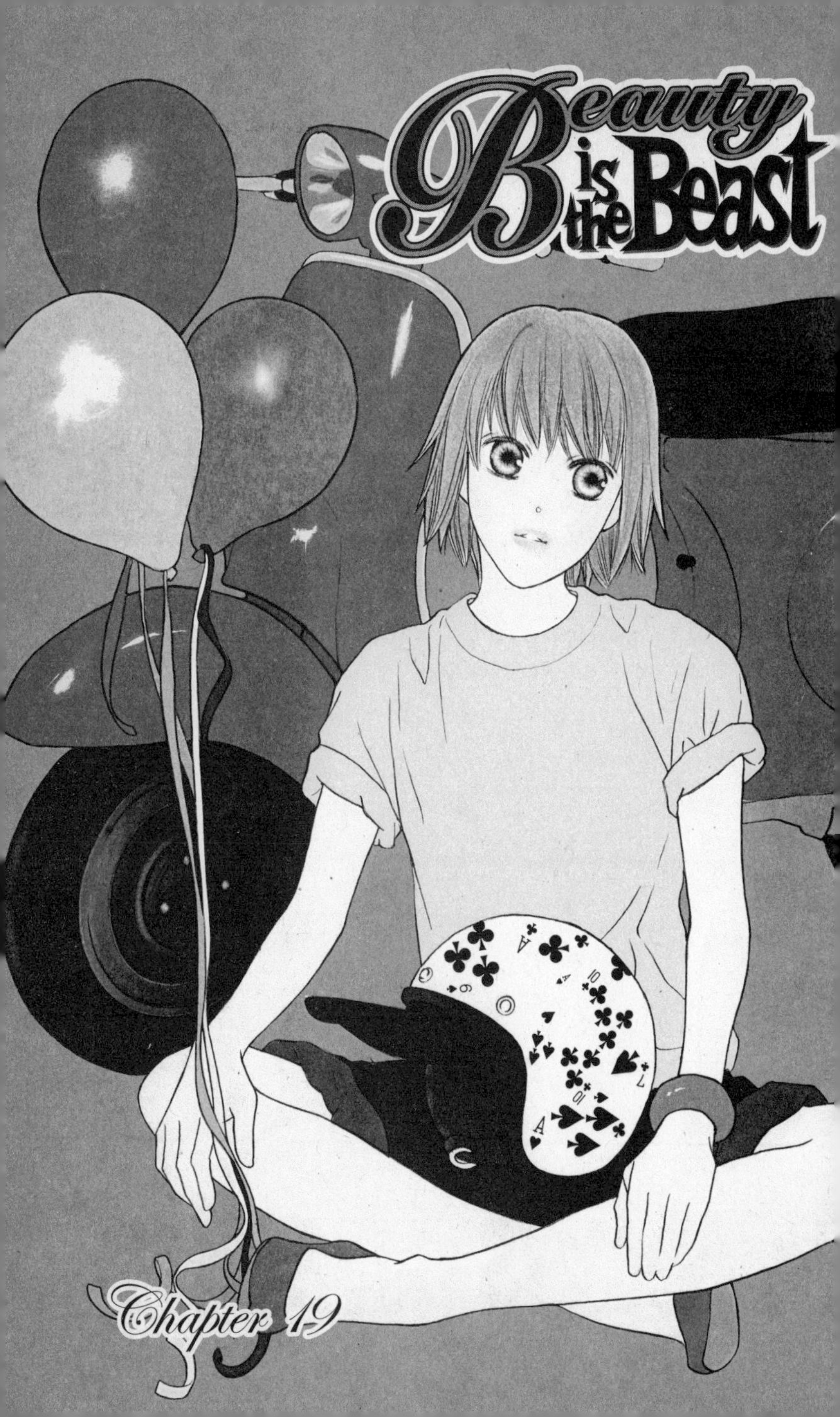
Beauty is the Beast
Chapter 19

南無阿弥陀仏

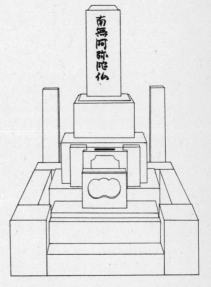

BEAUTY IS THE BEAST

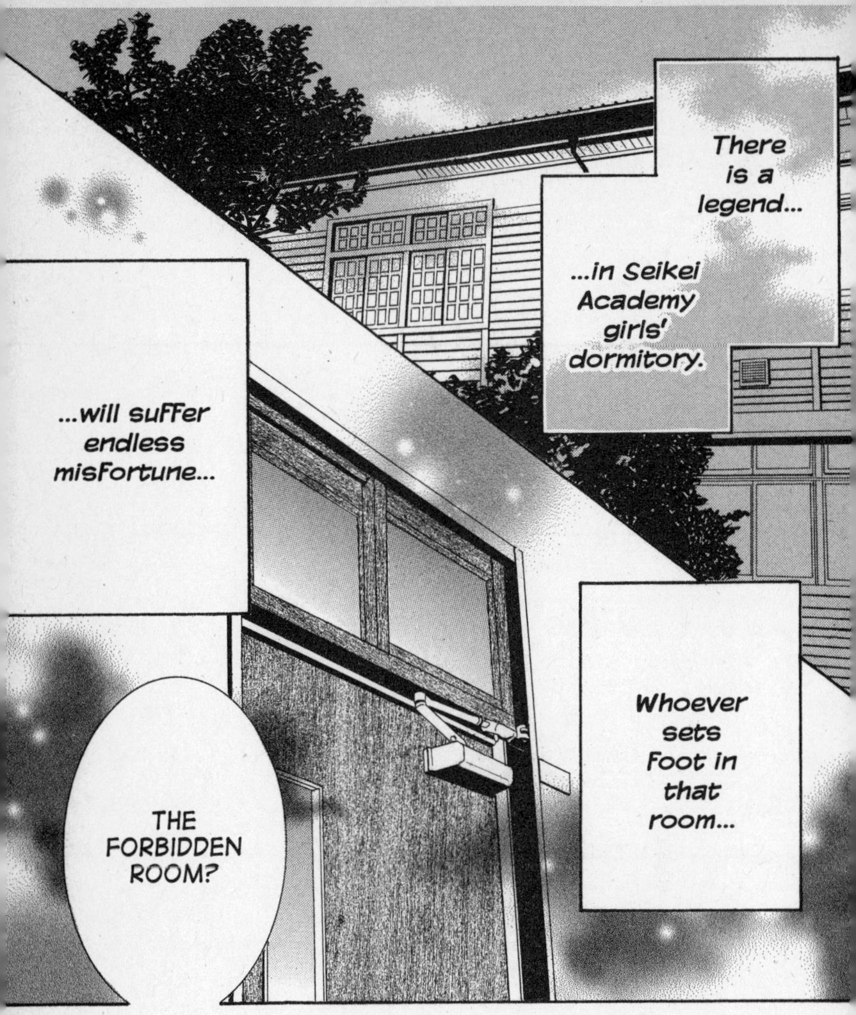
There is a legend...
...in Seikei Academy girls' dormitory.
Whoever sets foot in that room...
...will suffer endless misfortune...
THE FORBIDDEN ROOM?

About This Volume's Cover

Actually, I was going to draw male characters starting with the second volume, and I was doing the penciling for Fujitan. However, when my editor Taneoka-sama (just married) found out, he said, "No, Fujitan won't sell books." (☺)
Ah ha ha ha ha ha, poor Fujitan!!! (laughs out loud)
So it's Wanichin again, yes.

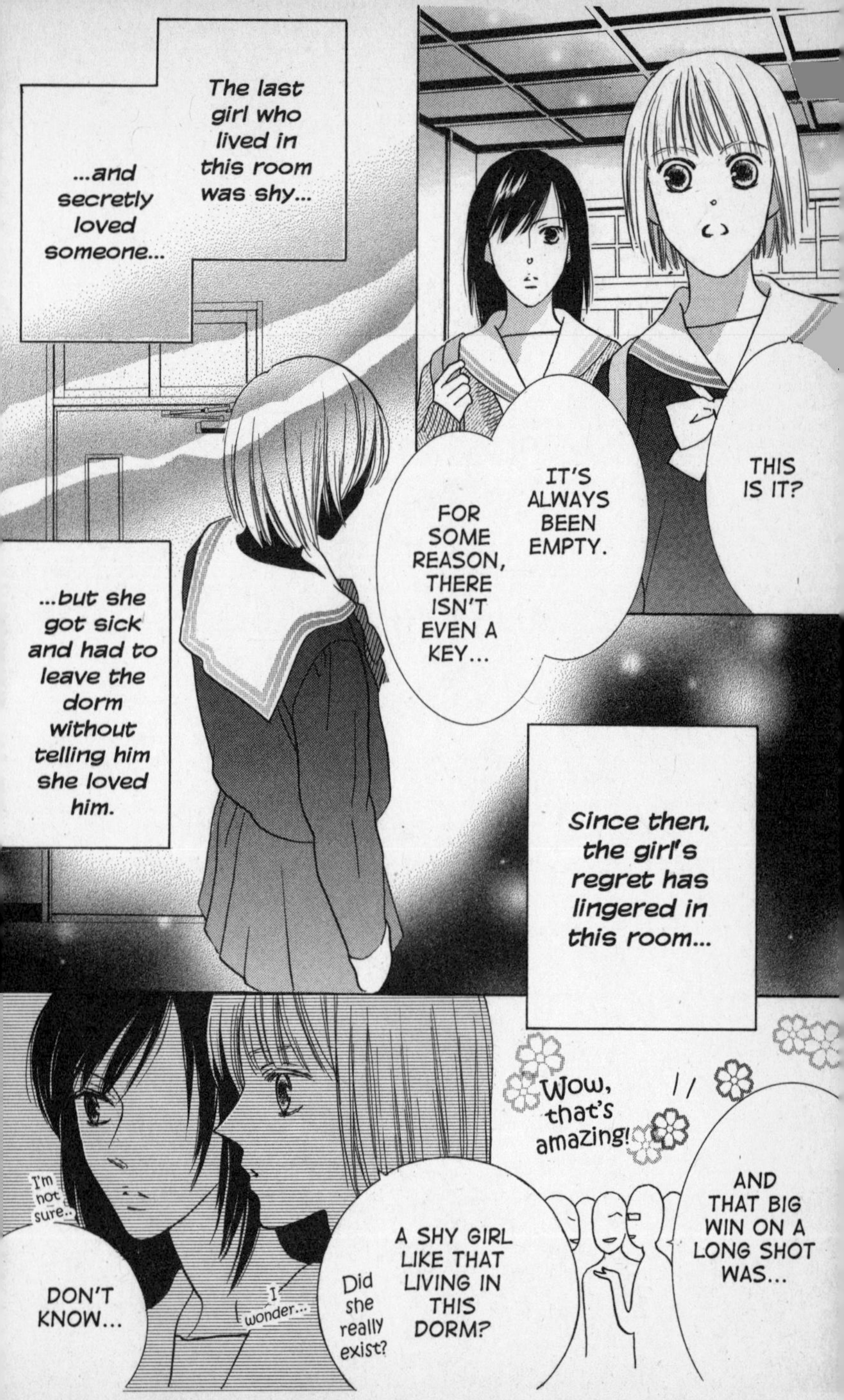
THIS IS IT?
IT'S ALWAYS BEEN EMPTY.
FOR SOME REASON, THERE ISN'T EVEN A KEY...
Since then, the girl's regret has lingered in this room...
The last girl who lived in this room was shy...
...and secretly loved someone...
...but she got sick and had to leave the dorm without telling him she loved him.
Wow, that's amazing!!
AND THAT BIG WIN ON A LONG SHOT WAS...
A SHY GIRL LIKE THAT LIVING IN THIS DORM?
Did she really exist?
I wonder...
I'm not sure..
DON'T KNOW...

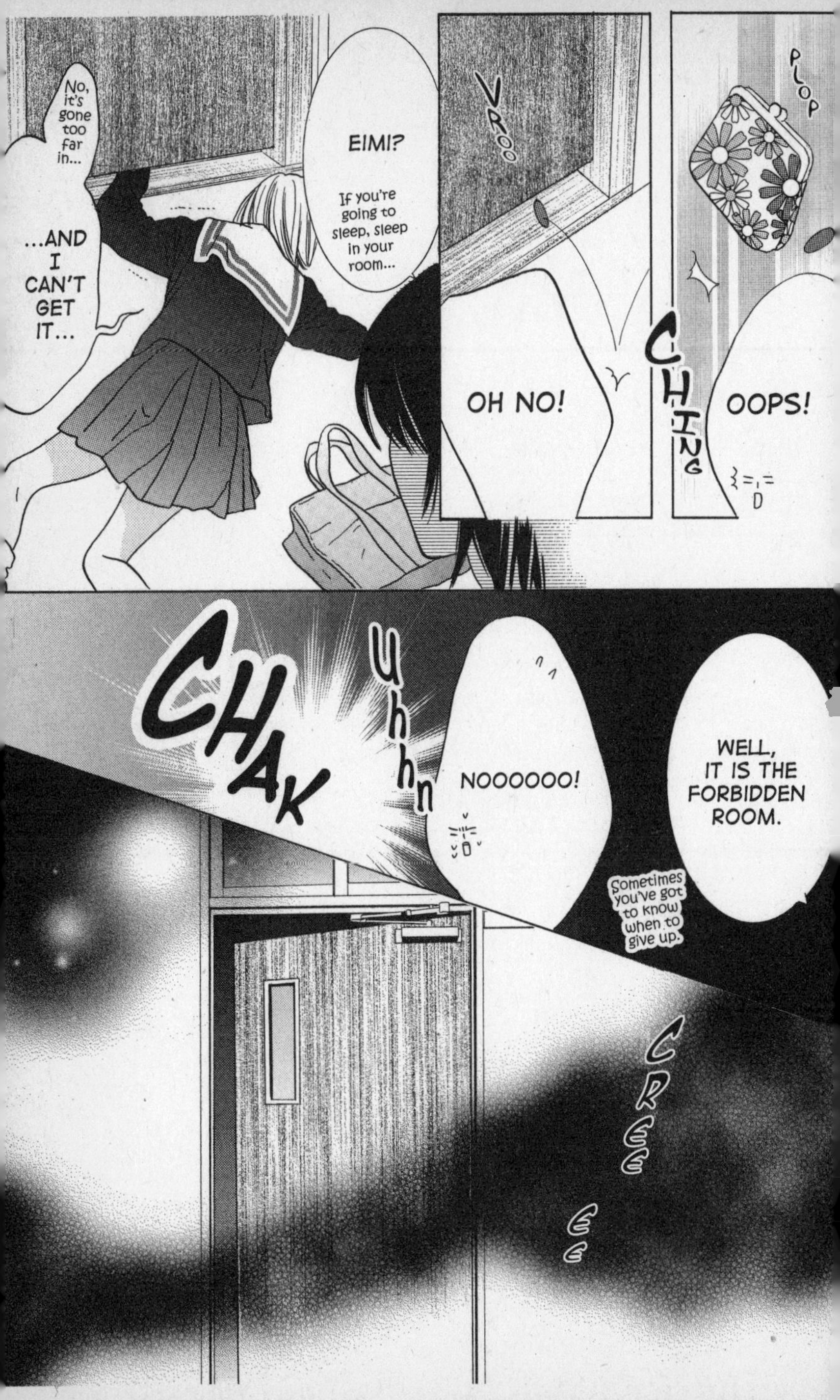
PLOP
OOPS!
VROOO
CHING
OH NO!
EIMI?
If you're going to sleep, sleep in your room...
No, it's gone too far in...
...AND I CAN'T GET IT...
WELL, IT IS THE FORBIDDEN ROOM.
Sometimes you've got to know when to give up.
NOOOOOO!
Uhhhn
CHAK
CREEEEE

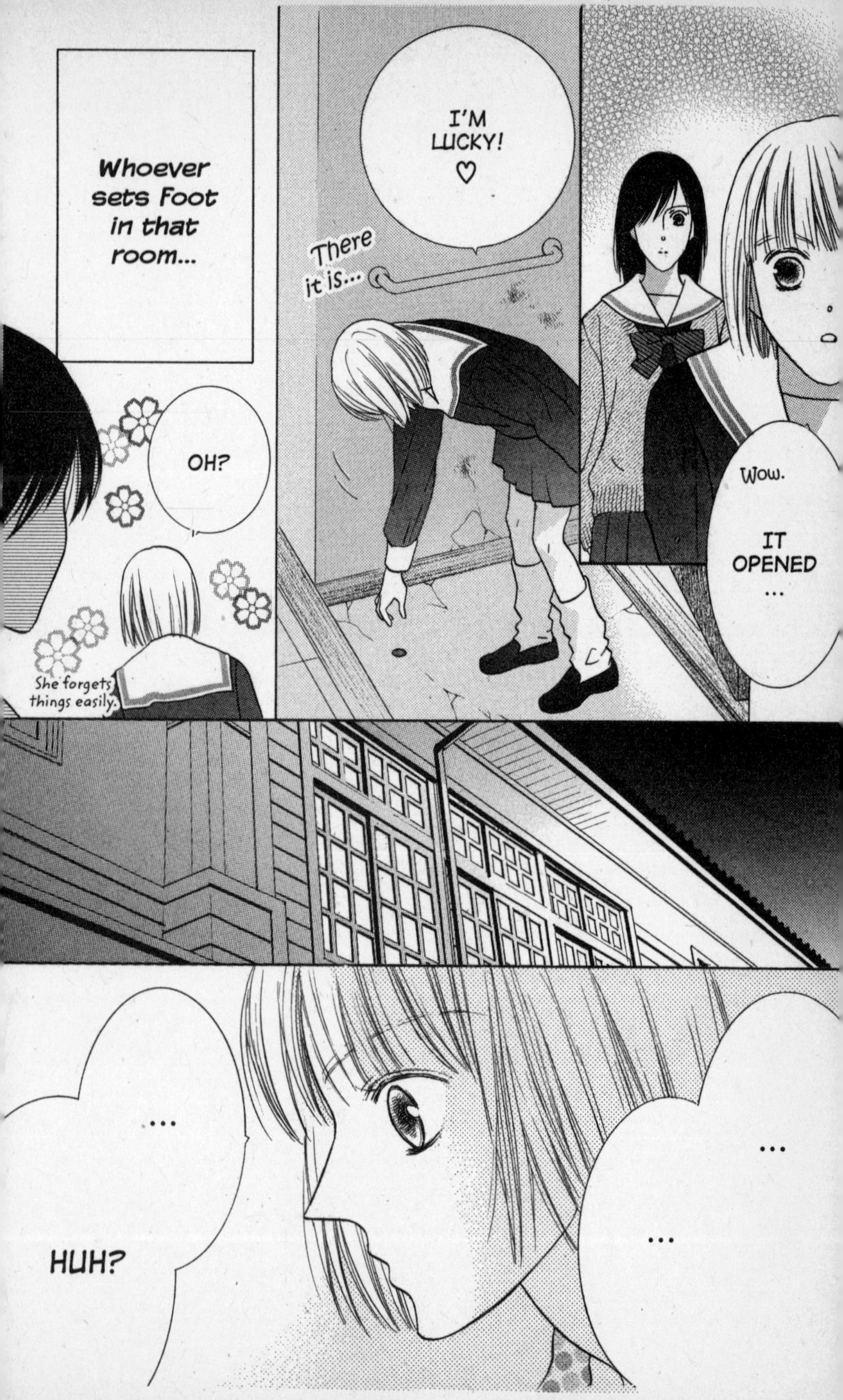
Wow. IT OPENED ...
I'M LUCKY! ♡
There it is...
Whoever sets foot in that room...
OH?
She forgets things easily.
...
...
... HUH?

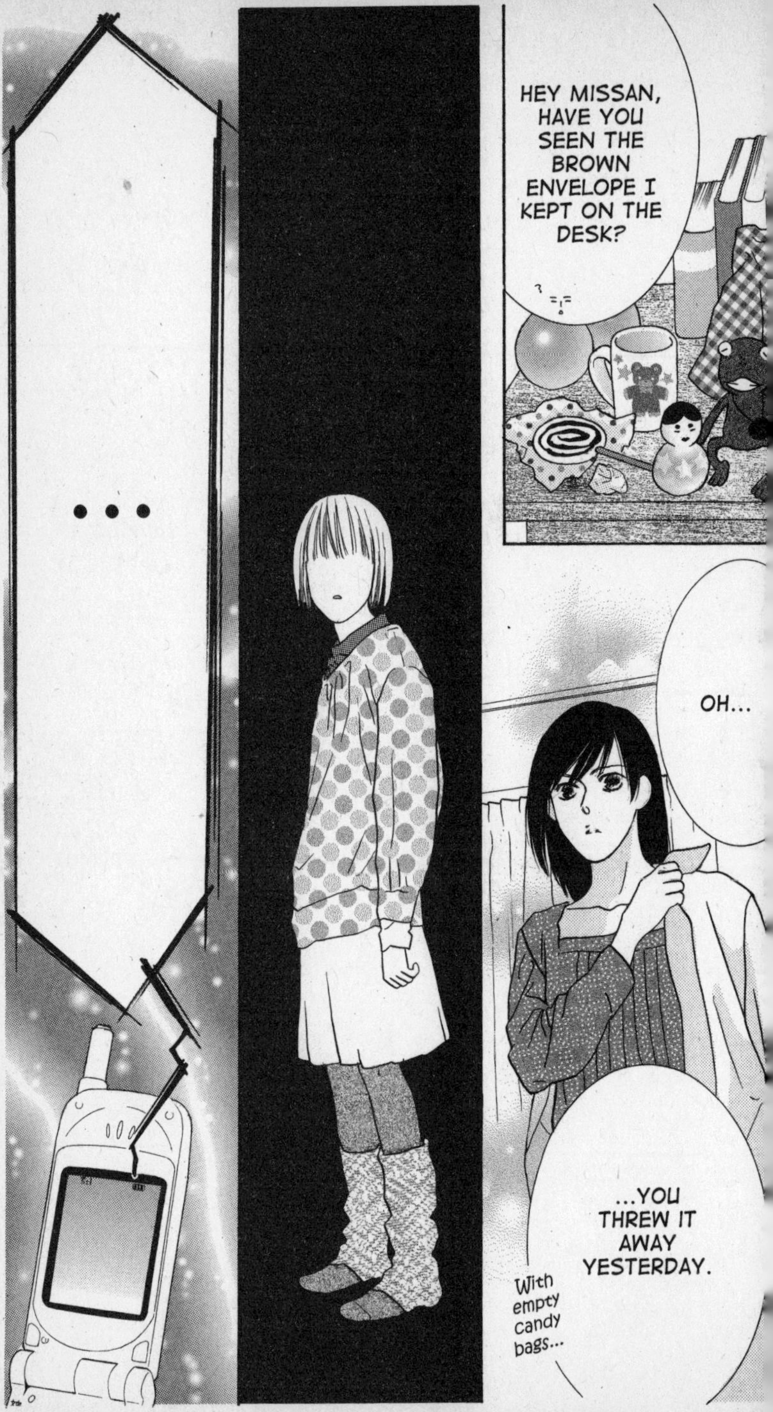
HEY MISSAN, HAVE YOU SEEN THE BROWN ENVELOPE I KEPT ON THE DESK?
OH...
...YOU THREW IT AWAY YESTERDAY.
With empty candy bags...
...

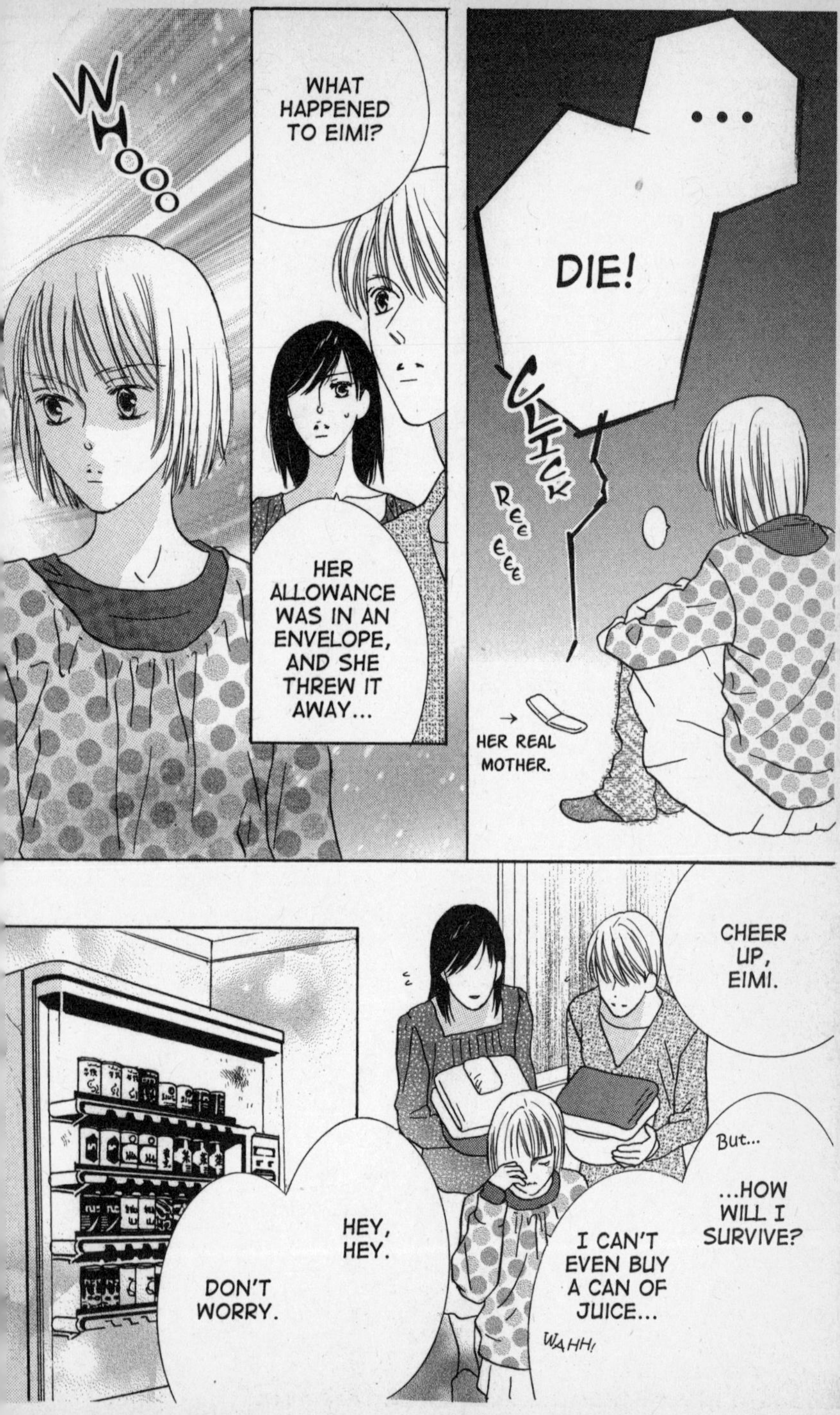

...
DIE!
CLICK
REEEEE
HER REAL MOTHER.
WHAT HAPPENED TO EIMI?
HER ALLOWANCE WAS IN AN ENVELOPE, AND SHE THREW IT AWAY...
WHOOO
CHEER UP, EIMI.
But...
...HOW WILL I SURVIVE?
I CAN'T EVEN BUY A CAN OF JUICE...
WAHH!
HEY, HEY.
DON'T WORRY.

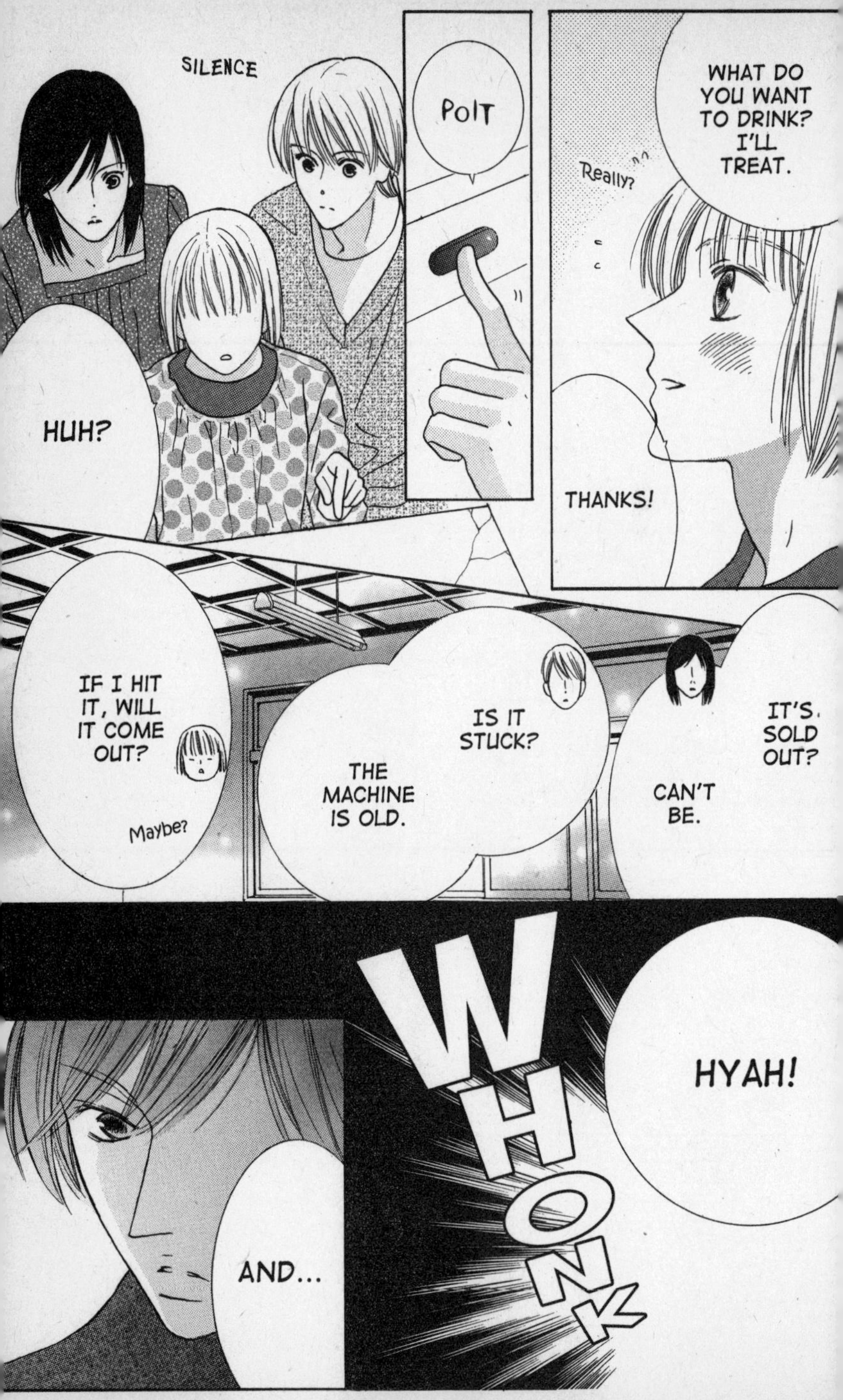
WHAT DO YOU WANT TO DRINK? I'LL TREAT.
Really?
THANKS!
POIT
SILENCE
HUH?
IT'S SOLD OUT?
CAN'T BE.
IS IT STUCK?
THE MACHINE IS OLD.
IF I HIT IT, WILL IT COME OUT?
Maybe?
HYAH!
WHONK
AND...

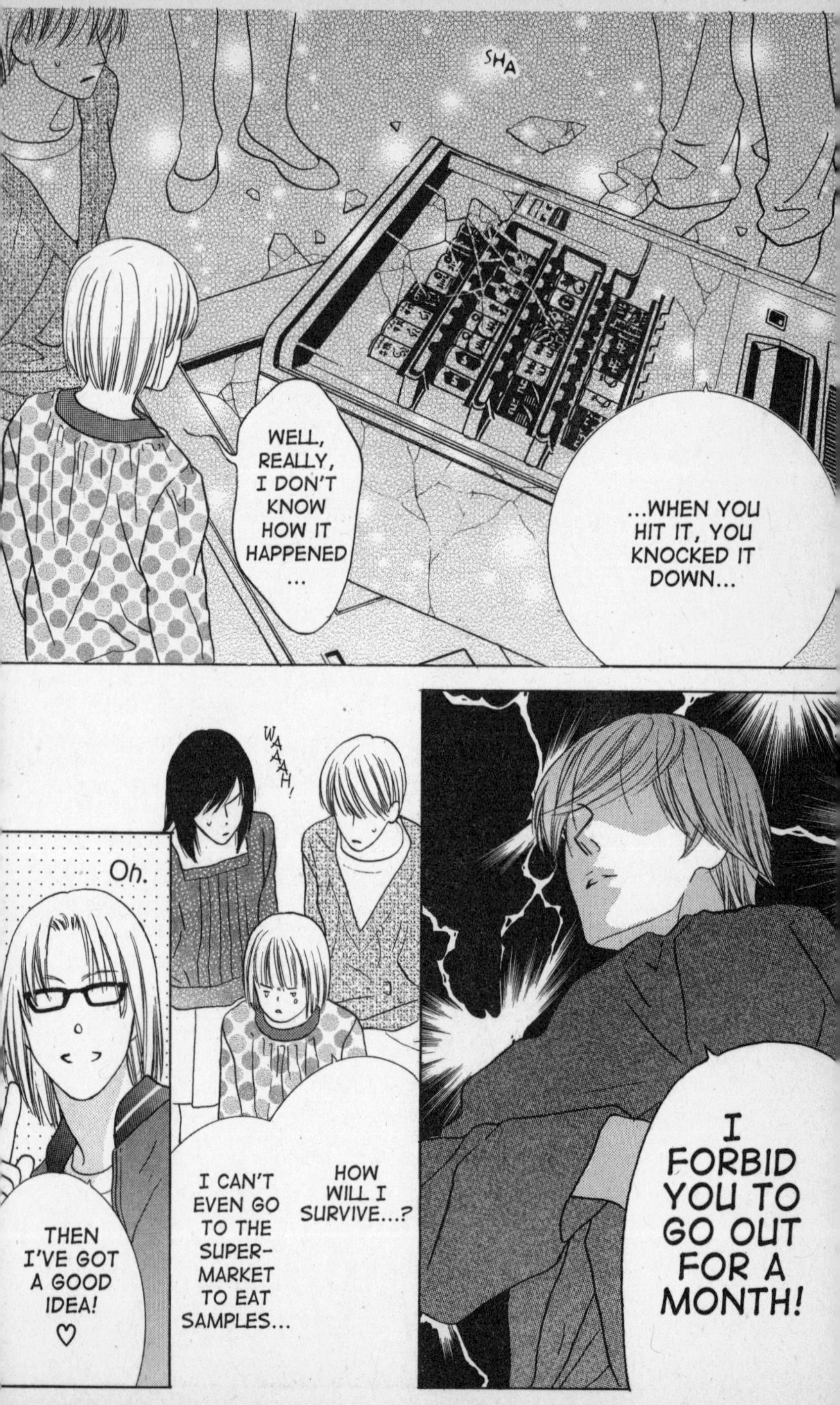
SHA
...WHEN YOU HIT IT, YOU KNOCKED IT DOWN...
WELL, REALLY, I DON'T KNOW HOW IT HAPPENED ...
I FORBID YOU TO GO OUT FOR A MONTH!
WAAAH!
HOW WILL I SURVIVE...?
I CAN'T EVEN GO TO THE SUPER-MARKET TO EAT SAMPLES...
Oh.
THEN I'VE GOT A GOOD IDEA! ♡

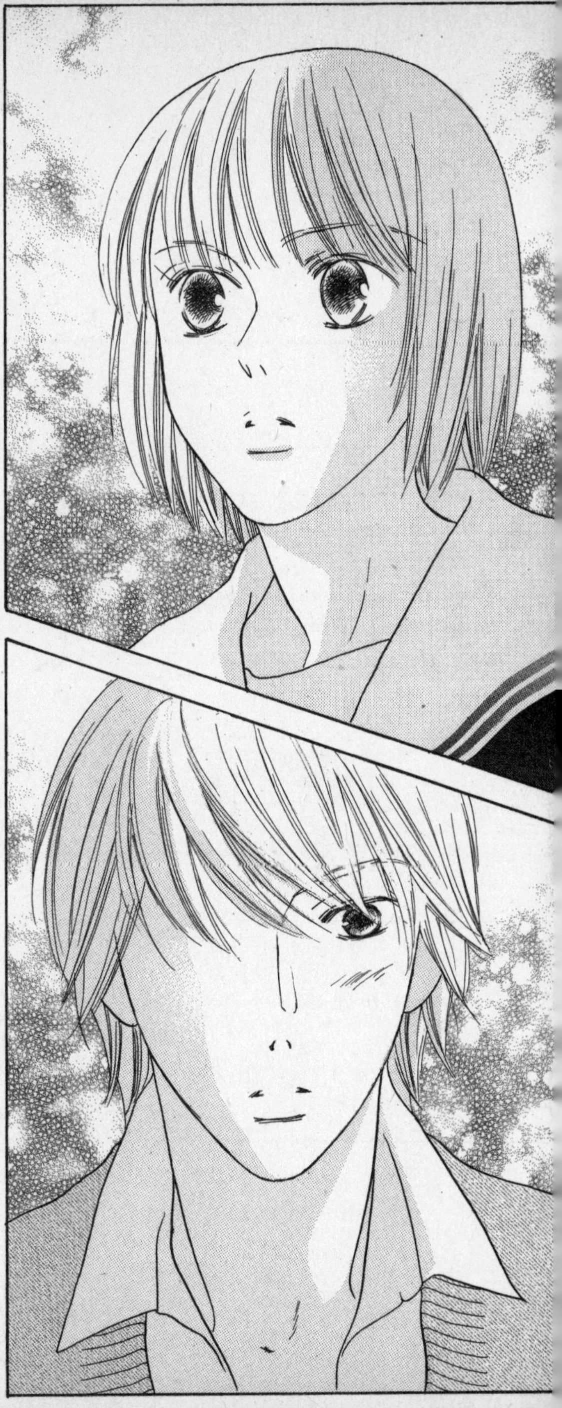

2

In my dorm, there was a room with a history, a room where ghosts supposedly appeared. But in reality, having upperclassmen yell at you was scarier (seriously) so I don't have any experience with ghosts. If asked, I do believe in ghosts. But there seems to be too many people who make that a business, and I feel I'll be their target right away (☺) so I won't believe in them.

But after I saw "Ringu," I was really scared. I thought Sadako might come. (You're believing in them!)

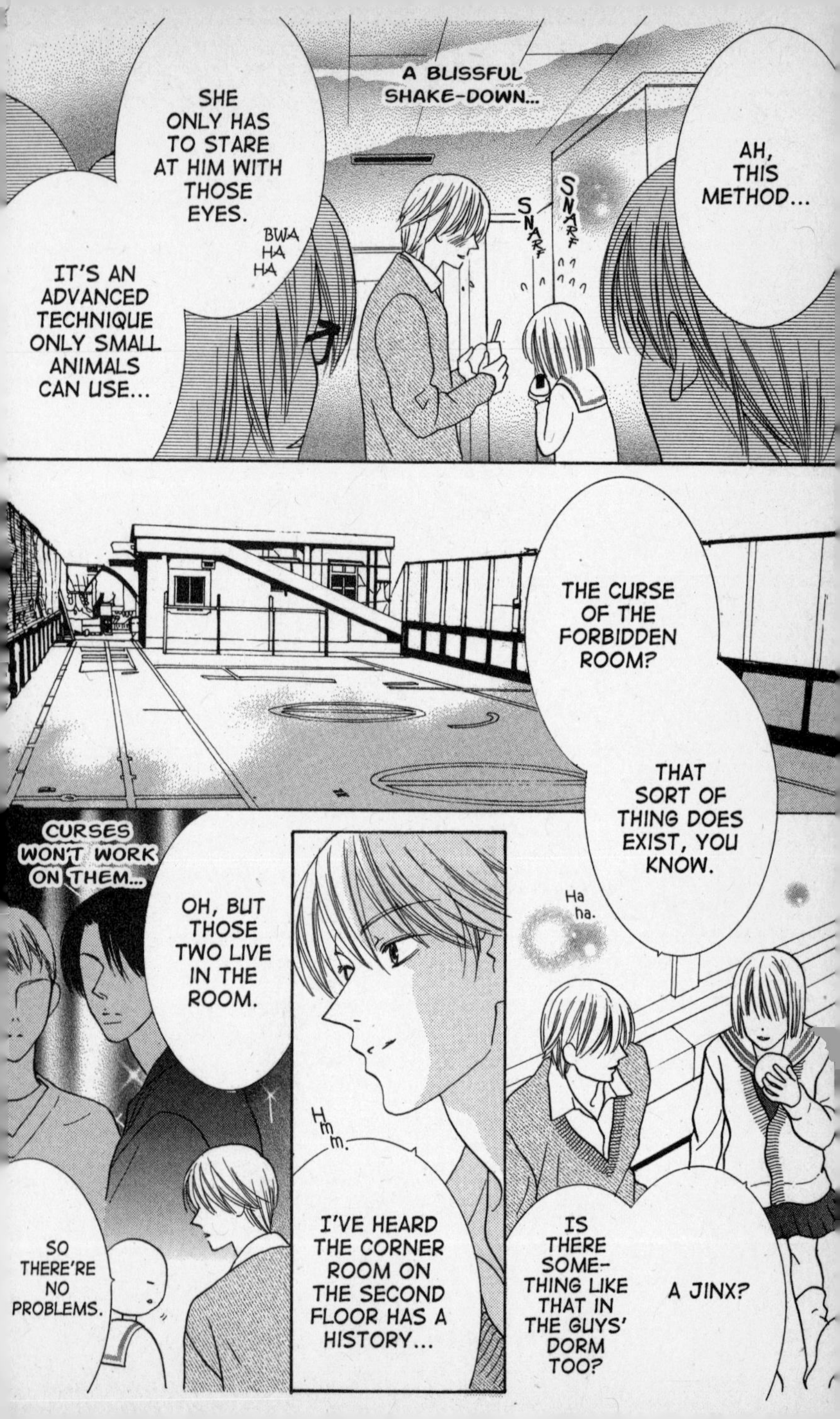
AH, THIS METHOD...
A BLISSFUL SHAKE-DOWN...
SNARF
SNARF
SHE ONLY HAS TO STARE AT HIM WITH THOSE EYES.
BWA HA HA
IT'S AN ADVANCED TECHNIQUE ONLY SMALL ANIMALS CAN USE...
THE CURSE OF THE FORBIDDEN ROOM?
THAT SORT OF THING DOES EXIST, YOU KNOW.
Ha ha.
A JINX?
IS THERE SOME-THING LIKE THAT IN THE GUYS' DORM TOO?
Hmm.
I'VE HEARD THE CORNER ROOM ON THE SECOND FLOOR HAS A HISTORY...
OH, BUT THOSE TWO LIVE IN THE ROOM.
CURSES WON'T WORK ON THEM...
SO THERE'RE NO PROBLEMS.

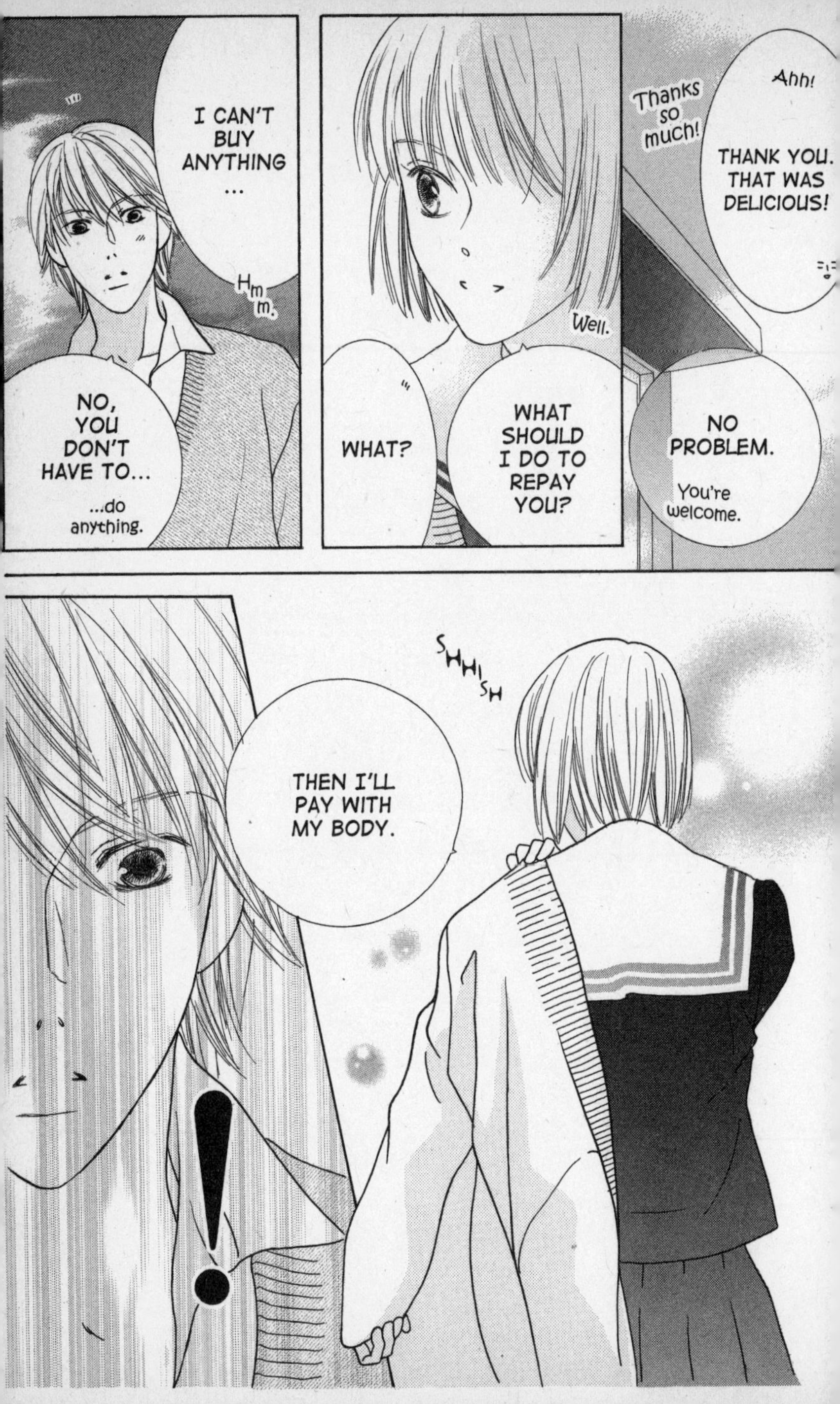
Ahh!
THANK YOU. THAT WAS DELICIOUS!
Thanks so much!
NO PROBLEM.
You're welcome.
Well.
WHAT SHOULD I DO TO REPAY YOU?
WHAT?
I CAN'T BUY ANYTHING ...
Hmm.
NO, YOU DON'T HAVE TO...
...do anything.
SHHISH
THEN I'LL PAY WITH MY BODY.

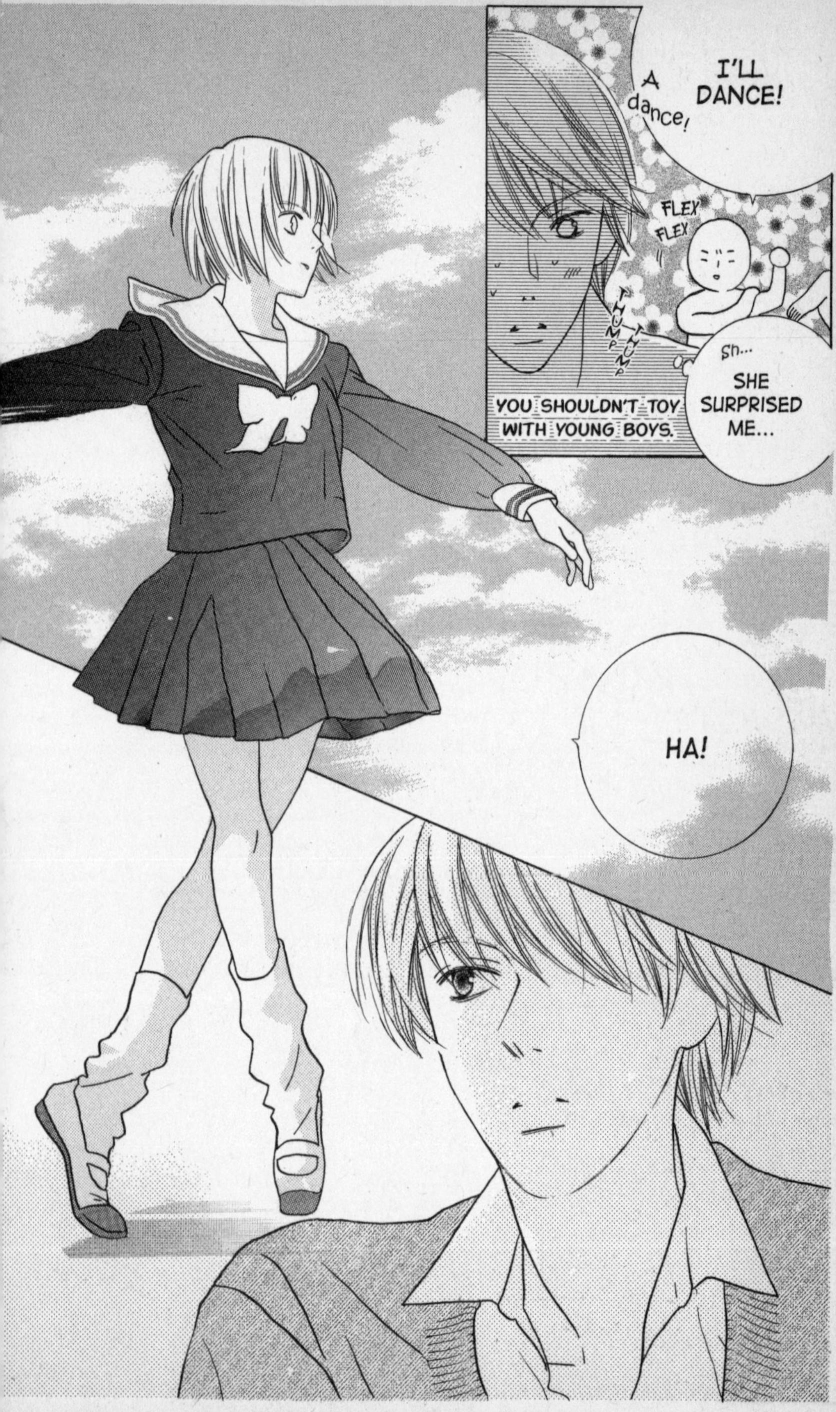
I'LL DANCE!
A dance!
FLEX FLEX
THUMP THUMP
Sh... SHE SURPRISED ME...
YOU SHOULDN'T TOY WITH YOUNG BOYS.
HA!

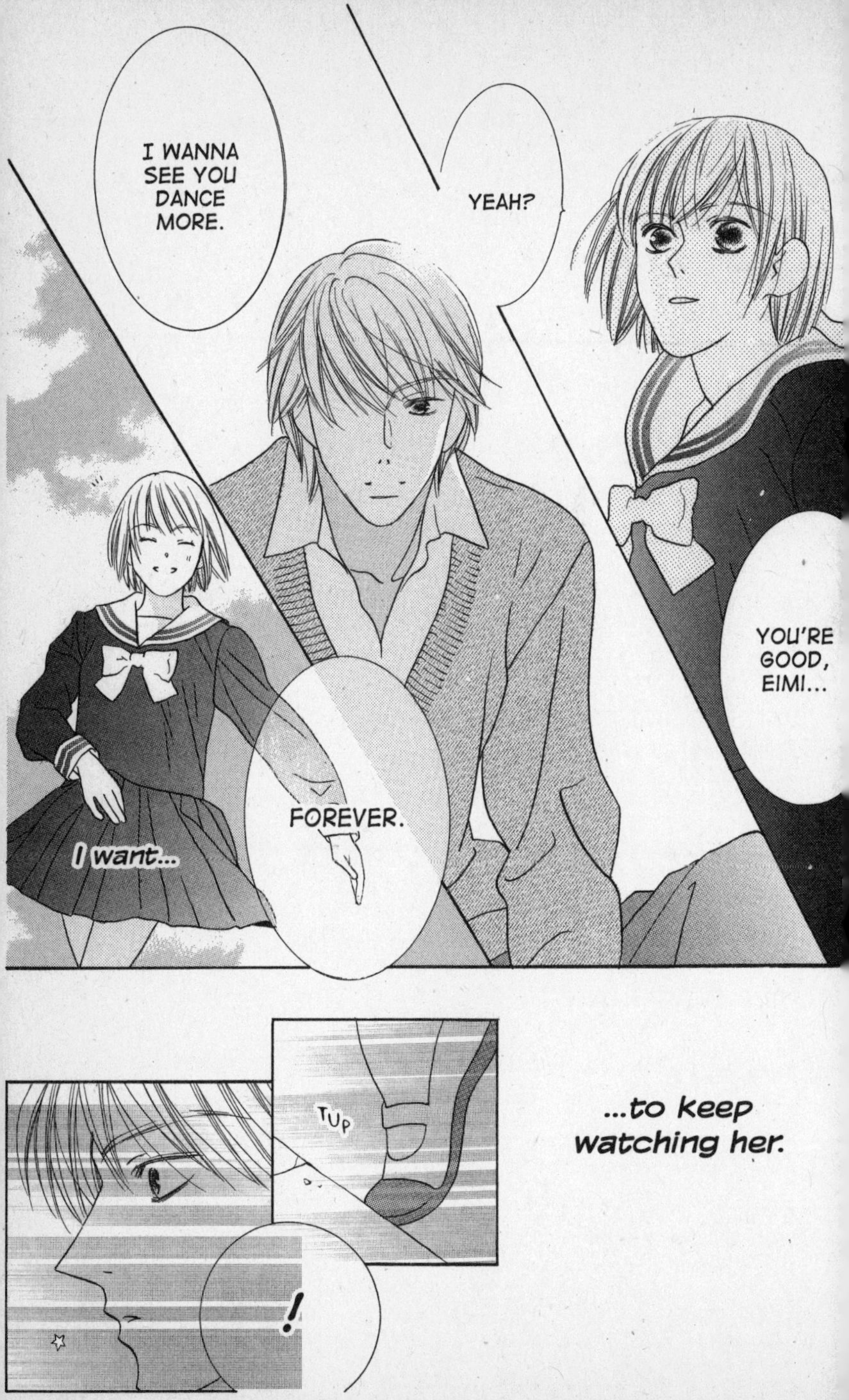
YOU'RE GOOD, EIMI...
YEAH?
I WANNA SEE YOU DANCE MORE.
FOREVER.
I want...
...to keep watching her.
TUP
!

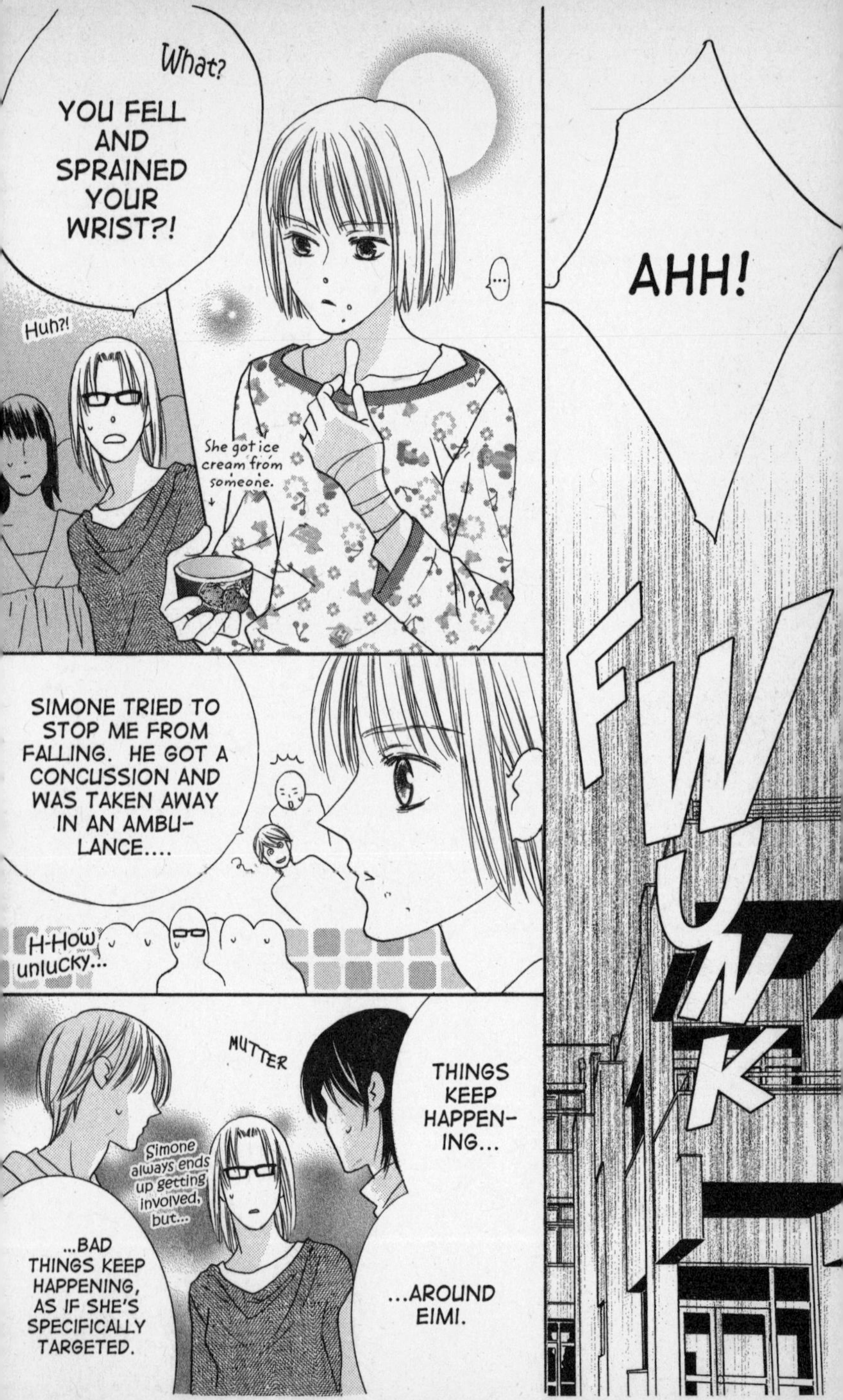
AHH!
FWUNK
What?
YOU FELL AND SPRAINED YOUR WRIST?!
...
Huh?!
She got ice cream from someone.
SIMONE TRIED TO STOP ME FROM FALLING. HE GOT A CONCUSSION AND WAS TAKEN AWAY IN AN AMBU-LANCE....
H-How unlucky...
THINGS KEEP HAPPEN-ING...
MUTTER
Simone always ends up getting involved, but...
...AROUND EIMI.
...BAD THINGS KEEP HAPPENING, AS IF SHE'S SPECIFICALLY TARGETED.

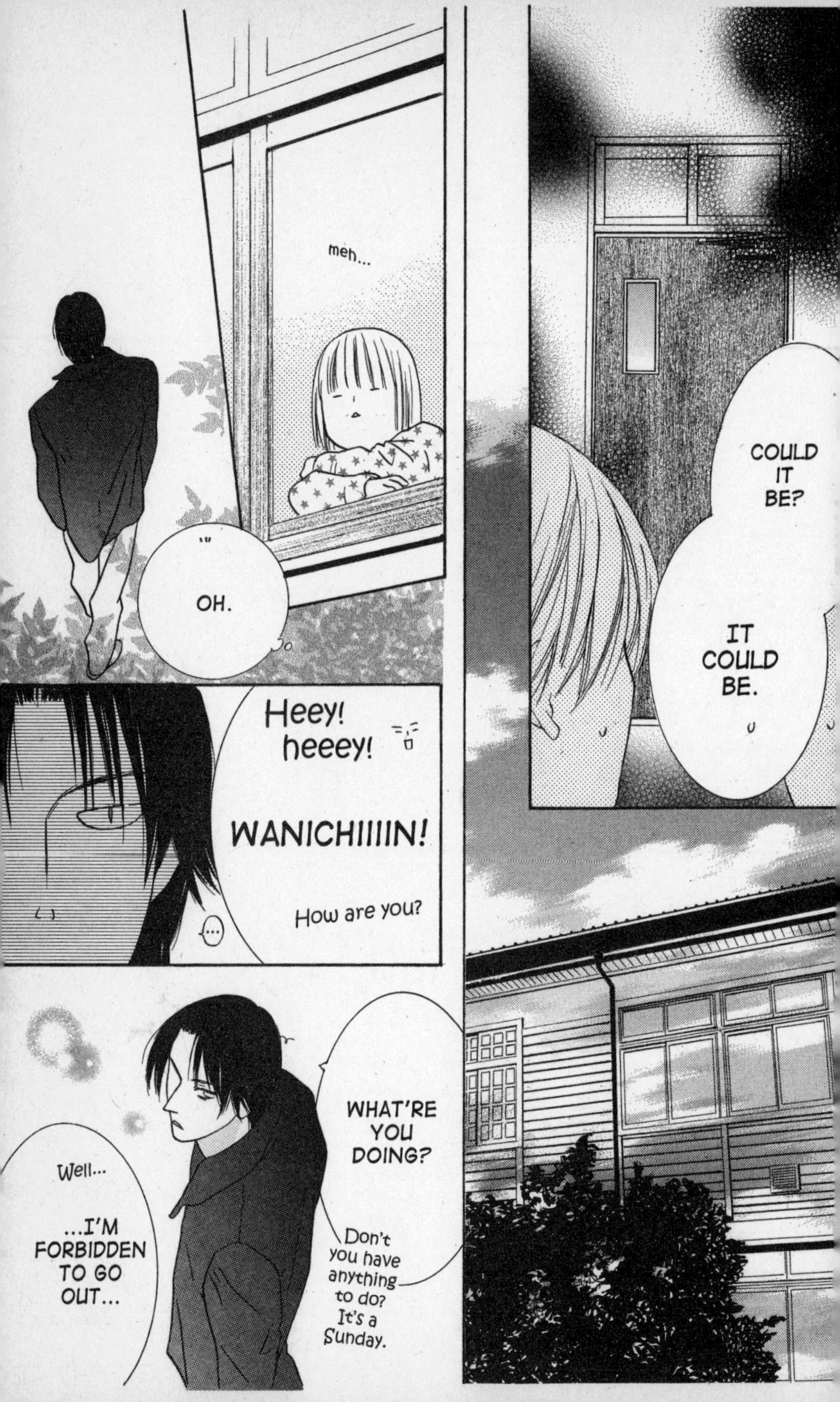
COULD IT BE?
IT COULD BE.
meh...
OH.
Heey! heeey!
WANICHIIIIN!
How are you?
...
WHAT'RE YOU DOING?
Don't you have anything to do? It's a Sunday.
Well...
...I'M FORBIDDEN TO GO OUT...

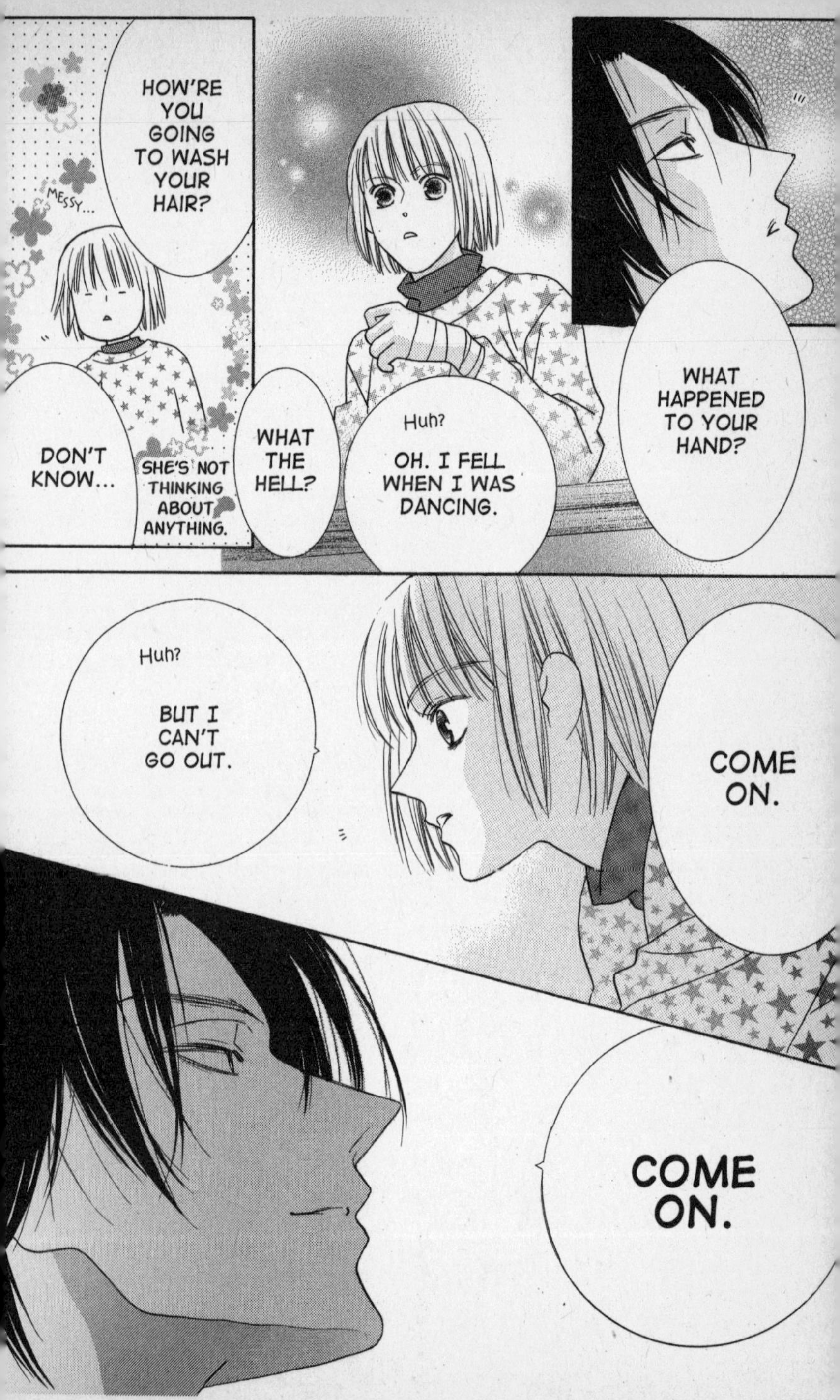
WHAT HAPPENED TO YOUR HAND?
Huh?
OH. I FELL WHEN I WAS DANCING.
WHAT THE HELL?
HOW'RE YOU GOING TO WASH YOUR HAIR?
MESSY...
DON'T KNOW...
SHE'S NOT THINKING ABOUT ANYTHING.
COME ON.
Huh?
BUT I CAN'T GO OUT.
COME ON.

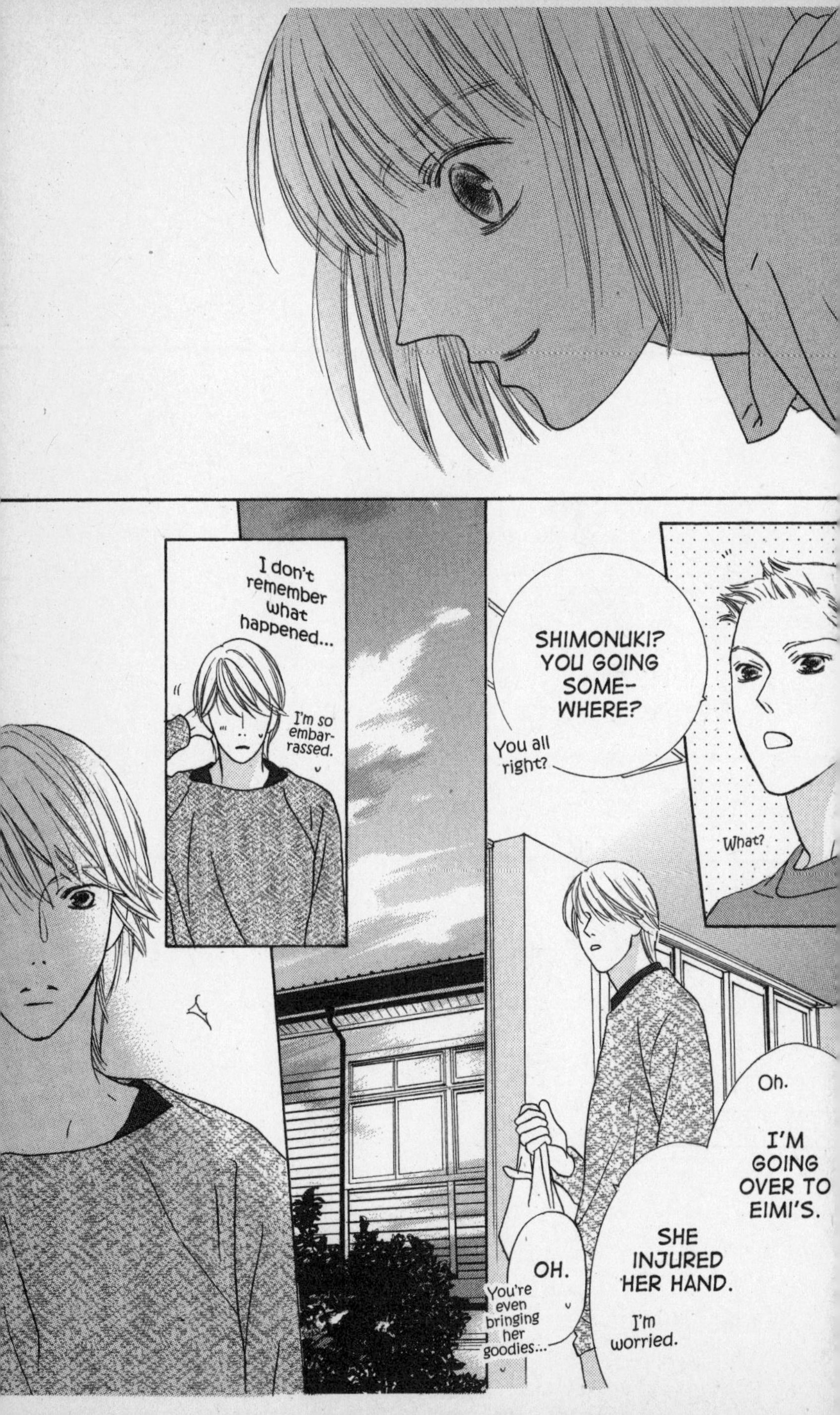
What?
SHIMONUKI? YOU GOING SOMEWHERE?
You all right?
Oh.
I'M GOING OVER TO EIMI'S.
SHE INJURED HER HAND.
I'm worried.
OH.
You're even bringing her goodies...
I don't remember what happened...
I'm so embarrassed.

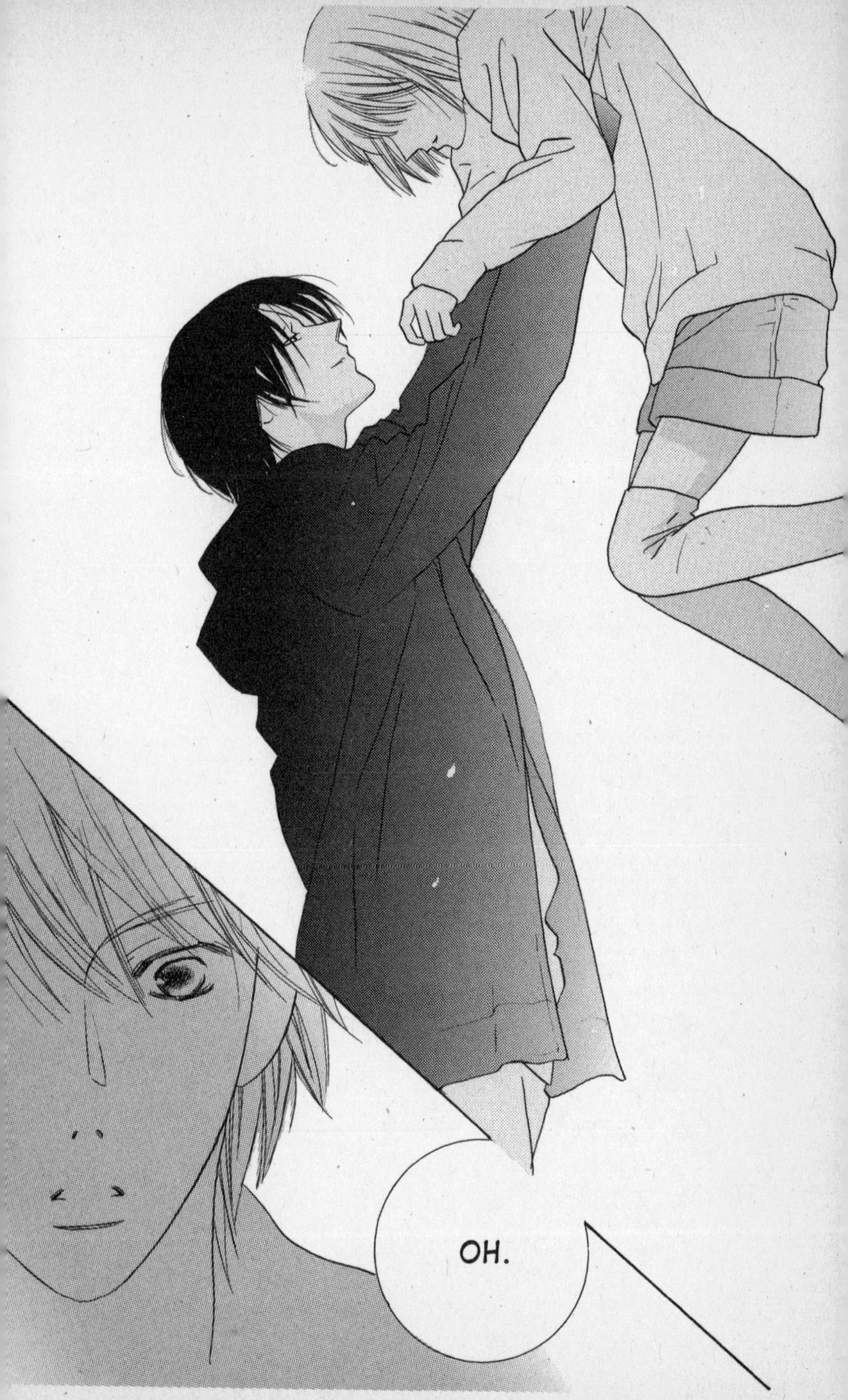
OH.

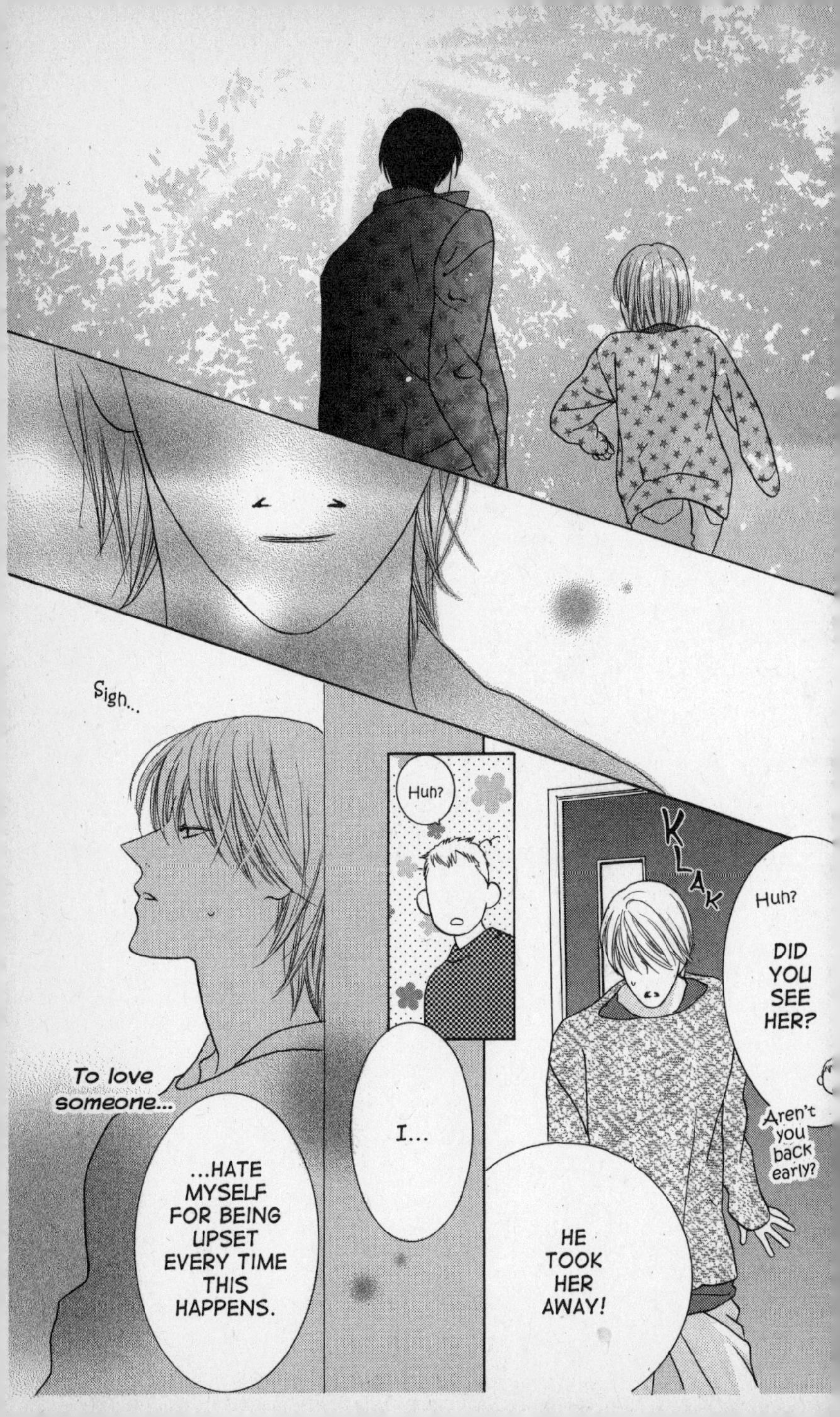
KLAK
Huh?
DID YOU SEE HER?
Aren't you back early?
HE TOOK HER AWAY!
Huh?
Sigh...
I...
...HATE MYSELF FOR BEING UPSET EVERY TIME THIS HAPPENS.
To love someone...

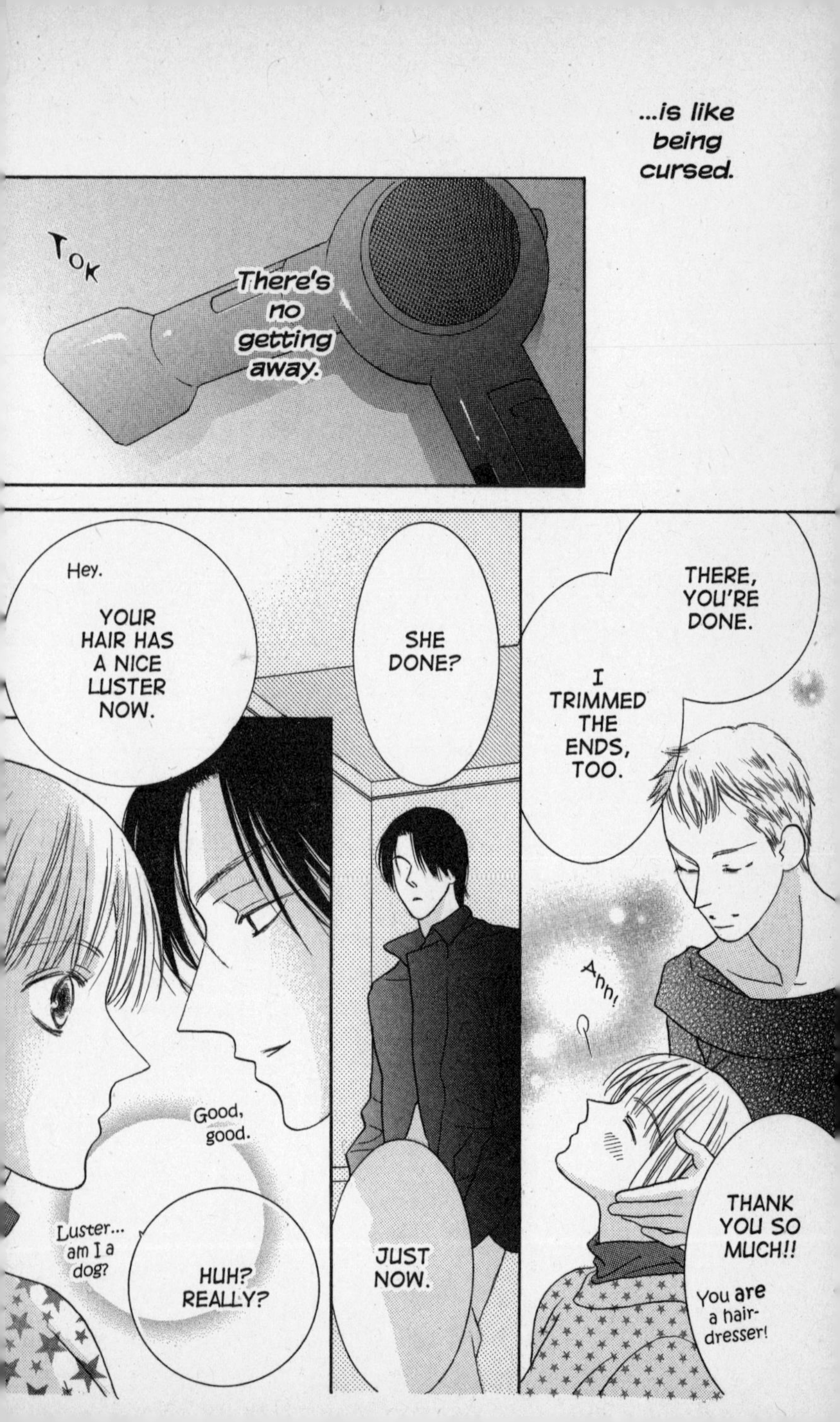
...is like being cursed.
TOK
There's no getting away.
THERE, YOU'RE DONE.
I TRIMMED THE ENDS, TOO.
Ahh!
THANK YOU SO MUCH!!
You are a hair-dresser!
SHE DONE?
JUST NOW.
Hey.
YOUR HAIR HAS A NICE LUSTER NOW.
Good, good.
HUH? REALLY?
Luster... am I a dog?

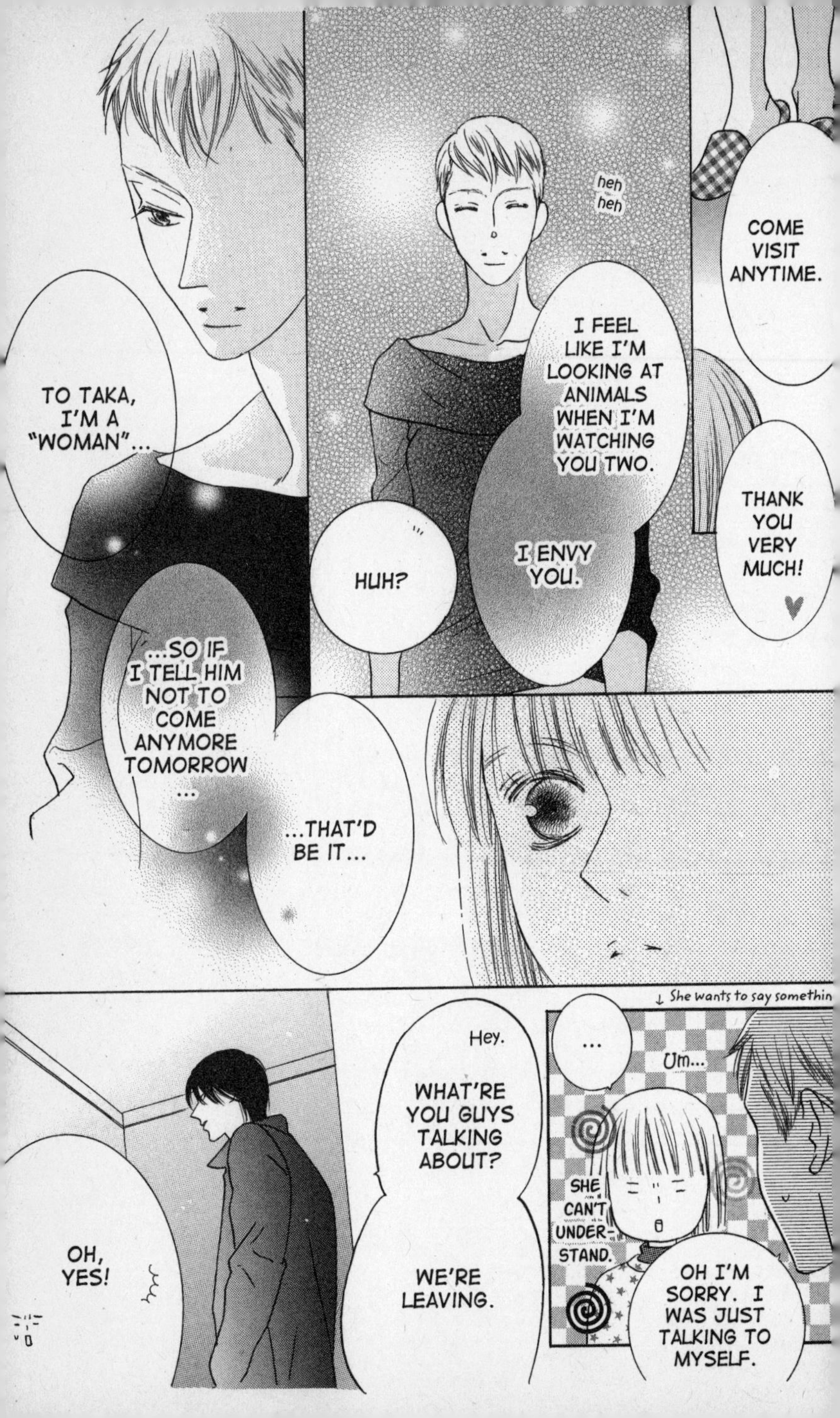
COME VISIT ANYTIME.
THANK YOU VERY MUCH! ♥
heh heh
I FEEL LIKE I'M LOOKING AT ANIMALS WHEN I'M WATCHING YOU TWO.
I ENVY YOU.
HUH?
TO TAKA, I'M A "WOMAN"...
...SO IF I TELL HIM NOT TO COME ANYMORE TOMORROW ...
...THAT'D BE IT...
↓ She wants to say somethin
...
Um...
SHE CAN'T UNDER-STAND.
OH I'M SORRY. I WAS JUST TALKING TO MYSELF.
Hey.
WHAT'RE YOU GUYS TALKING ABOUT?
WE'RE LEAVING.
OH, YES!

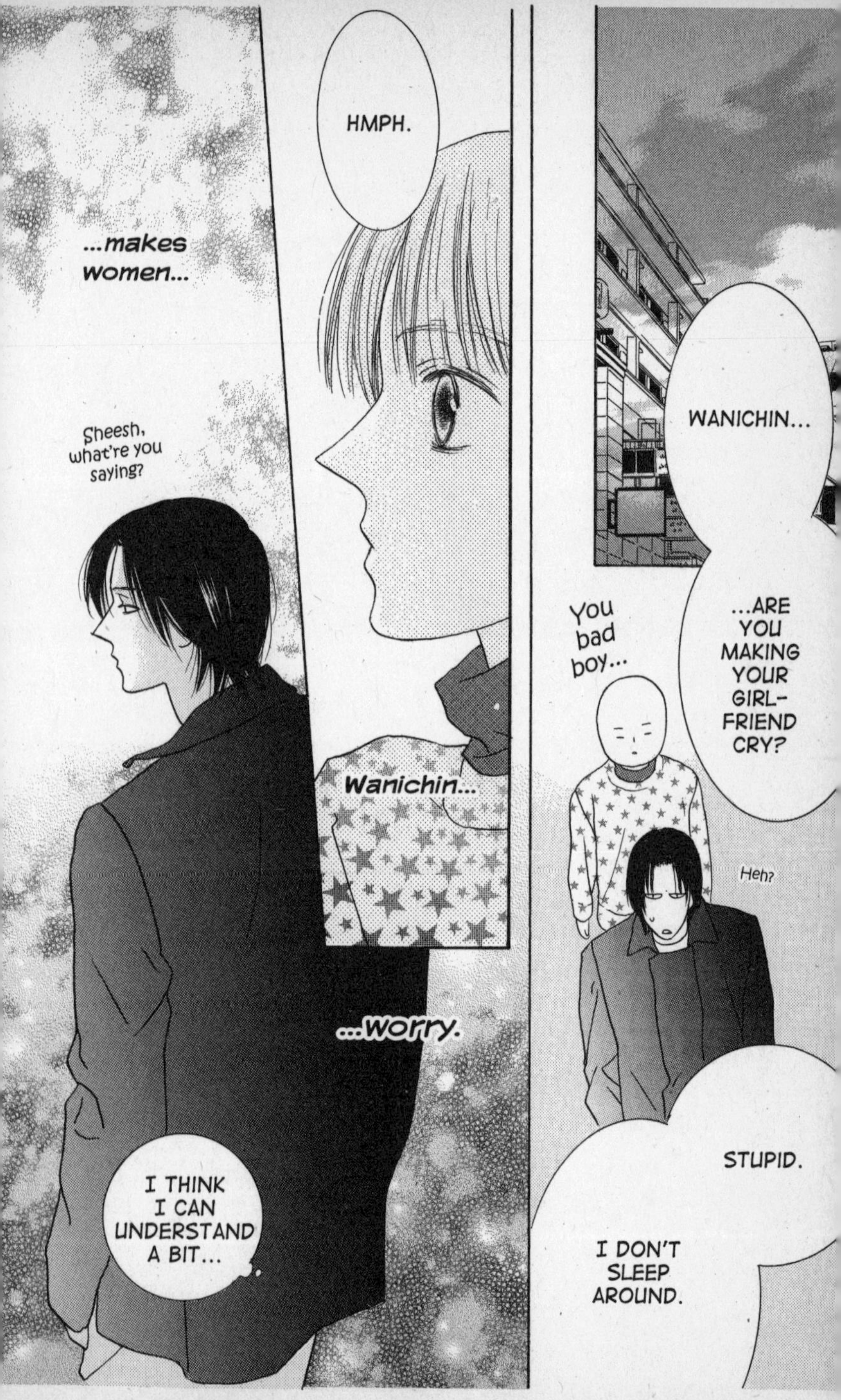
WANICHIN...
...ARE YOU MAKING YOUR GIRL-FRIEND CRY?
You bad boy...
Heh?
STUPID.
I DON'T SLEEP AROUND.
HMPH.
Wanichin...
...makes women...
Sheesh, what're you saying?
...worry.
I THINK I CAN UNDERSTAND A BIT...

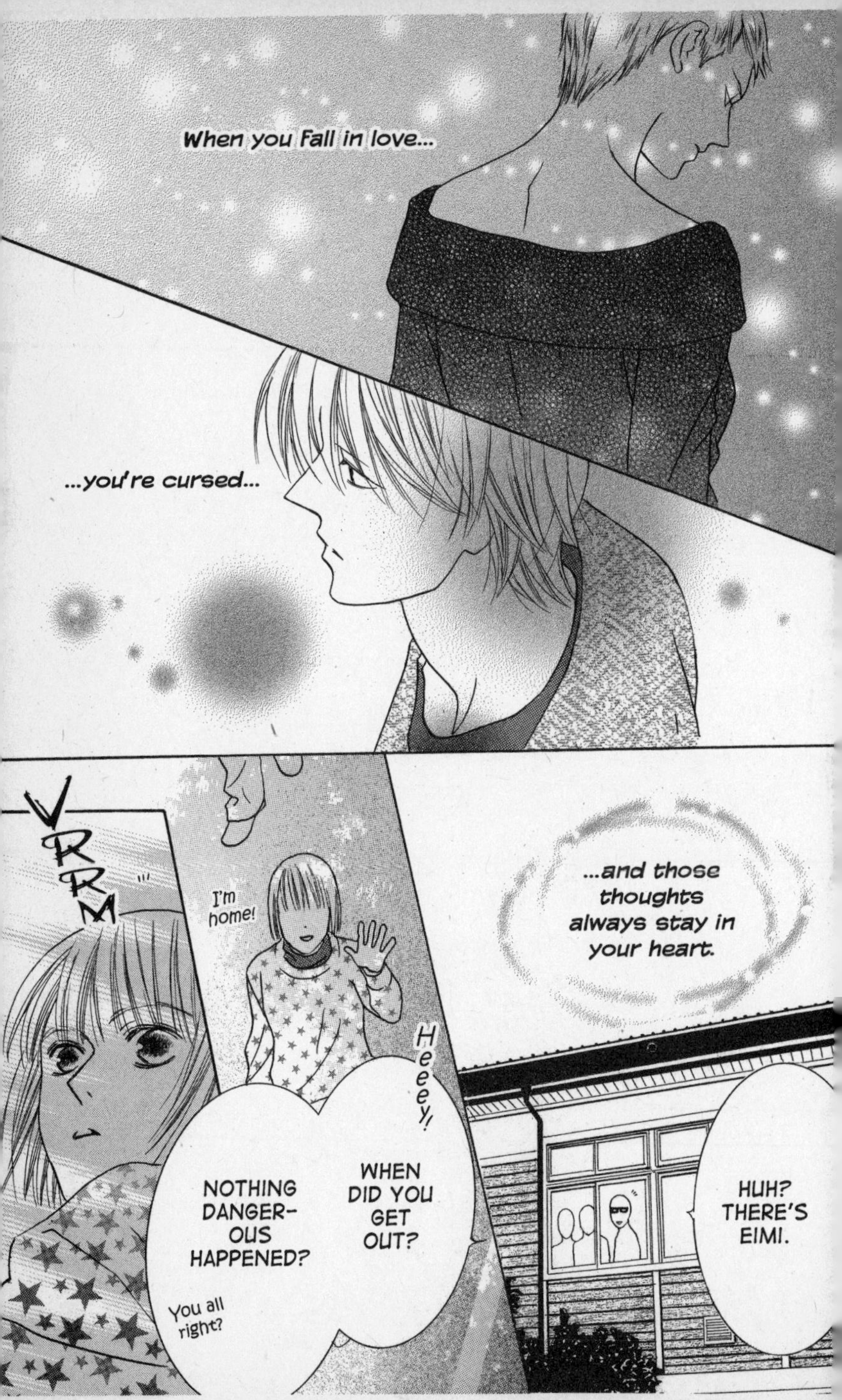
When you fall in love...
...you're cursed...
...and those thoughts always stay in your heart.
HUH? THERE'S EIMI.
I'm home!
Heeeey!
WHEN DID YOU GET OUT?
NOTHING DANGER-OUS HAPPENED?
You all right?
VRRM

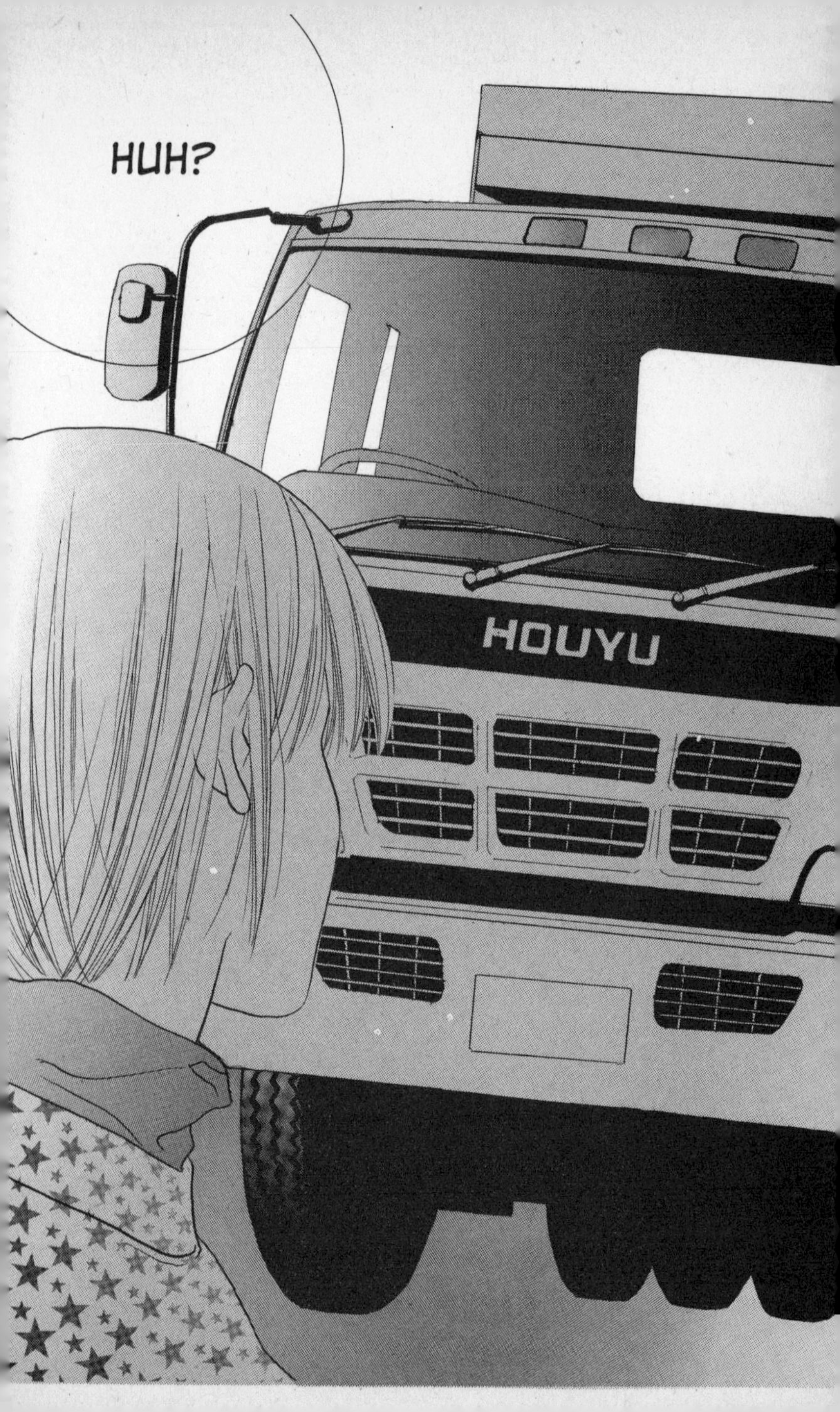
HUH?
HOUYU

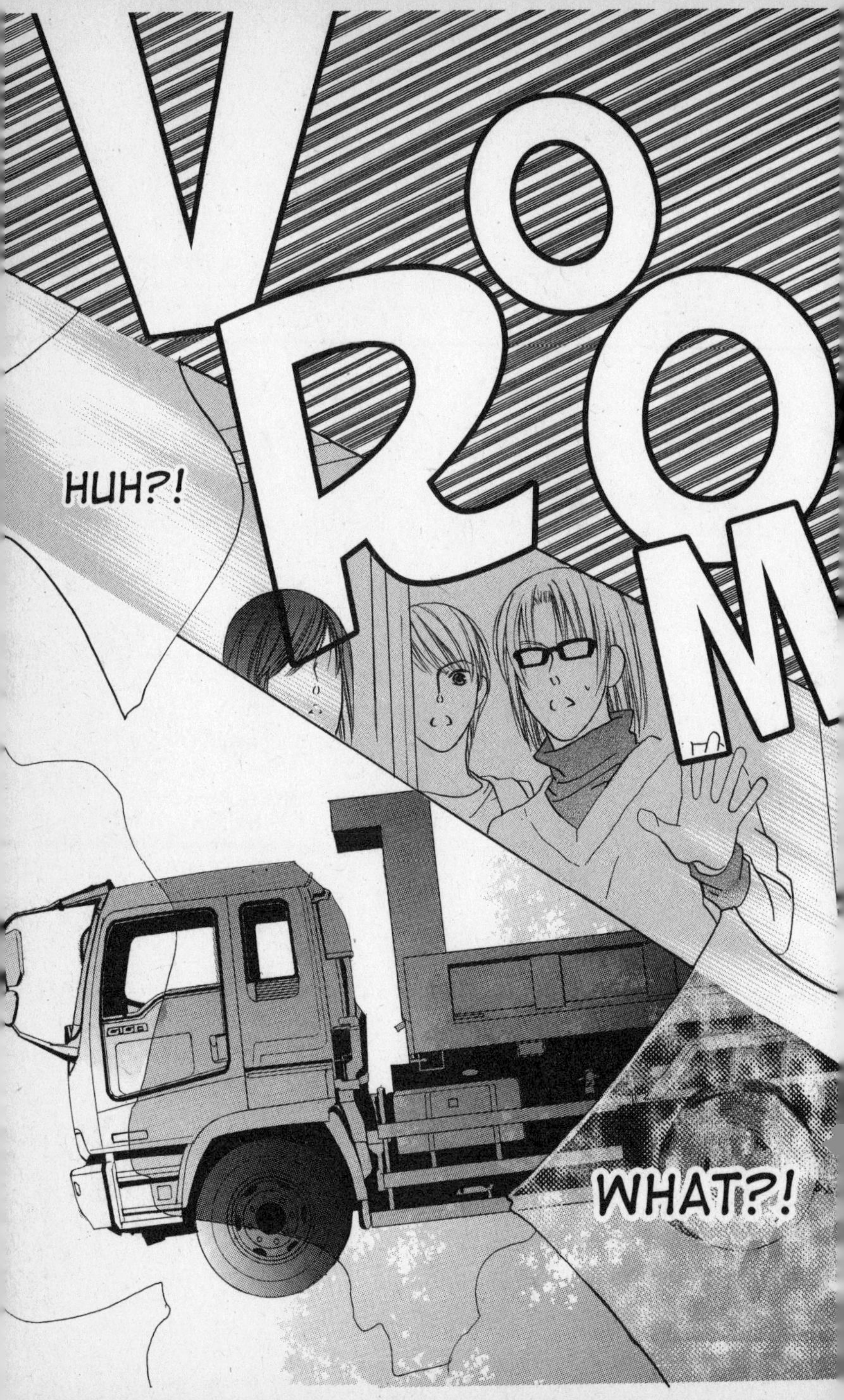
VROOM
HUH?!
WHAT?!

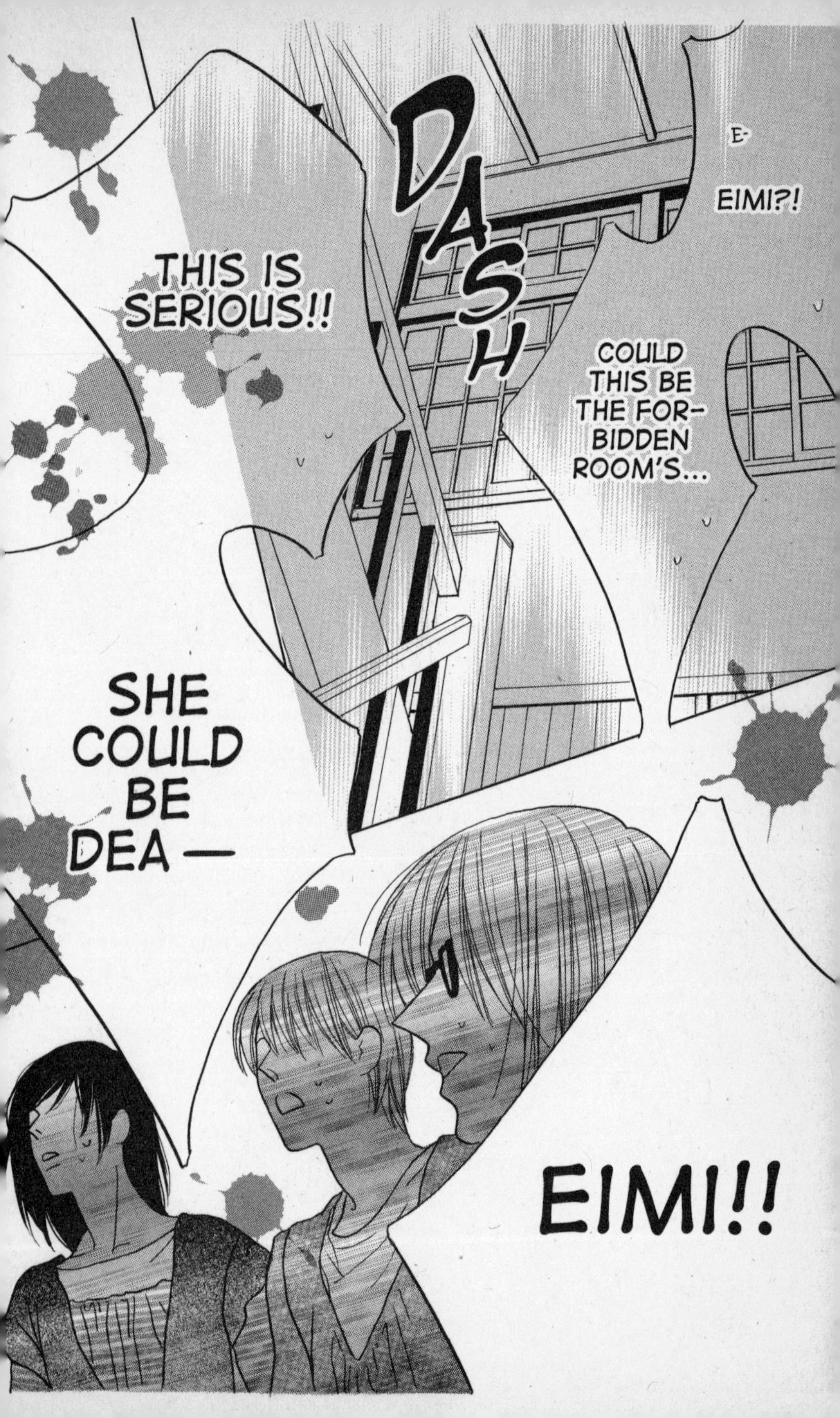
E-
EIMI?!
DASH
COULD THIS BE THE FOR-BIDDEN ROOM'S...
THIS IS SERIOUS!!
SHE COULD BE DEA—
EIMI!!

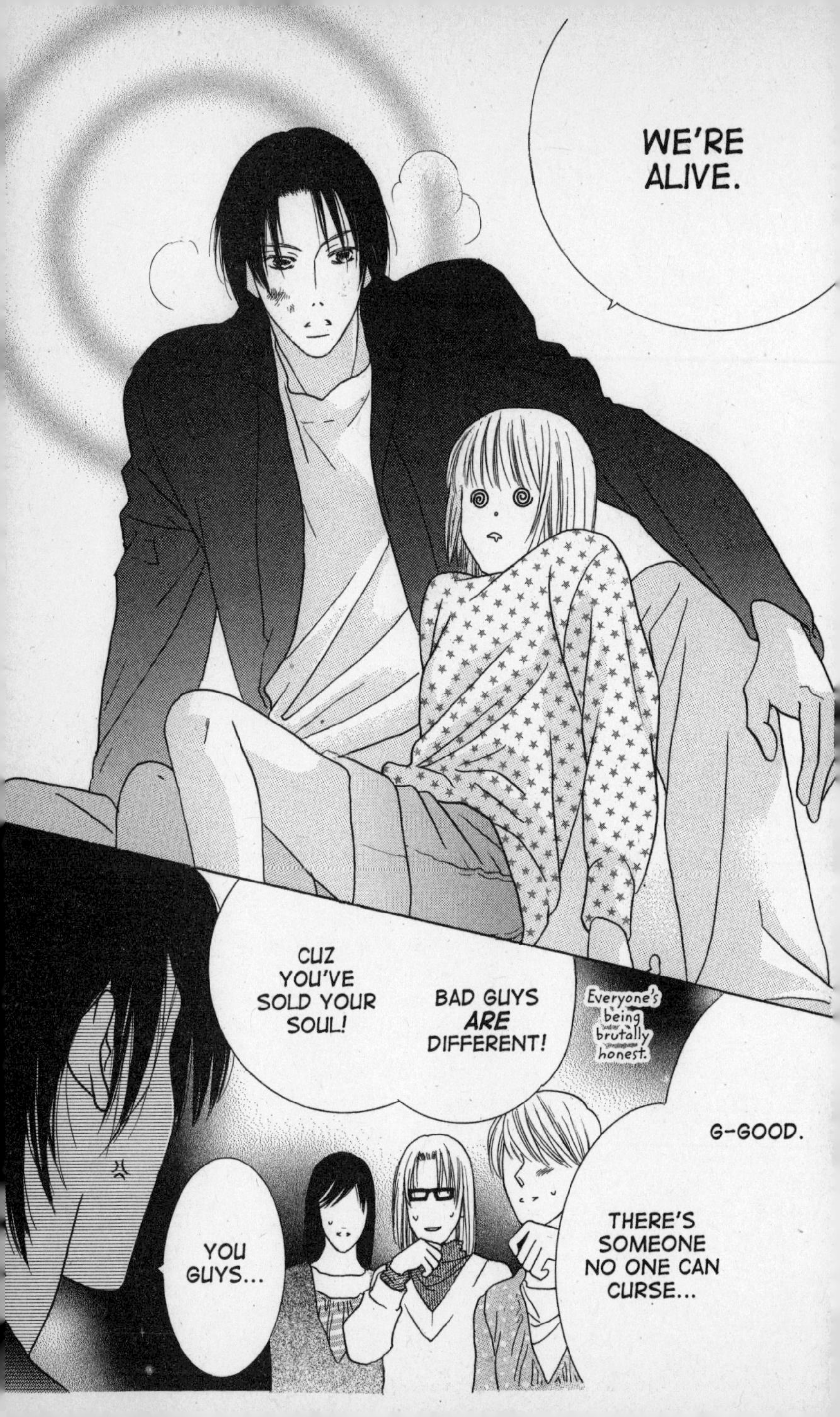
WE'RE ALIVE.
G-GOOD.
THERE'S SOMEONE NO ONE CAN CURSE...
Everyone's being brutally honest.
BAD GUYS **ARE** DIFFERENT!
CUZ YOU'VE SOLD YOUR SOUL!
YOU GUYS...

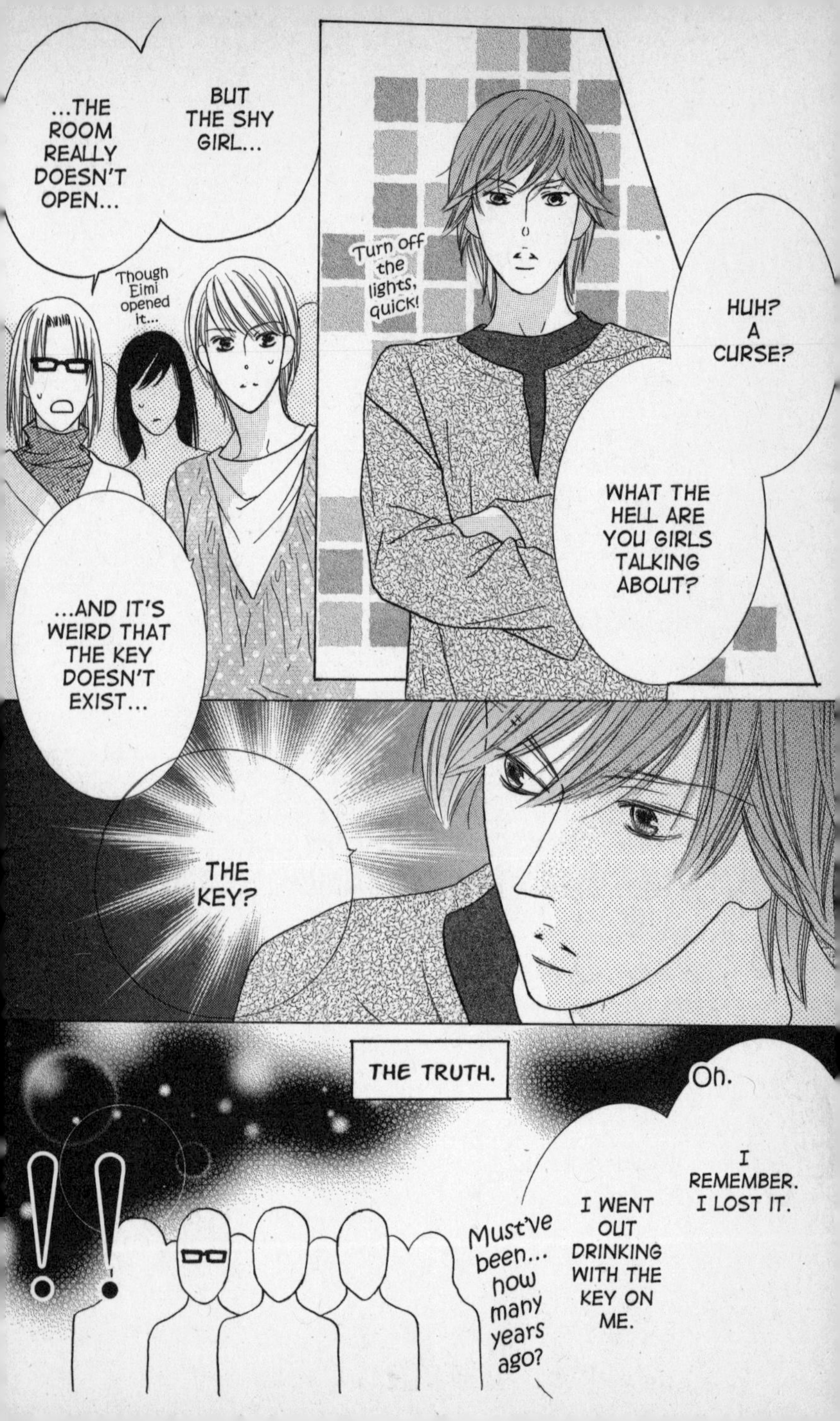
HUH? A CURSE?
WHAT THE HELL ARE YOU GIRLS TALKING ABOUT?
Turn off the lights, quick!
BUT THE SHY GIRL...
...THE ROOM REALLY DOESN'T OPEN...
Though Eimi opened it...
...AND IT'S WEIRD THAT THE KEY DOESN'T EXIST...
THE KEY?
Oh.
I REMEMBER. I LOST IT.
I WENT OUT DRINKING WITH THE KEY ON ME.
Must've been... how many years ago?
THE TRUTH.
!!

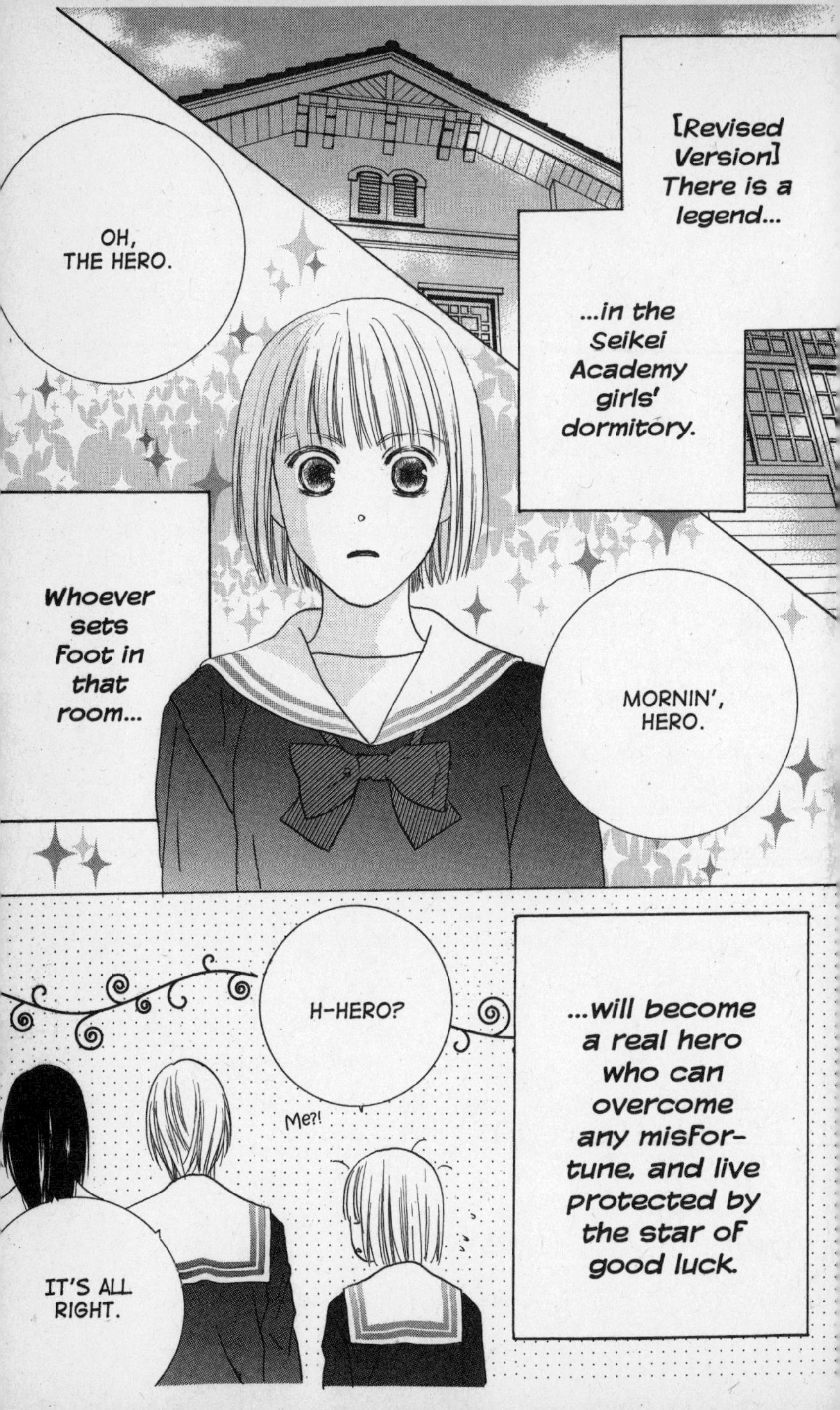
[Revised Version] There is a legend...
...in the Seikei Academy girls' dormitory.
OH, THE HERO.
MORNIN', HERO.
Whoever sets foot in that room...
...will become a real hero who can overcome any misfor-tune, and live protected by the star of good luck.
H-HERO?
Me?!
IT'S ALL RIGHT.

100 g
200 g
300 g
400 g
500 g
600 g
700 g
800 g

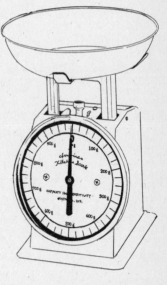

BEAUTY IS THE BEAST

Beauty is the Beast

There are two guys and a girl ...

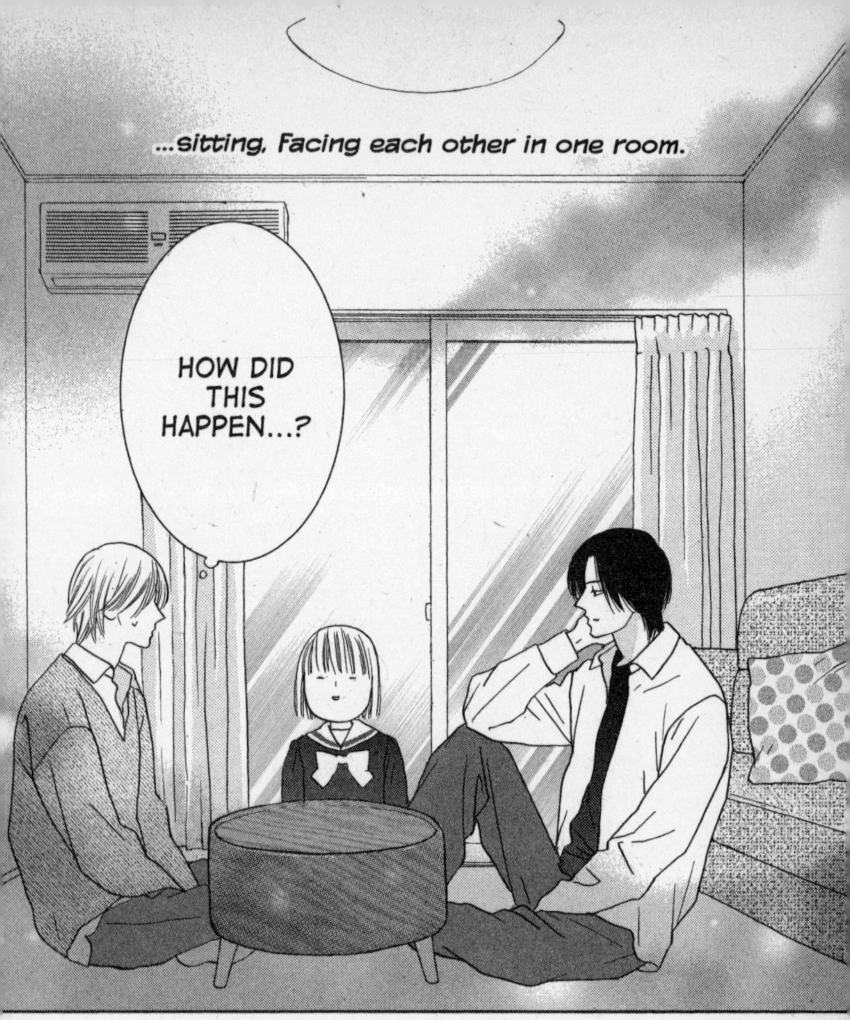
...sitting, Facing each other in one room.
HOW DID THIS HAPPEN...?

My backgournd music during work this time was curiously traditional(?), and I listened to Usher, Alicia Keys, Prince, and Maroon 5.

I really love Maroon 5. I've been listening to them since I got the first relase of their import album.
The way I listen to music is to listen to the one song I liked about 1500-2000 times in the first month. If I still want to listen to it, it is "Certified as a Song I Really Love." (☺) An amazing persistence!

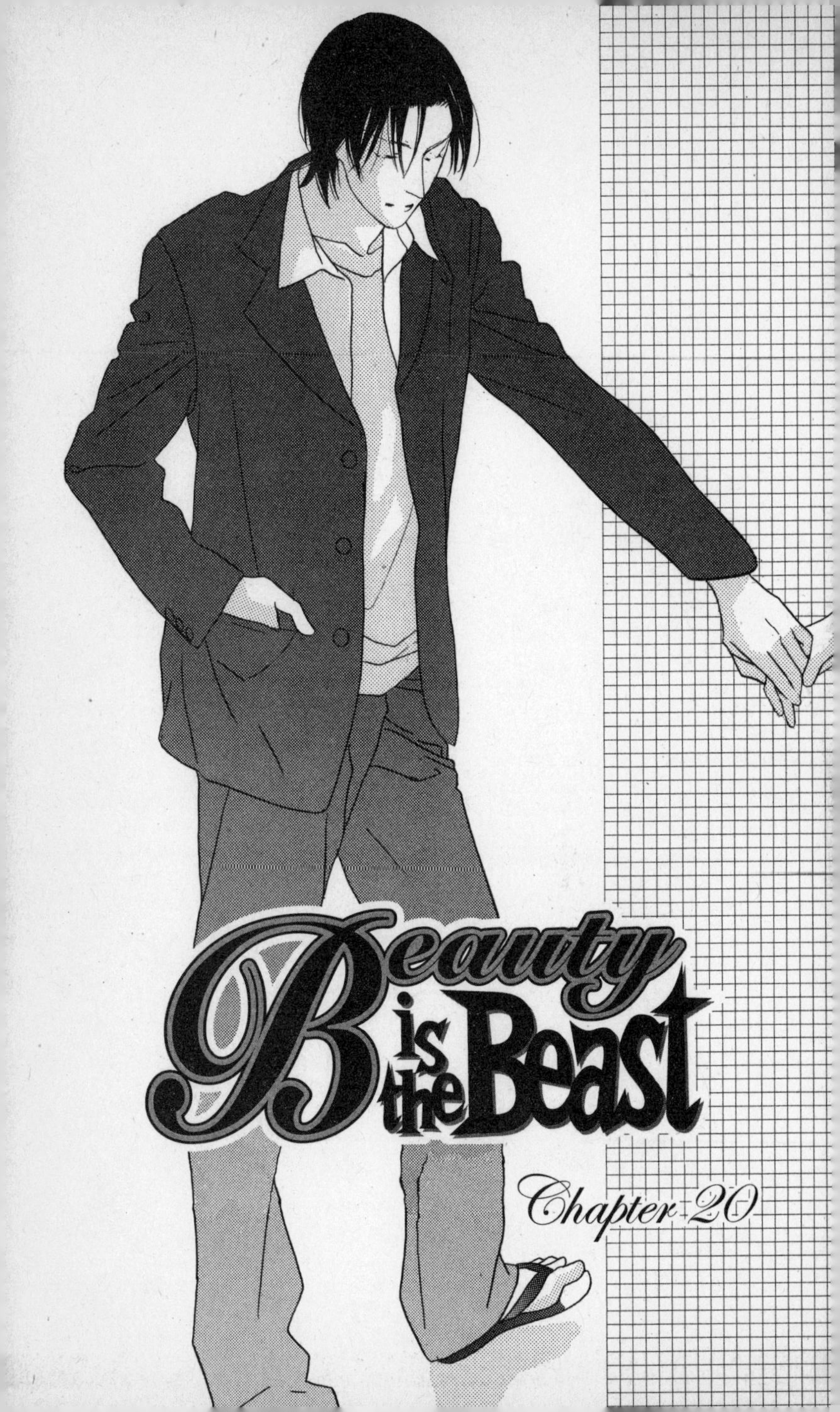
Beauty is the Beast
Chapter 20

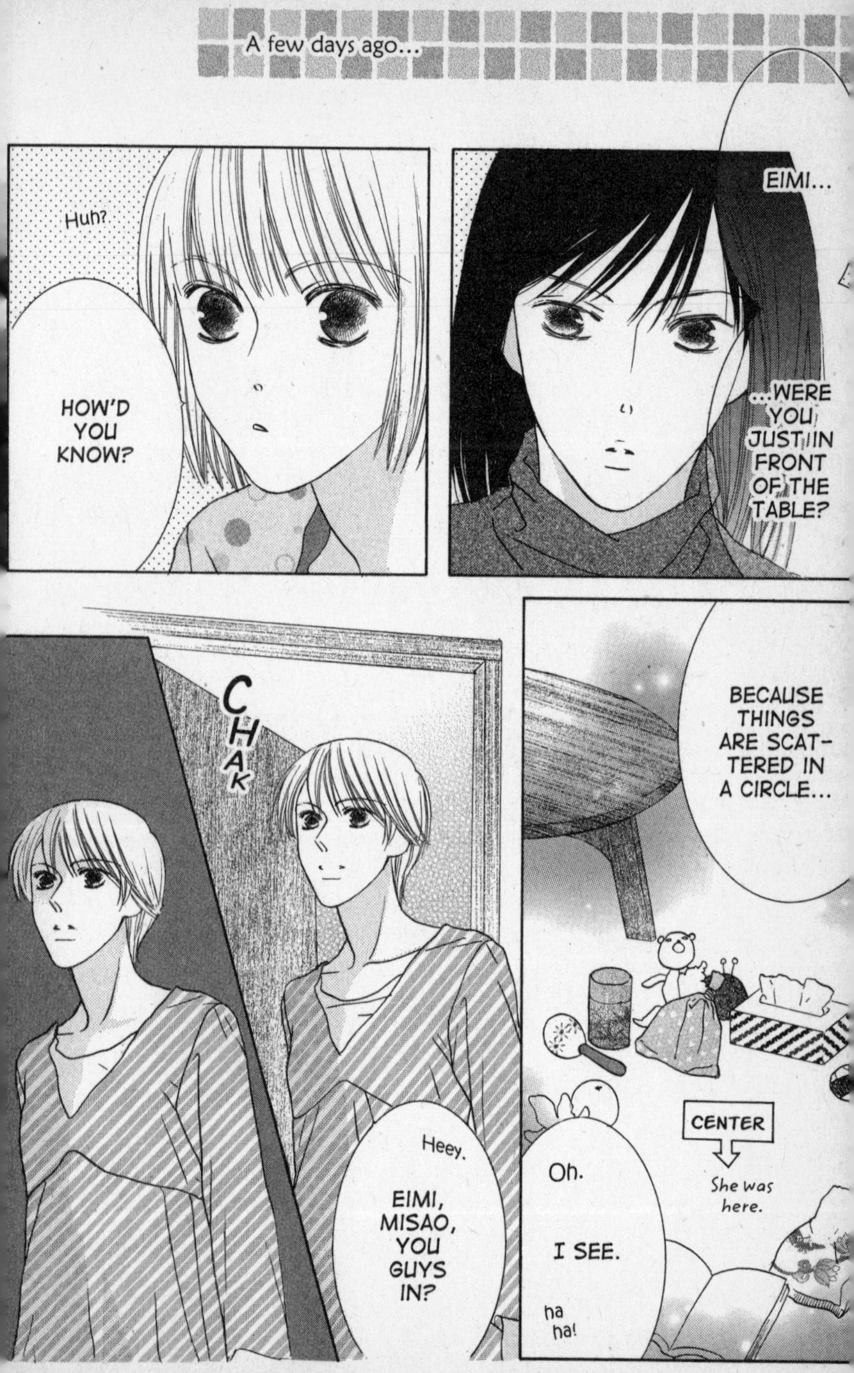
A few days ago...
EIMI...
...WERE YOU JUST IN FRONT OF THE TABLE?
Huh?
HOW'D YOU KNOW?
BECAUSE THINGS ARE SCAT-TERED IN A CIRCLE...
CENTER
She was here.
Oh.
I SEE.
ha ha!
CHAK
Heey.
EIMI, MISAO, YOU GUYS IN?

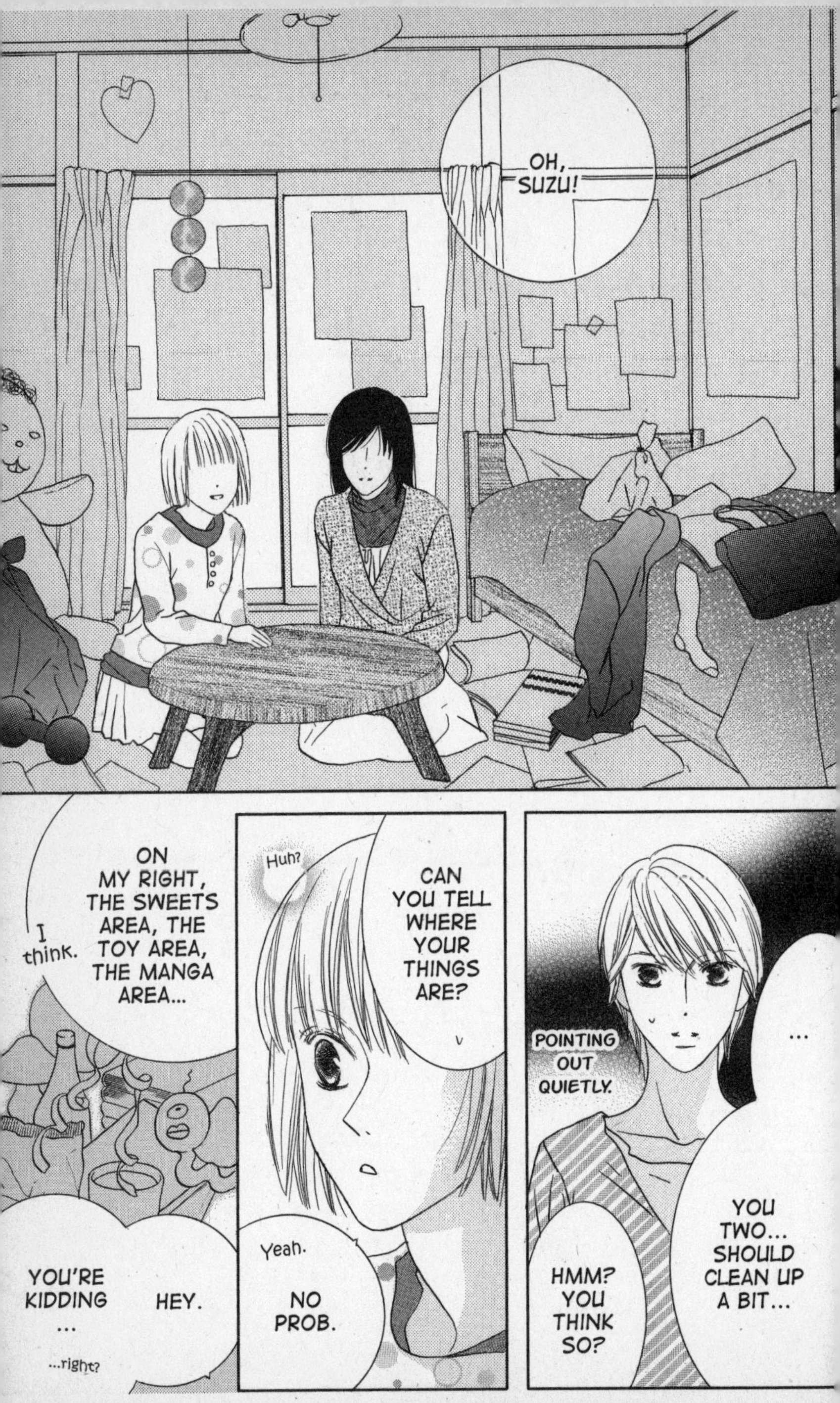
OH, SUZU!
...
YOU TWO... SHOULD CLEAN UP A BIT...
POINTING OUT QUIETLY.
HMM? YOU THINK SO?
CAN YOU TELL WHERE YOUR THINGS ARE?
Huh?
Yeah.
NO PROB.
ON MY RIGHT, THE SWEETS AREA, THE TOY AREA, THE MANGA AREA...
I think.
HEY.
YOU'RE KIDDING ...
...right?

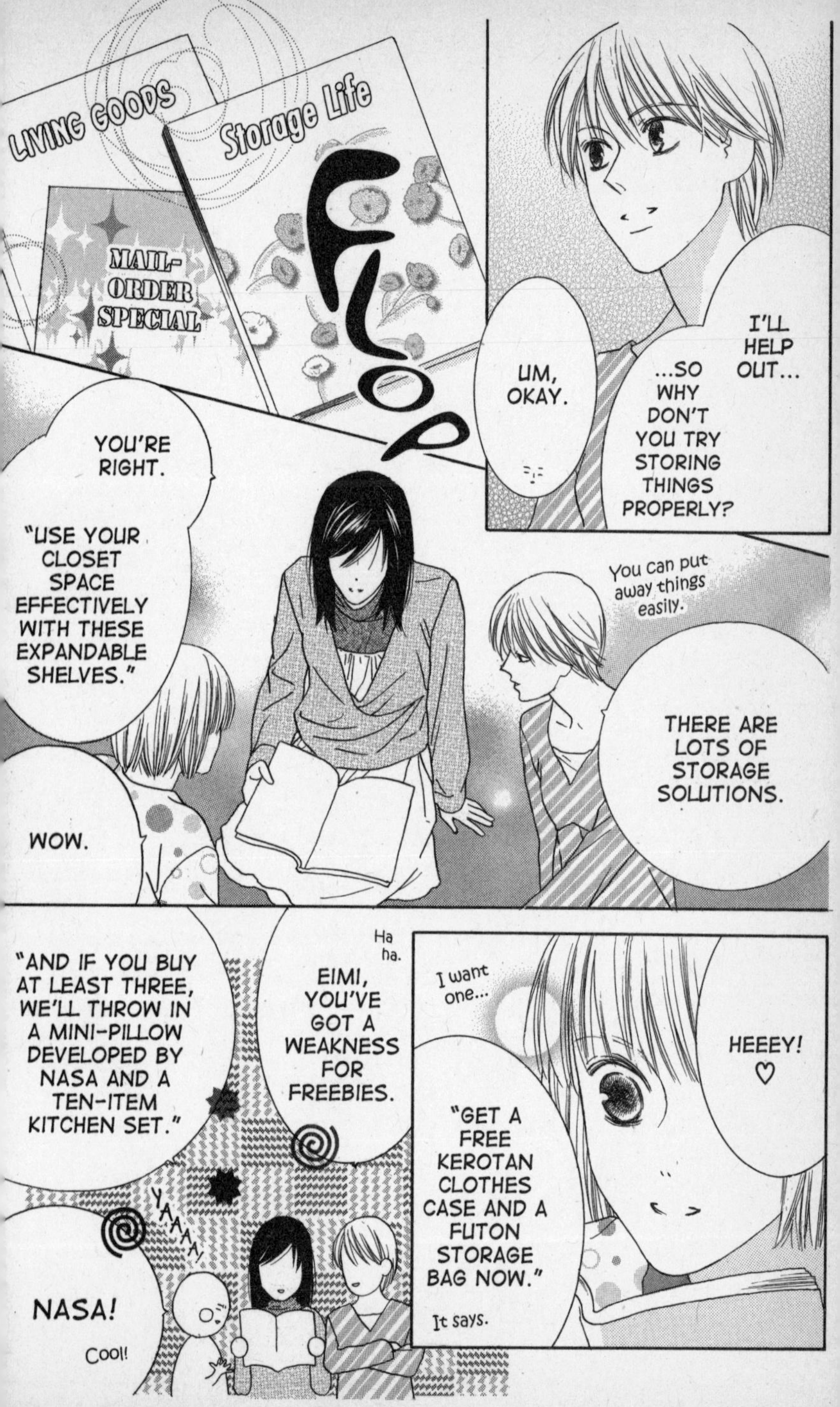
I'LL HELP OUT...
...SO WHY DON'T YOU TRY STORING THINGS PROPERLY?
UM, OKAY.
Storage Life
LIVING GOODS
MAIL-ORDER SPECIAL
FLOP
You can put away things easily.
THERE ARE LOTS OF STORAGE SOLUTIONS.
YOU'RE RIGHT.
"USE YOUR CLOSET SPACE EFFECTIVELY WITH THESE EXPANDABLE SHELVES."
WOW.
HEEEY! ♡
I want one...
"GET A FREE KEROTAN CLOTHES CASE AND A FUTON STORAGE BAG NOW."
It says.
Ha ha.
EIMI, YOU'VE GOT A WEAKNESS FOR FREEBIES.
"AND IF YOU BUY AT LEAST THREE, WE'LL THROW IN A MINI-PILLOW DEVELOPED BY NASA AND A TEN-ITEM KITCHEN SET."
YAAAA!
NASA!
Cool!

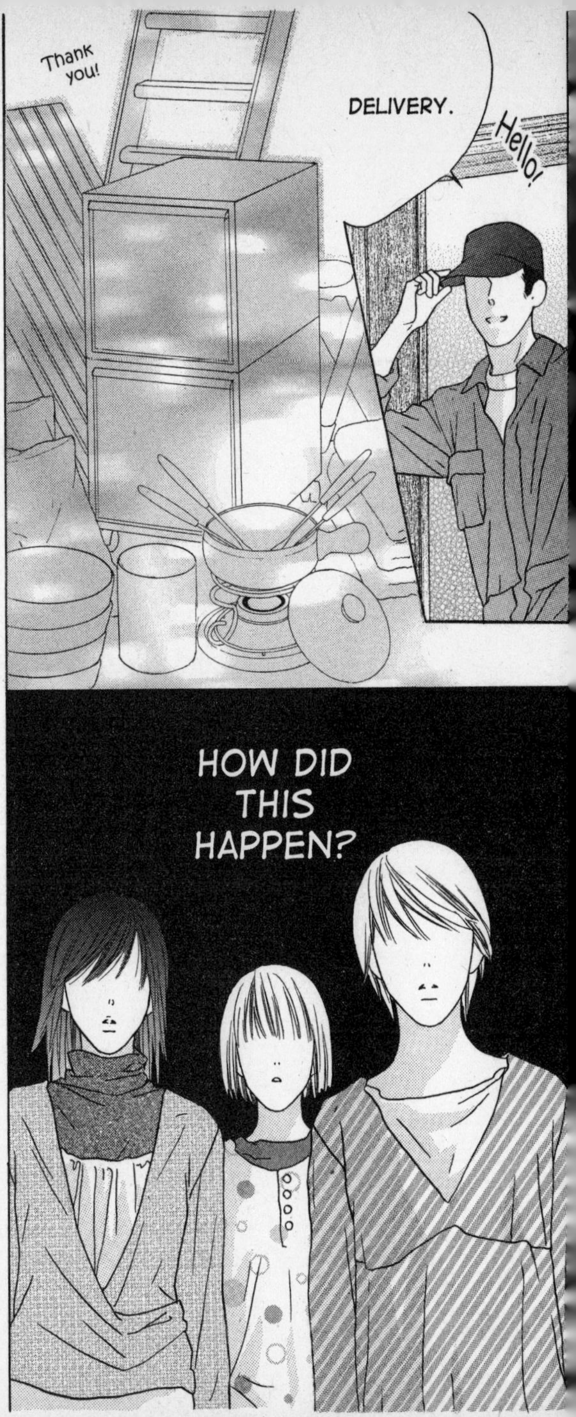
Hello!
DELIVERY.
Thank you!
HOW DID THIS HAPPEN?

3

I love love love interior decorations!
I like looking at mail-order magazines. I like DIY centers too.
My grandfather was a carpenter and maybe because of that, I get excited when I see timber or metal arranged in rows.
I'm not that strong, so I can't work on big stuff, but doing things like replacing the handles on furniture to change the atmosphere is fun. And I go to a 100 yen bargain store and buy hinges for no reason. (Are you stupid?!)
By the way, the desk and curtains in my current studio are handmade. People try to talk me out of doing things (bitter smile), but I don't care.

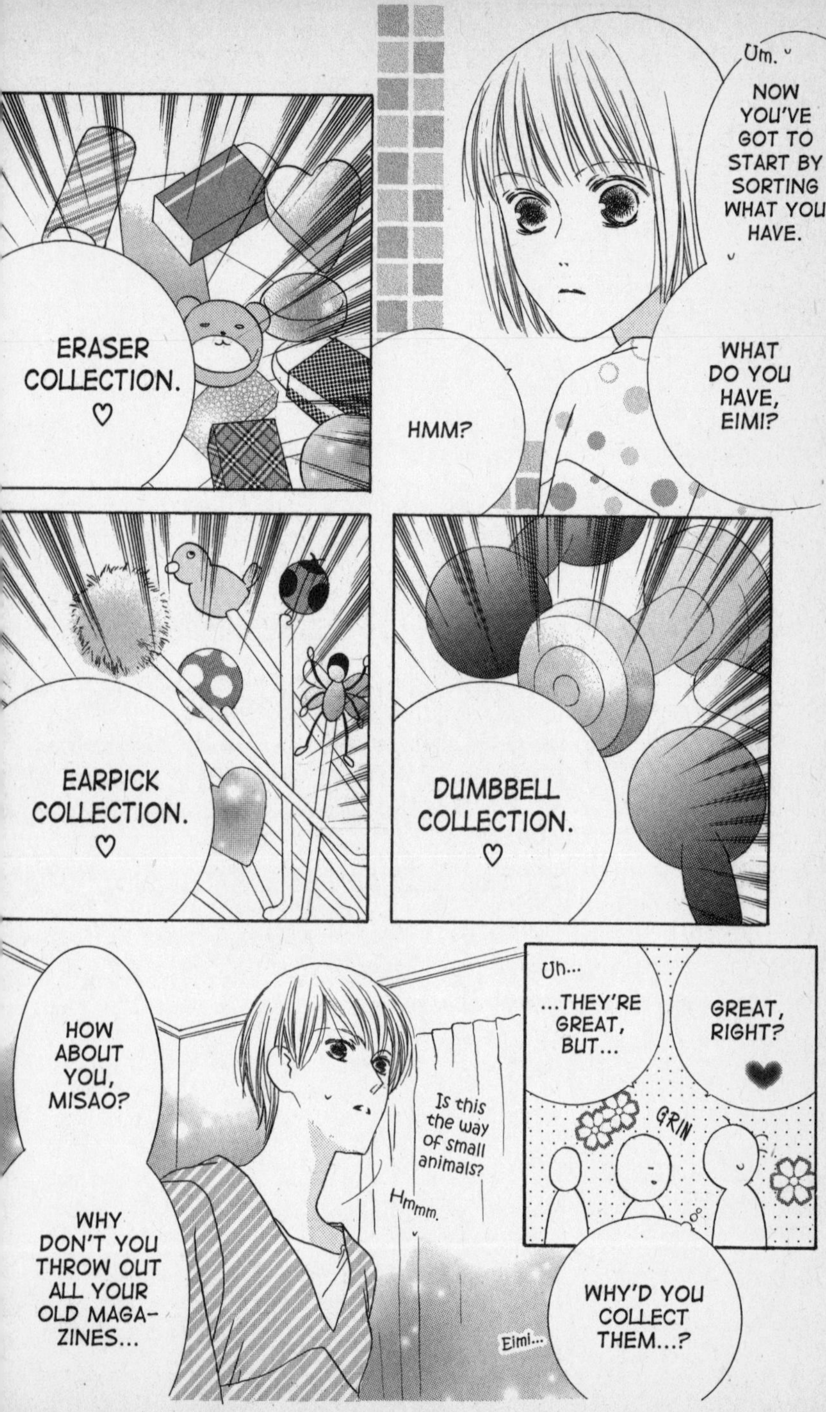
Um.
NOW YOU'VE GOT TO START BY SORTING WHAT YOU HAVE.
WHAT DO YOU HAVE, EIMI?
HMM?
ERASER COLLECTION. ♡
DUMBBELL COLLECTION. ♡
EARPICK COLLECTION. ♡
GREAT, RIGHT? ♥
Uh...
...THEY'RE GREAT, BUT...
GRIN
WHY'D YOU COLLECT THEM...?
Eimi...
Hmmm.
Is this the way of small animals?
HOW ABOUT YOU, MISAO?
WHY DON'T YOU THROW OUT ALL YOUR OLD MAGA-ZINES...

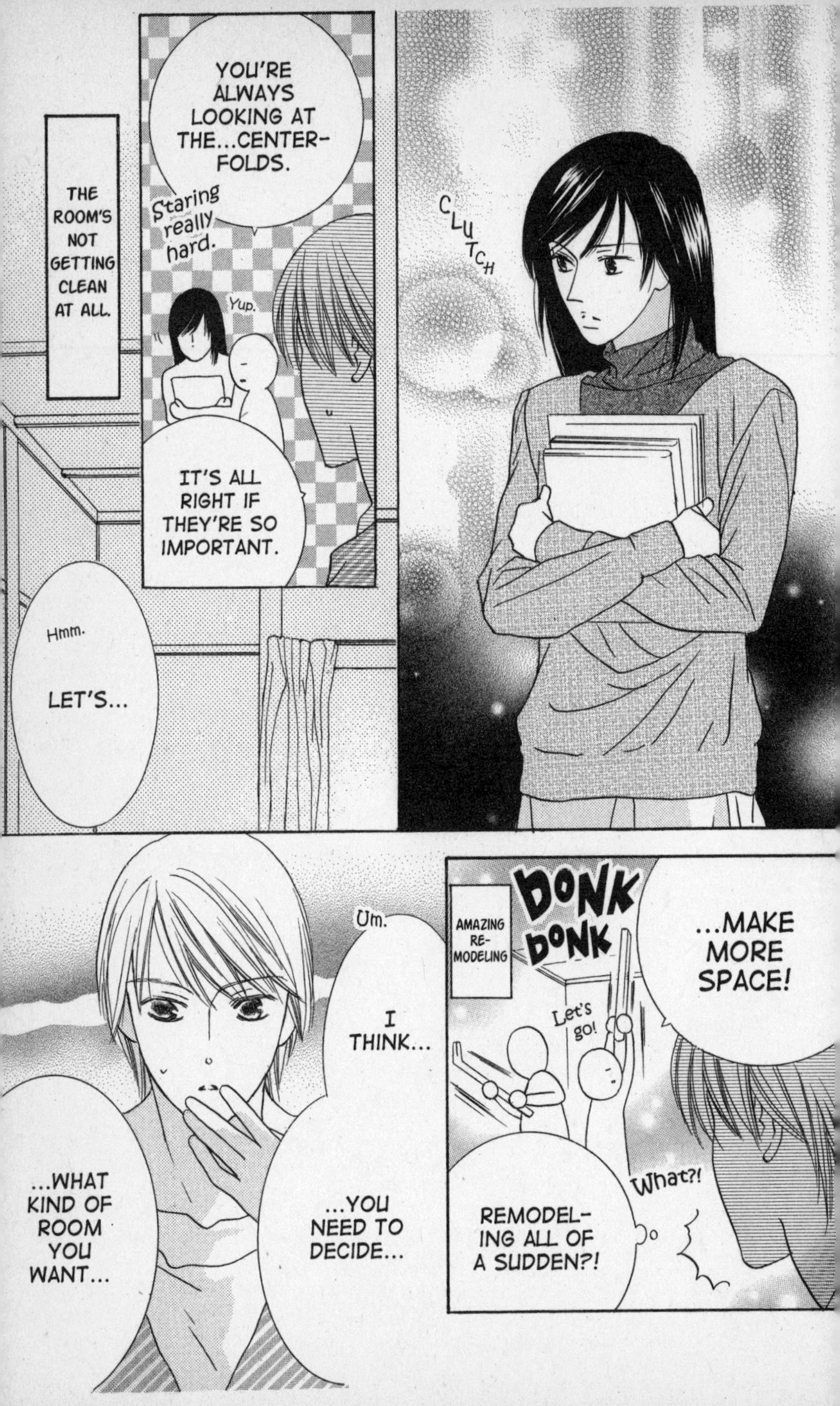
CLUTCH
YOU'RE ALWAYS LOOKING AT THE...CENTERFOLDS.
Staring really hard.
Yup.
IT'S ALL RIGHT IF THEY'RE SO IMPORTANT.
THE ROOM'S NOT GETTING CLEAN AT ALL.
Hmm.
LET'S...
...MAKE MORE SPACE!
DONK DONK
AMAZING RE-MODELING
Let's go!
What?!
REMODELING ALL OF A SUDDEN?!
Um.
I THINK...
...YOU NEED TO DECIDE...
...WHAT KIND OF ROOM YOU WANT...

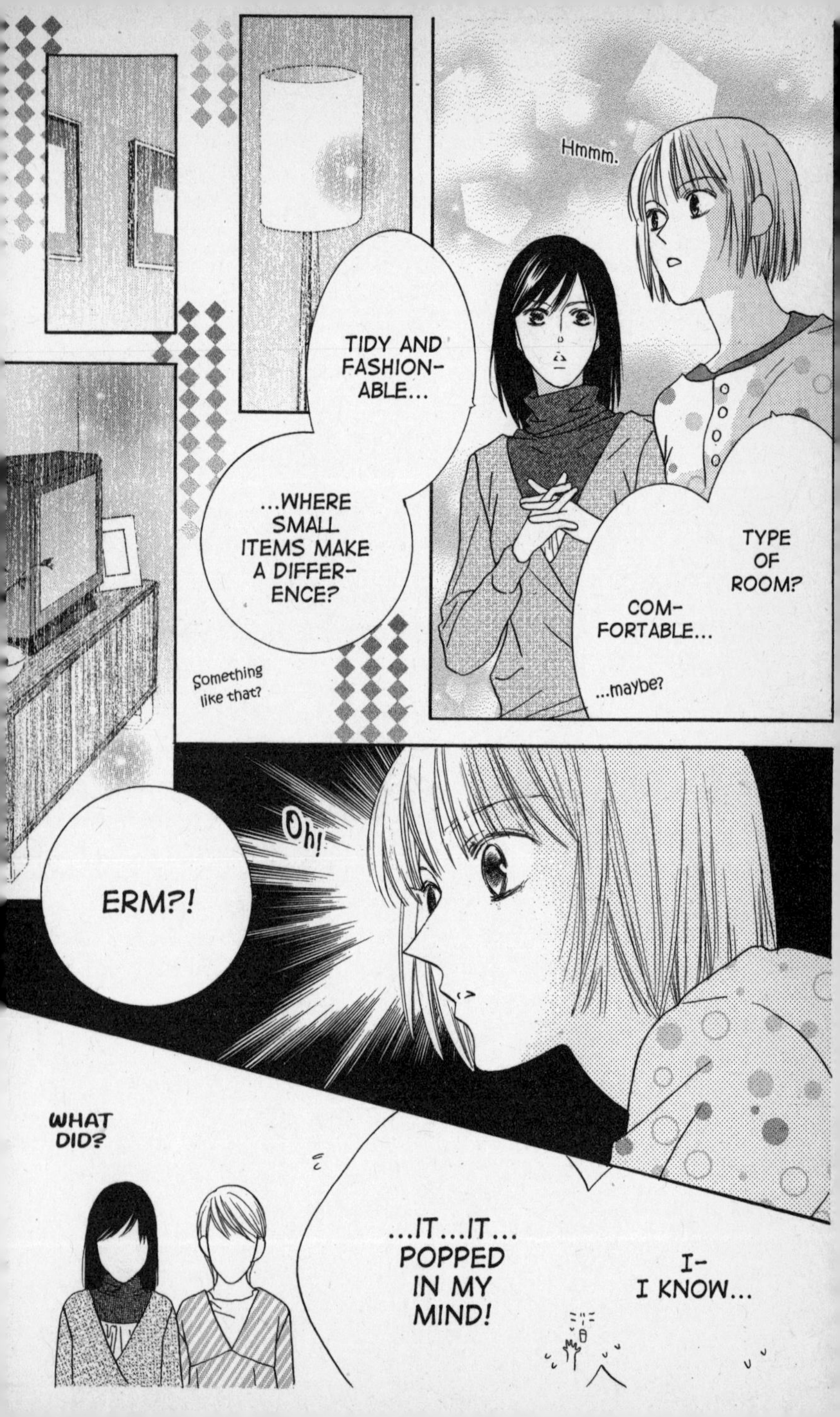

Hmmm.
TYPE OF ROOM?
COM-FORTABLE...
...maybe?
TIDY AND FASHION-ABLE...
...WHERE SMALL ITEMS MAKE A DIFFER-ENCE?
Something like that?
Oh!
ERM?!
I- I KNOW...
...IT...IT... POPPED IN MY MIND!
WHAT DID?

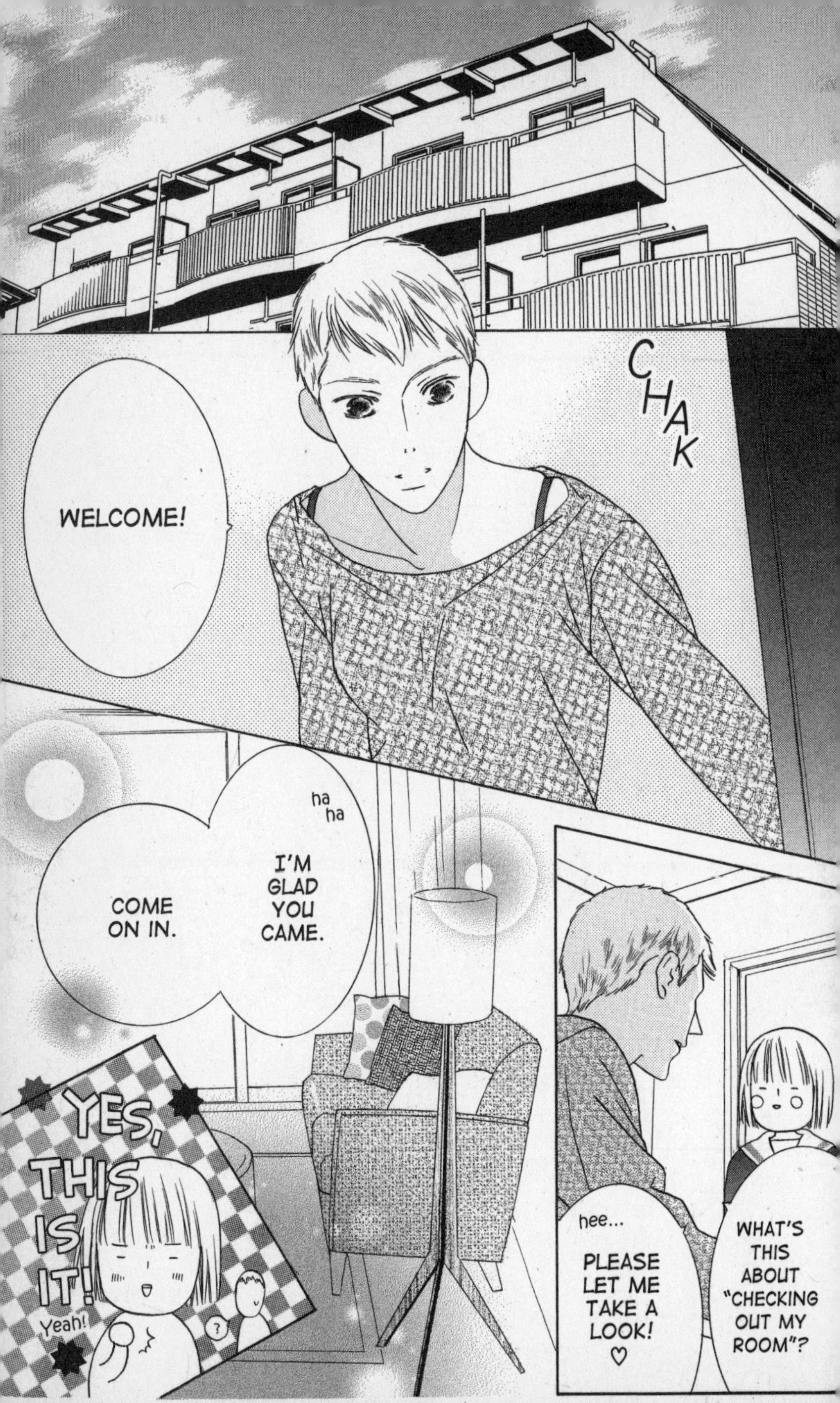
CHAK
WELCOME!
ha ha
I'M GLAD YOU CAME.
COME ON IN.
WHAT'S THIS ABOUT "CHECKING OUT MY ROOM"?
hee...
PLEASE LET ME TAKE A LOOK! ♡
YES, THIS IS IT!
Yeah!

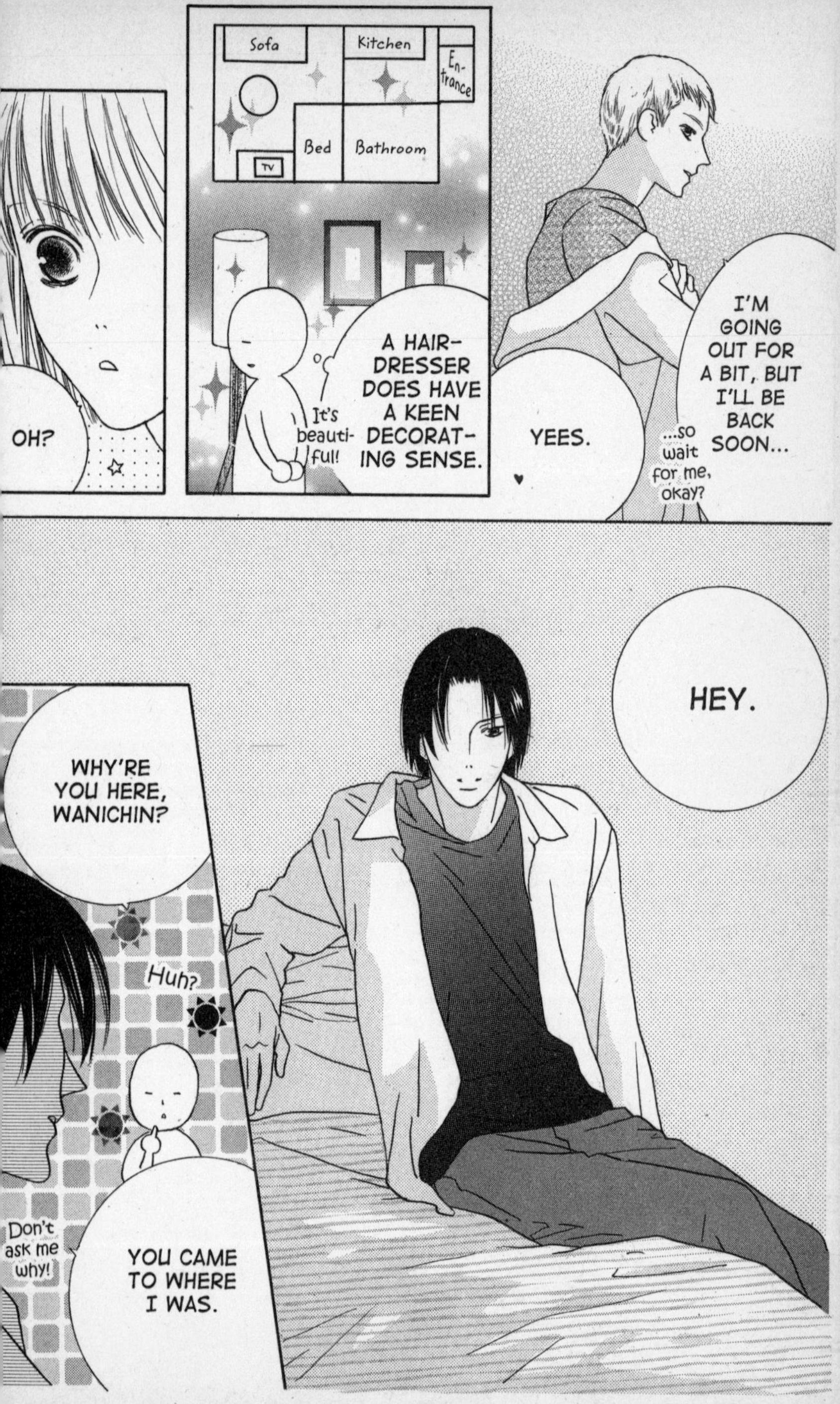
I'M GOING OUT FOR A BIT, BUT I'LL BE BACK SOON...
...so wait for me, okay?
YEES.
Sofa
Kitchen
En-trance
Bed
Bathroom
TV
A HAIR-DRESSER DOES HAVE A KEEN DECORATING SENSE.
It's beautiful!
OH?
HEY.
WHY'RE YOU HERE, WANICHIN?
Huh?
YOU CAME TO WHERE I WAS.
Don't ask me why!

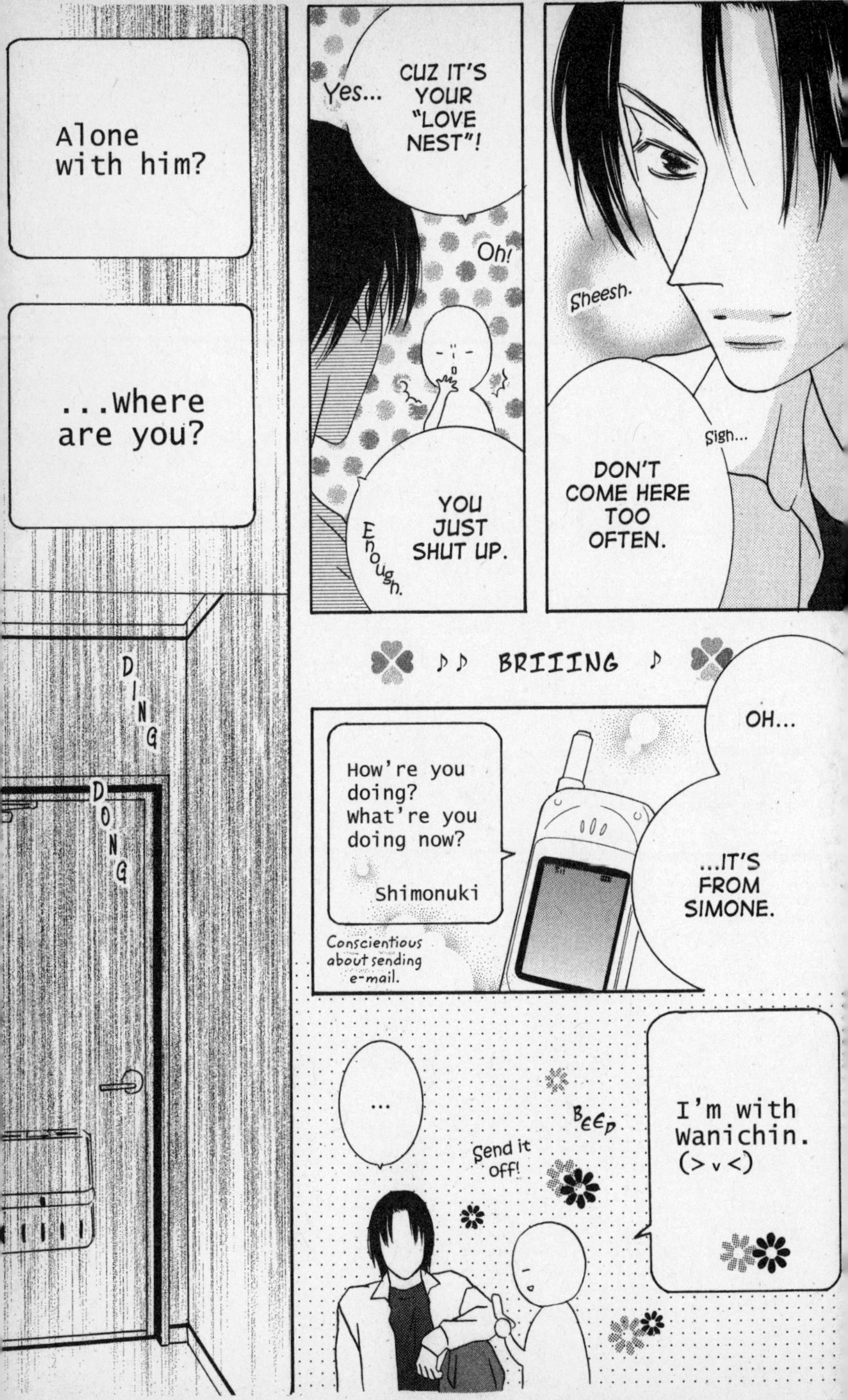
Sheesh.
Sigh...
DON'T COME HERE TOO OFTEN.
CUZ IT'S YOUR "LOVE NEST"!
Yes...
Oh!
YOU JUST SHUT UP.
Enough.
BRIIING
OH...
...IT'S FROM SIMONE.
How're you doing? What're you doing now? Shimonuki
Conscientious about sending e-mail.
I'm with Wanichin. (>v<)
BEEP
Send it off!
...
Alone with him?
...Where are you?
DING
DONG

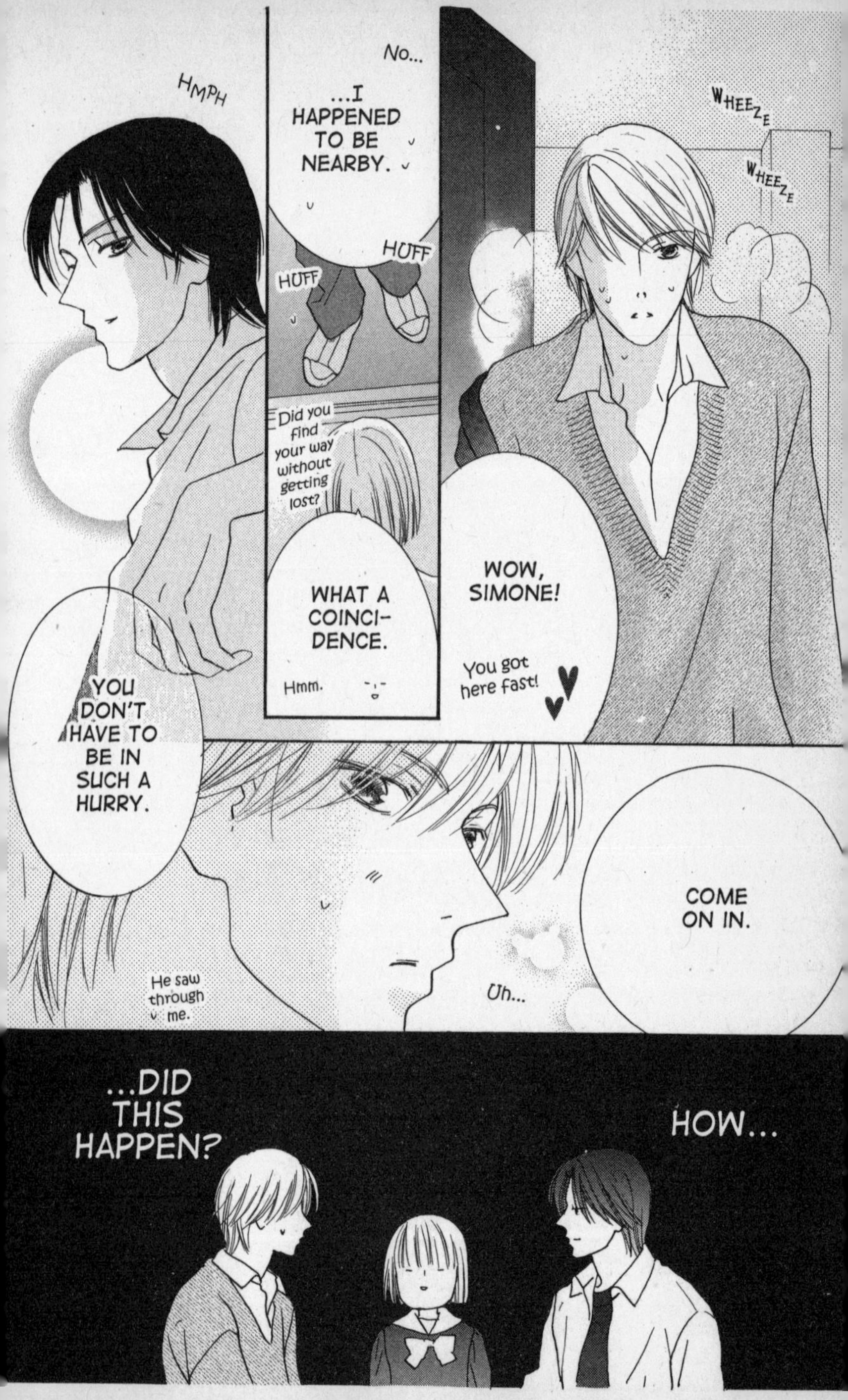
WHEEZE
WHEEZE
WOW, SIMONE!
You got here fast!
No...
...I HAPPENED TO BE NEARBY.
HUFF
HUFF
Did you find your way without getting lost?
WHAT A COINCIDENCE.
Hmm.
HMPH
YOU DON'T HAVE TO BE IN SUCH A HURRY.
COME ON IN.
Uh...
He saw through me.
HOW...
...DID THIS HAPPEN?

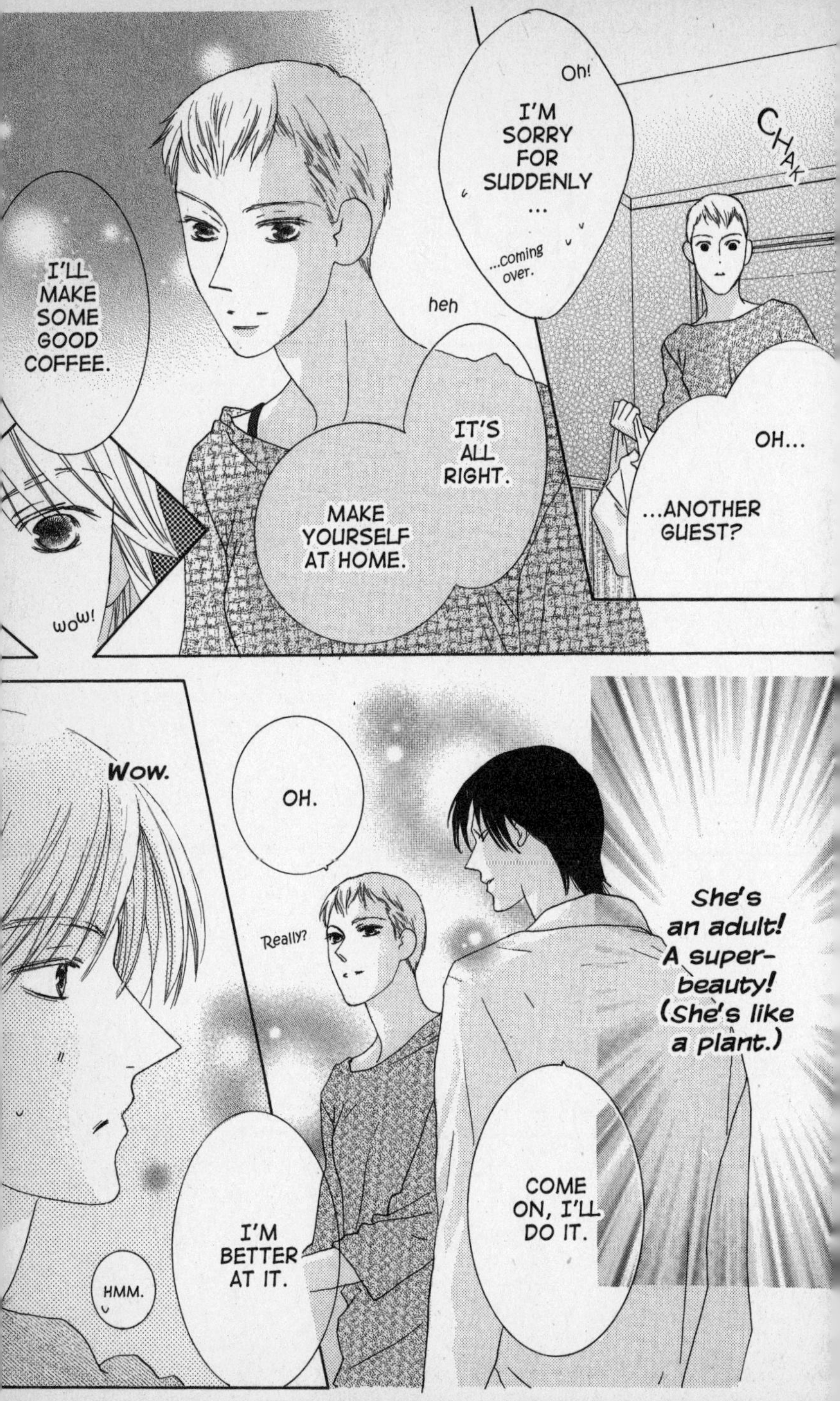
CHAK
OH...
...ANOTHER GUEST?
Oh!
I'M SORRY FOR SUDDENLY ...
...coming over.
heh
IT'S ALL RIGHT.
MAKE YOURSELF AT HOME.
I'LL MAKE SOME GOOD COFFEE.
WOW!
She's an adult! A super-beauty! (She's like a plant.)
COME ON, I'LL DO IT.
OH.
Really?
I'M BETTER AT IT.
Wow.
HMM.

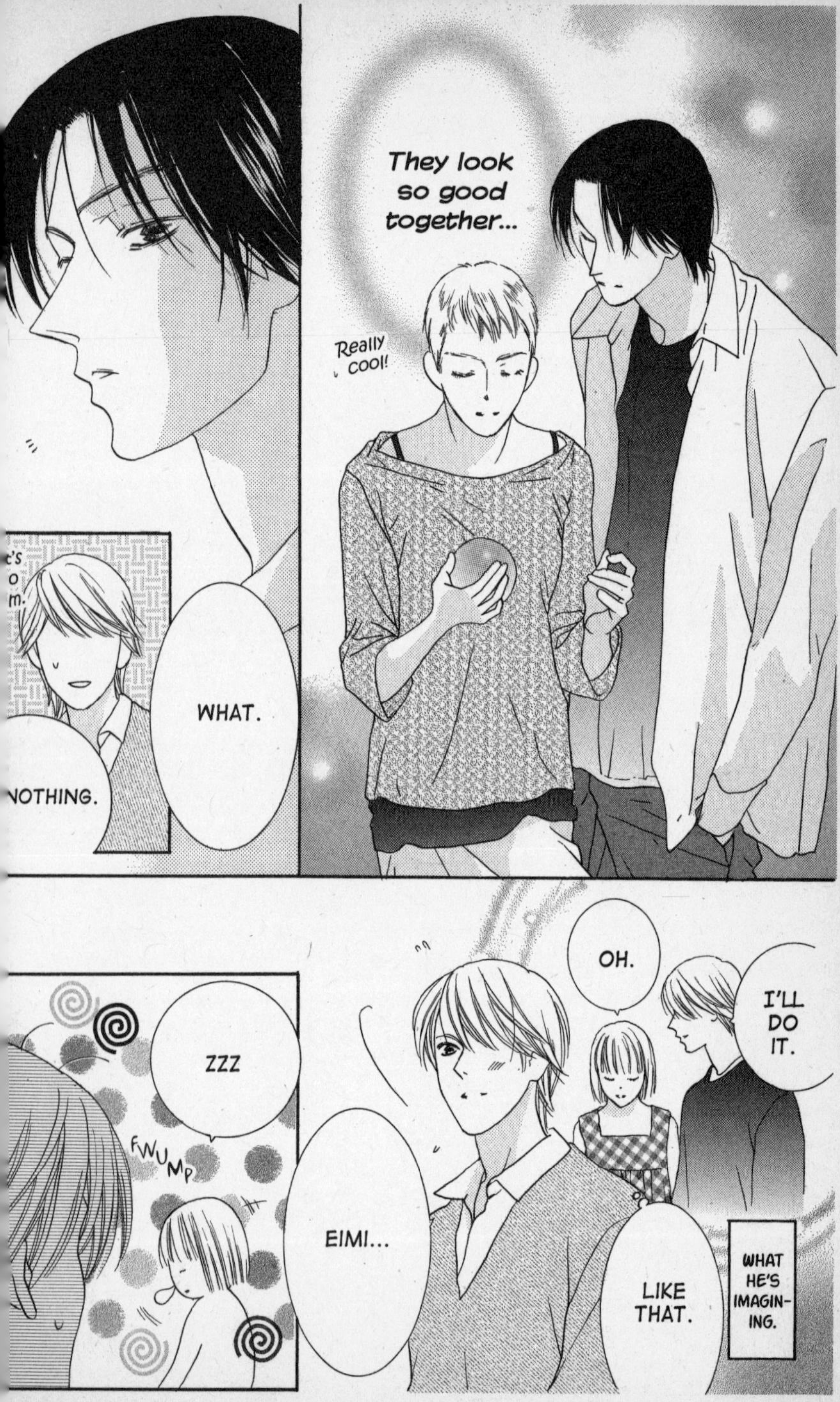
They look so good together...
Really cool!
WHAT.
NOTHING.
I'LL DO IT.
OH.
WHAT HE'S IMAGINING.
LIKE THAT.
EIMI...
ZZZ
FWUMP

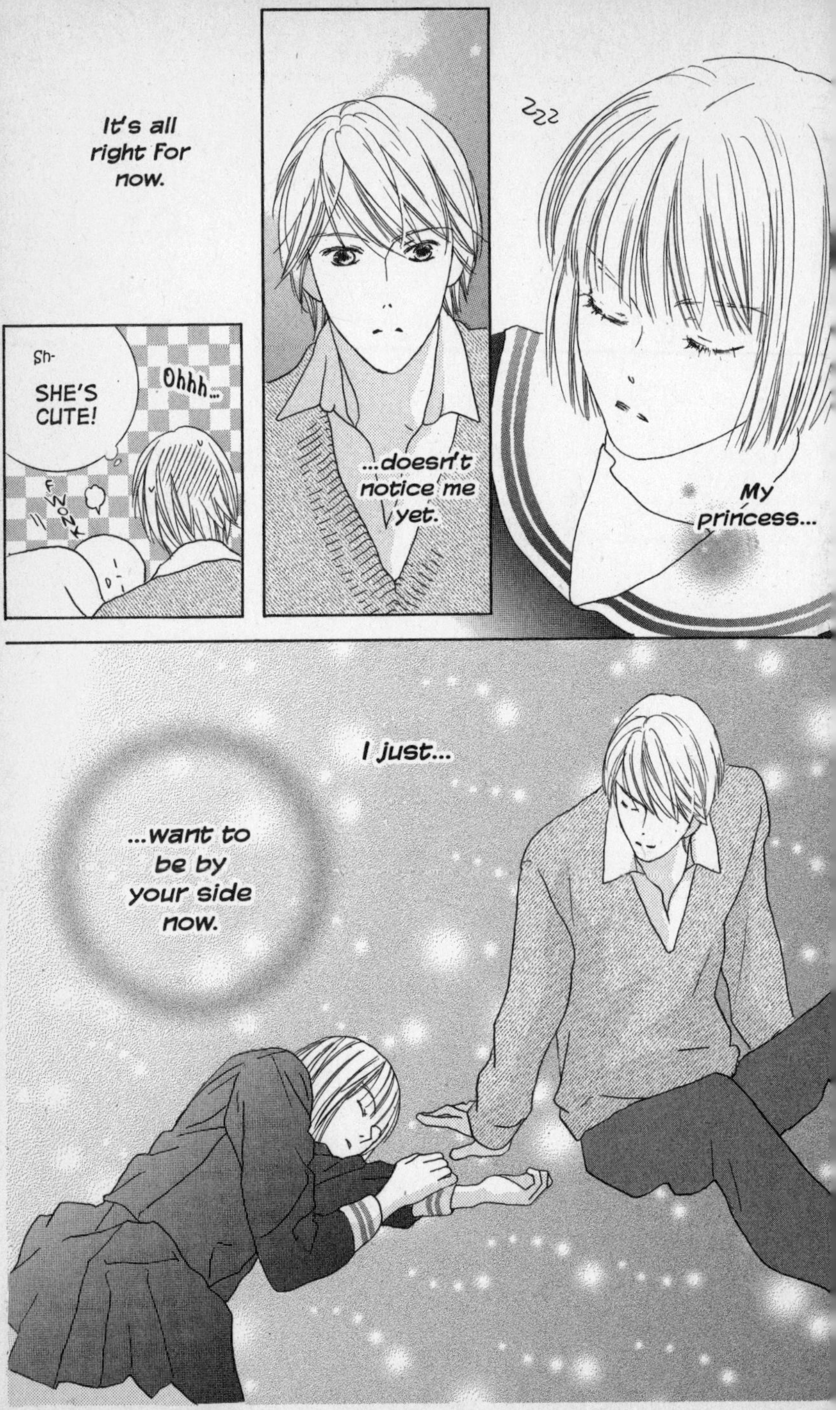

ZZZ
My princess...
...doesn't notice me yet.
It's all right for now.
Sh-
SHE'S CUTE!
Ohhh...
FWONK
I just...
...want to be by your side now.

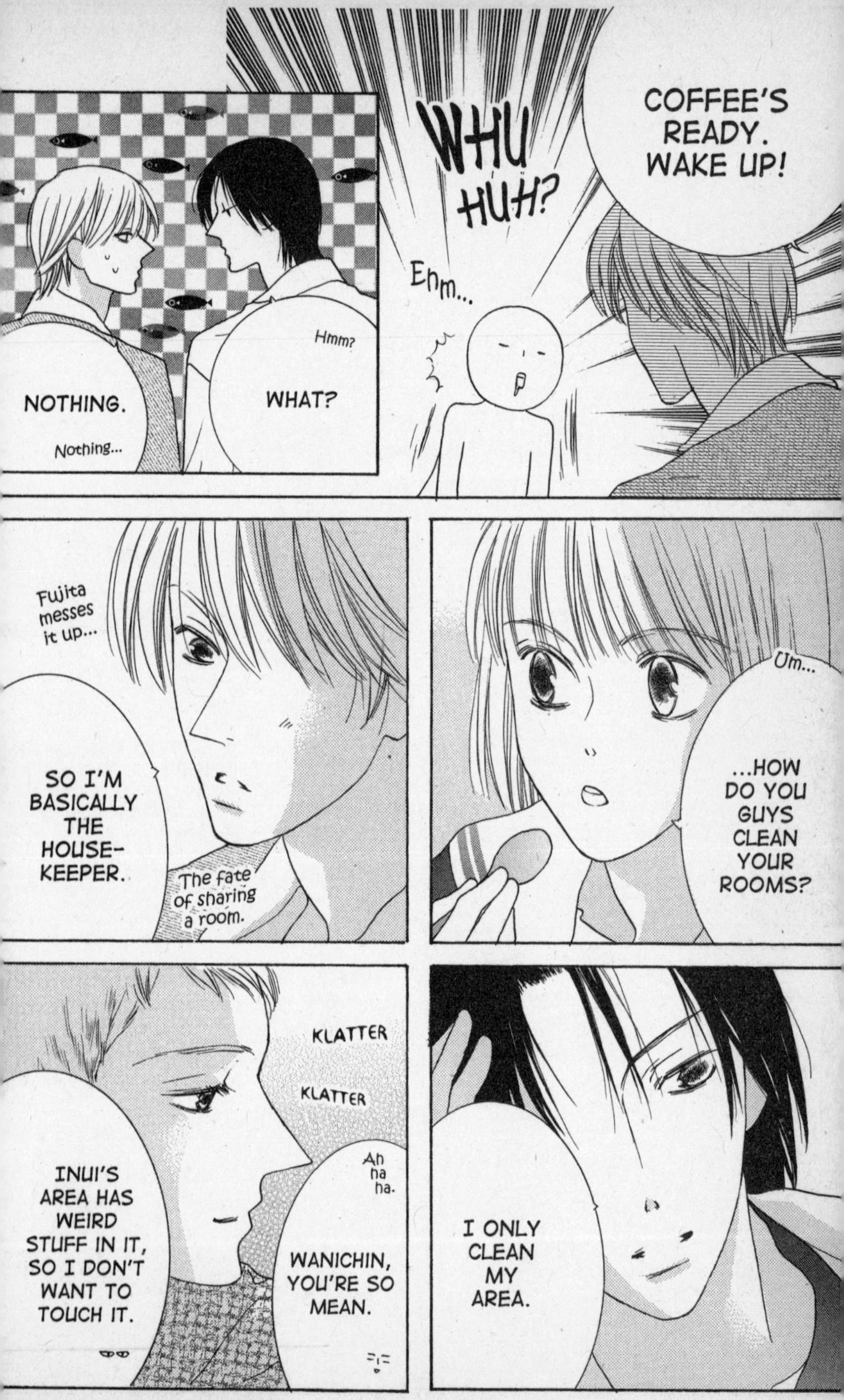
COFFEE'S READY. WAKE UP!
WHU HUH?
Enm...
Hmm?
WHAT?
NOTHING.
Nothing...
Um...
...HOW DO YOU GUYS CLEAN YOUR ROOMS?
Fujita messes it up...
SO I'M BASICALLY THE HOUSE-KEEPER.
The fate of sharing a room.
I ONLY CLEAN MY AREA.
KLATTER
KLATTER
Ah ha ha.
WANICHIN, YOU'RE SO MEAN.
INUI'S AREA HAS WEIRD STUFF IN IT, SO I DON'T WANT TO TOUCH IT.

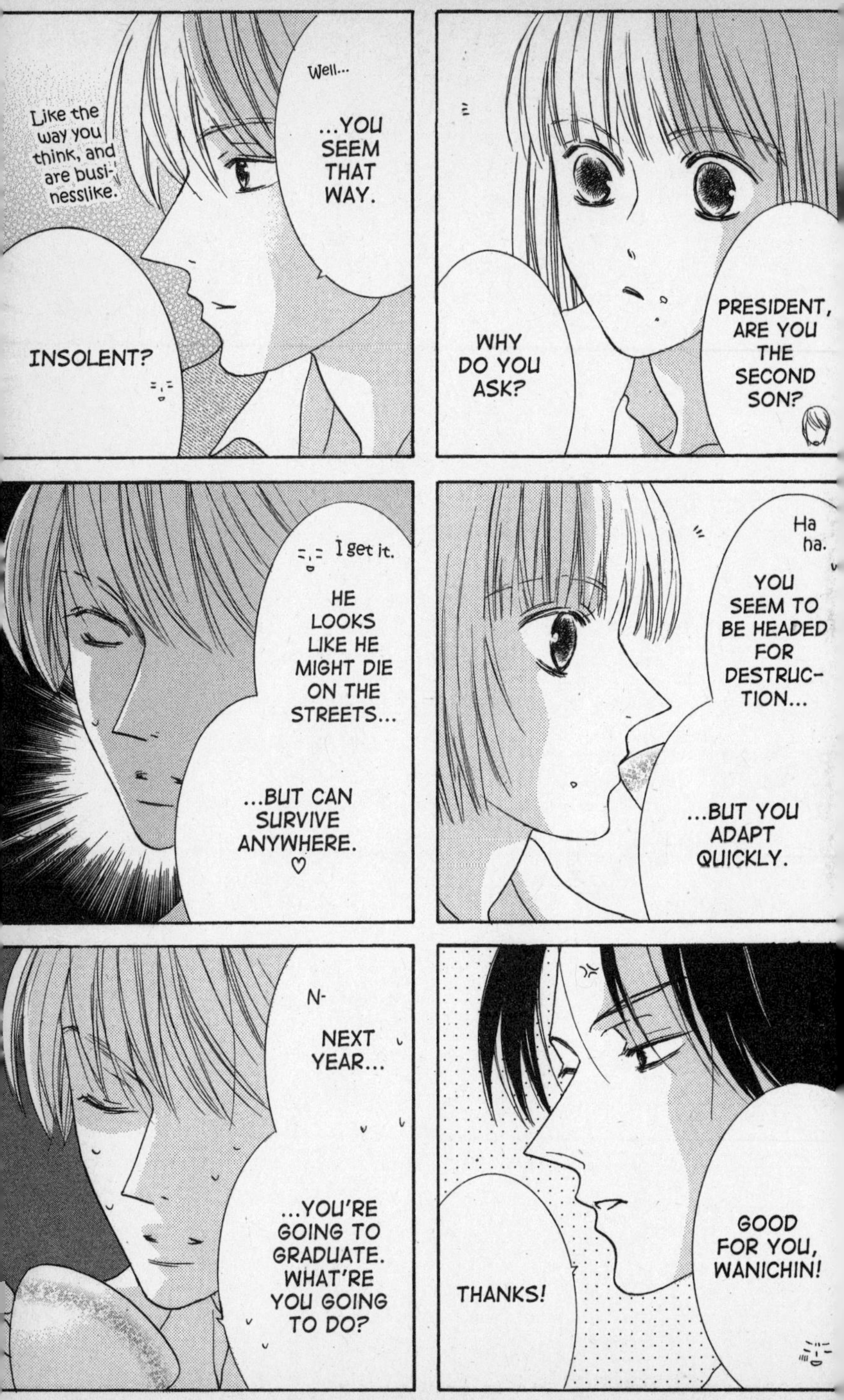
PRESIDENT, ARE YOU THE SECOND SON?
WHY DO YOU ASK?
Well...
...YOU SEEM THAT WAY.
Like the way you think, and are busi-nesslike.
INSOLENT?
Ha ha.
YOU SEEM TO BE HEADED FOR DESTRUCTION...
...BUT YOU ADAPT QUICKLY.
I get it.
HE LOOKS LIKE HE MIGHT DIE ON THE STREETS...
...BUT CAN SURVIVE ANYWHERE. ♡
GOOD FOR YOU, WANICHIN!
THANKS!
N-
NEXT YEAR...
...YOU'RE GOING TO GRADUATE. WHAT'RE YOU GOING TO DO?

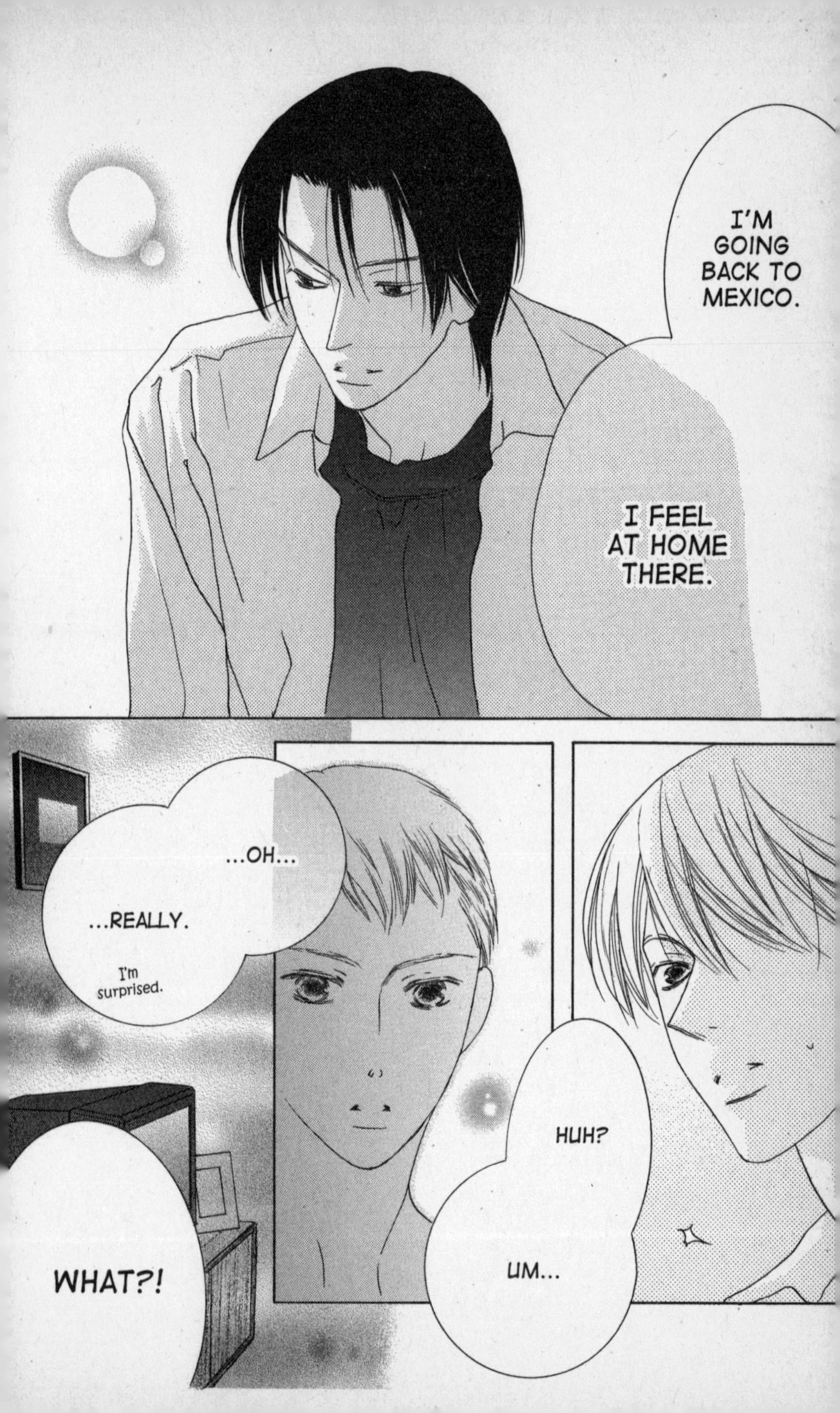
I'M GOING BACK TO MEXICO.
I FEEL AT HOME THERE.
HUH?
UM...
...OH...
...REALLY.
I'm surprised.
WHAT?!

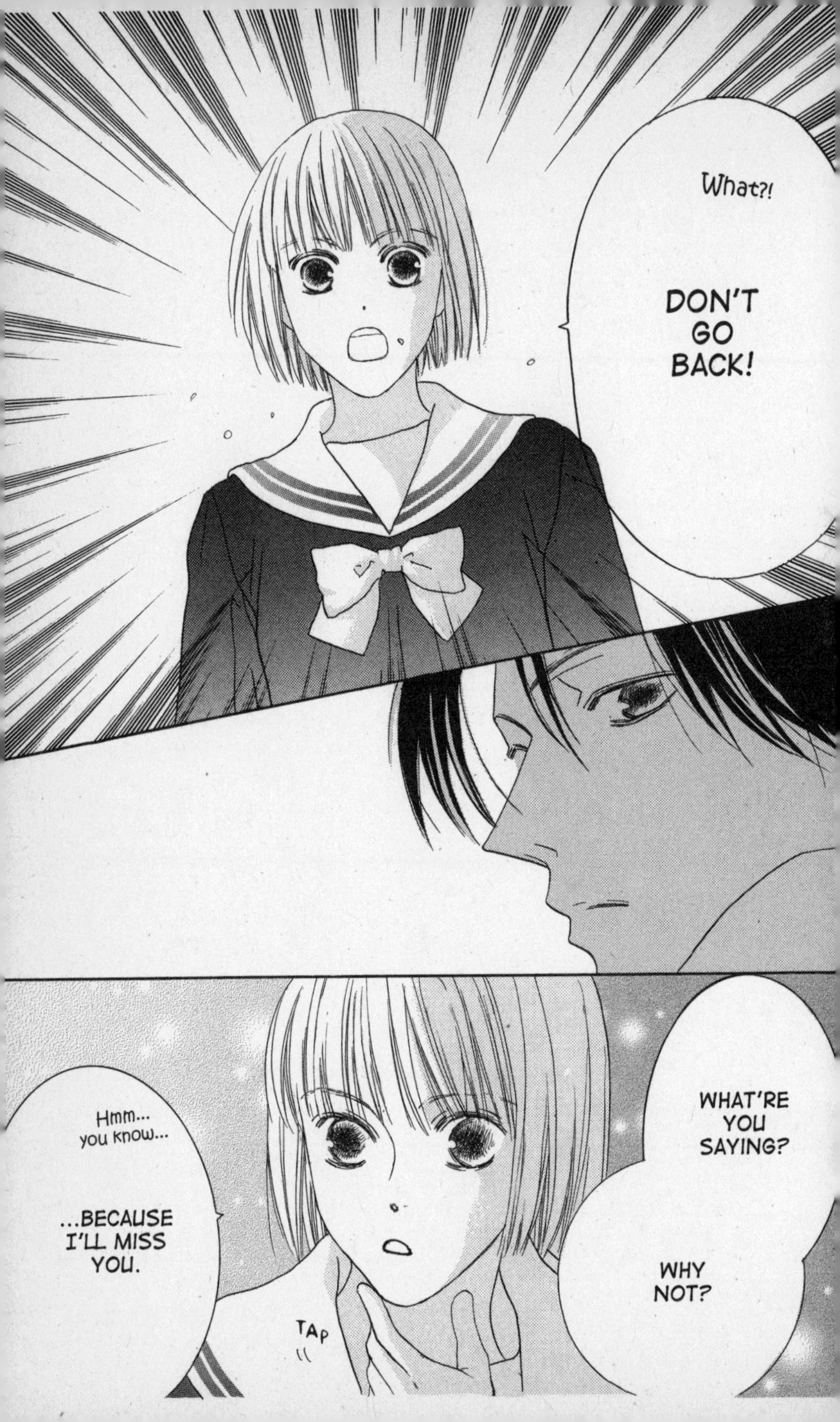
What?!
DON'T GO BACK!
WHAT'RE YOU SAYING?
WHY NOT?
Hmm... you know...
...BECAUSE I'LL MISS YOU.
TAP

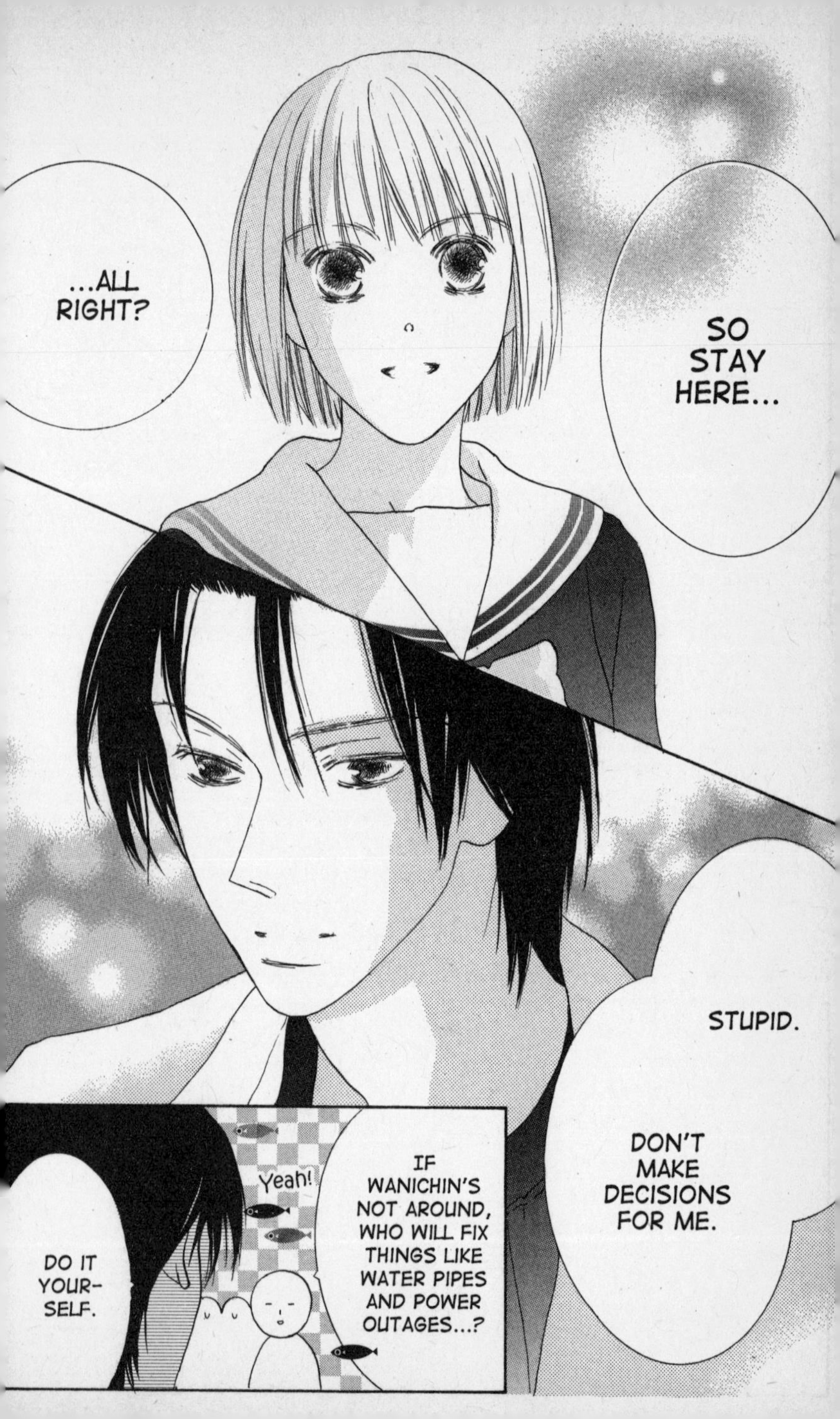
SO STAY HERE...
...ALL RIGHT?
STUPID.
DON'T MAKE DECISIONS FOR ME.
IF WANICHIN'S NOT AROUND, WHO WILL FIX THINGS LIKE WATER PIPES AND POWER OUTAGES...?
Yeah!
DO IT YOUR-SELF.

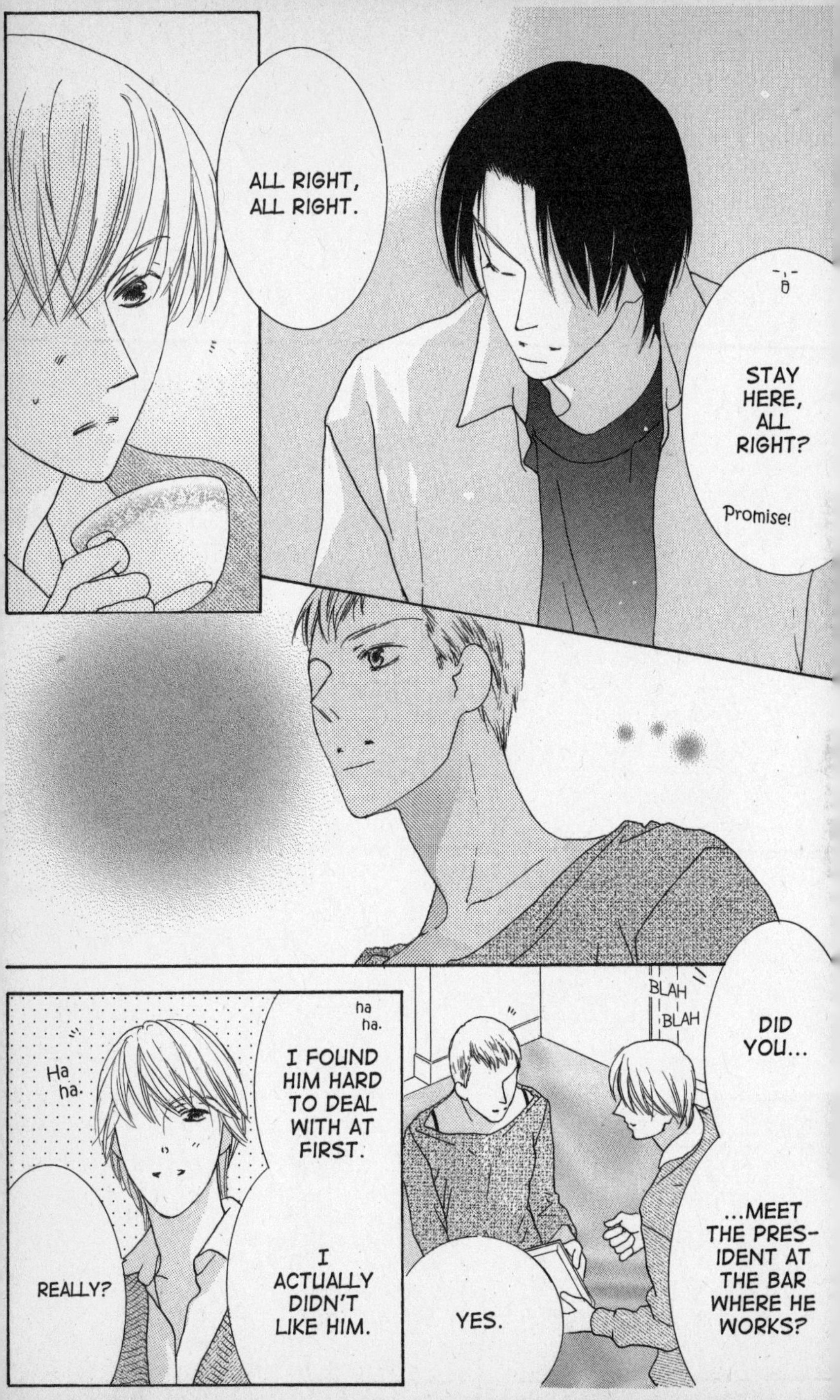
STAY HERE, ALL RIGHT?
Promise!
ALL RIGHT, ALL RIGHT.
BLAH BLAH
DID YOU...
...MEET THE PRESIDENT AT THE BAR WHERE HE WORKS?
YES.
ha ha.
I FOUND HIM HARD TO DEAL WITH AT FIRST.
I ACTUALLY DIDN'T LIKE HIM.
Ha ha.
REALLY?

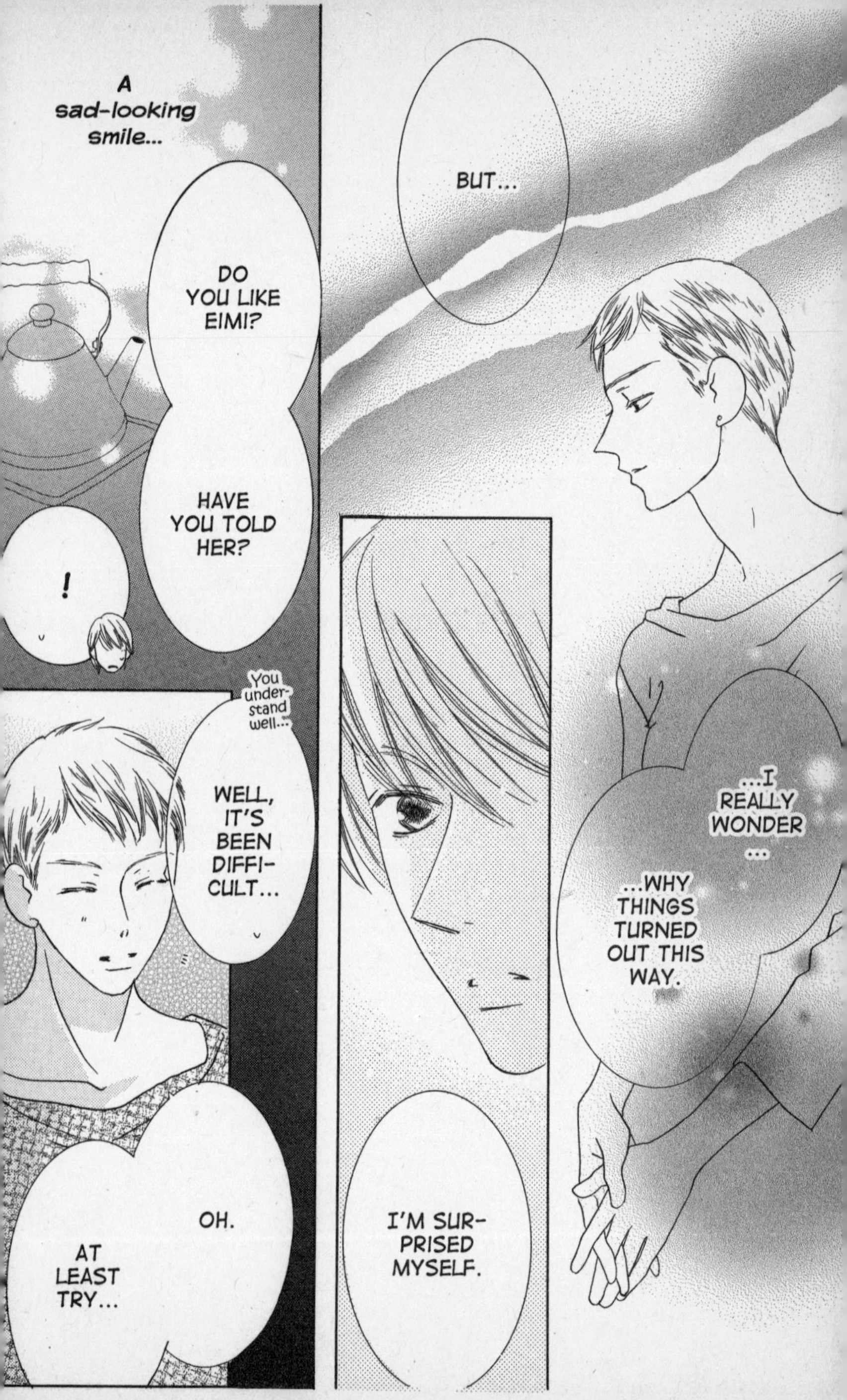
BUT...
...I REALLY WONDER...
...WHY THINGS TURNED OUT THIS WAY.
I'M SURPRISED MYSELF.
A sad-looking smile...
DO YOU LIKE EIMI?
HAVE YOU TOLD HER?
!
You understand well...
WELL, IT'S BEEN DIFFICULT...
OH.
AT LEAST TRY...

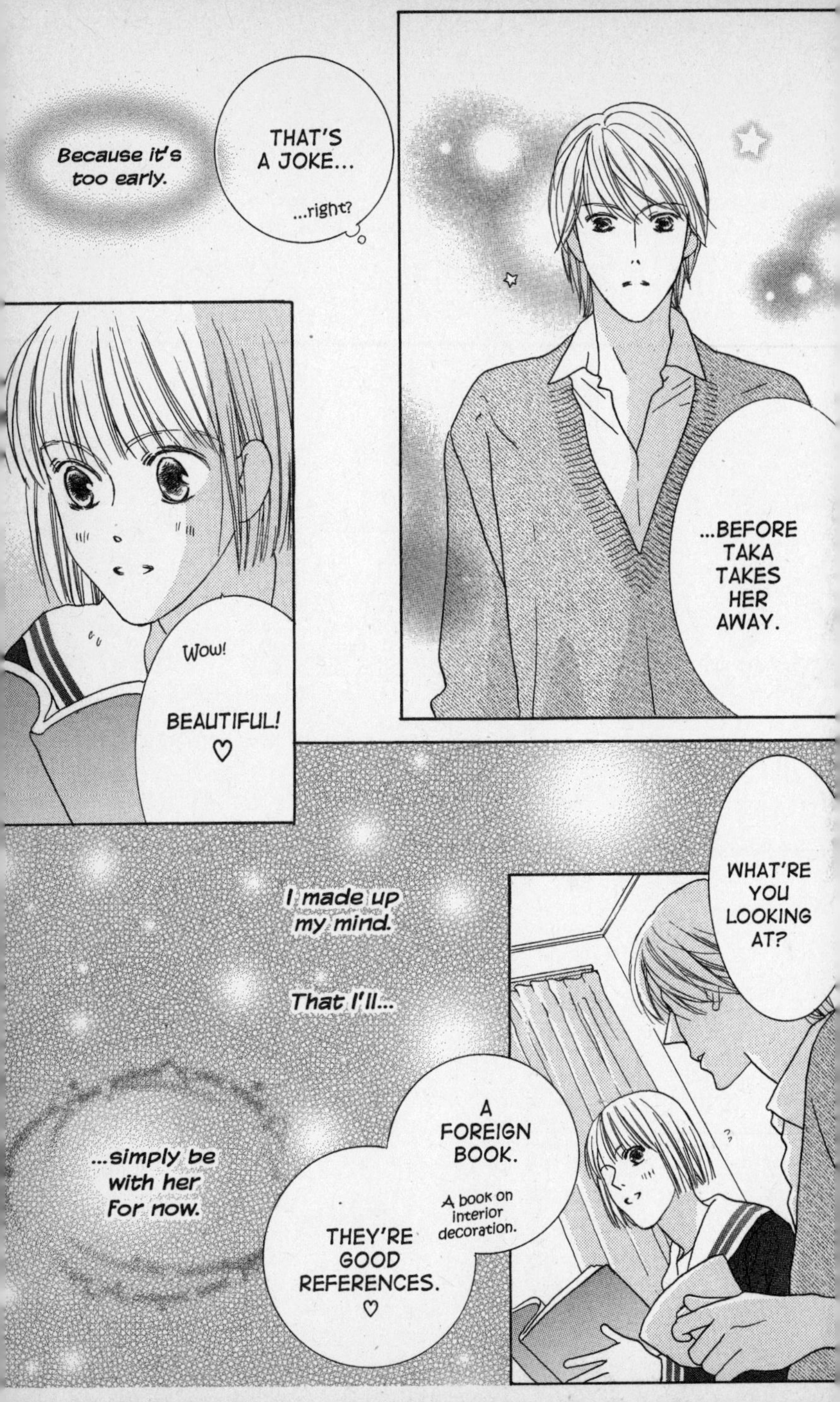
...BEFORE TAKA TAKES HER AWAY.
Because it's too early.
THAT'S A JOKE...
...right?
Wow!
BEAUTIFUL! ♡
WHAT'RE YOU LOOKING AT?
A FOREIGN BOOK.
A book on interior decoration.
THEY'RE GOOD REFERENCES. ♡
I made up my mind.
That I'll...
...simply be with her for now.

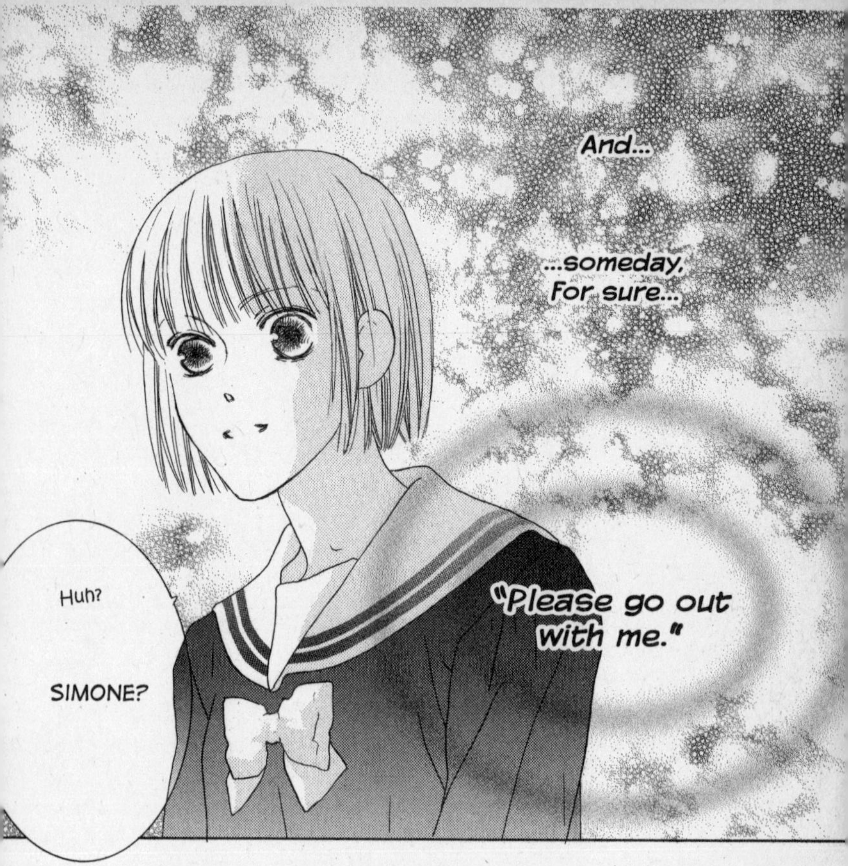
And...
...someday, For sure...
"Please go out with me."
Huh?
SIMONE?

! A question to everyone. Have you ever just blurted out something that you were thinking?

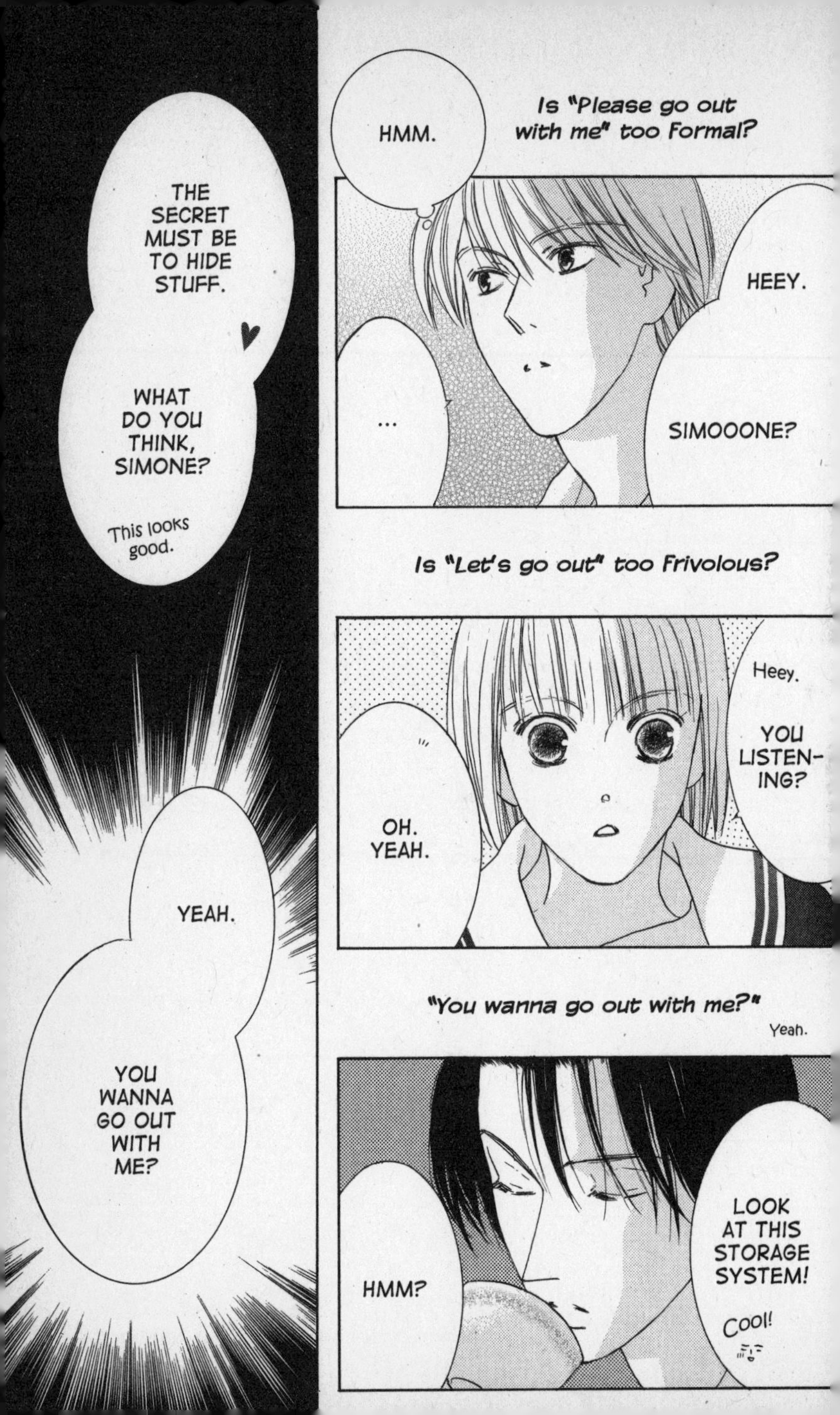
Is "Please go out with me" too formal?
HMM.
HEEY.
SIMOOONE?
...
Is "Let's go out" too frivolous?
Heey.
YOU LISTENING?
OH. YEAH.
"You wanna go out with me?"
Yeah.
LOOK AT THIS STORAGE SYSTEM!
Cool!
HMM?
THE SECRET MUST BE TO HIDE STUFF.
WHAT DO YOU THINK, SIMONE?
This looks good.
YEAH.
YOU WANNA GO OUT WITH ME?

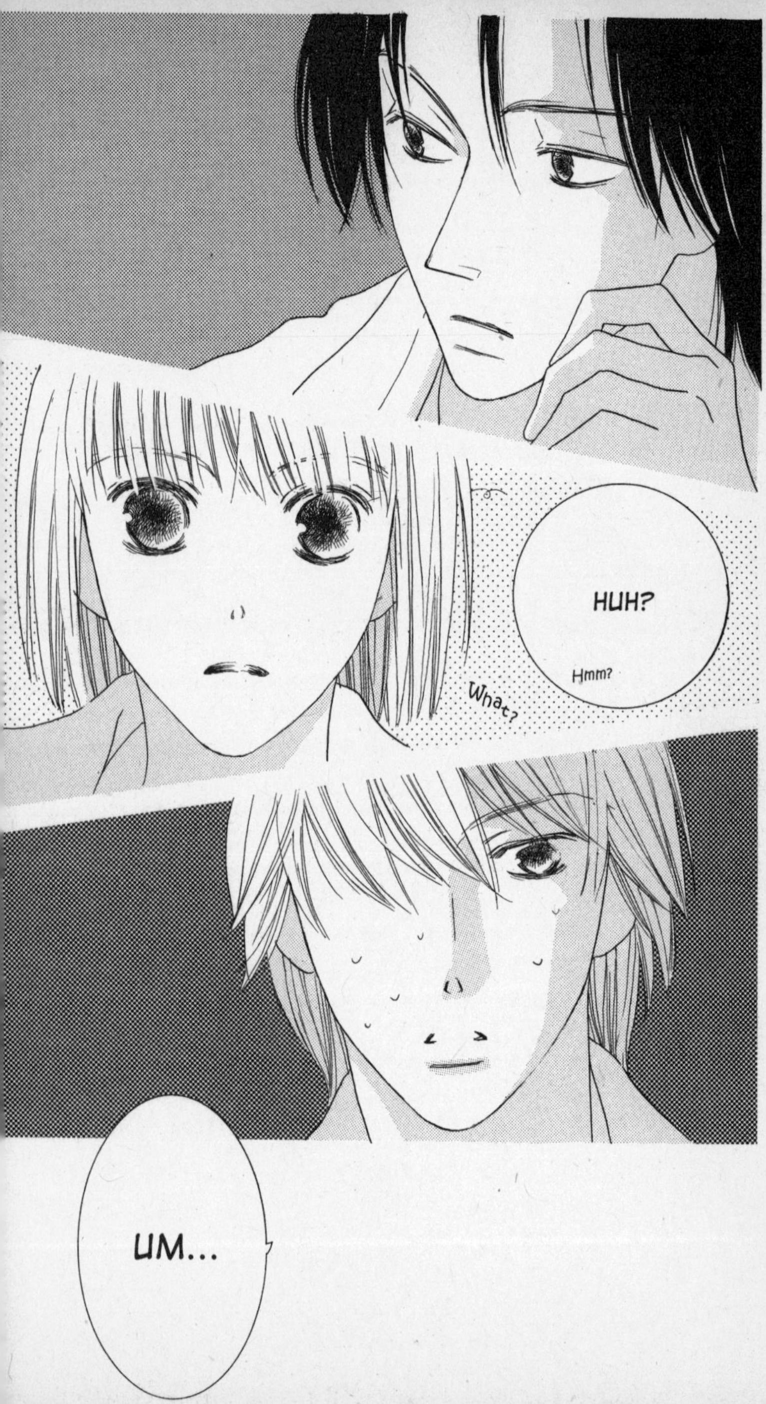
HUH?
Hmm?
What?
UM...

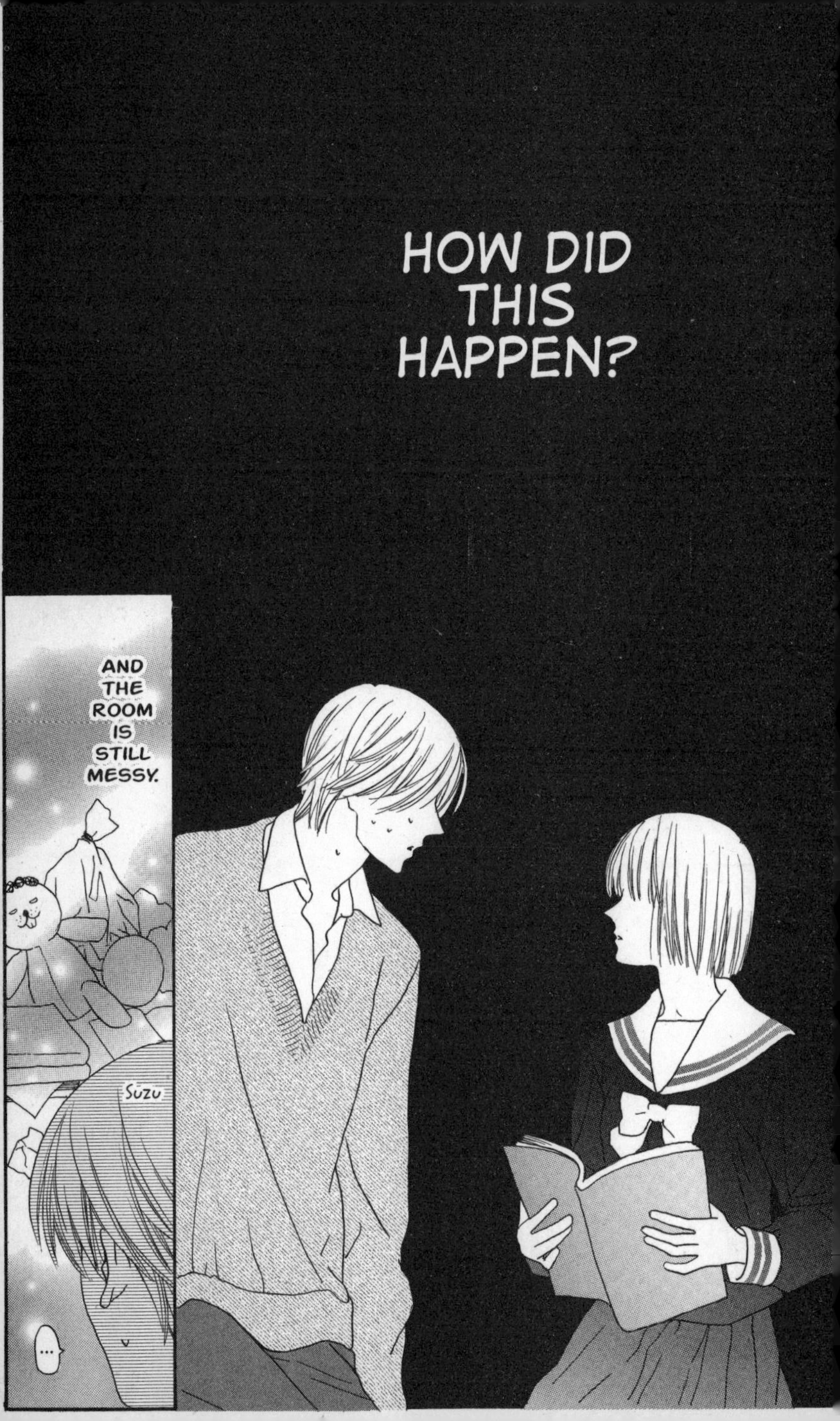
HOW DID THIS HAPPEN?
AND THE ROOM IS STILL MESSY.
SUZU
...

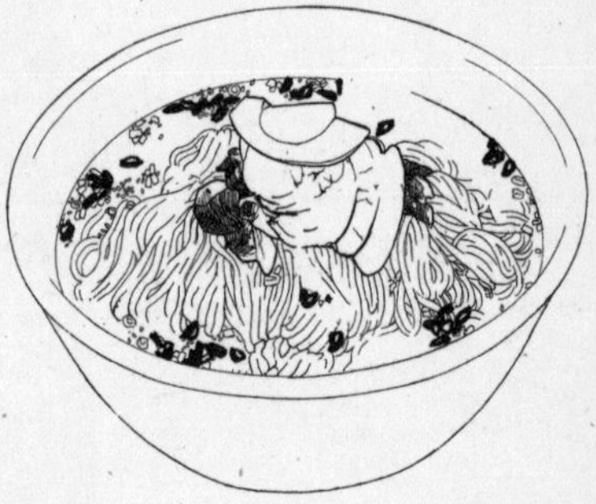

BEAUTY **IS THE BEAST**

EIMI YAMASHITA'S REPLIES.

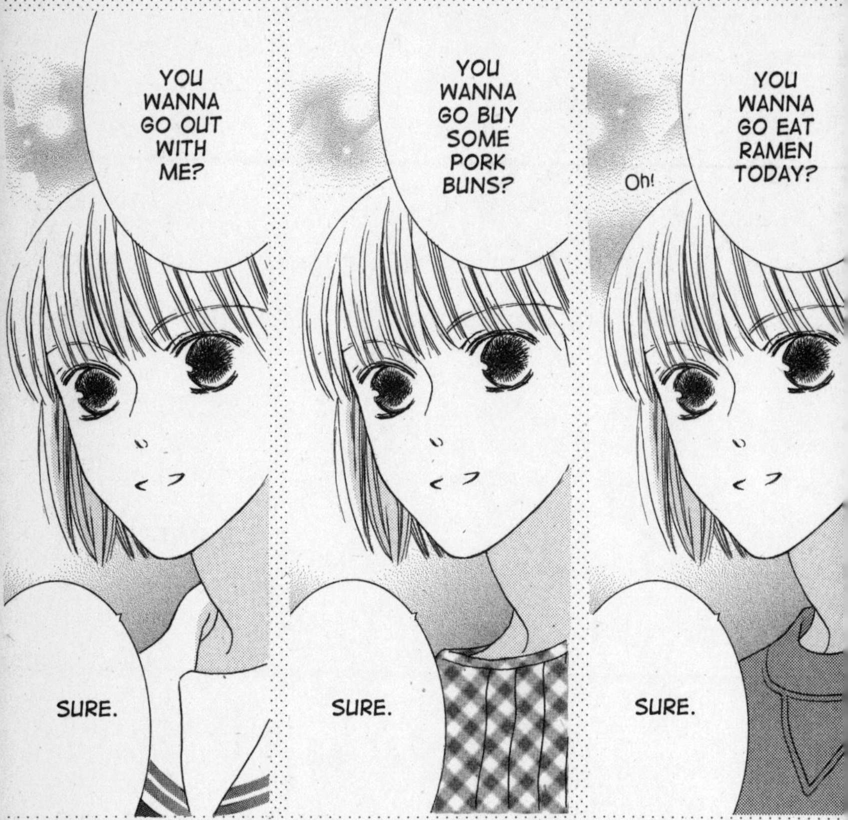
YOU WANNA GO EAT RAMEN TODAY?
Oh!
SURE.
YOU WANNA GO BUY SOME PORK BUNS?
SURE.
YOU WANNA GO OUT WITH ME?
SURE.

So Maroon 5's "This Love" and Prince's "LIFE O' THE PARTY" are on super-heavy rotation, and are songs that I truly love. Prince I'd hardly listened to, and I didn't know him much. I had the preconception that his '80s songs were maniac (?), but when I saw his promo clips in 2004, they were so cool, I was surprised. I really liked the funkiness.

How can he create those songs? He must be pretty old by now. ↑ (Unwanted comment.)

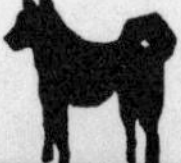

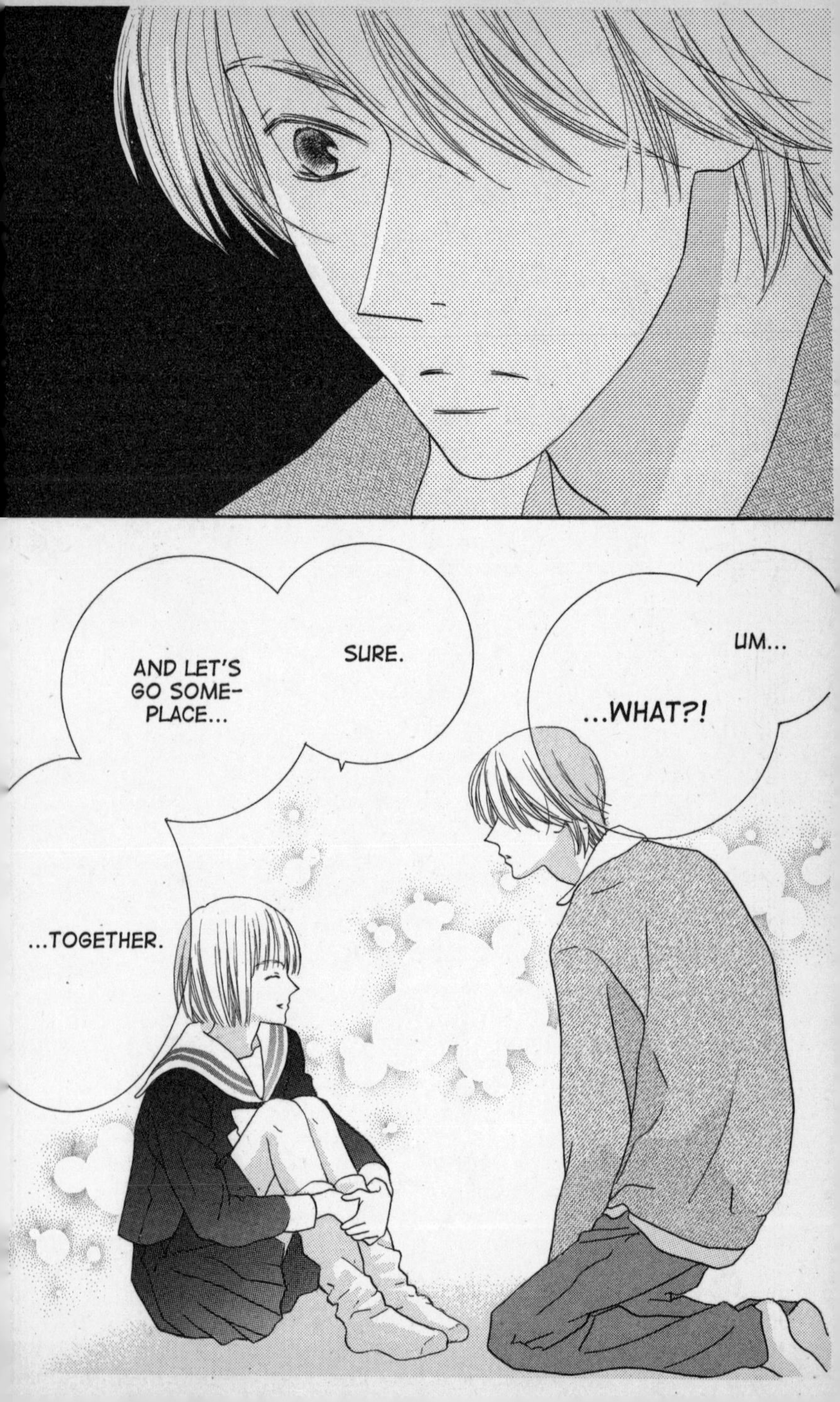
UM...
...WHAT?!
SURE.
AND LET'S GO SOME-PLACE...
...TOGETHER.

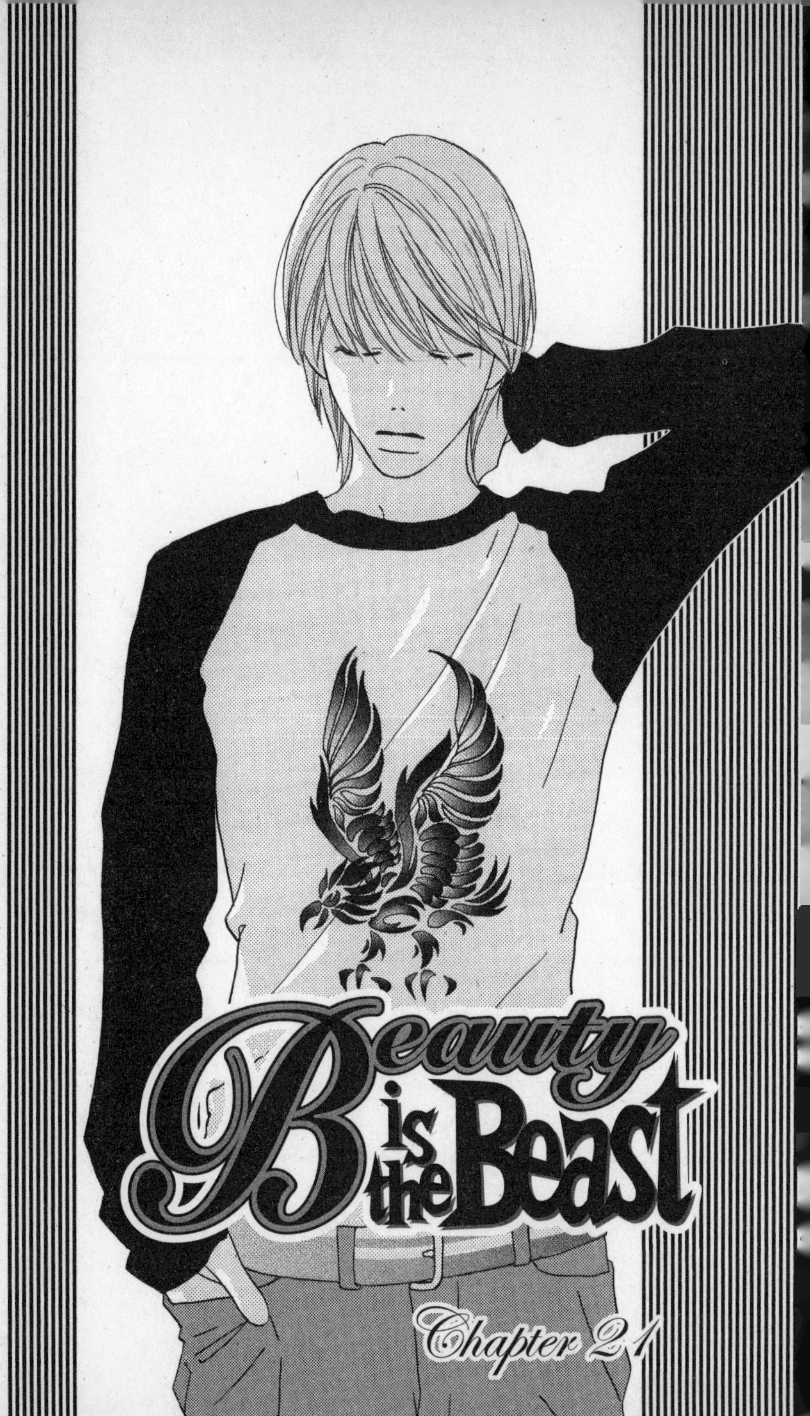
Beauty is the Beast
Chapter 21

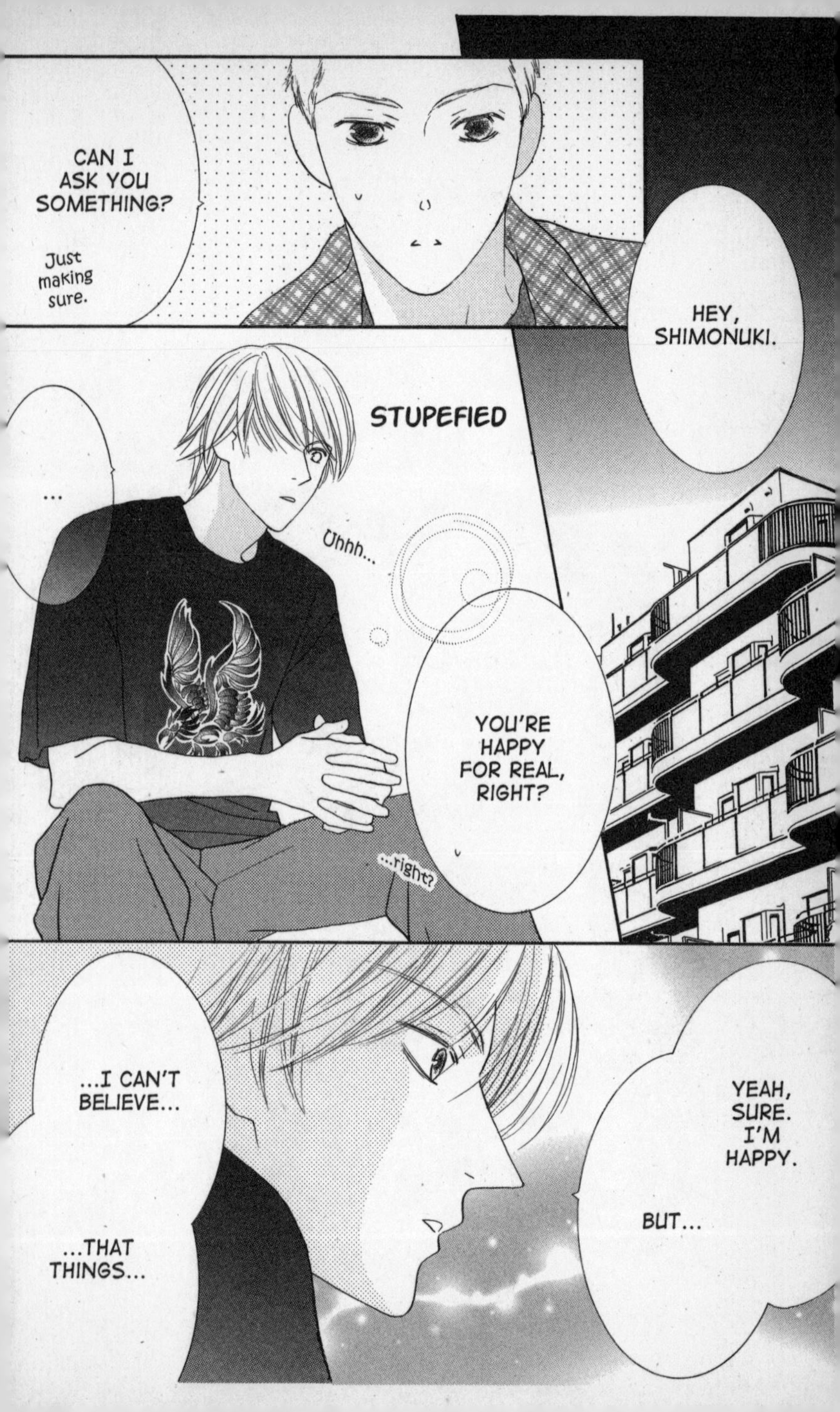

HEY, SHIMONUKI.
CAN I ASK YOU SOMETHING?
Just making sure.
YOU'RE HAPPY FOR REAL, RIGHT?
...right?
STUPEFIED
Uhhh...
...
YEAH, SURE. I'M HAPPY.
BUT...
...I CAN'T BELIEVE...
...THAT THINGS...

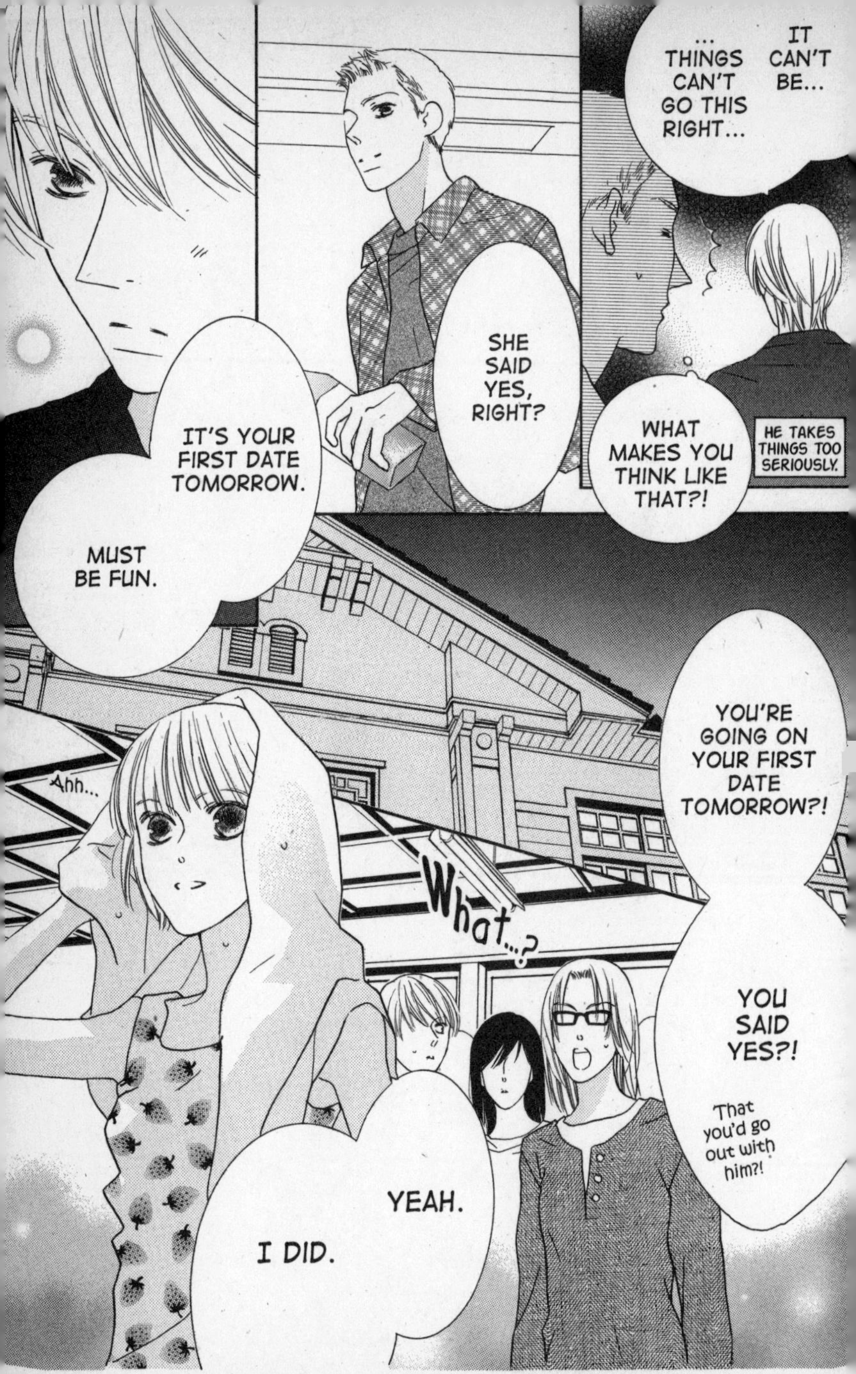
IT CAN'T BE... ...THINGS CAN'T GO THIS RIGHT...
HE TAKES THINGS TOO SERIOUSLY.
WHAT MAKES YOU THINK LIKE THAT?!
SHE SAID YES, RIGHT?
IT'S YOUR FIRST DATE TOMORROW.
MUST BE FUN.
YOU'RE GOING ON YOUR FIRST DATE TOMORROW?!
YOU SAID YES?!
That you'd go out with him?!
What...?
Ahh...
YEAH.
I DID.

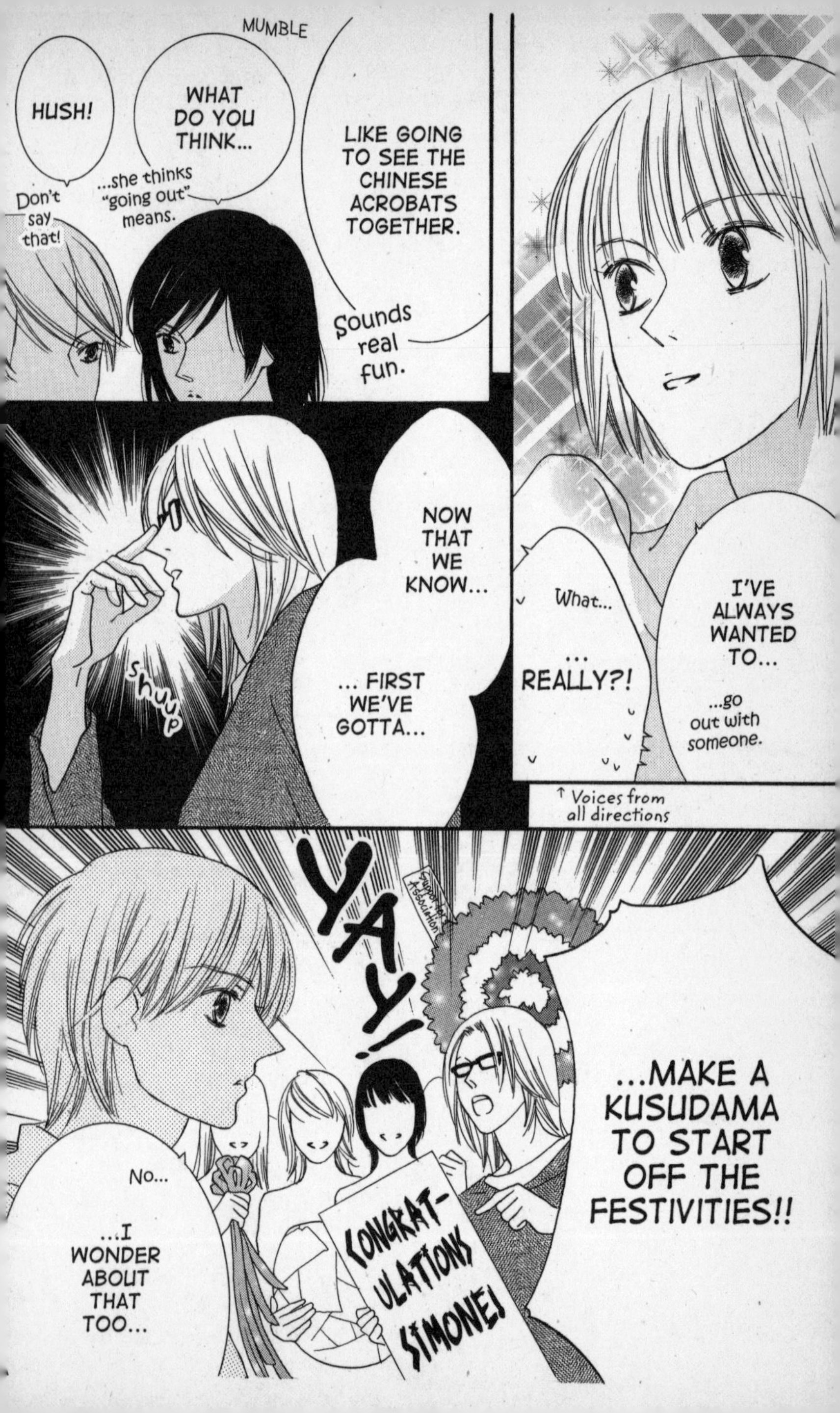
I'VE ALWAYS WANTED TO...
...go out with someone.
What...
... REALLY?!
↑ Voices from all directions
MUMBLE
LIKE GOING TO SEE THE CHINESE ACROBATS TOGETHER.
Sounds real fun.
WHAT DO YOU THINK...
...she thinks "going out" means.
HUSH!
Don't say that!
NOW THAT WE KNOW...
... FIRST WE'VE GOTTA...
Shuup
...MAKE A KUSUDAMA TO START OFF THE FESTIVITIES!!
YAY!
Support Association
CONGRAT-ULATIONS SIMONE!
No...
...I WONDER ABOUT THAT TOO...

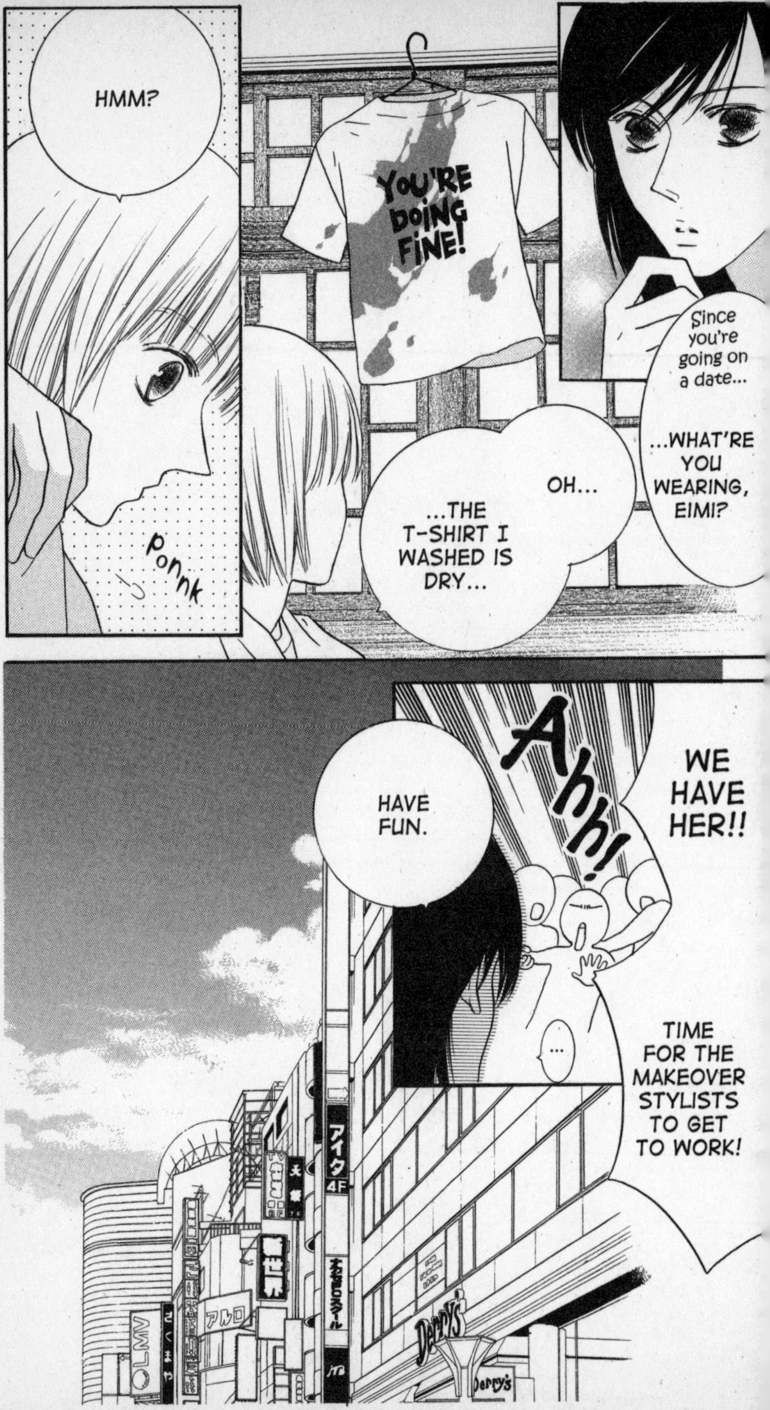
Since you're going on a date...
...WHAT'RE YOU WEARING, EIMI?
OH...
...THE T-SHIRT I WASHED IS DRY...
YOU'RE DOING FINE!
HMM?
Ponnk
WE HAVE HER!!
Ahh!
HAVE FUN.
...
TIME FOR THE MAKEOVER STYLISTS TO GET TO WORK!
アイタ 4F
Derry's
Derry's

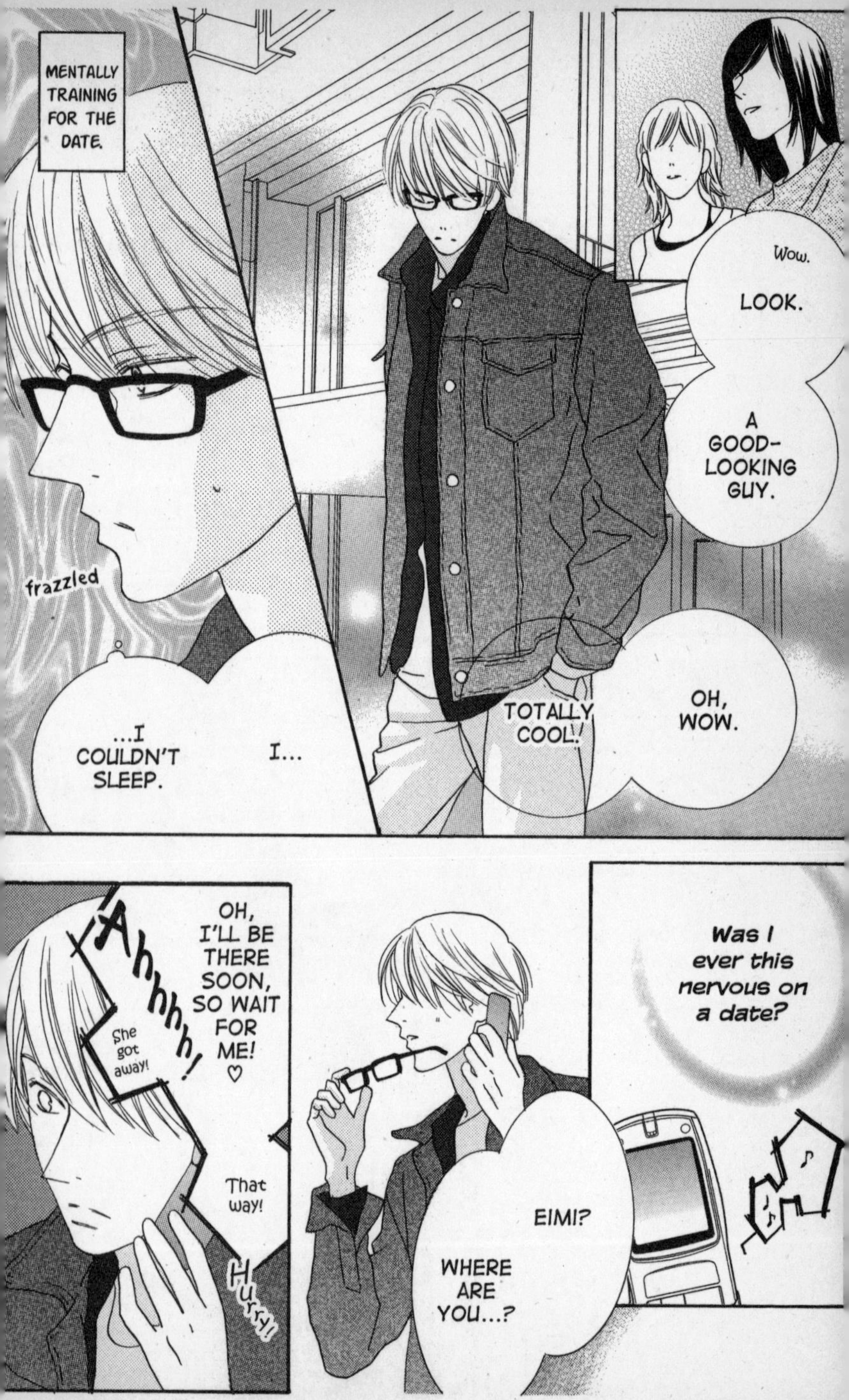
Wow.
LOOK.
A GOOD-LOOKING GUY.
OH, WOW.
TOTALLY COOL!
MENTALLY TRAINING FOR THE DATE.
frazzled
I...
...I COULDN'T SLEEP.
Was I ever this nervous on a date?
EIMI?
WHERE ARE YOU...?
OH, I'LL BE THERE SOON, SO WAIT FOR ME! ♡
Ahhhh!
She got away!
That way!
Hurry!

4

I like mail order because I can't go out much. During a 30-day month, I can only go out 2-4 days. I'm working on my pages for about 4 days (penciling, inking, finishing up), so I'm at home thinking up the story for over 20 days. Apparently, my manga looks like I draw it in one shot, with momentum. So when I tell them how I do my work, people say "seri-ously?!" I'm serious, yes. And when I'm holed up at home, I watch videos and read books. It's okay if they help me with my story, but I'm so worried about my work not progressing, that nothing I see or read stays in my head, so it's useless. Ha ha ha. (Don't say "ha ha ha.")

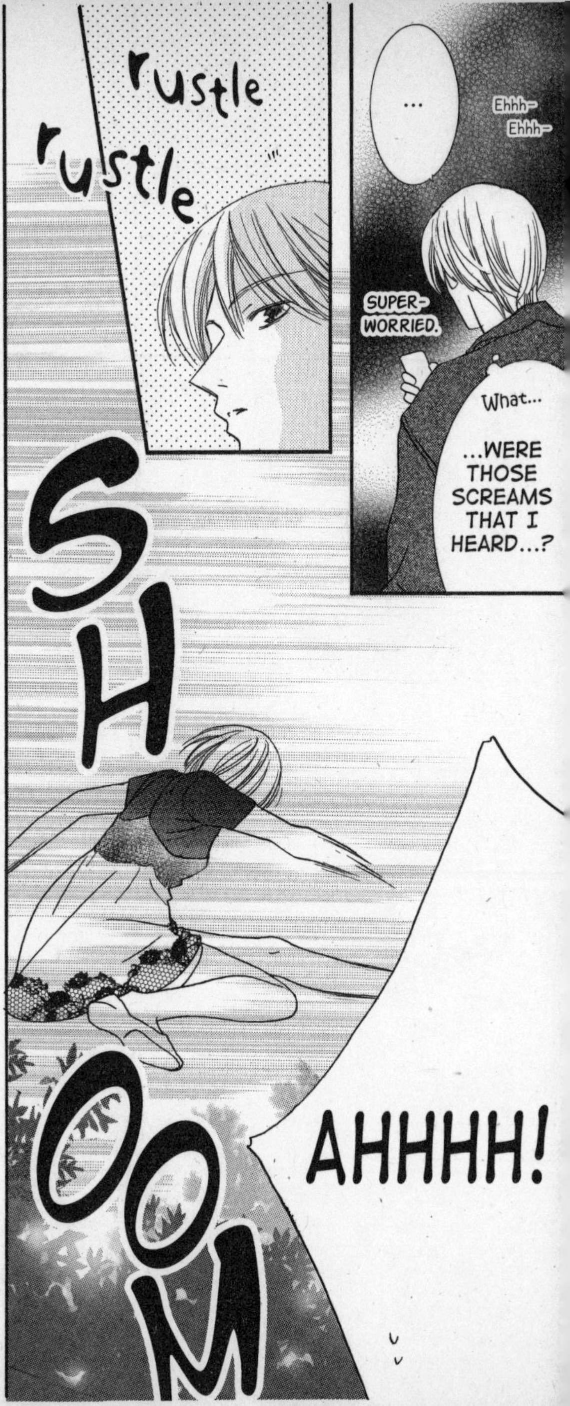
...
Ehhh-
Ehhh-
SUPER-WORRIED.
What...
...WERE THOSE SCREAMS THAT I HEARD...?
rustle
rustle
AHHHH!
SHOOM

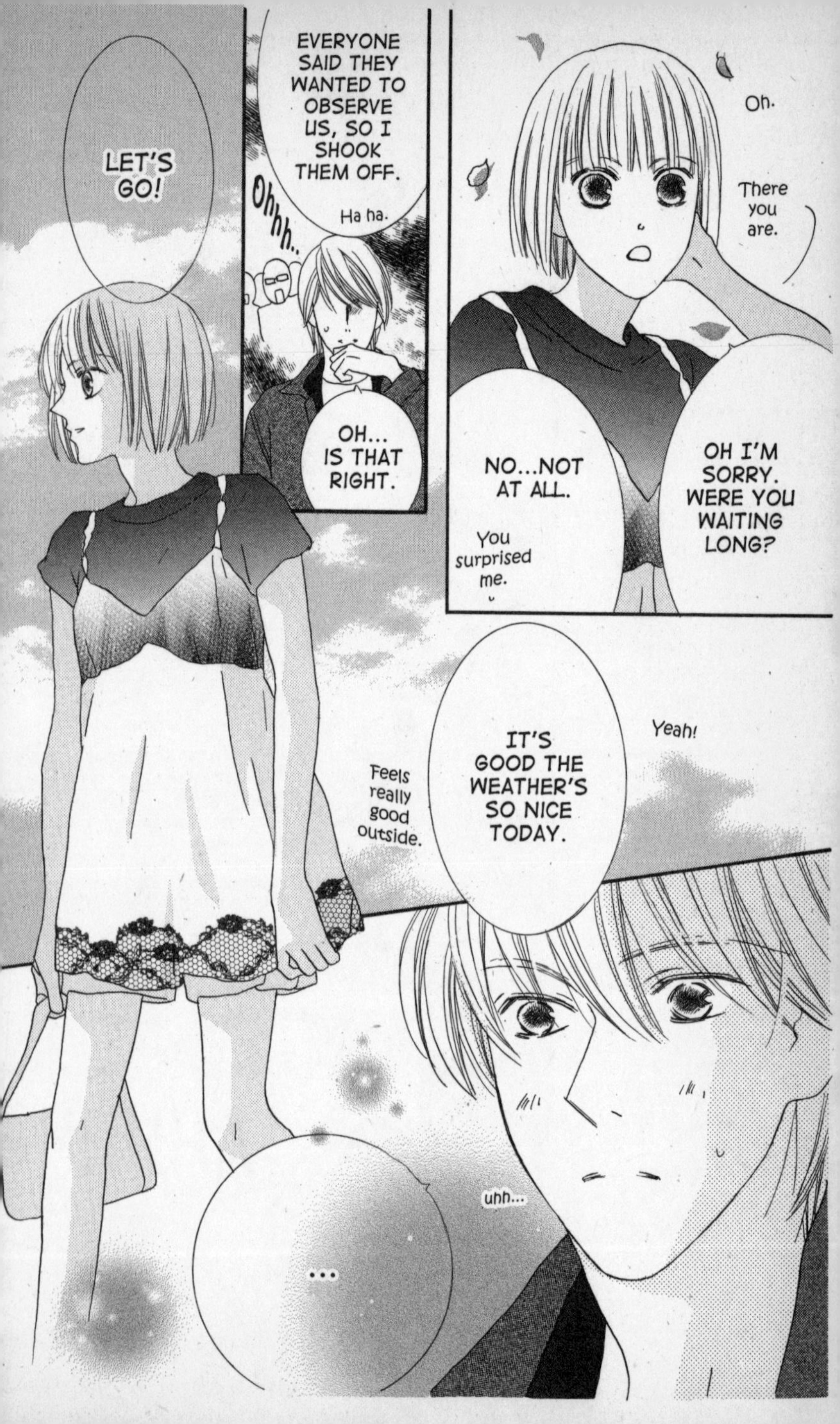
Oh.
There you are.
OH I'M SORRY. WERE YOU WAITING LONG?
NO...NOT AT ALL.
You surprised me.
EVERYONE SAID THEY WANTED TO OBSERVE US, SO I SHOOK THEM OFF.
Ha ha.
Ohhhh..
OH... IS THAT RIGHT.
IT'S GOOD THE WEATHER'S SO NICE TODAY.
Yeah!
Feels really good outside.
uhn...
...
LET'S GO!

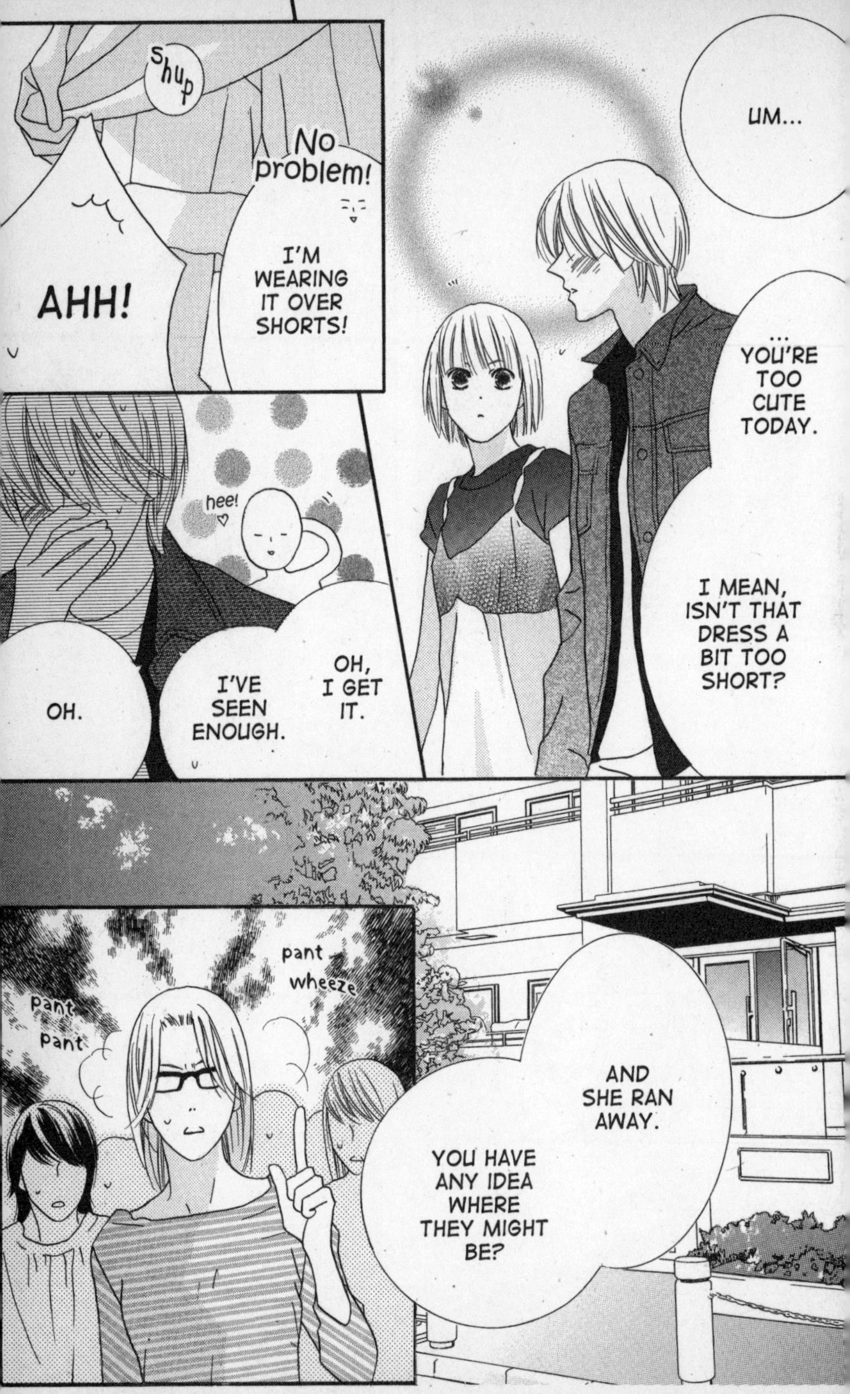
UM...
...YOU'RE TOO CUTE TODAY.
I MEAN, ISN'T THAT DRESS A BIT TOO SHORT?
shup
No problem!
I'M WEARING IT OVER SHORTS!
AHH!
hee!
OH, I GET IT.
I'VE SEEN ENOUGH.
OH.
AND SHE RAN AWAY.
YOU HAVE ANY IDEA WHERE THEY MIGHT BE?
pant wheeze
pant pant

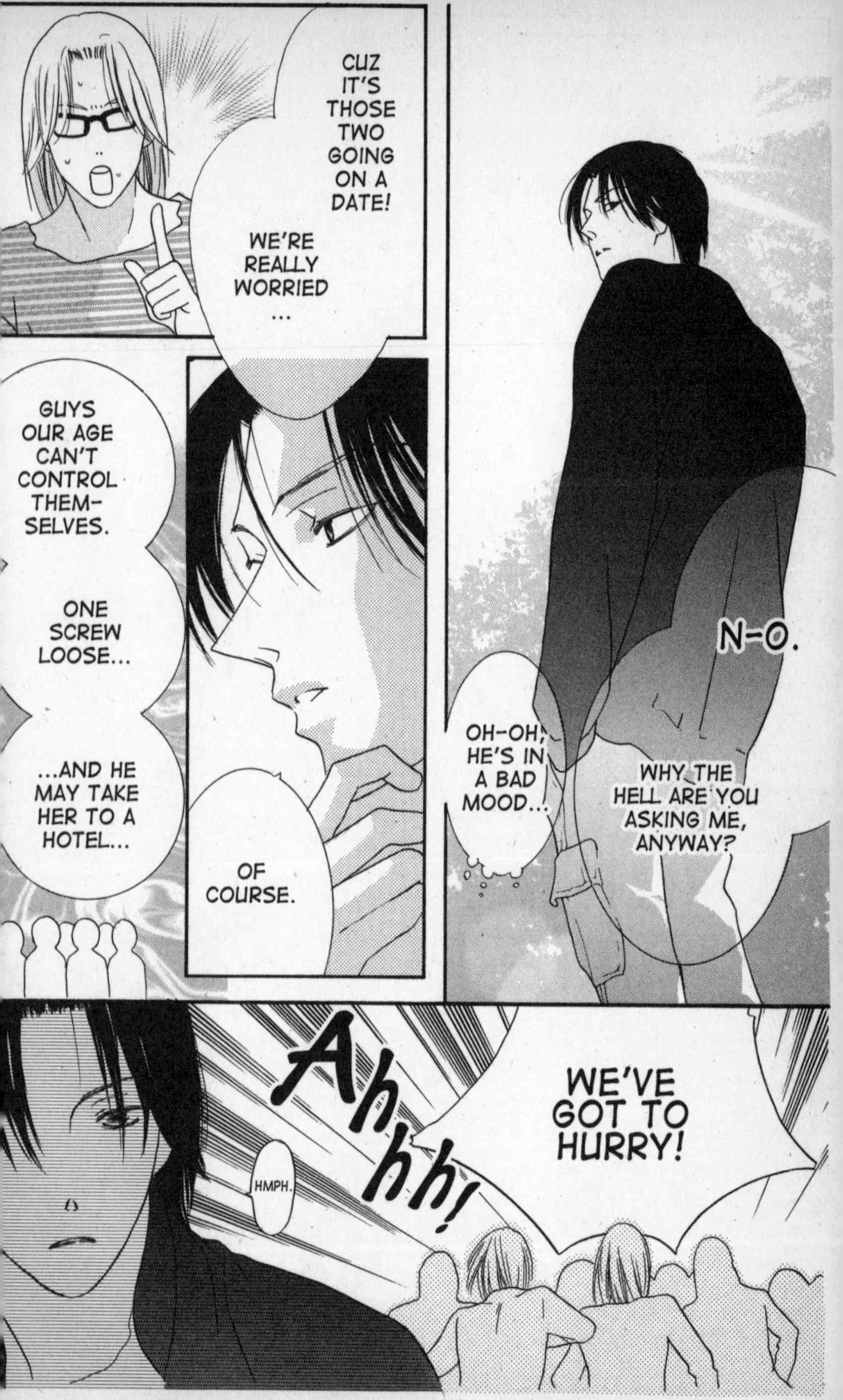
N-O.
WHY THE HELL ARE YOU ASKING ME, ANYWAY?
OH-OH, HE'S IN A BAD MOOD...
CUZ IT'S THOSE TWO GOING ON A DATE!
WE'RE REALLY WORRIED ...
OF COURSE.
GUYS OUR AGE CAN'T CONTROL THEM-SELVES.
ONE SCREW LOOSE...
...AND HE MAY TAKE HER TO A HOTEL...
WE'VE GOT TO HURRY!
Ahhh!
HMPH.

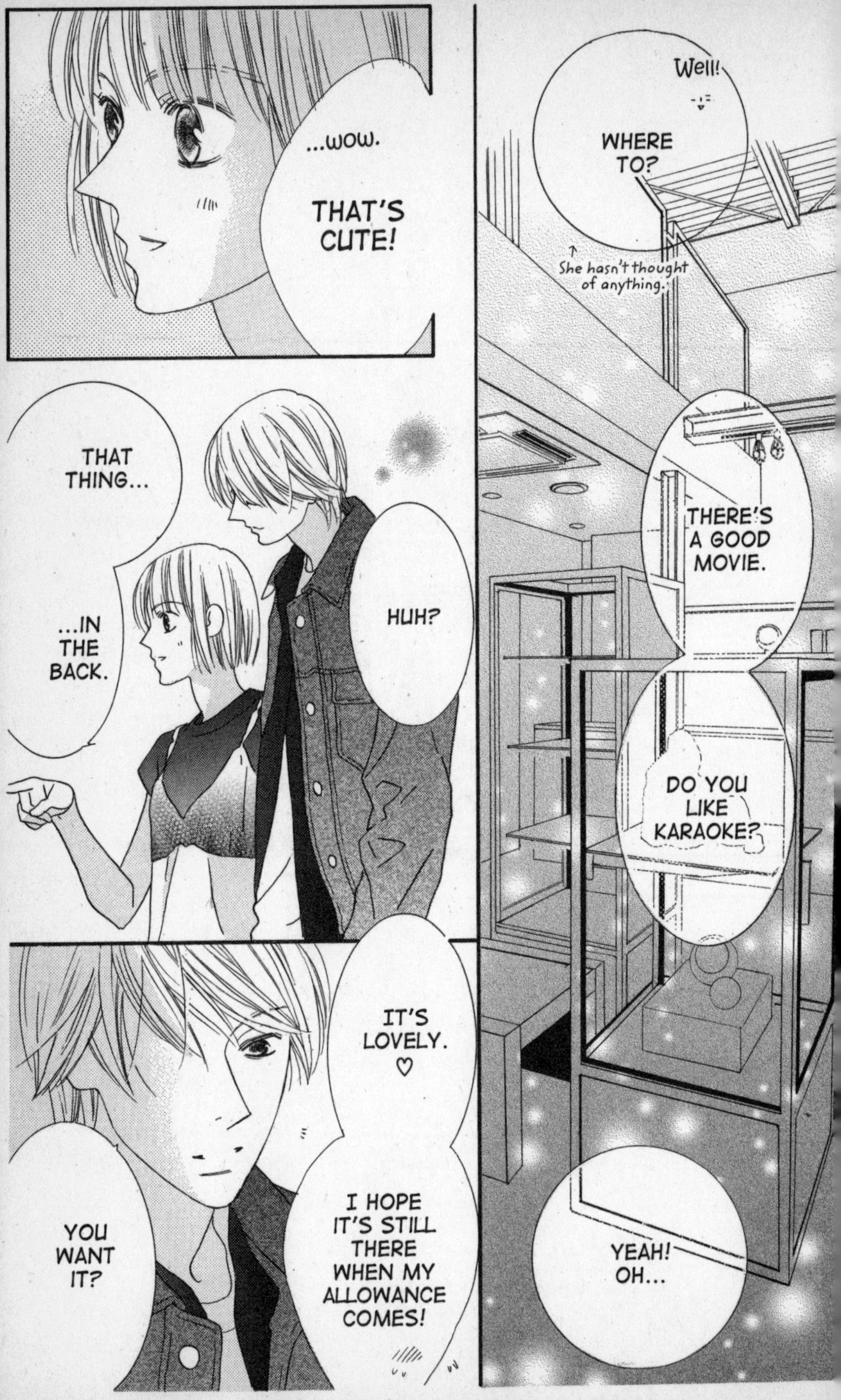
Well!
WHERE TO?
She hasn't thought of anything.
THERE'S A GOOD MOVIE.
DO YOU LIKE KARAOKE?
YEAH! OH...
...WOW.
THAT'S CUTE!
THAT THING...
...IN THE BACK.
HUH?
IT'S LOVELY. ♡
I HOPE IT'S STILL THERE WHEN MY ALLOWANCE COMES!
YOU WANT IT?

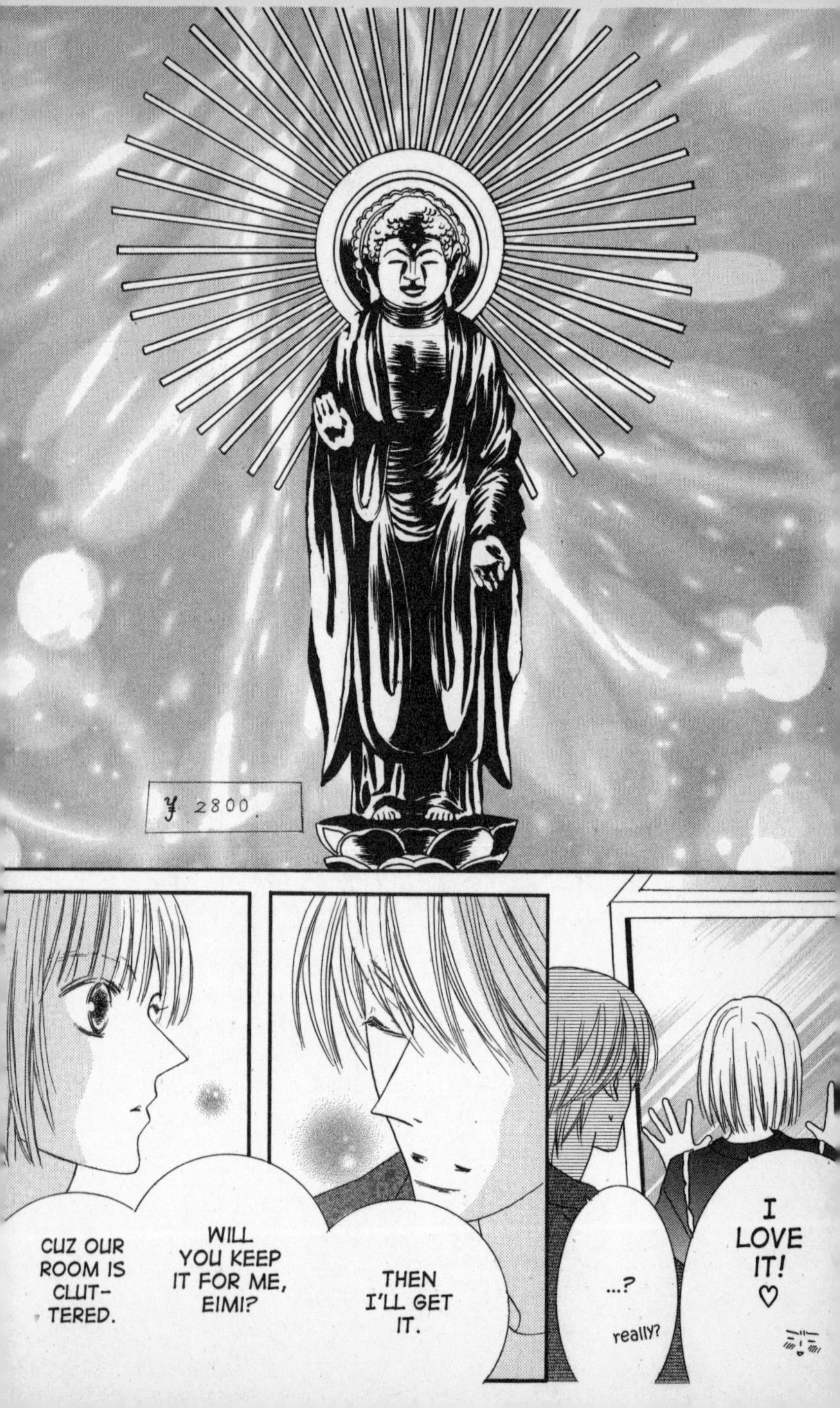
¥ 2800
I LOVE IT! ♡
...?
really?
THEN I'LL GET IT.
WILL YOU KEEP IT FOR ME, EIMI?
CUZ OUR ROOM IS CLUT-TERED.

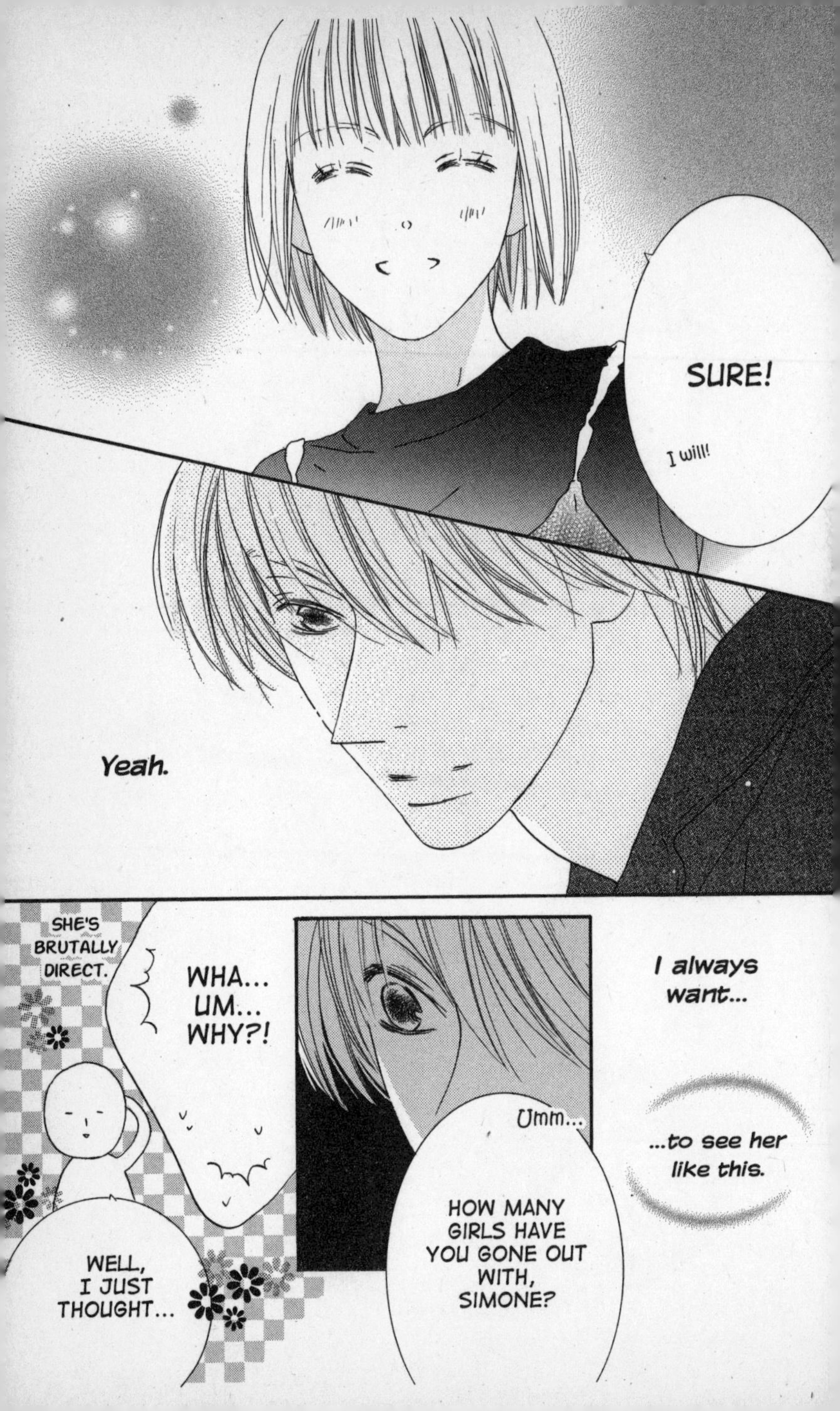
SURE!
I will!
Yeah.
I always want...
...to see her like this.
Umm...
HOW MANY GIRLS HAVE YOU GONE OUT WITH, SIMONE?
WHA... UM... WHY?!
SHE'S BRUTALLY DIRECT.
WELL, I JUST THOUGHT...

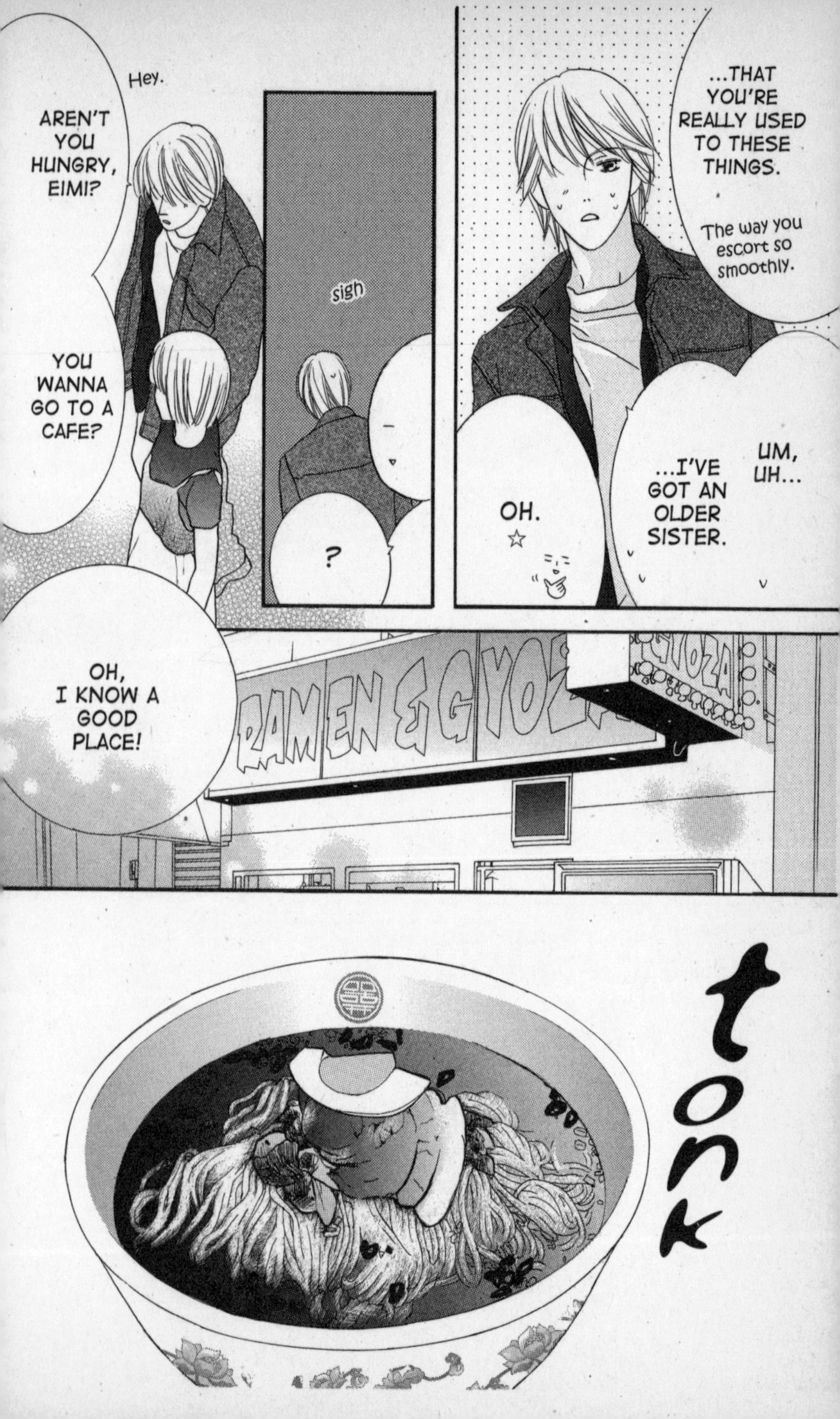
...THAT YOU'RE REALLY USED TO THESE THINGS.
The way you escort so smoothly.
UM, UH...
...I'VE GOT AN OLDER SISTER.
OH.
sigh
?
Hey.
AREN'T YOU HUNGRY, EIMI?
YOU WANNA GO TO A CAFE?
OH, I KNOW A GOOD PLACE!
RAMEN & GYOZ
GYOZA
tonk

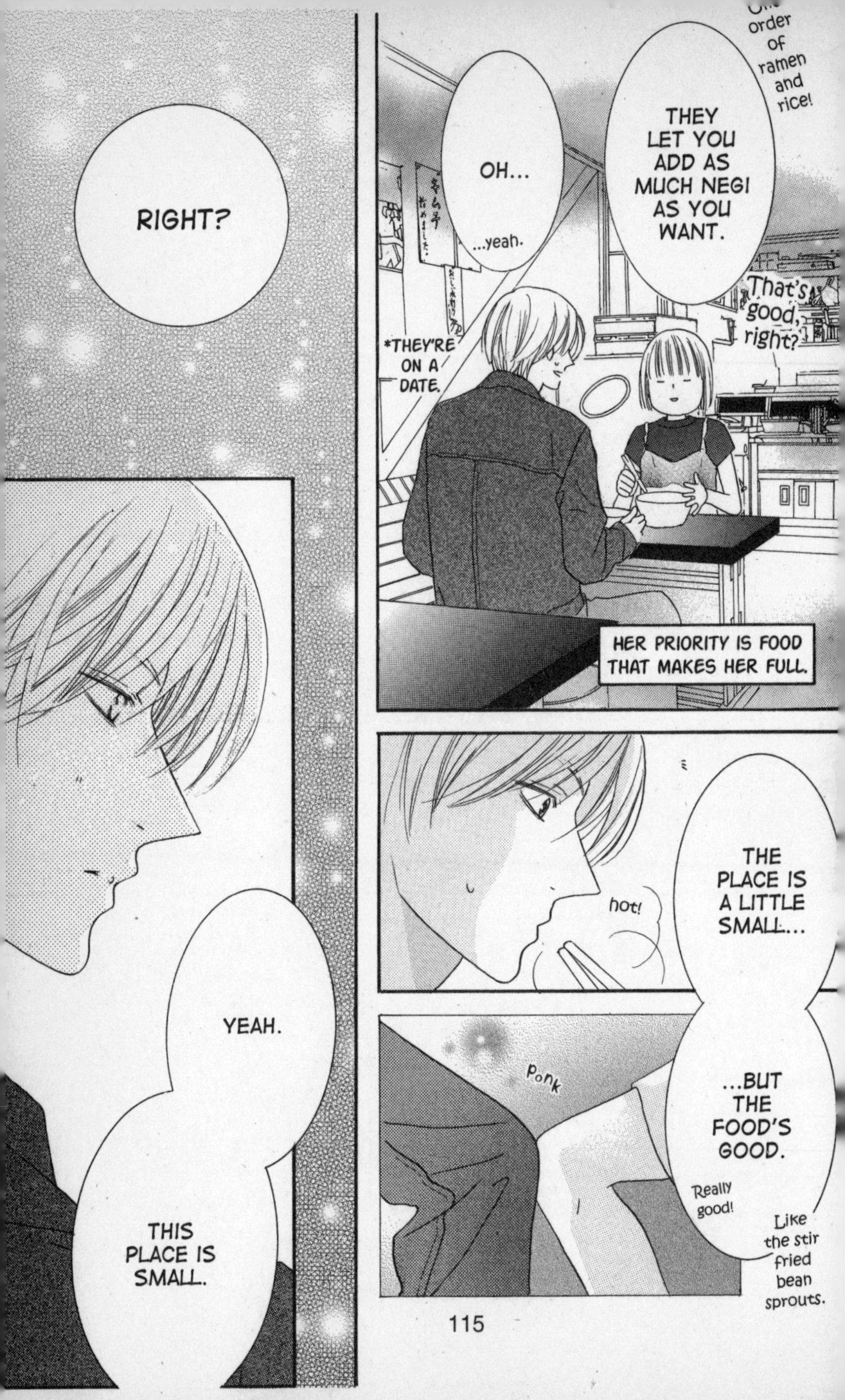
order of ramen and rice!
THEY LET YOU ADD AS MUCH NEGI AS YOU WANT.
That's good, right?
OH...
...yeah.
*THEY'RE ON A DATE.
HER PRIORITY IS FOOD THAT MAKES HER FULL.
THE PLACE IS A LITTLE SMALL...
hot!
...BUT THE FOOD'S GOOD.
Like the stir fried bean sprouts.
Really good!
Ponk
RIGHT?
YEAH.
THIS PLACE IS SMALL.

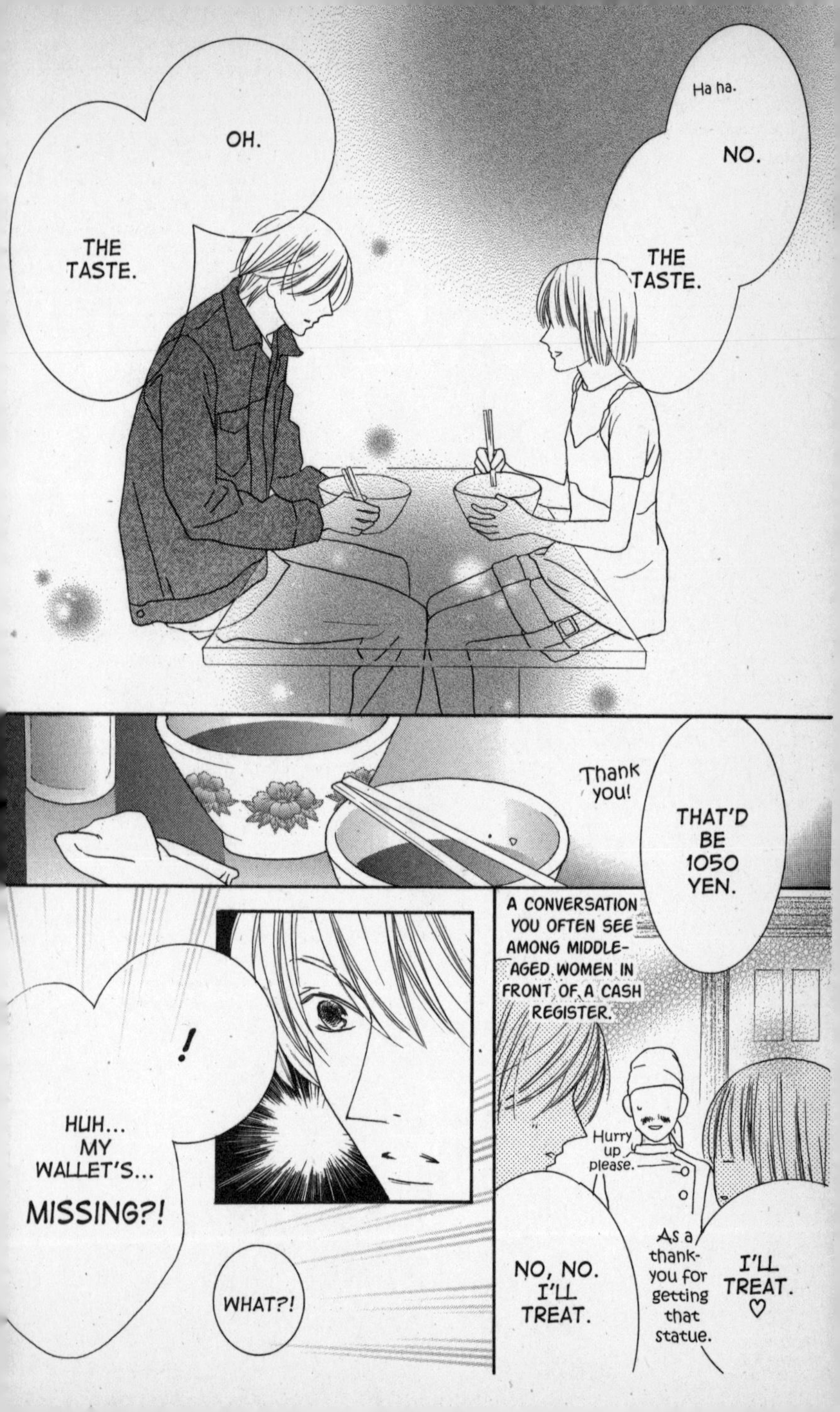
Ha ha.
NO.
THE TASTE.
OH.
THE TASTE.
THAT'D BE 1050 YEN.
Thank you!
A CONVERSATION YOU OFTEN SEE AMONG MIDDLE-AGED WOMEN IN FRONT OF A CASH REGISTER.
Hurry up please.
I'LL TREAT. ♡
As a thank-you for getting that statue.
NO, NO. I'LL TREAT.
!
HUH... MY WALLET'S... MISSING?!
WHAT?!

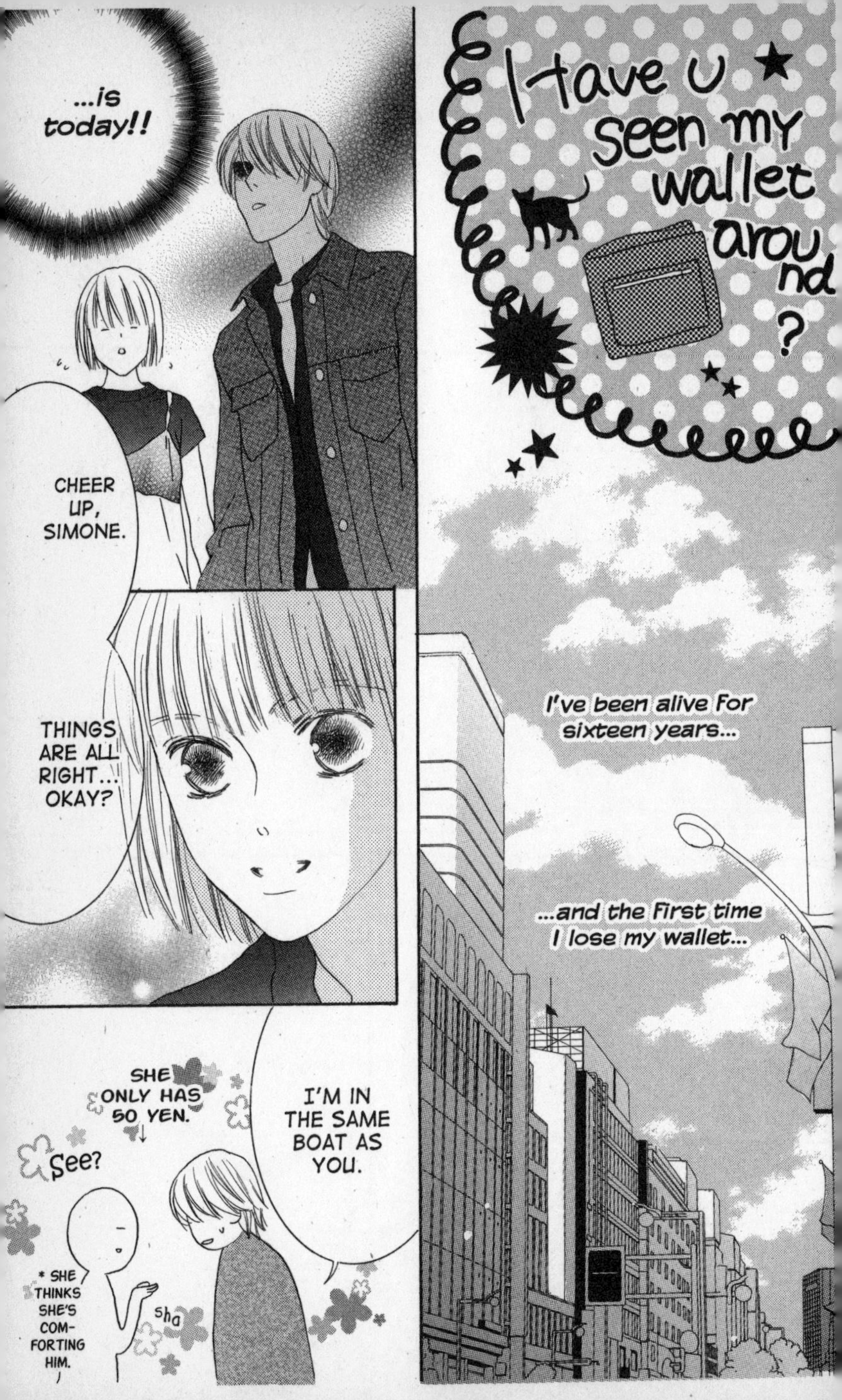
Have U seen my wallet around?
I've been alive for sixteen years...
...and the first time I lose my wallet...
...is today!!
CHEER UP, SIMONE.
THINGS ARE ALL RIGHT... OKAY?
I'M IN THE SAME BOAT AS YOU.
SHE ONLY HAS 50 YEN.
See?
sha
* SHE THINKS SHE'S COM-FORTING HIM.

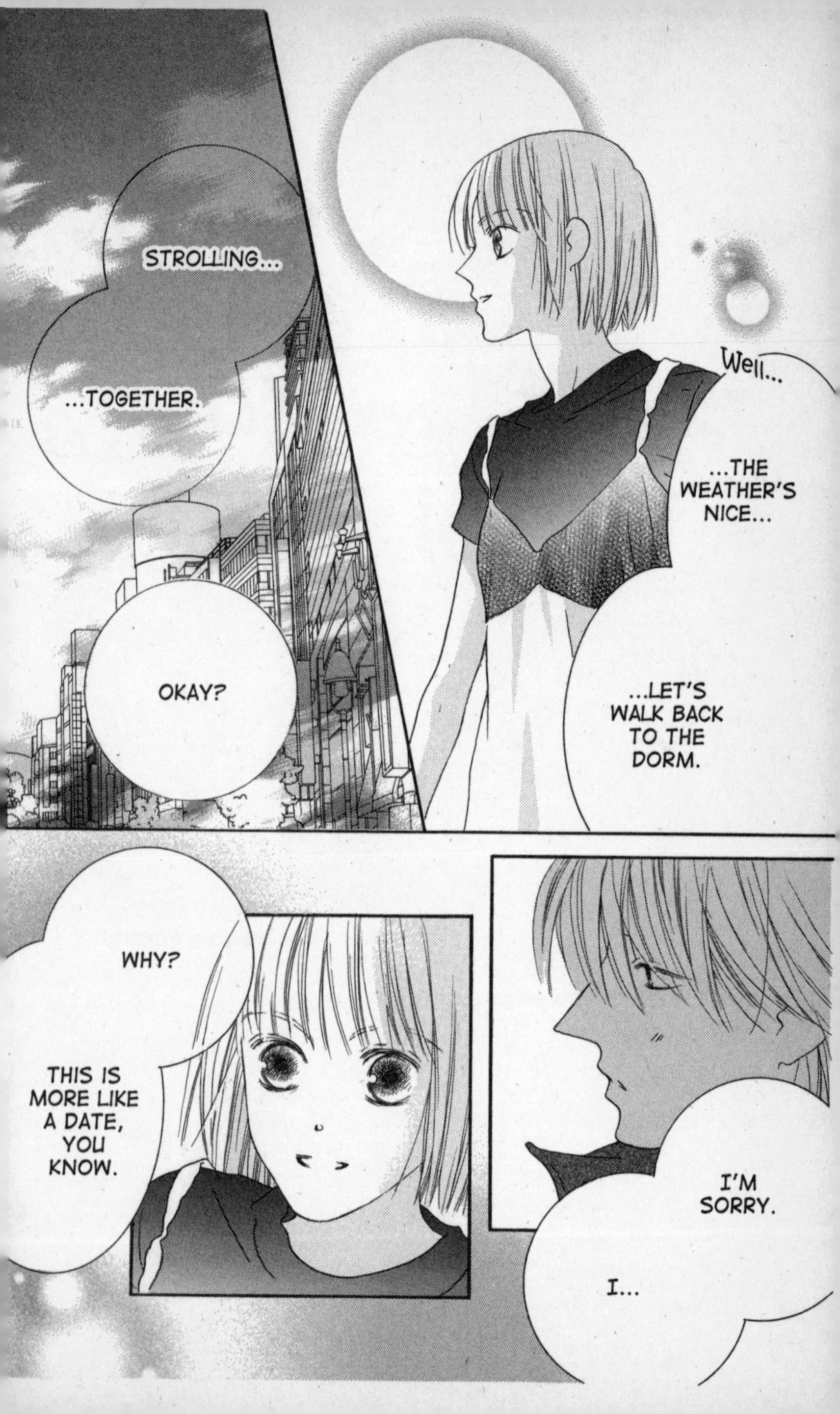
Well...
...THE WEATHER'S NICE...
...LET'S WALK BACK TO THE DORM.
STROLLING...
...TOGETHER.
OKAY?
I'M SORRY.
I...
WHY?
THIS IS MORE LIKE A DATE, YOU KNOW.

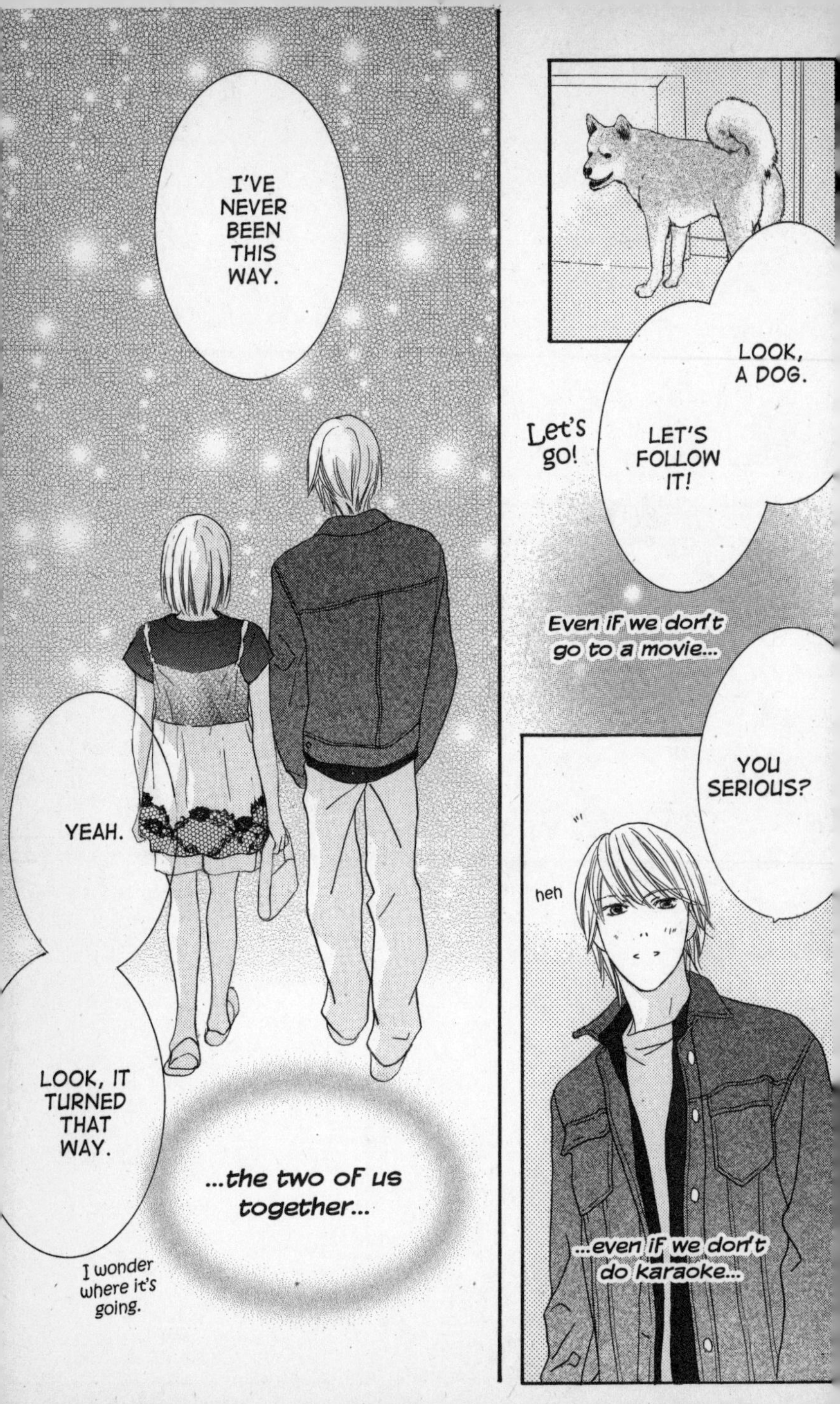
LOOK, A DOG.
LET'S FOLLOW IT!
Let's go!
Even if we don't go to a movie...
YOU SERIOUS?
heh
...even if we don't do karaoke...
I'VE NEVER BEEN THIS WAY.
YEAH.
LOOK, IT TURNED THAT WAY.
I wonder where it's going.
...the two of us together...

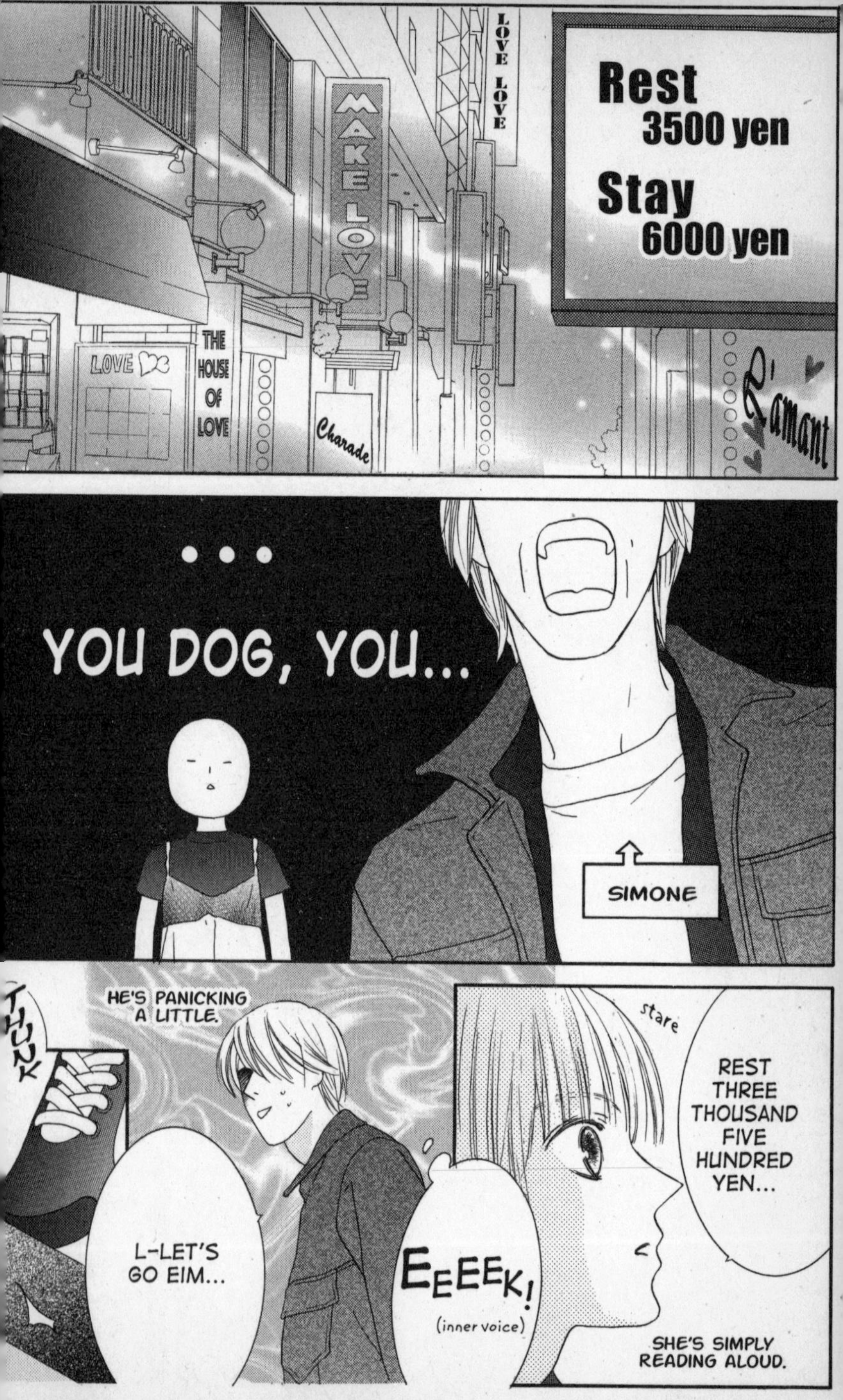
Rest
3500 yen
Stay
6000 yen
L'amant
LOVE LOVE
MAKE LOVE
Charade
THE HOUSE OF LOVE
LOVE
• • •
YOU DOG, YOU...
SIMONE
stare
REST THREE THOUSAND FIVE HUNDRED YEN...
SHE'S SIMPLY READING ALOUD.
EEEEK!
(inner voice)
HE'S PANICKING A LITTLE.
L-LET'S GO EIM...
THUNK

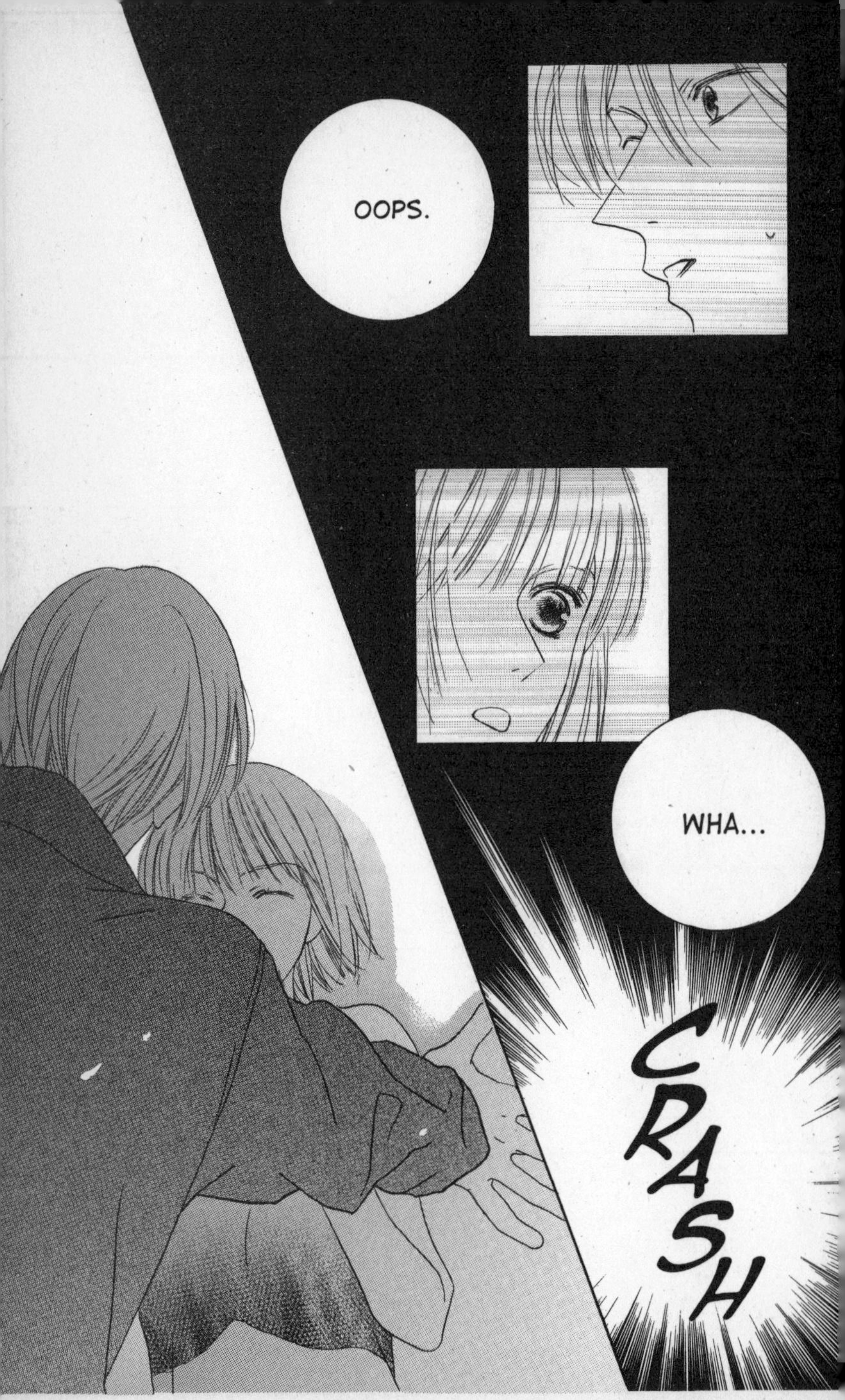
OOPS.
WHA...
CRASH

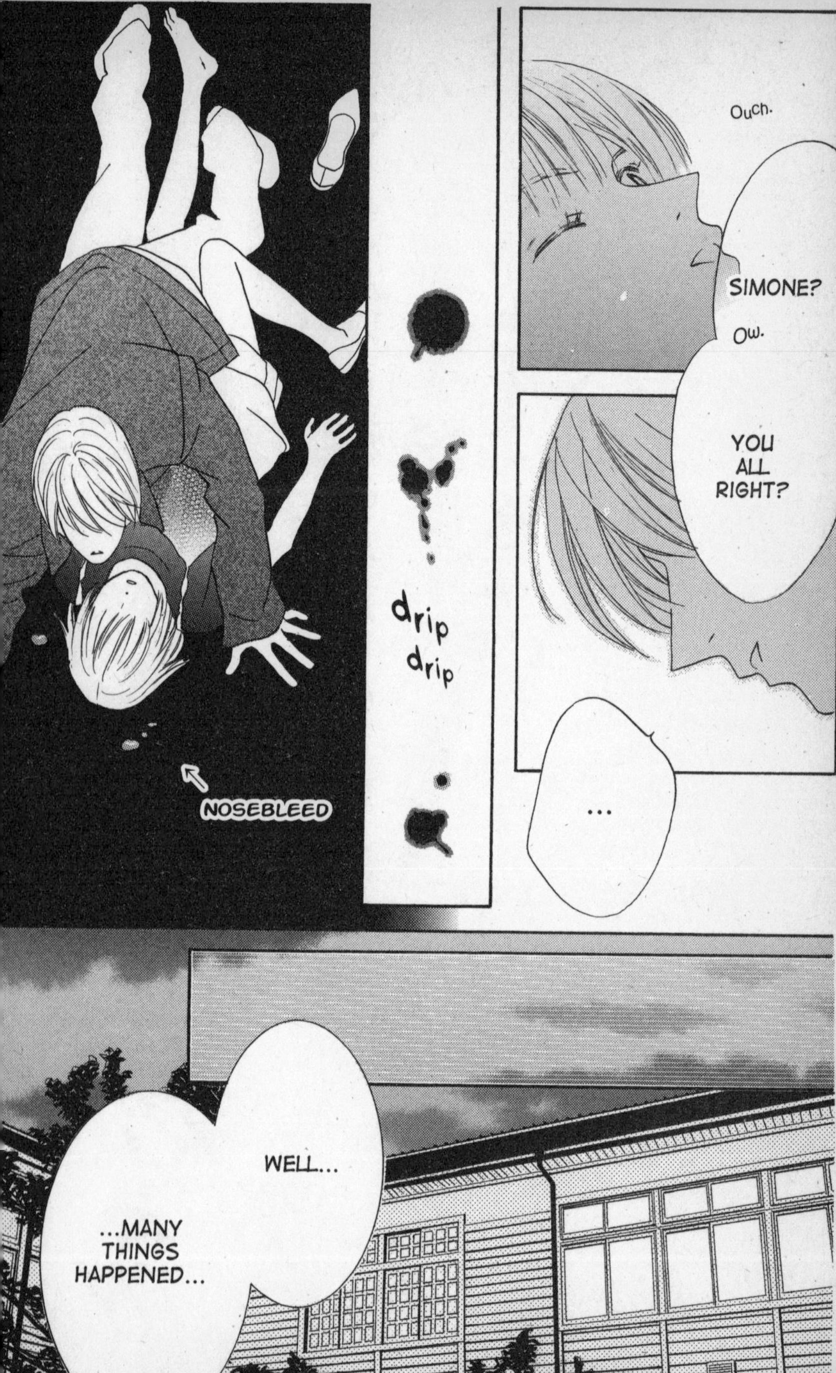
Ouch.
SIMONE?
Ow.
YOU ALL RIGHT?
...
drip drip
NOSEBLEED
WELL...
...MANY THINGS HAPPENED...

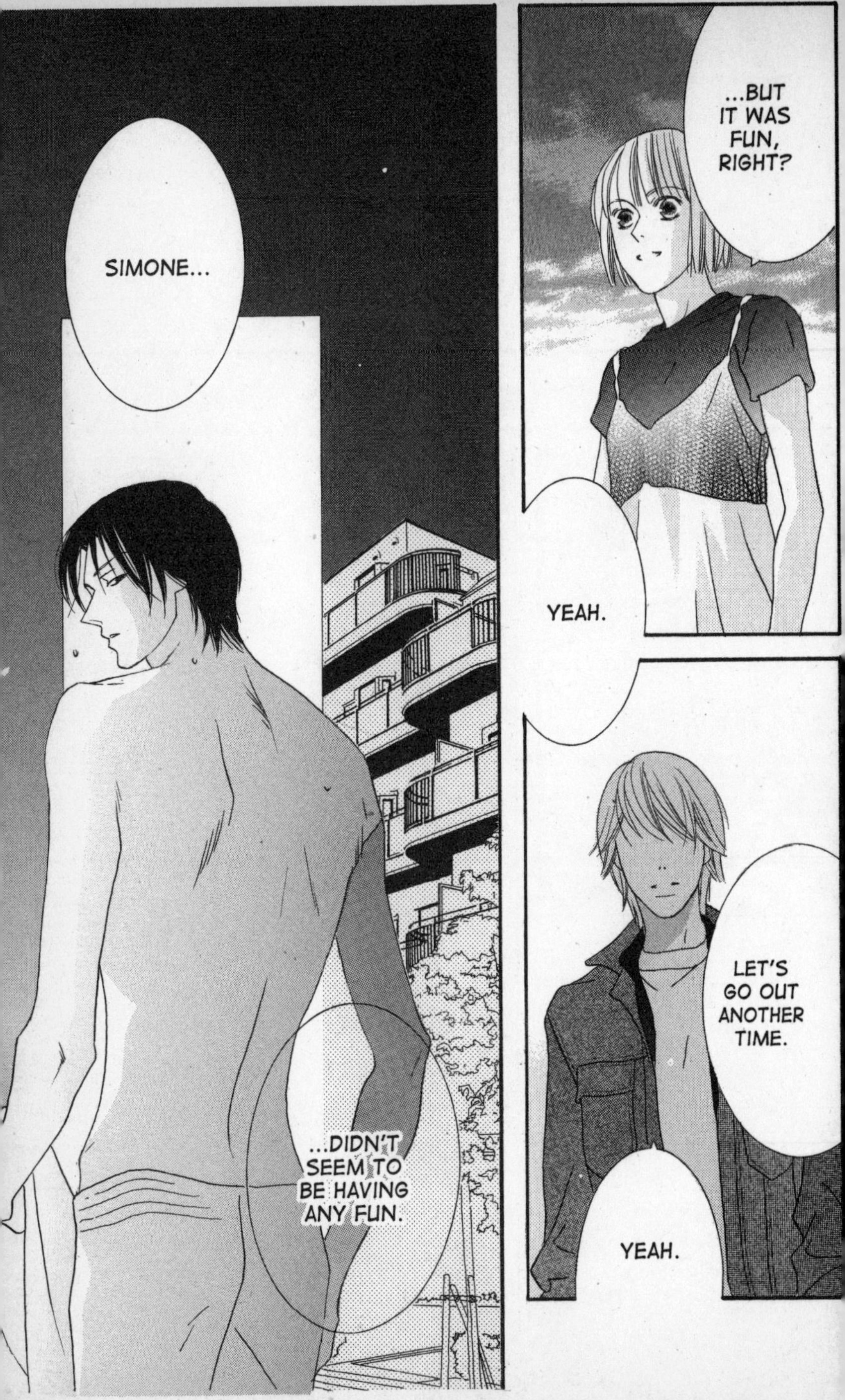
...BUT IT WAS FUN, RIGHT?
YEAH.
LET'S GO OUT ANOTHER TIME.
YEAH.
SIMONE...
...DIDN'T SEEM TO BE HAVING ANY FUN.

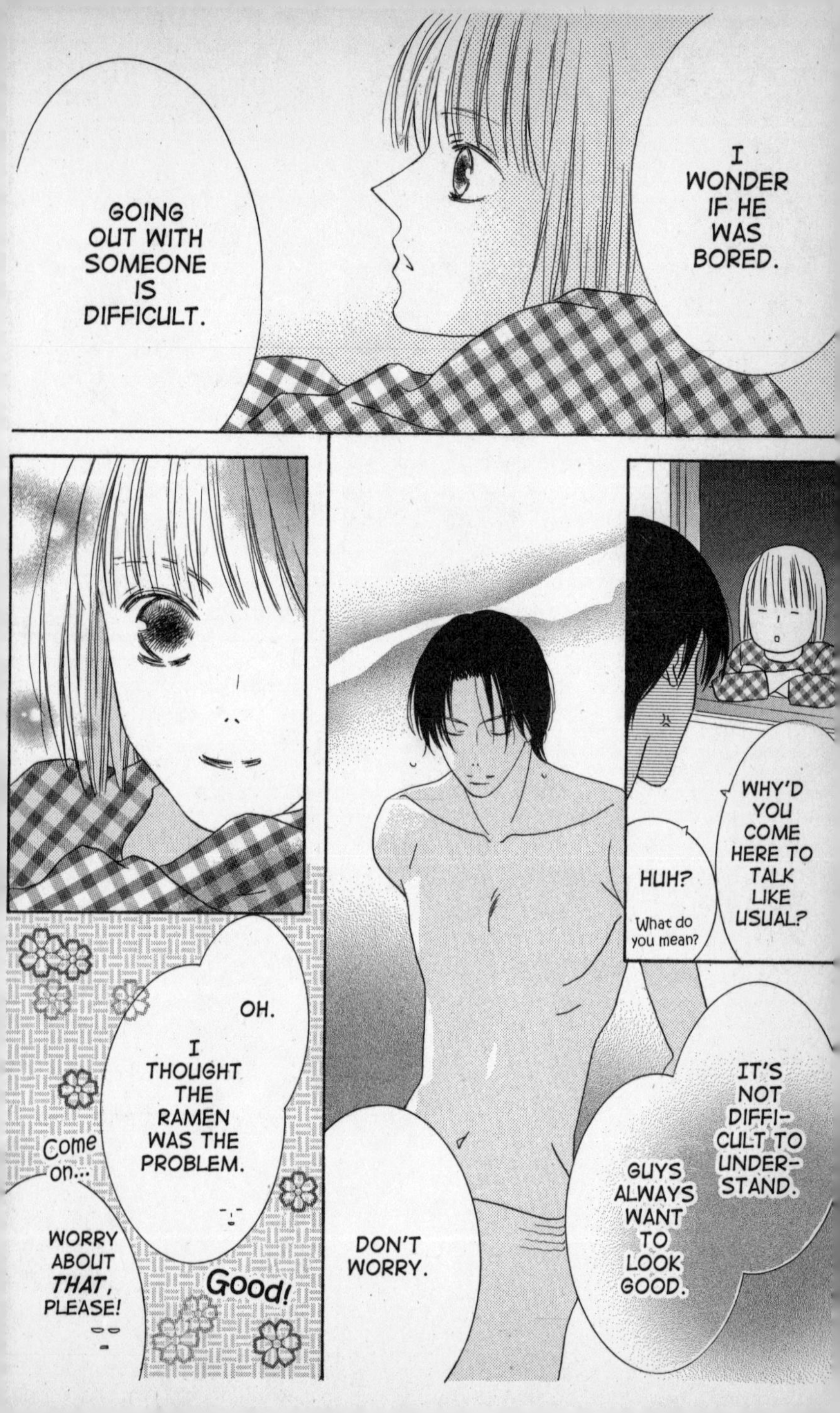
I WONDER IF HE WAS BORED.
GOING OUT WITH SOMEONE IS DIFFICULT.
WHY'D YOU COME HERE TO TALK LIKE USUAL?
HUH?
What do you mean?
IT'S NOT DIFFI-CULT TO UNDER-STAND.
GUYS ALWAYS WANT TO LOOK GOOD.
DON'T WORRY.
OH.
I THOUGHT THE RAMEN WAS THE PROBLEM.
Good!
Come on...
WORRY ABOUT *THAT*, PLEASE!

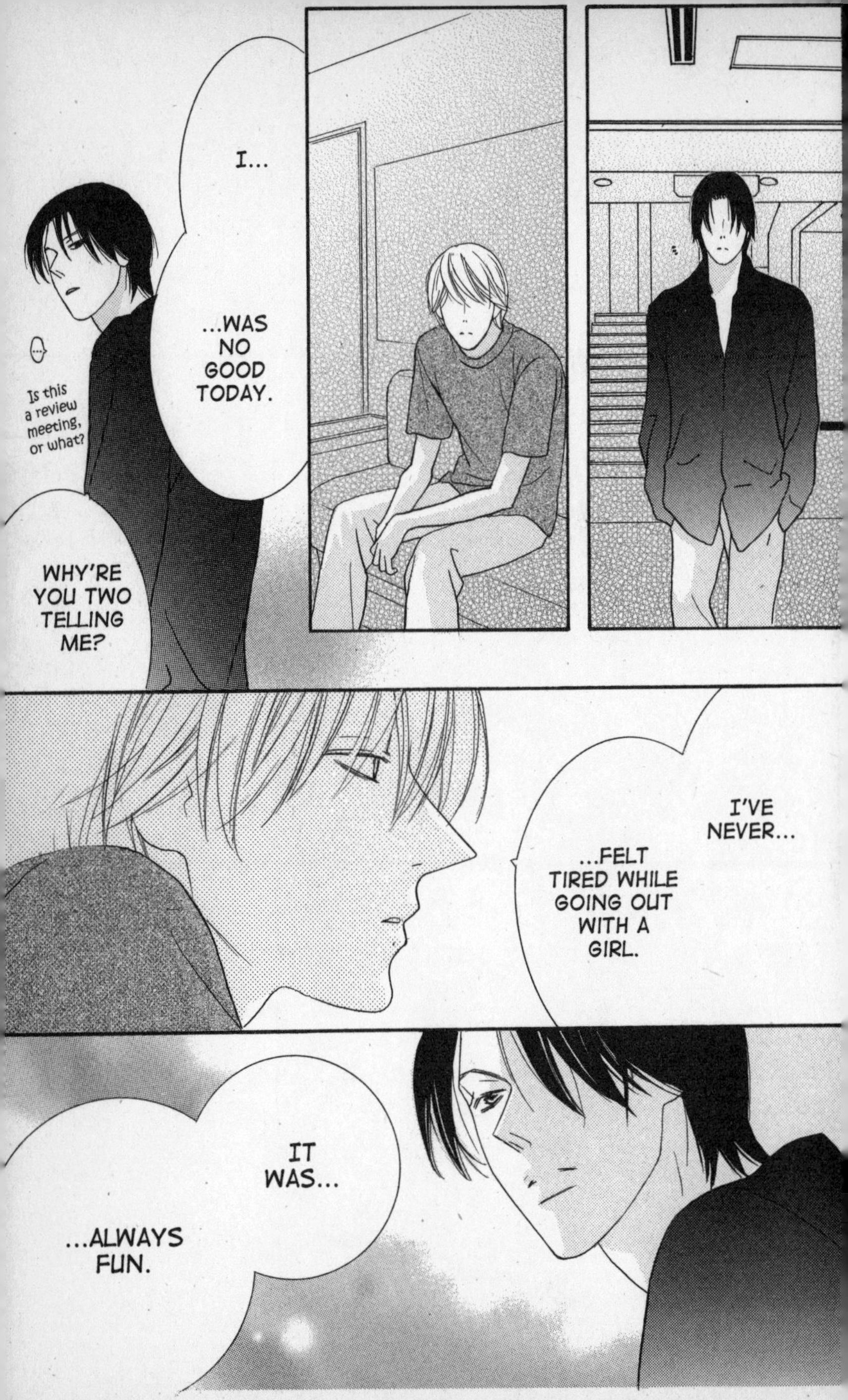
I...
...WAS NO GOOD TODAY.
...
Is this a review meeting, or what?
WHY'RE YOU TWO TELLING ME?
I'VE NEVER...
...FELT TIRED WHILE GOING OUT WITH A GIRL.
IT WAS...
...ALWAYS FUN.

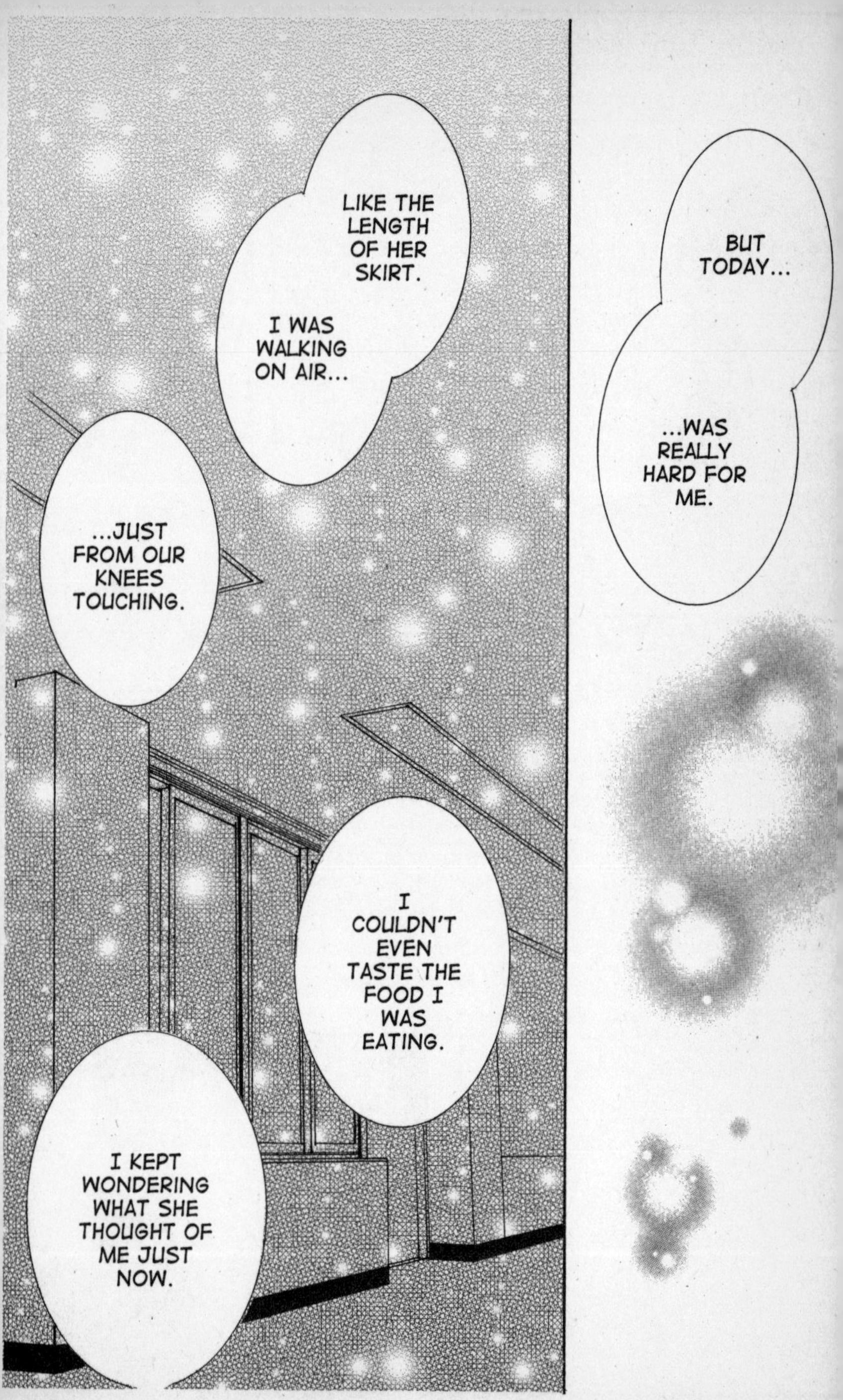
BUT TODAY...
...WAS REALLY HARD FOR ME.
LIKE THE LENGTH OF HER SKIRT.
I WAS WALKING ON AIR...
...JUST FROM OUR KNEES TOUCHING.
I COULDN'T EVEN TASTE THE FOOD I WAS EATING.
I KEPT WONDERING WHAT SHE THOUGHT OF ME JUST NOW.

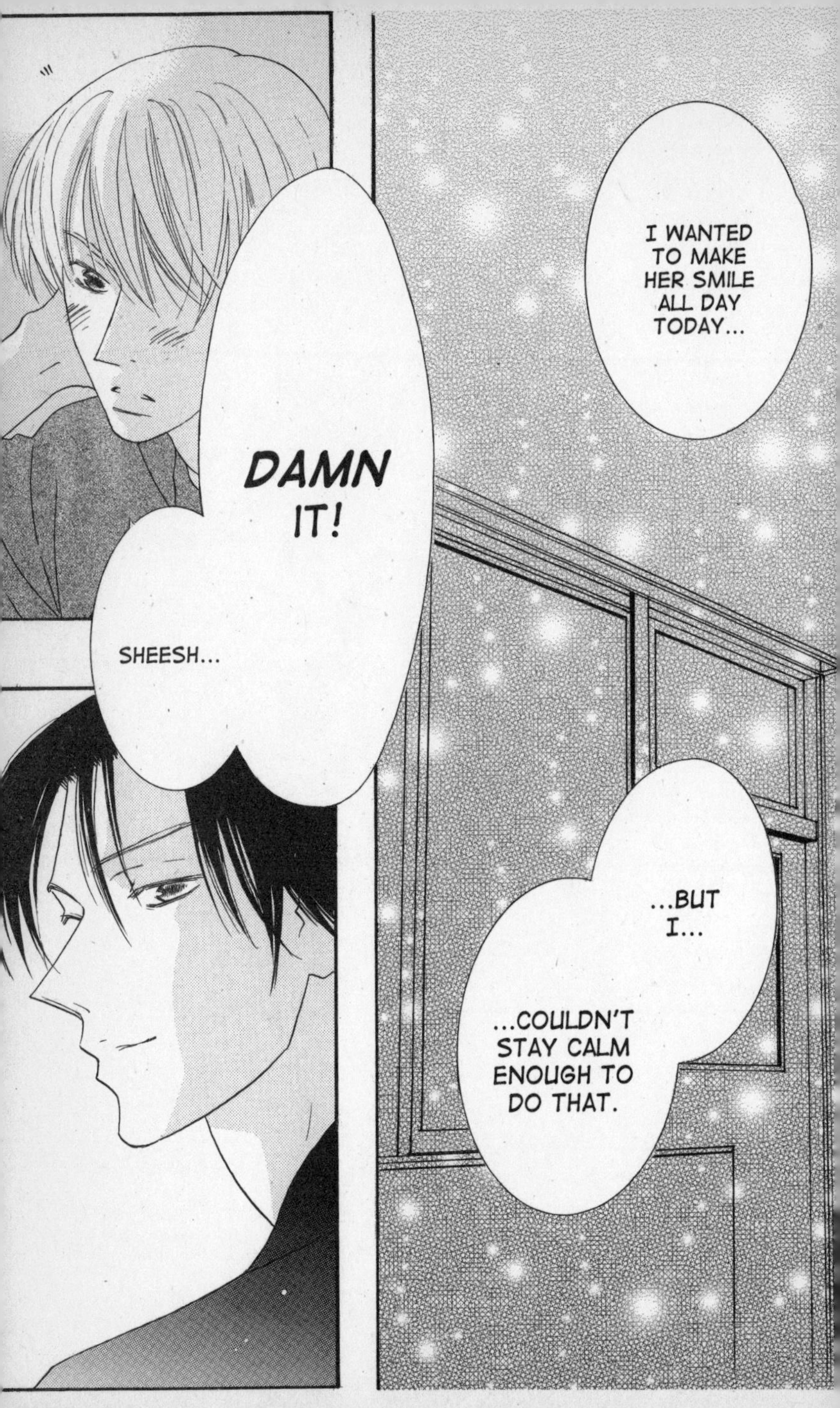
I WANTED TO MAKE HER SMILE ALL DAY TODAY...
...BUT I...
...COULDN'T STAY CALM ENOUGH TO DO THAT.
DAMN IT!
SHEESH...

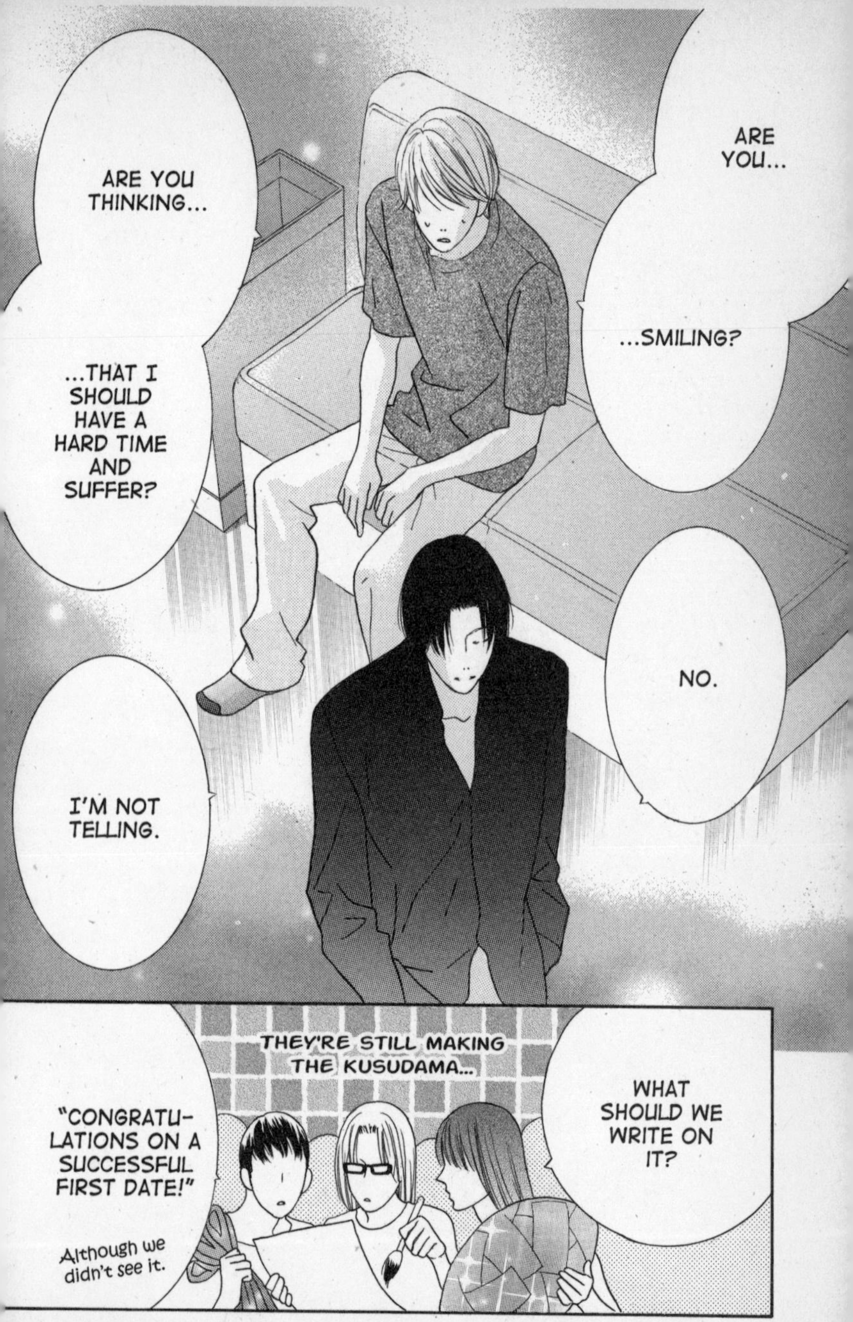
ARE YOU...
...SMILING?
ARE YOU THINKING...
...THAT I SHOULD HAVE A HARD TIME AND SUFFER?
NO.
I'M NOT TELLING.
THEY'RE STILL MAKING THE KUSUDAMA...
WHAT SHOULD WE WRITE ON IT?
"CONGRATU-LATIONS ON A SUCCESSFUL FIRST DATE!"
Although we didn't see it.

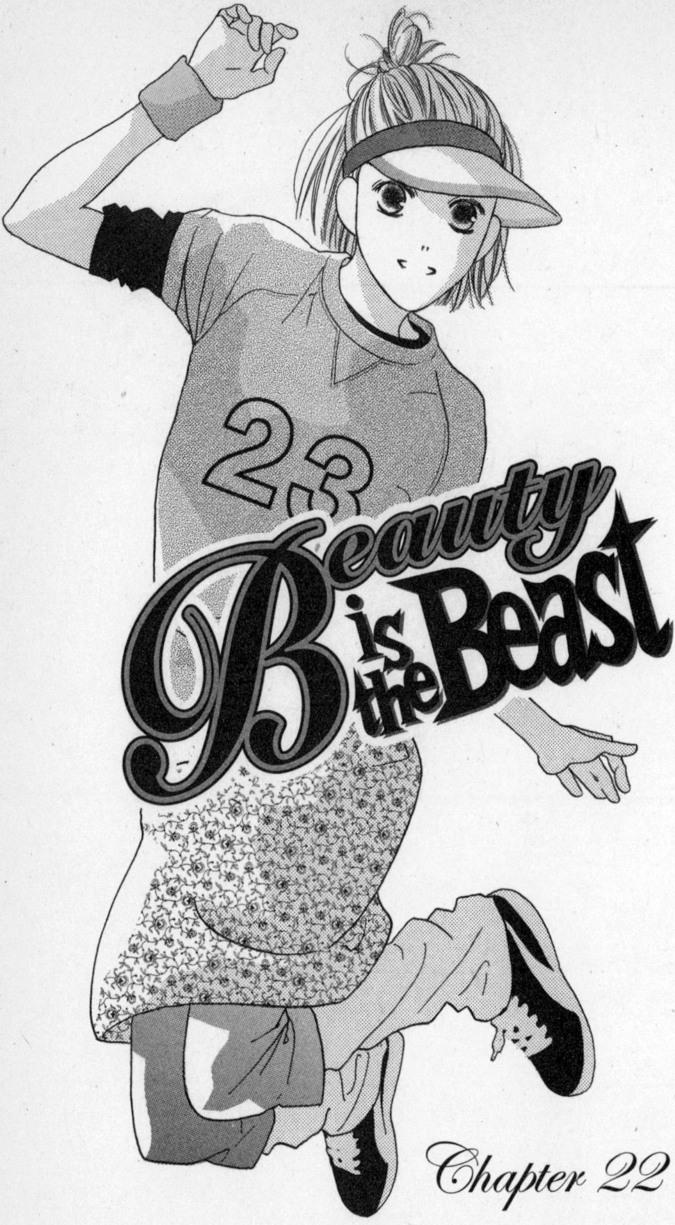

Beauty is the Beast

Chapter 22

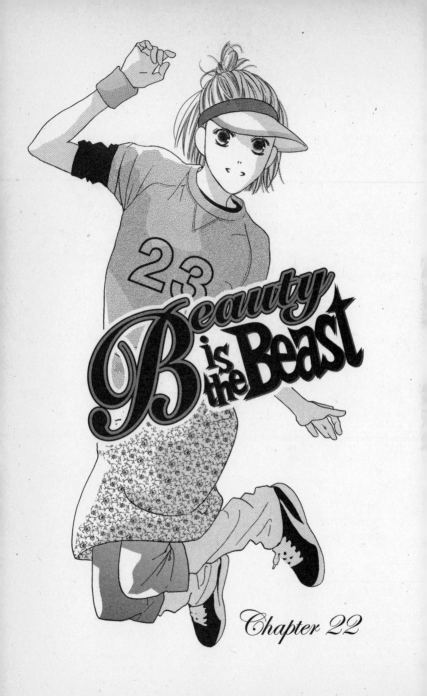

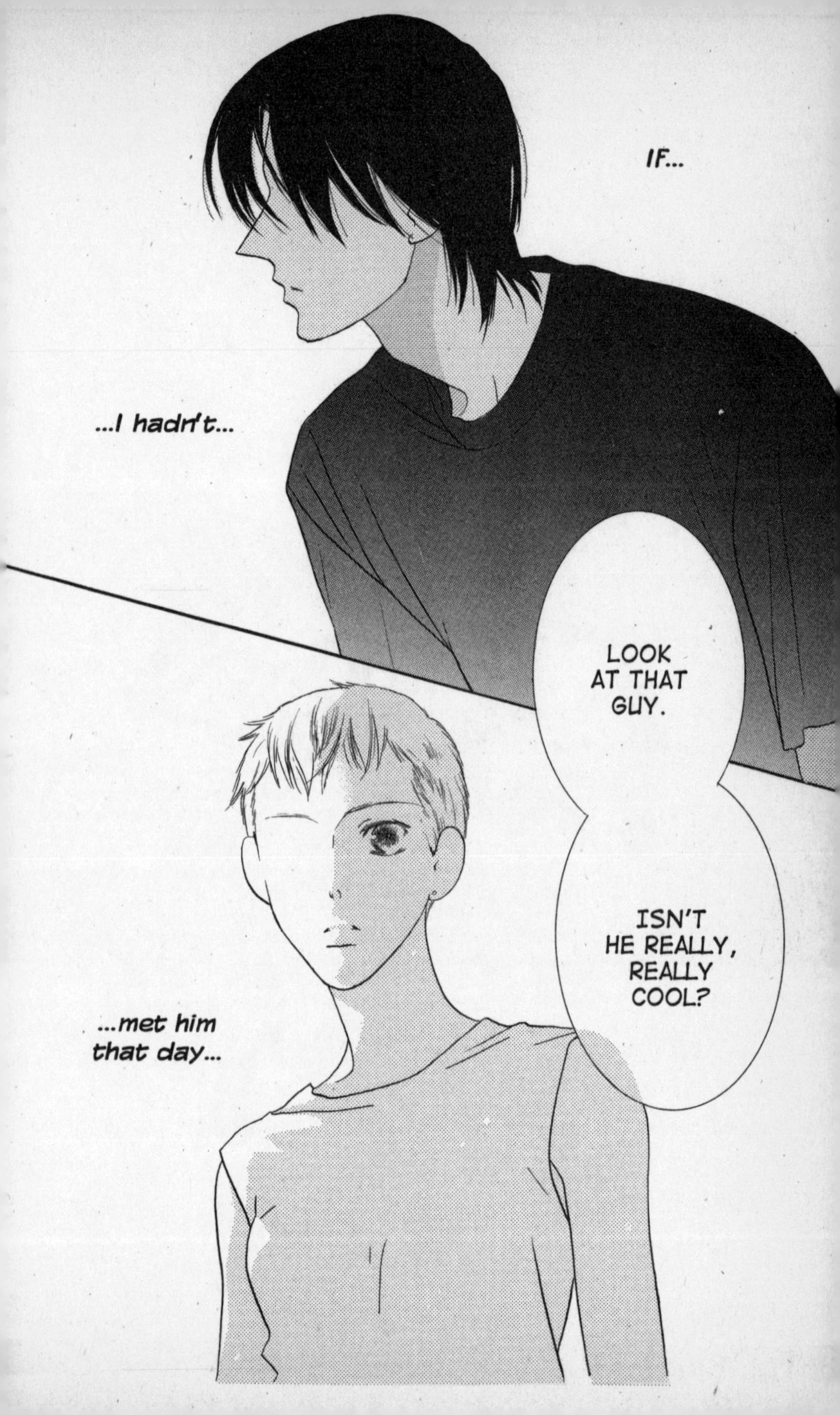
IF...
...I hadn't...
LOOK AT THAT GUY.
ISN'T HE REALLY, REALLY COOL?
...met him that day...

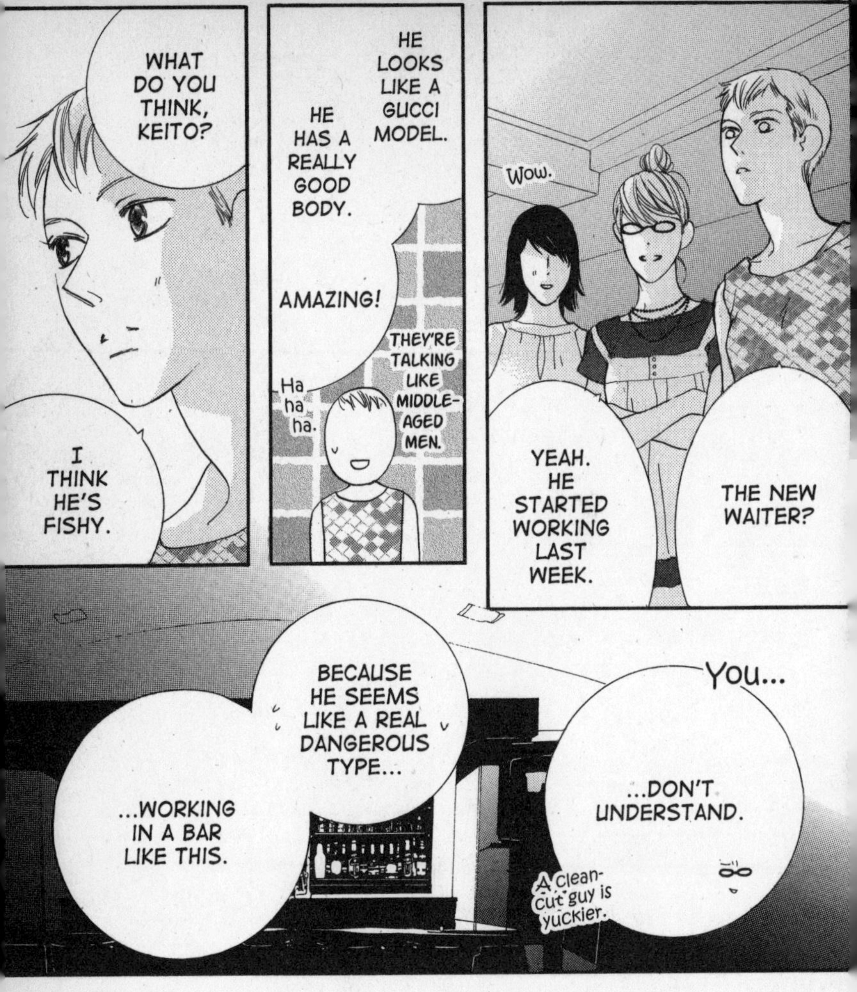
Wow.
THE NEW WAITER?
YEAH. HE STARTED WORKING LAST WEEK.
HE LOOKS LIKE A GUCCI MODEL.
HE HAS A REALLY GOOD BODY.
AMAZING!
THEY'RE TALKING LIKE MIDDLE-AGED MEN.
Ha ha ha.
WHAT DO YOU THINK, KEITO?
I THINK HE'S FISHY.
You...
...DON'T UNDERSTAND.
A clean-cut guy is yuckier.
BECAUSE HE SEEMS LIKE A REAL DANGEROUS TYPE...
...WORKING IN A BAR LIKE THIS.

"Natural Woman," the song that appears in this chapter, was written and composed by Carole King and sung by Aretha Franklin. Carole sung it herself later, and I have her version.
It might not satisfy people who are used to hearing the low tones of R&B, but I like it. It tastes like dried seaweed and squid. On the other hand, Aretha's has a meaty presence.
Mary J. Blige has apparently covered it, too. (A reader told me!☆) I've gotta check it out.
Good songs get covered by many people, so it's fun listening and comparing the various versions.

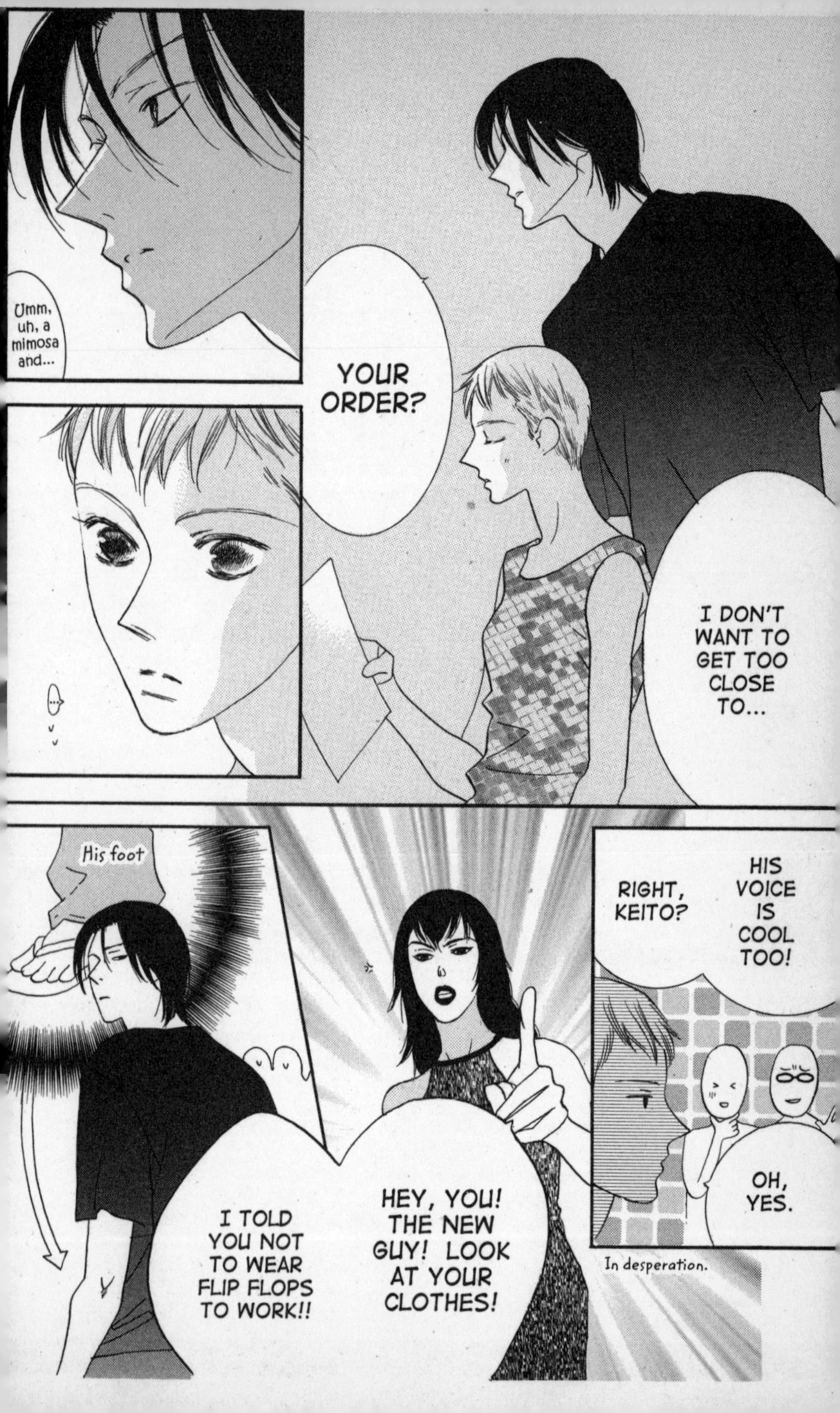
YOUR ORDER?
I DON'T WANT TO GET TOO CLOSE TO...
Umm, uh, a mimosa and...
...
HIS VOICE IS COOL TOO!
RIGHT, KEITO?
OH, YES.
In desperation.
HEY, YOU! THE NEW GUY! LOOK AT YOUR CLOTHES!
I TOLD YOU NOT TO WEAR FLIP FLOPS TO WORK!!
His foot

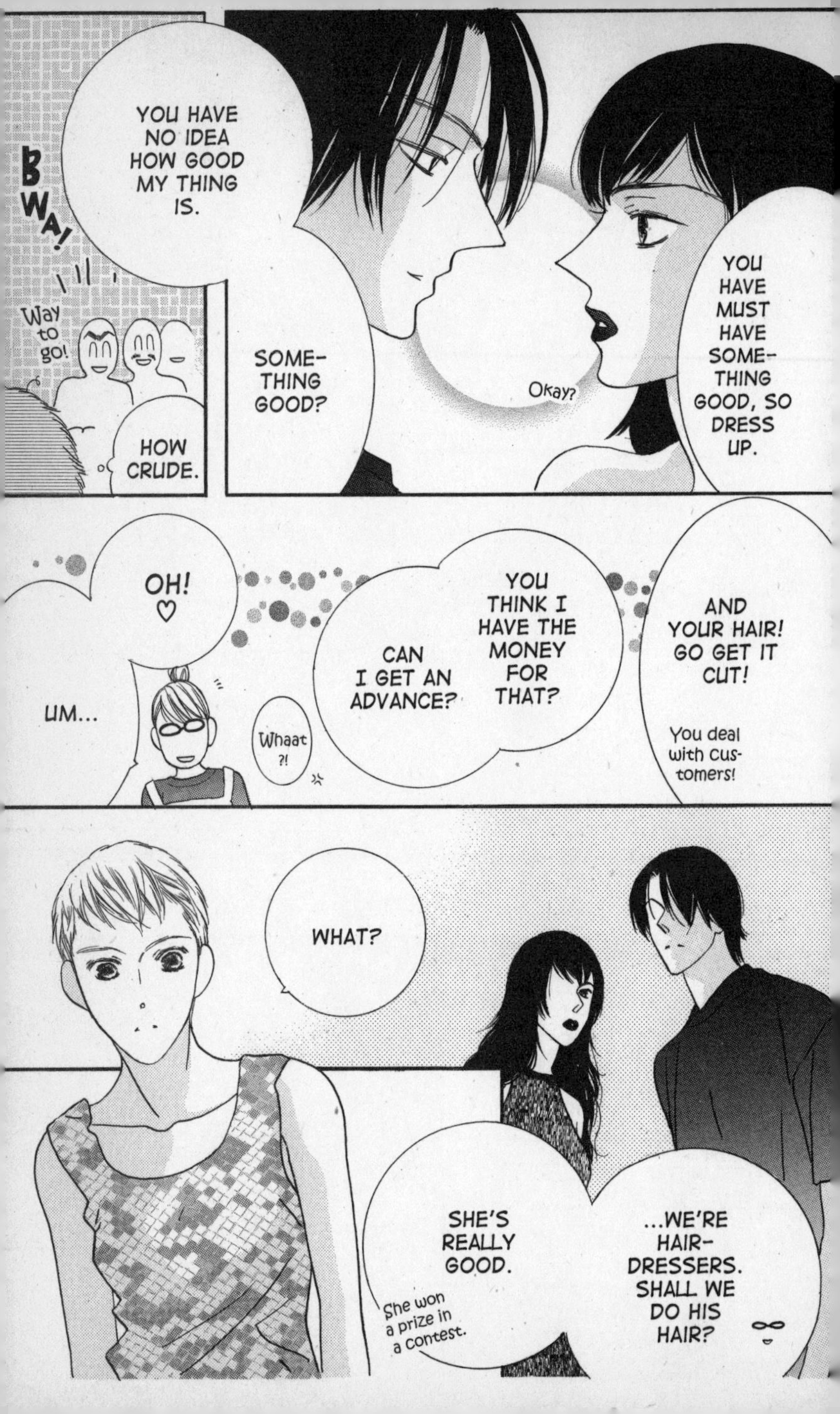
YOU HAVE MUST HAVE SOME-THING GOOD, SO DRESS UP.
Okay?
SOME-THING GOOD?
YOU HAVE NO IDEA HOW GOOD MY THING IS.
BWA!
Way to go!
HOW CRUDE.
AND YOUR HAIR! GO GET IT CUT!
You deal with cus-tomers!
YOU THINK I HAVE THE MONEY FOR THAT?
CAN I GET AN ADVANCE?
Whaat?!
OH! ♡
UM...
WHAT?
...WE'RE HAIR-DRESSERS. SHALL WE DO HIS HAIR?
SHE'S REALLY GOOD.
She won a prize in a contest.

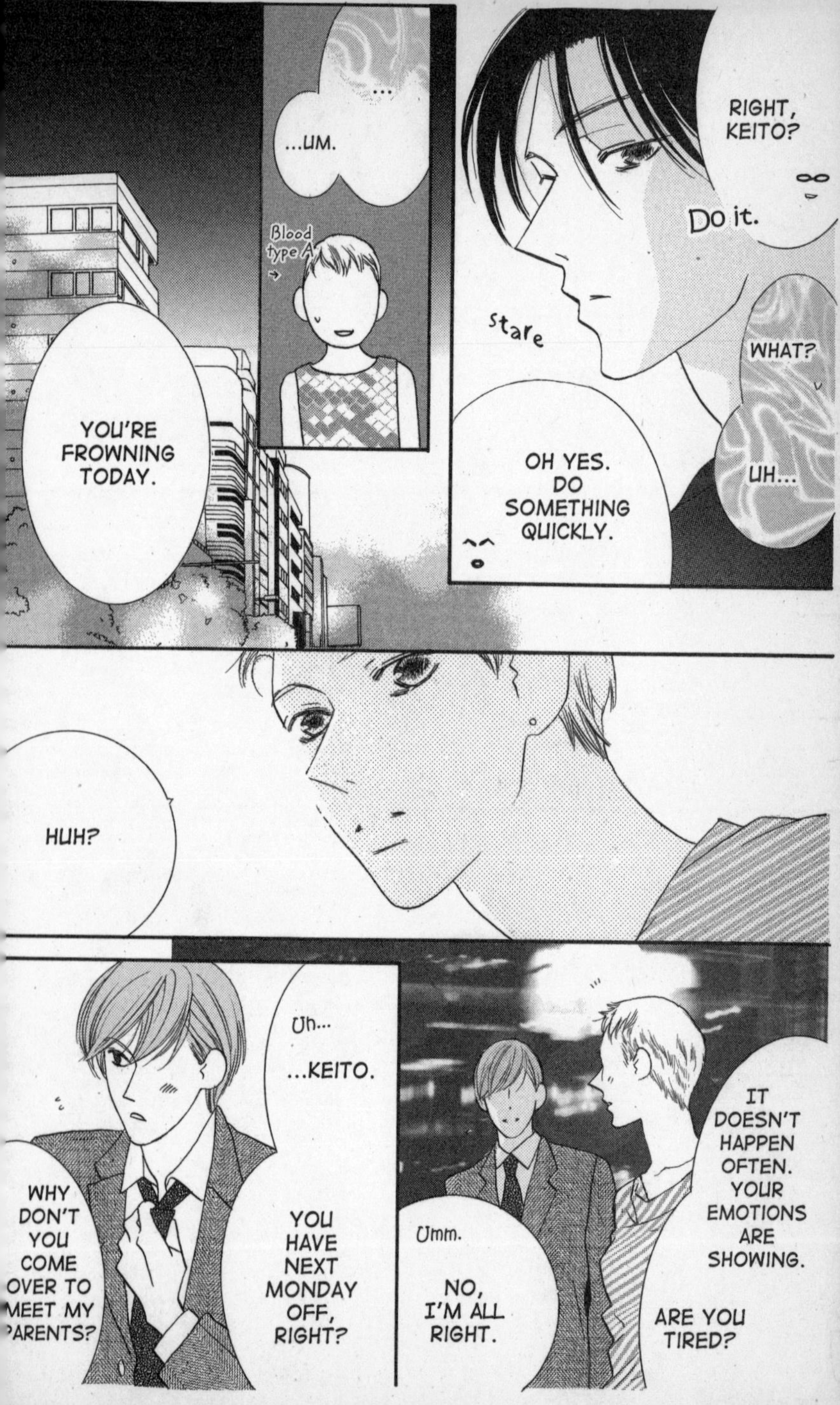
RIGHT, KEITO?
Do it.
stare
WHAT?
UH...
OH YES. DO SOMETHING QUICKLY.
...
...UM.
Blood type A →
YOU'RE FROWNING TODAY.
HUH?
IT DOESN'T HAPPEN OFTEN. YOUR EMOTIONS ARE SHOWING.
ARE YOU TIRED?
Umm.
NO, I'M ALL RIGHT.
Uh...
...KEITO.
YOU HAVE NEXT MONDAY OFF, RIGHT?
WHY DON'T YOU COME OVER TO MEET MY PARENTS?

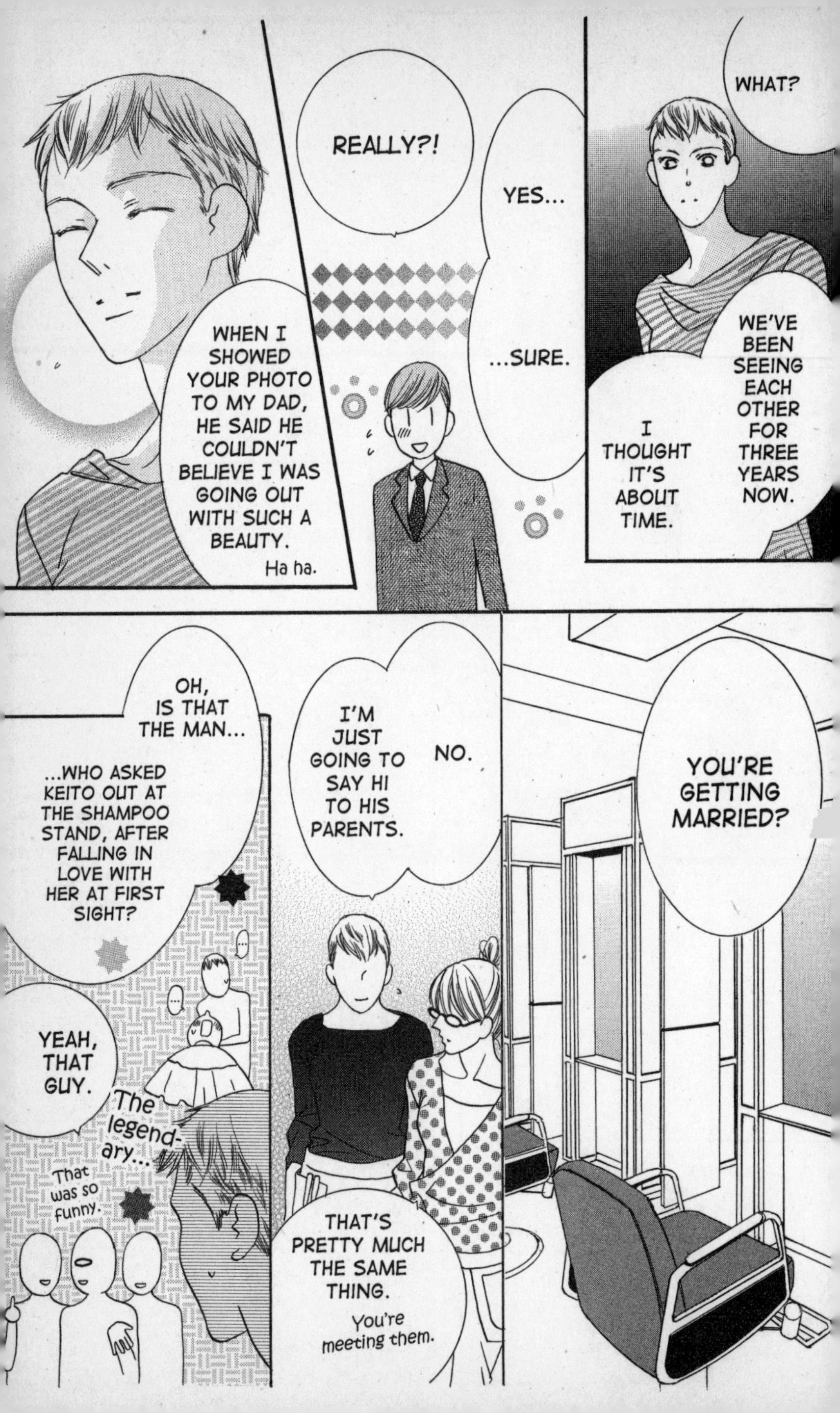
WHAT?
WE'VE BEEN SEEING EACH OTHER FOR THREE YEARS NOW.
I THOUGHT IT'S ABOUT TIME.
REALLY?!
YES...
...SURE.
WHEN I SHOWED YOUR PHOTO TO MY DAD, HE SAID HE COULDN'T BELIEVE I WAS GOING OUT WITH SUCH A BEAUTY.
Ha ha.
YOU'RE GETTING MARRIED?
NO.
I'M JUST GOING TO SAY HI TO HIS PARENTS.
THAT'S PRETTY MUCH THE SAME THING.
You're meeting them.
OH, IS THAT THE MAN...
...WHO ASKED KEITO OUT AT THE SHAMPOO STAND, AFTER FALLING IN LOVE WITH HER AT FIRST SIGHT?
YEAH, THAT GUY.
The legend-ary...
That was so funny.

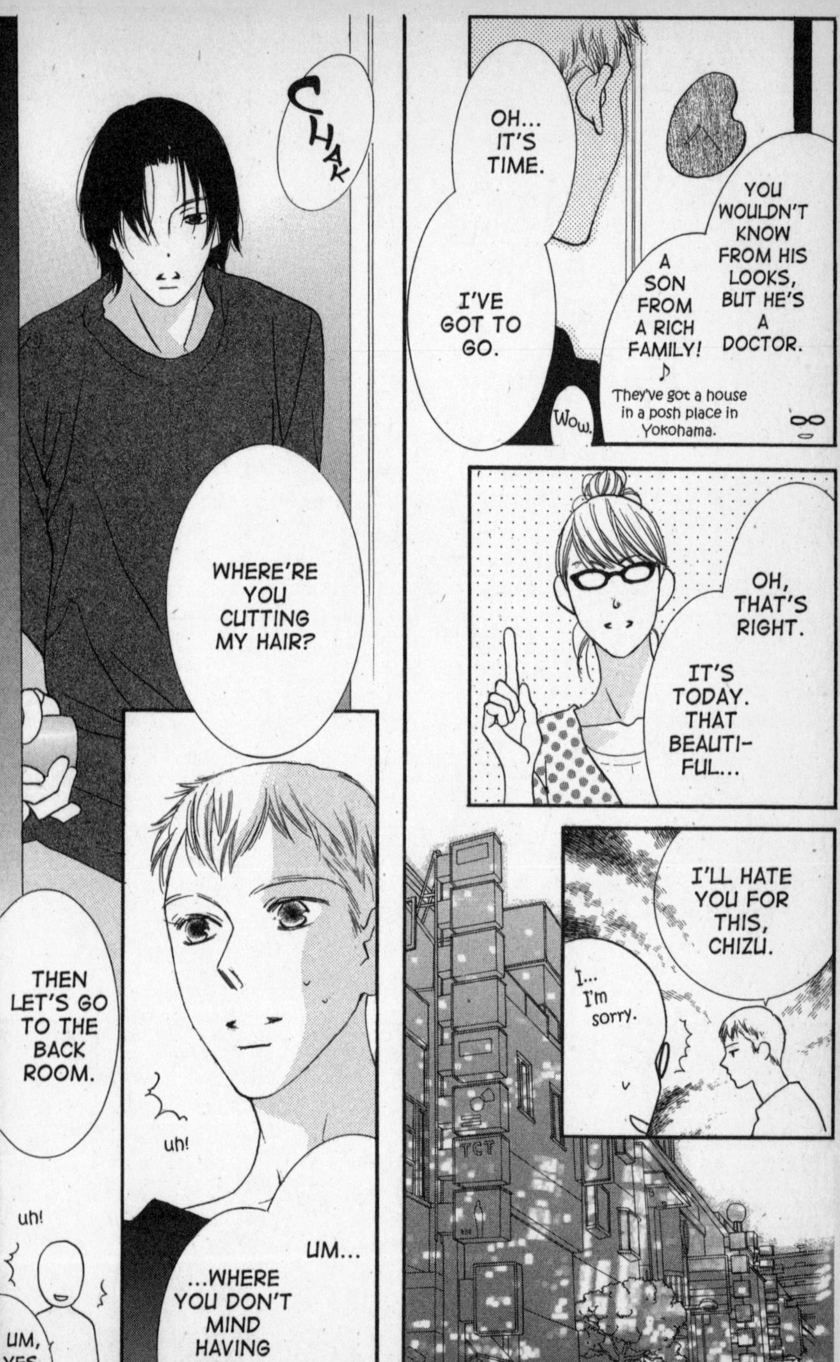

YOU WOULDN'T KNOW FROM HIS LOOKS, BUT HE'S A DOCTOR.
A SON FROM A RICH FAMILY! ♪
They've got a house in a posh place in Yokohama.
Wow.
OH... IT'S TIME.
I'VE GOT TO GO.
OH, THAT'S RIGHT.
IT'S TODAY. THAT BEAUTI-FUL...
I'LL HATE YOU FOR THIS, CHIZU.
I... I'm sorry.
CHAK
WHERE'RE YOU CUTTING MY HAIR?
UM...
...WHERE YOU DON'T MIND HAVING HAIR FALL.
uh!
THEN LET'S GO TO THE BACK ROOM.
uh!
UM, YES.

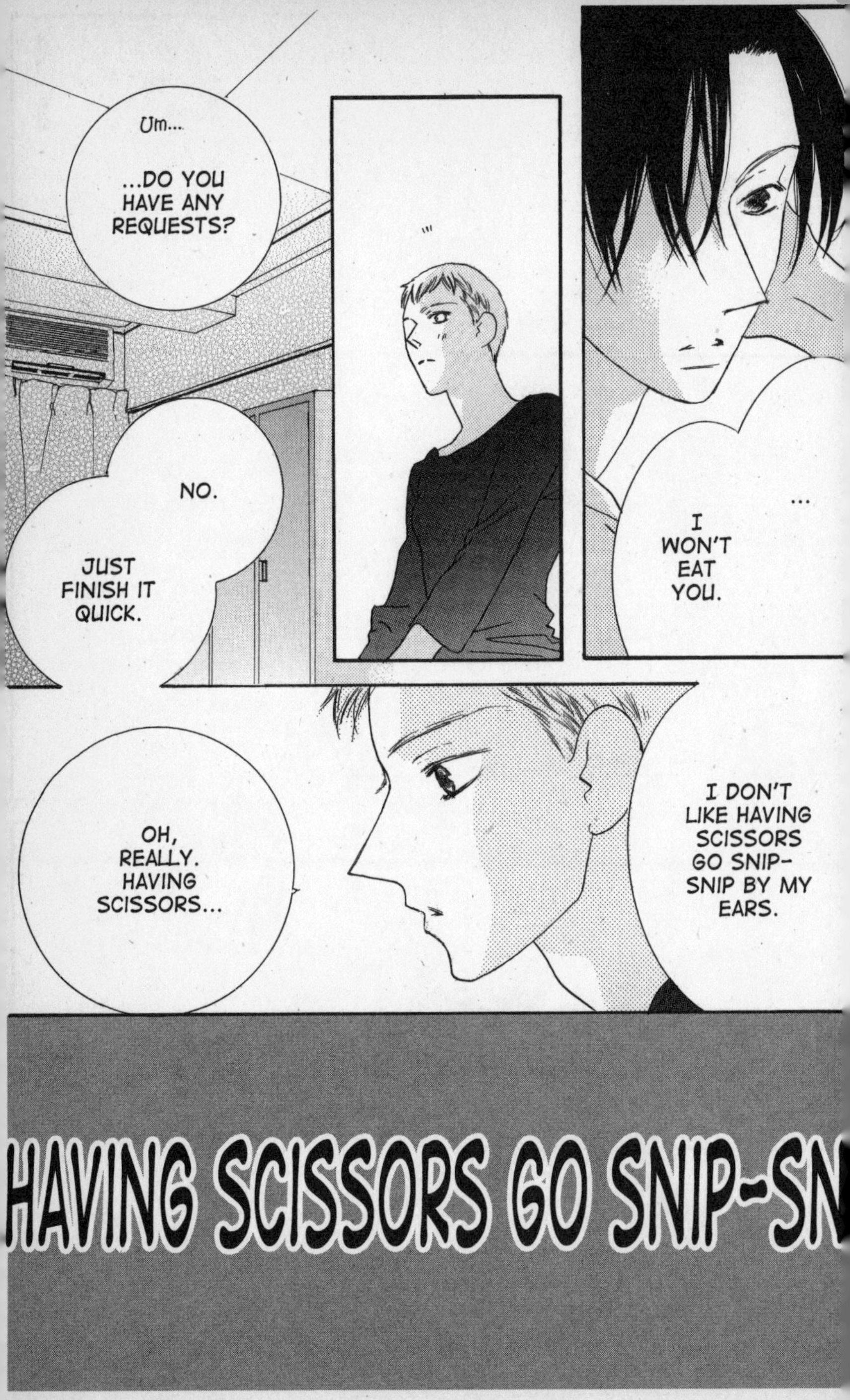
...
I WON'T EAT YOU.
Um...
...DO YOU HAVE ANY REQUESTS?
NO.
JUST FINISH IT QUICK.
I DON'T LIKE HAVING SCISSORS GO SNIP-SNIP BY MY EARS.
OH, REALLY. HAVING SCISSORS...
HAVING SCISSORS GO SNIP-SN

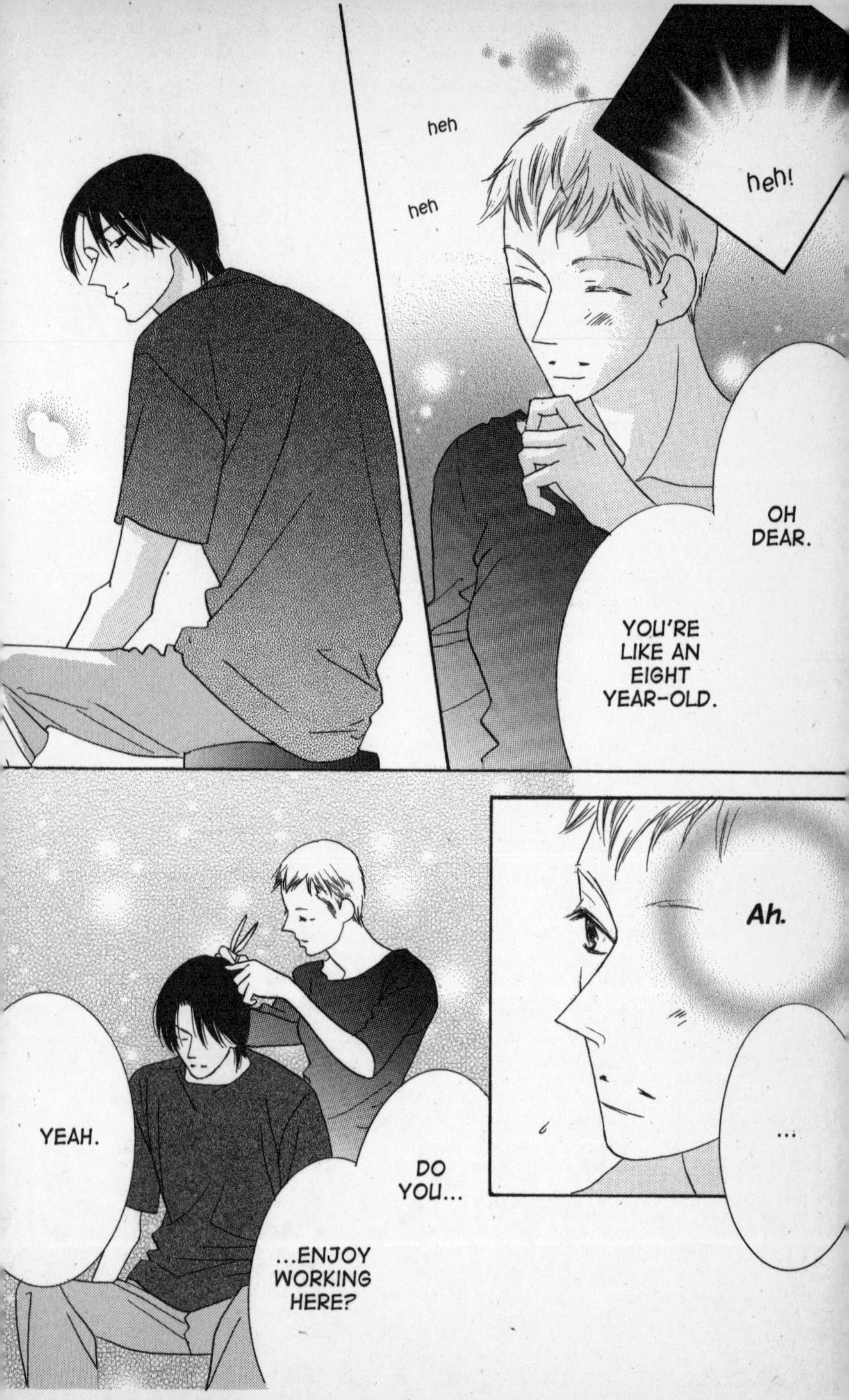
heh!
heh
heh
OH DEAR.
YOU'RE LIKE AN EIGHT YEAR-OLD.
Ah.
...
DO YOU...
...ENJOY WORKING HERE?
YEAH.

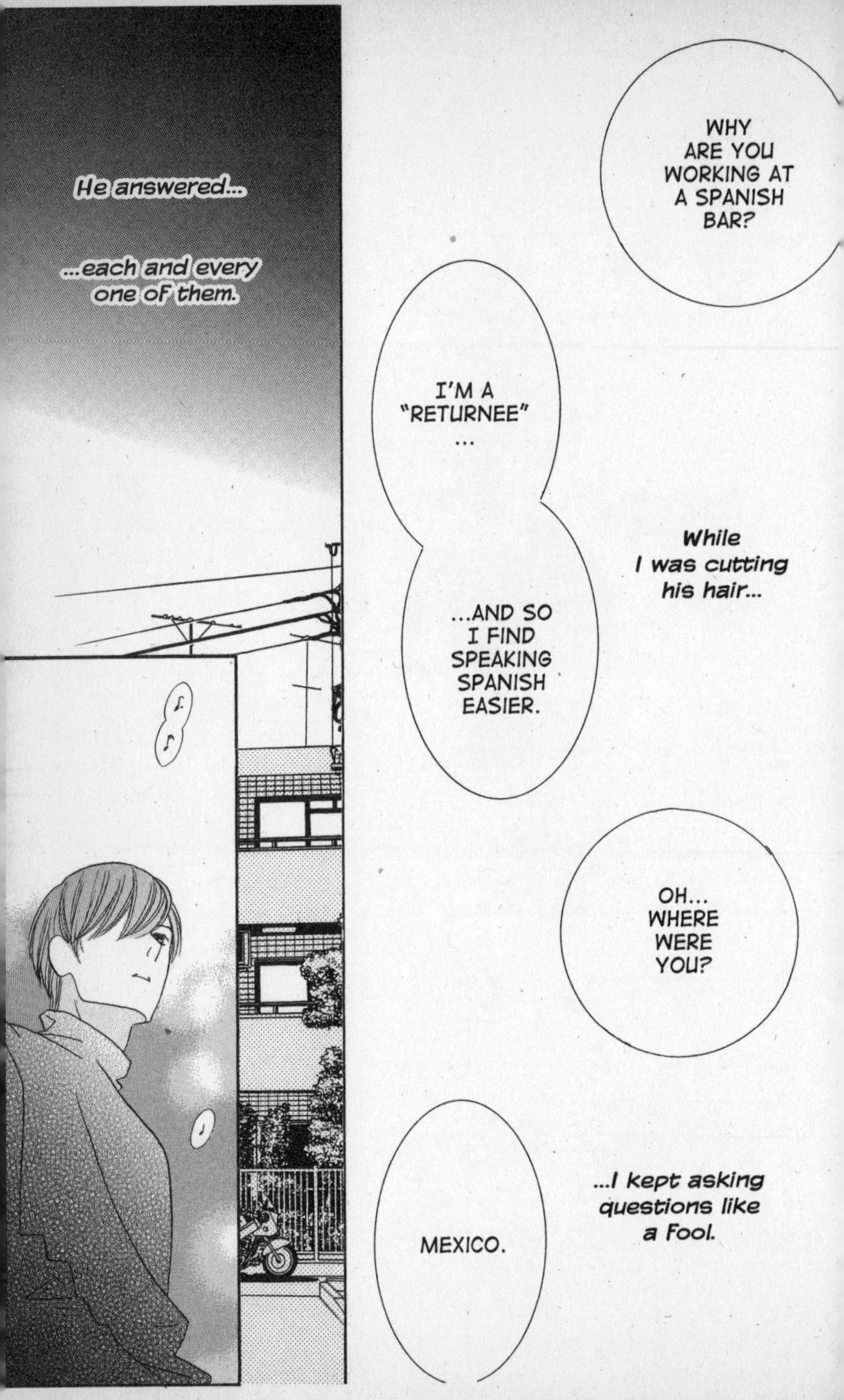
WHY ARE YOU WORKING AT A SPANISH BAR?
While I was cutting his hair...
I'M A "RETURNEE"...
...AND SO I FIND SPEAKING SPANISH EASIER.
OH... WHERE WERE YOU?
...I kept asking questions like a fool.
MEXICO.
He answered...
...each and every one of them.

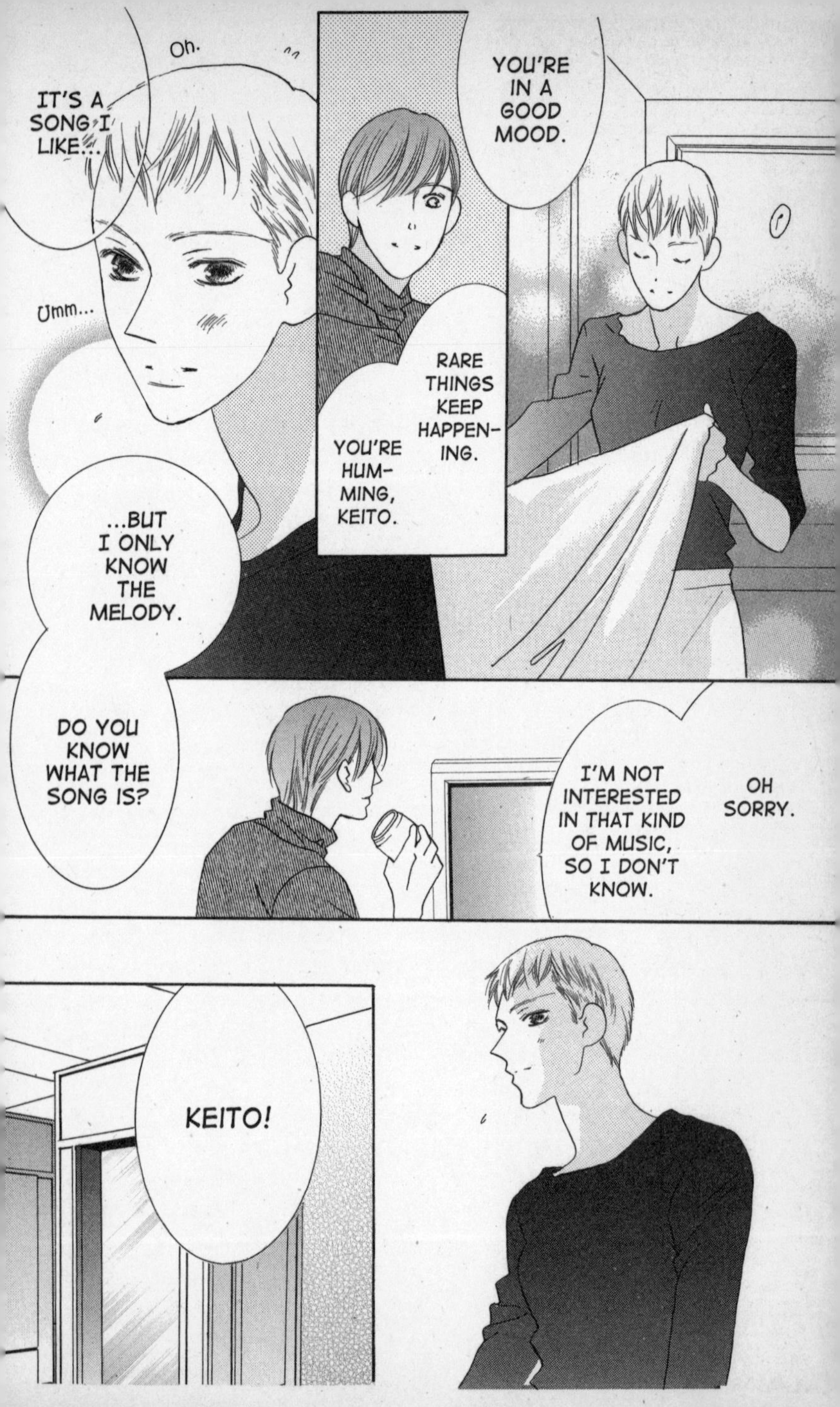
YOU'RE IN A GOOD MOOD.
RARE THINGS KEEP HAPPEN-ING.
YOU'RE HUM-MING, KEITO.
Oh.
IT'S A SONG I LIKE...
Umm...
...BUT I ONLY KNOW THE MELODY.
DO YOU KNOW WHAT THE SONG IS?
I'M NOT INTERESTED IN THAT KIND OF MUSIC, SO I DON'T KNOW.
OH SORRY.
KEITO!

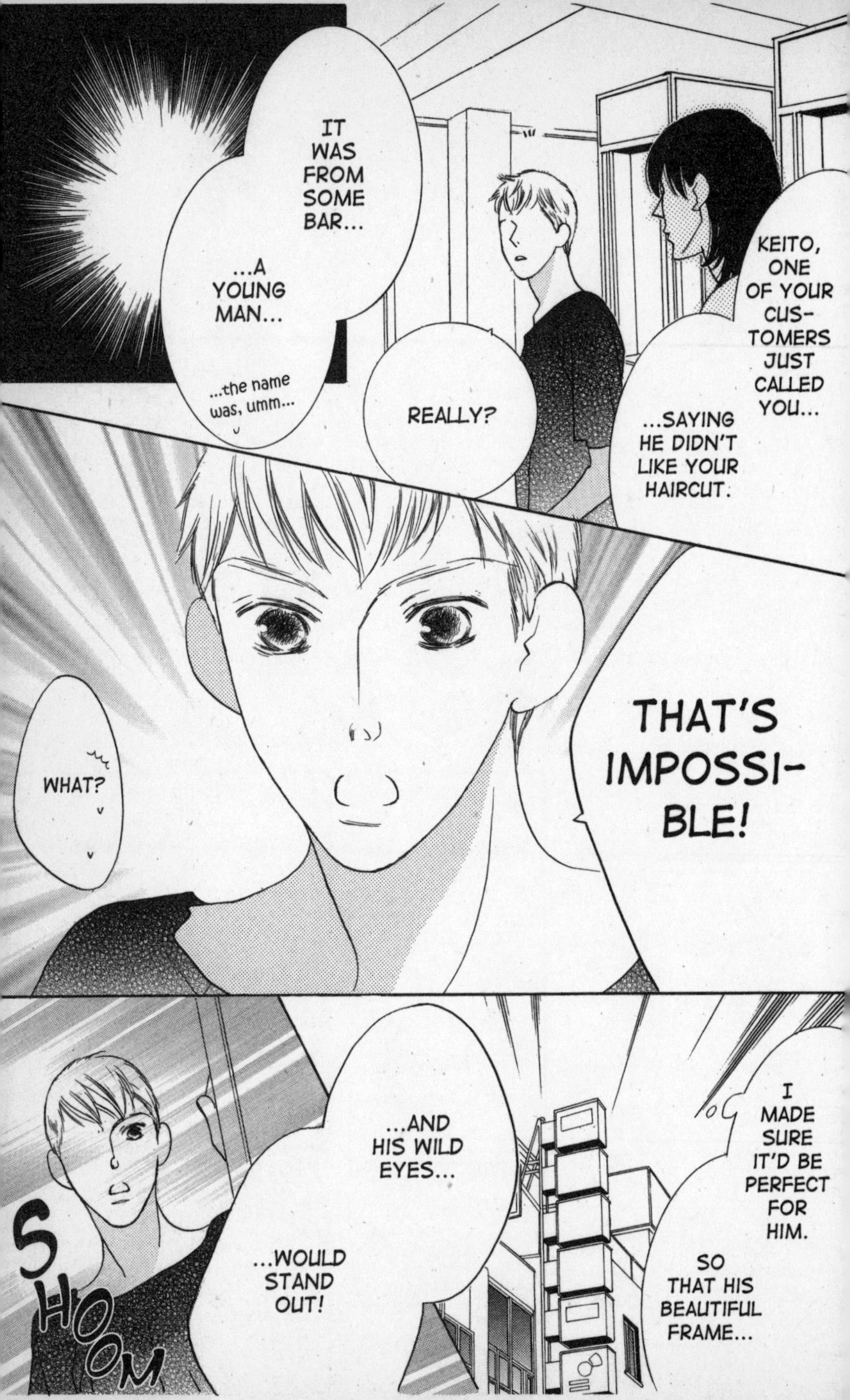
KEITO, ONE OF YOUR CUS-TOMERS JUST CALLED YOU...
...SAYING HE DIDN'T LIKE YOUR HAIRCUT.
REALLY?
IT WAS FROM SOME BAR...
...A YOUNG MAN...
...the name was, umm...
THAT'S IMPOSSI-BLE!
WHAT?
I MADE SURE IT'D BE PERFECT FOR HIM.
SO THAT HIS BEAUTIFUL FRAME...
...AND HIS WILD EYES...
...WOULD STAND OUT!
SHOOM

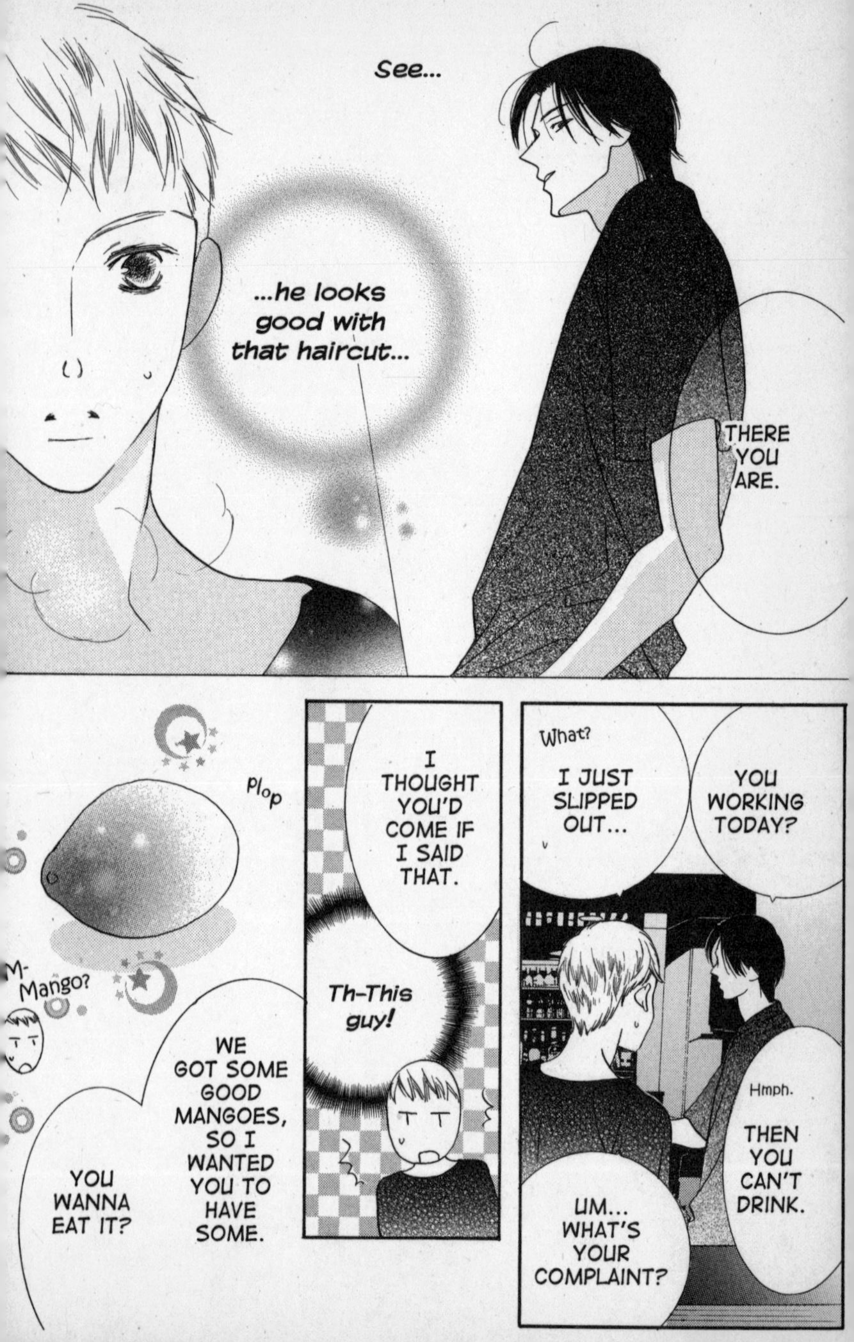
THERE YOU ARE.
See...
...he looks good with that haircut...
YOU WORKING TODAY?
What?
I JUST SLIPPED OUT...
Hmph.
THEN YOU CAN'T DRINK.
UM... WHAT'S YOUR COMPLAINT?
I THOUGHT YOU'D COME IF I SAID THAT.
Th-This guy!
Plop
WE GOT SOME GOOD MANGOES, SO I WANTED YOU TO HAVE SOME.
M-Mango?
YOU WANNA EAT IT?

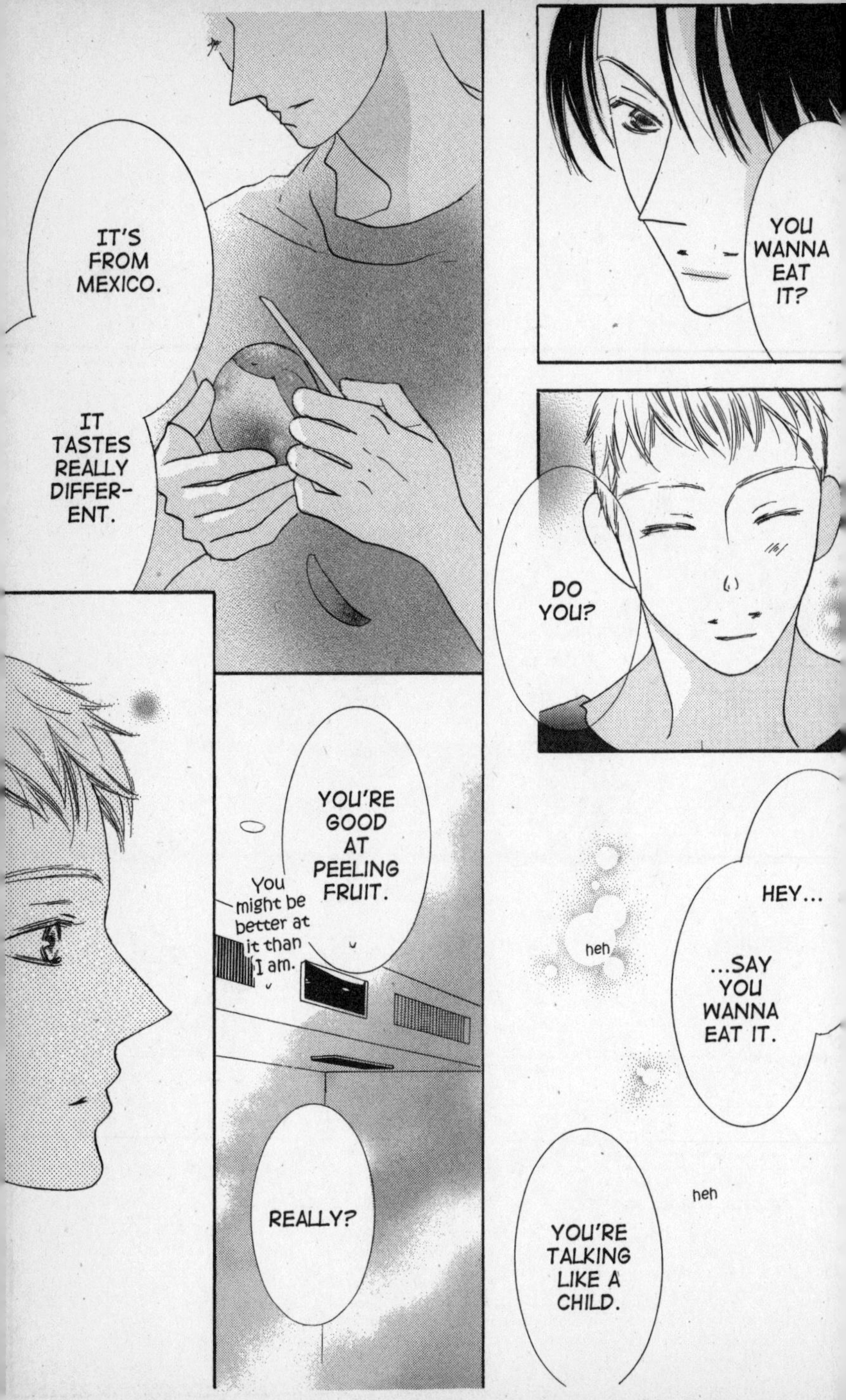

YOU WANNA EAT IT?
DO YOU?
HEY...
...SAY YOU WANNA EAT IT.
heh
heh
YOU'RE TALKING LIKE A CHILD.
IT'S FROM MEXICO.
IT TASTES REALLY DIFFER-ENT.
YOU'RE GOOD AT PEELING FRUIT.
You might be better at it than I am.
REALLY?

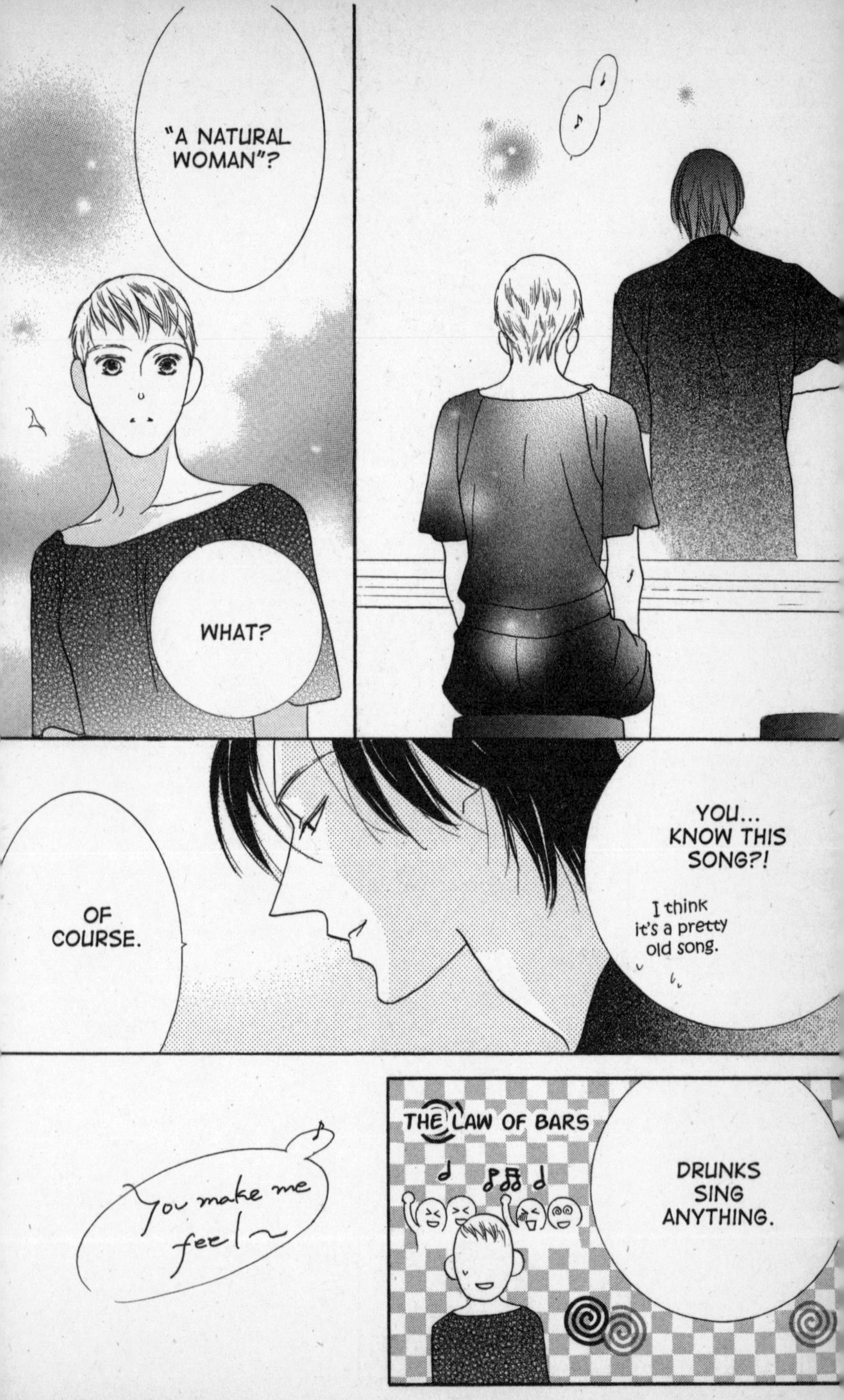
"A NATURAL WOMAN"?
WHAT?
YOU... KNOW THIS SONG?!
I think it's a pretty old song.
OF COURSE.
THE LAW OF BARS
DRUNKS SING ANYTHING.
You make me feel ~

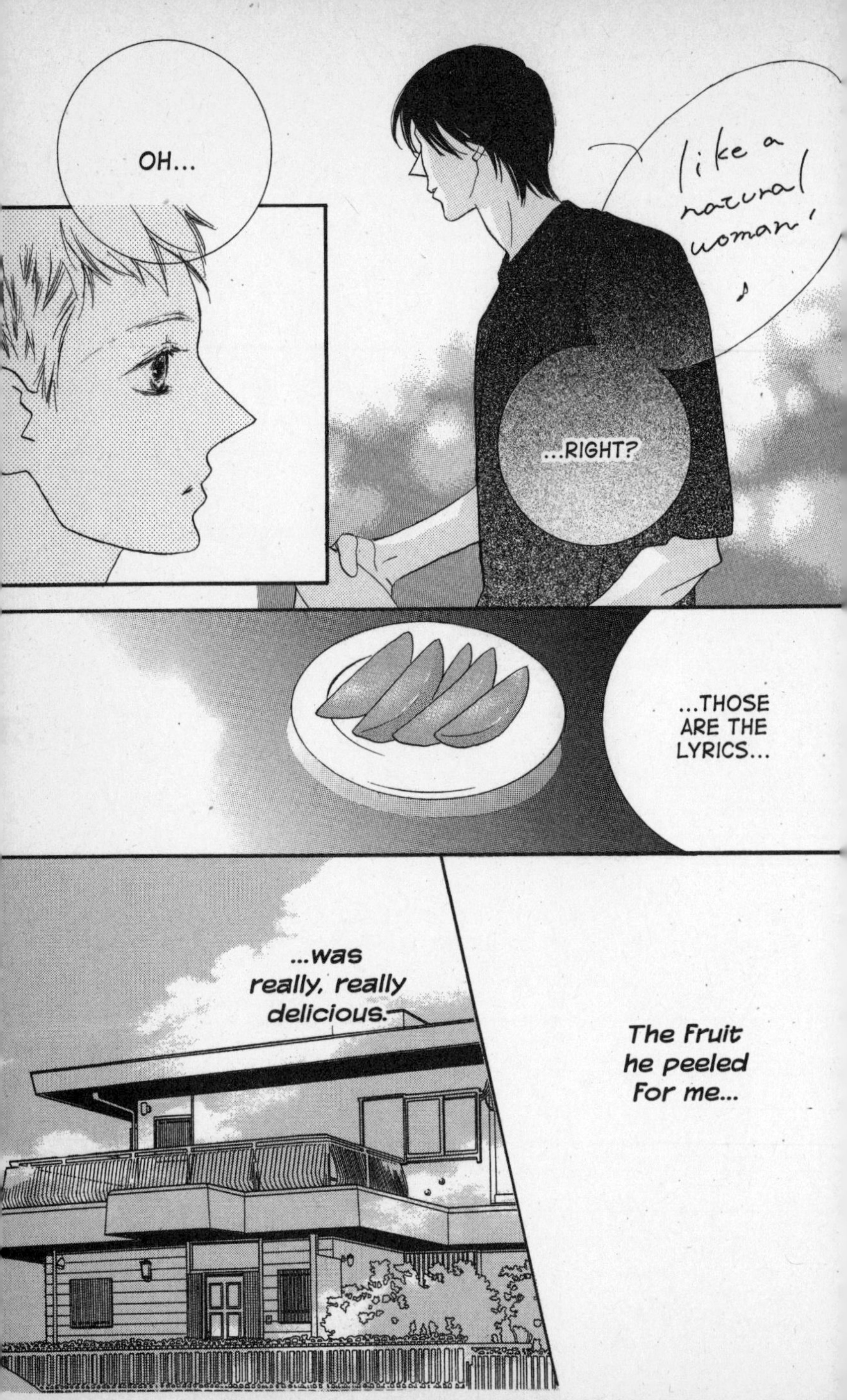
like a natural woman ♪
...RIGHT?
OH...
...THOSE ARE THE LYRICS...
The Fruit he peeled For me...
...was really, really delicious.

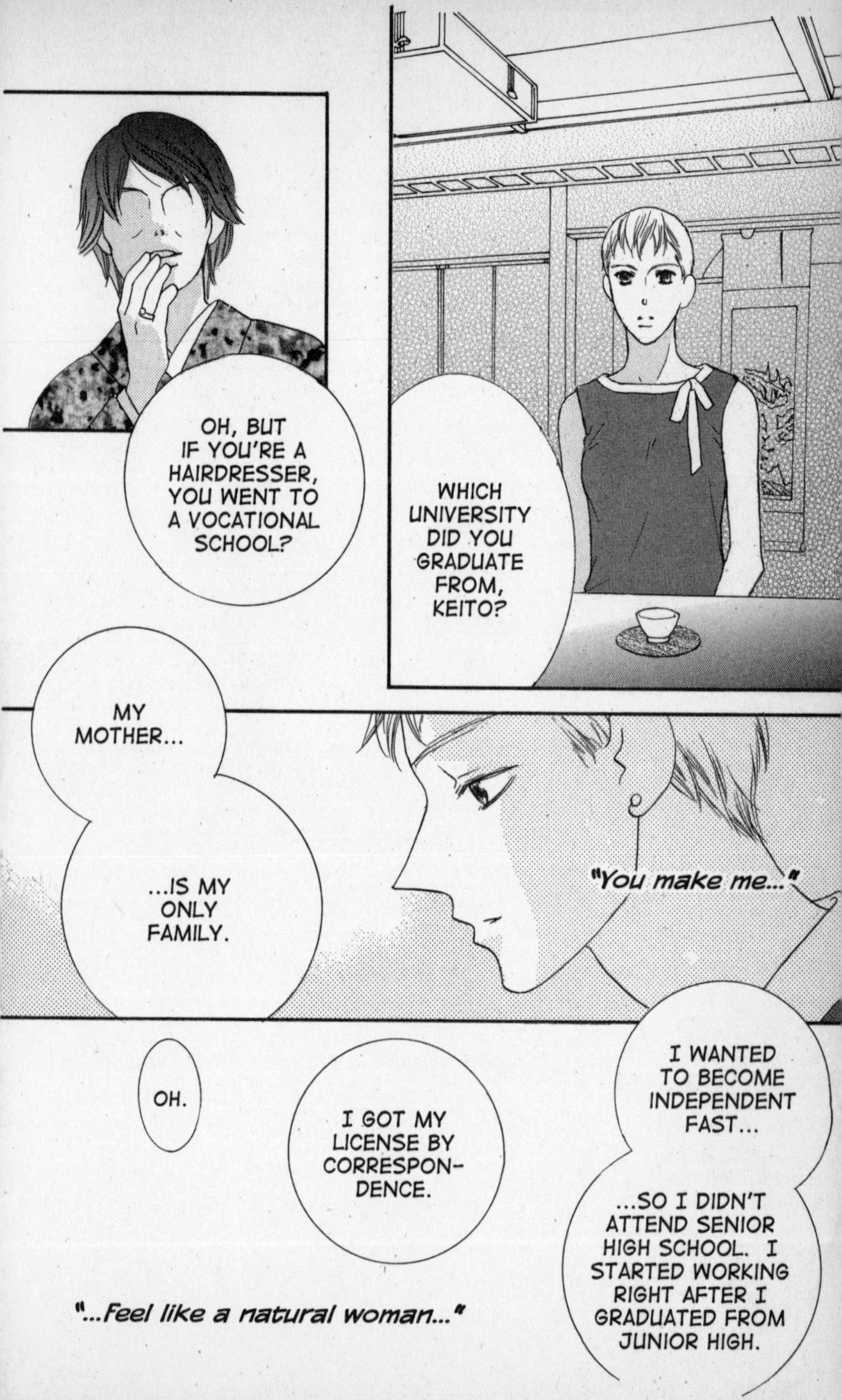
WHICH UNIVERSITY DID YOU GRADUATE FROM, KEITO?
OH, BUT IF YOU'RE A HAIRDRESSER, YOU WENT TO A VOCATIONAL SCHOOL?
MY MOTHER...
...IS MY ONLY FAMILY.
"You make me..."
I WANTED TO BECOME INDEPENDENT FAST...
...SO I DIDN'T ATTEND SENIOR HIGH SCHOOL. I STARTED WORKING RIGHT AFTER I GRADUATED FROM JUNIOR HIGH.
I GOT MY LICENSE BY CORRESPONDENCE.
OH.
"...Feel like a natural woman..."

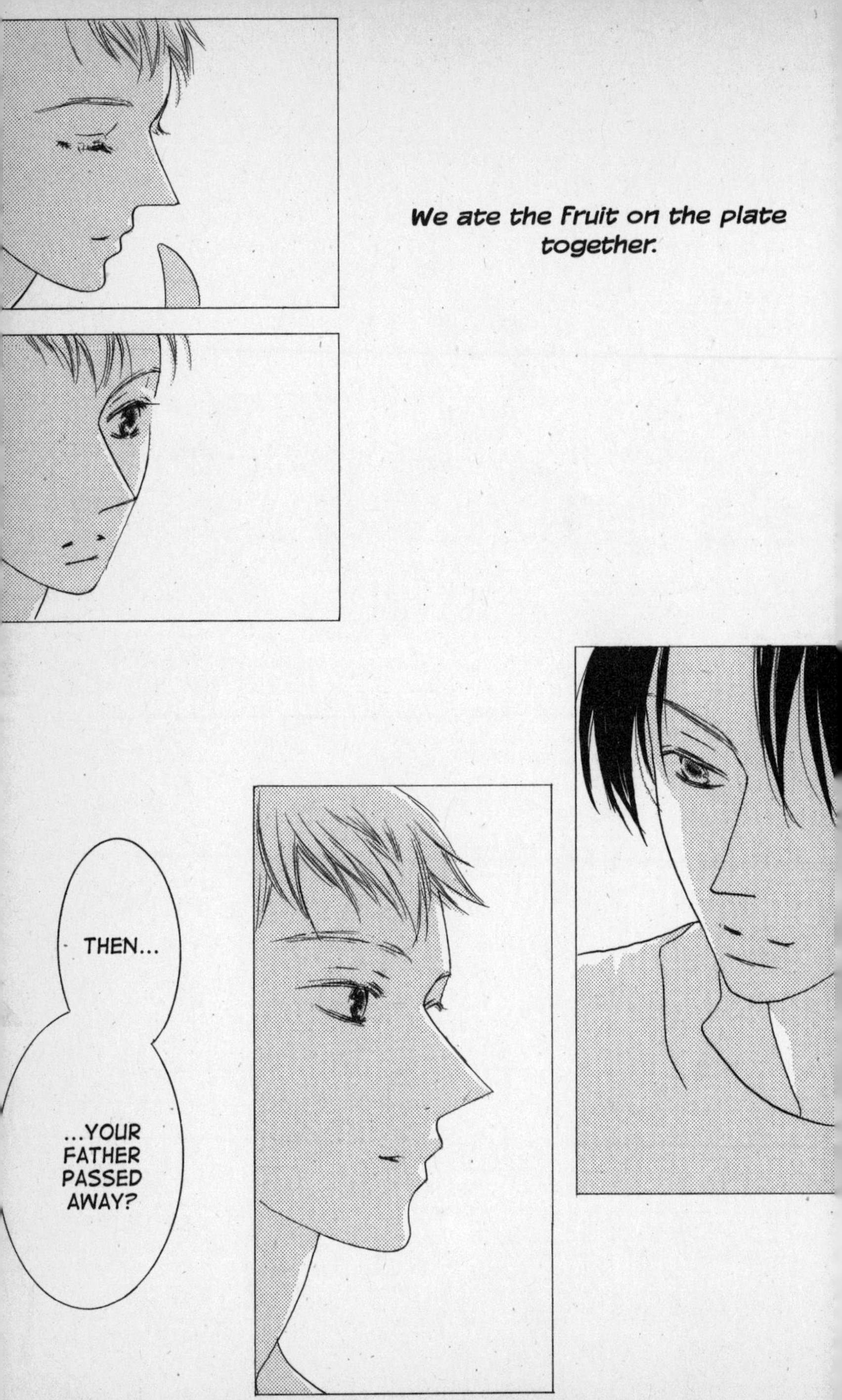
We ate the fruit on the plate together.
THEN...
...YOUR FATHER PASSED AWAY?

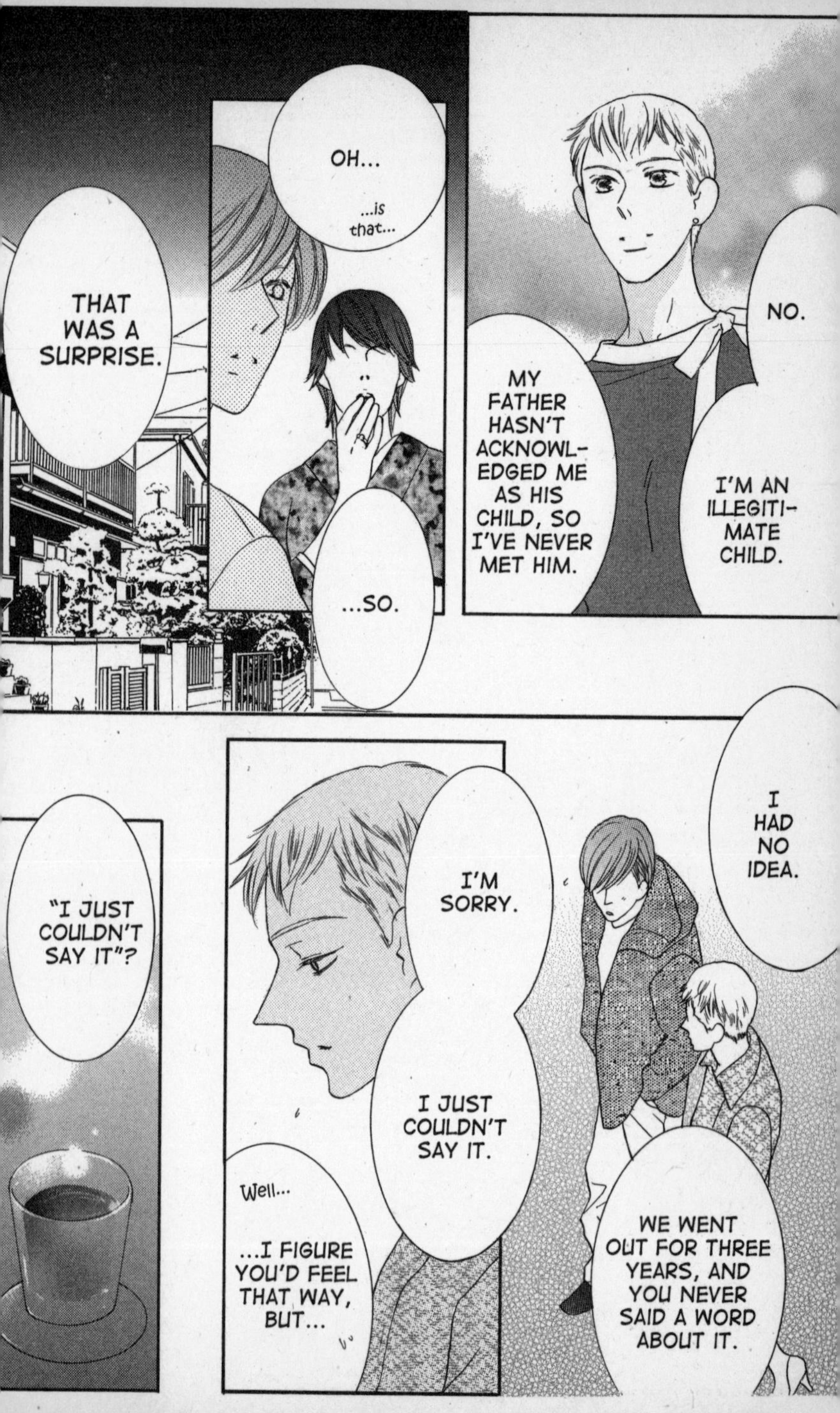
NO.
I'M AN ILLEGITIMATE CHILD.
MY FATHER HASN'T ACKNOWLEDGED ME AS HIS CHILD, SO I'VE NEVER MET HIM.
OH...
...is that...
...SO.
THAT WAS A SURPRISE.
I HAD NO IDEA.
WE WENT OUT FOR THREE YEARS, AND YOU NEVER SAID A WORD ABOUT IT.
I'M SORRY.
I JUST COULDN'T SAY IT.
Well...
...I FIGURE YOU'D FEEL THAT WAY, BUT...
"I JUST COULDN'T SAY IT"?

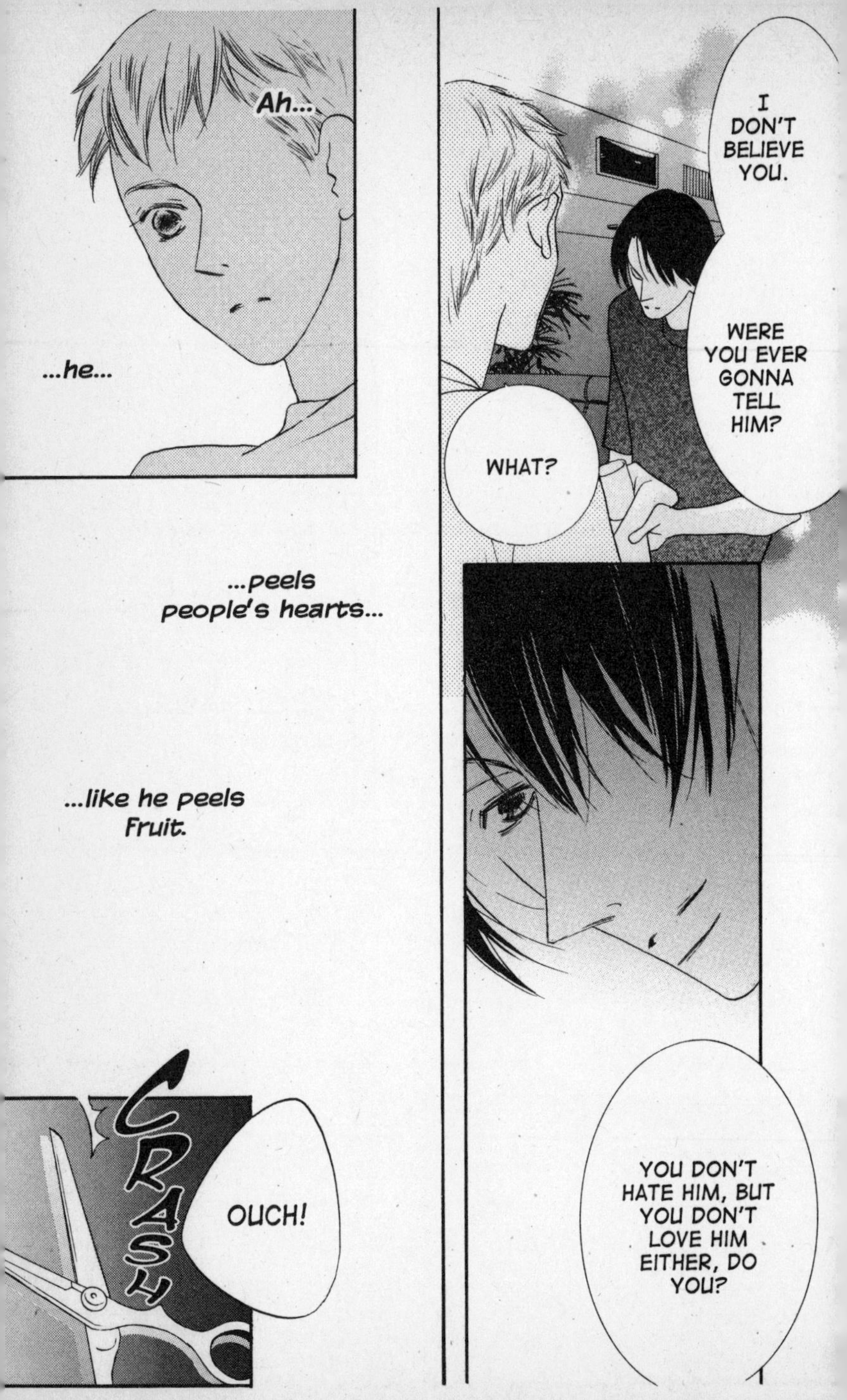
I DON'T BELIEVE YOU.
WERE YOU EVER GONNA TELL HIM?
WHAT?
YOU DON'T HATE HIM, BUT YOU DON'T LOVE HIM EITHER, DO YOU?
Ah...
...he...
...peels people's hearts...
...like he peels fruit.
CRASH
OUCH!

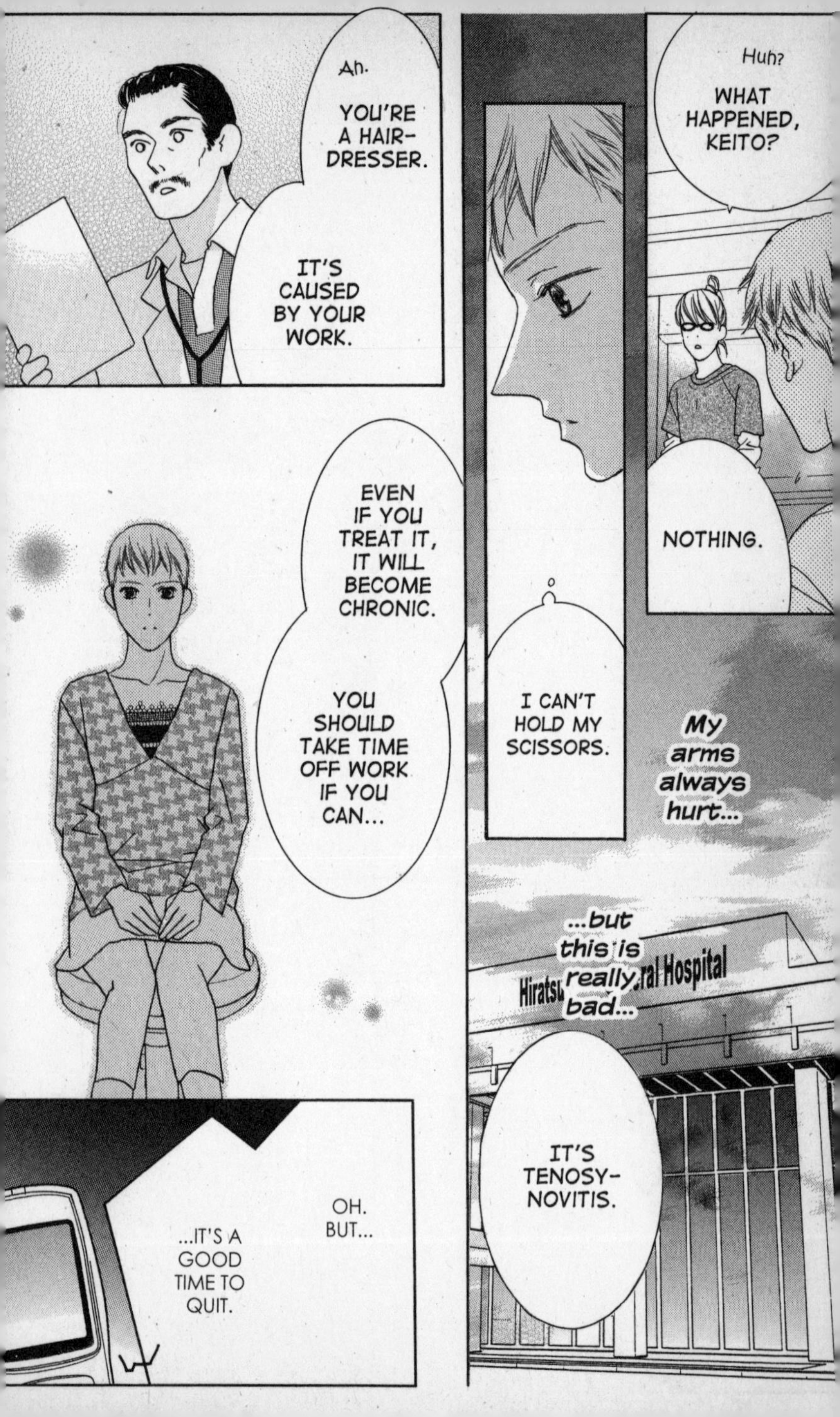
Huh?
WHAT HAPPENED, KEITO?
NOTHING.
I CAN'T HOLD MY SCISSORS.
My arms always hurt...
...but this is really bad...
IT'S TENOSY-NOVITIS.
Ah.
YOU'RE A HAIR-DRESSER.
IT'S CAUSED BY YOUR WORK.
EVEN IF YOU TREAT IT, IT WILL BECOME CHRONIC.
YOU SHOULD TAKE TIME OFF WORK IF YOU CAN...
OH. BUT...
...IT'S A GOOD TIME TO QUIT.

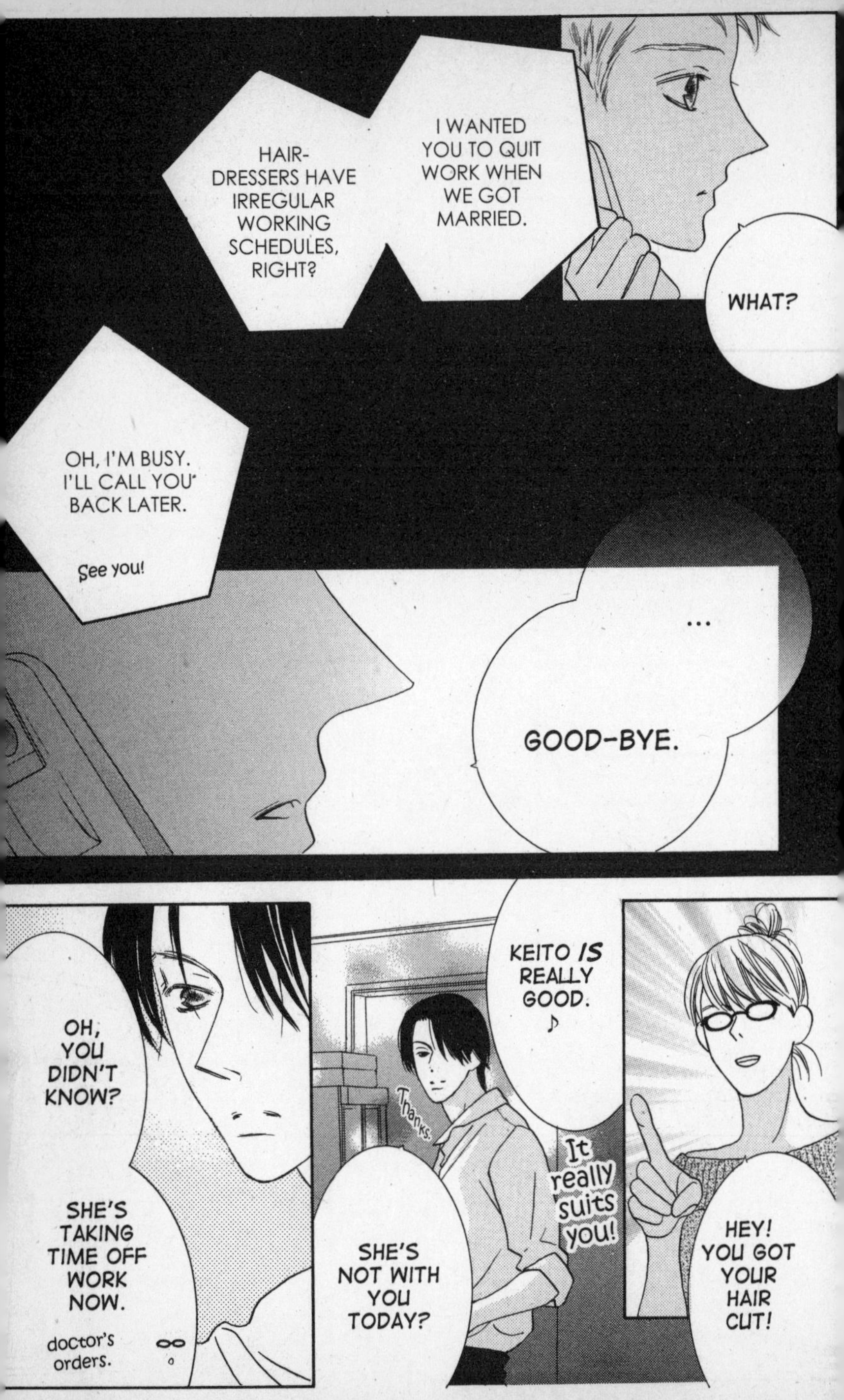

WHAT?
I WANTED YOU TO QUIT WORK WHEN WE GOT MARRIED.
HAIR-DRESSERS HAVE IRREGULAR WORKING SCHEDULES, RIGHT?
OH, I'M BUSY. I'LL CALL YOU BACK LATER.
See you!
...
GOOD-BYE.
HEY! YOU GOT YOUR HAIR CUT!
It really suits you!
KEITO *IS* REALLY GOOD. ♪
Thanks.
SHE'S NOT WITH YOU TODAY?
OH, YOU DIDN'T KNOW?
SHE'S TAKING TIME OFF WORK NOW.
doctor's orders.

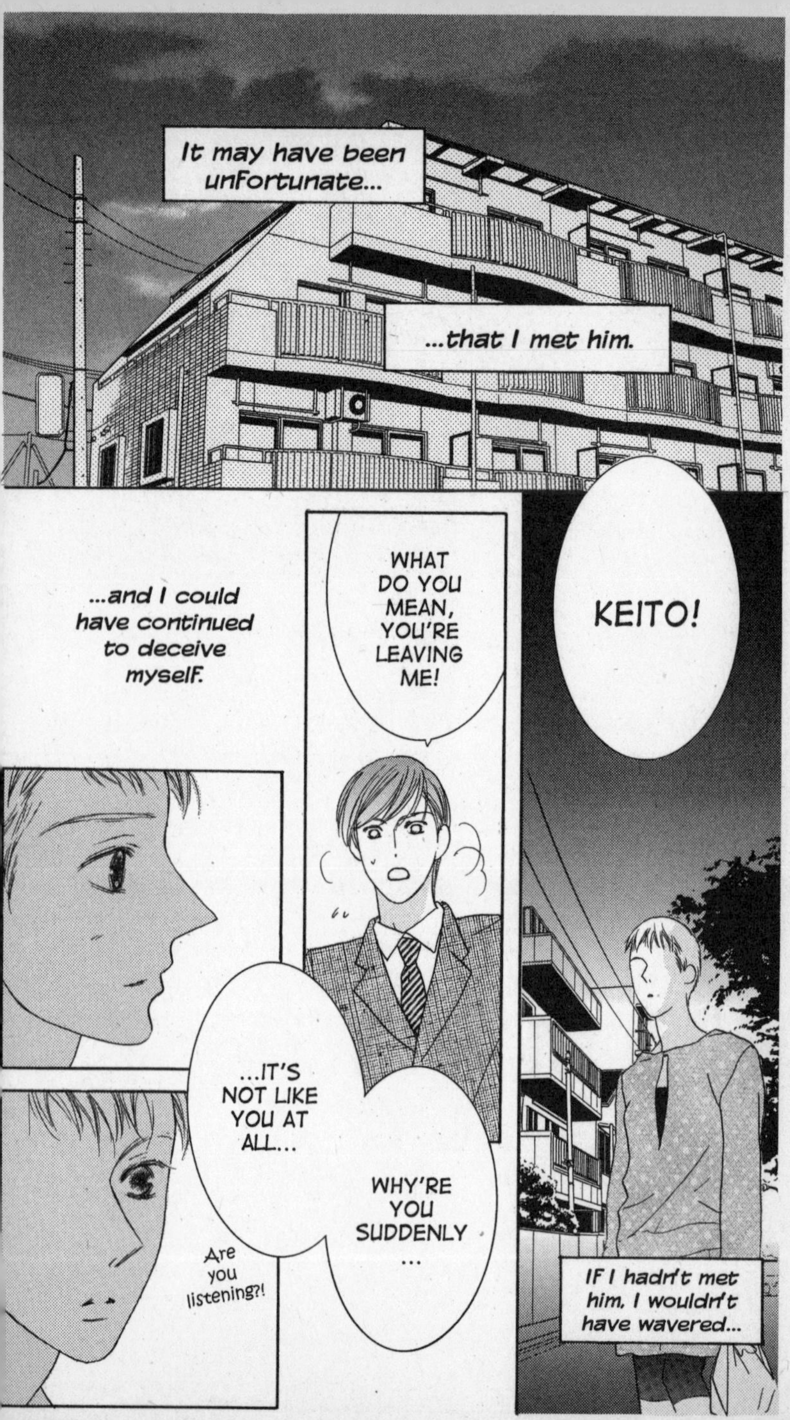
It may have been unfortunate...
...that I met him.
KEITO!
IF I hadn't met him, I wouldn't have wavered...
WHAT DO YOU MEAN, YOU'RE LEAVING ME!
...and I could have continued to deceive myself.
...IT'S NOT LIKE YOU AT ALL...
WHY'RE YOU SUDDENLY ...
Are you listening?!

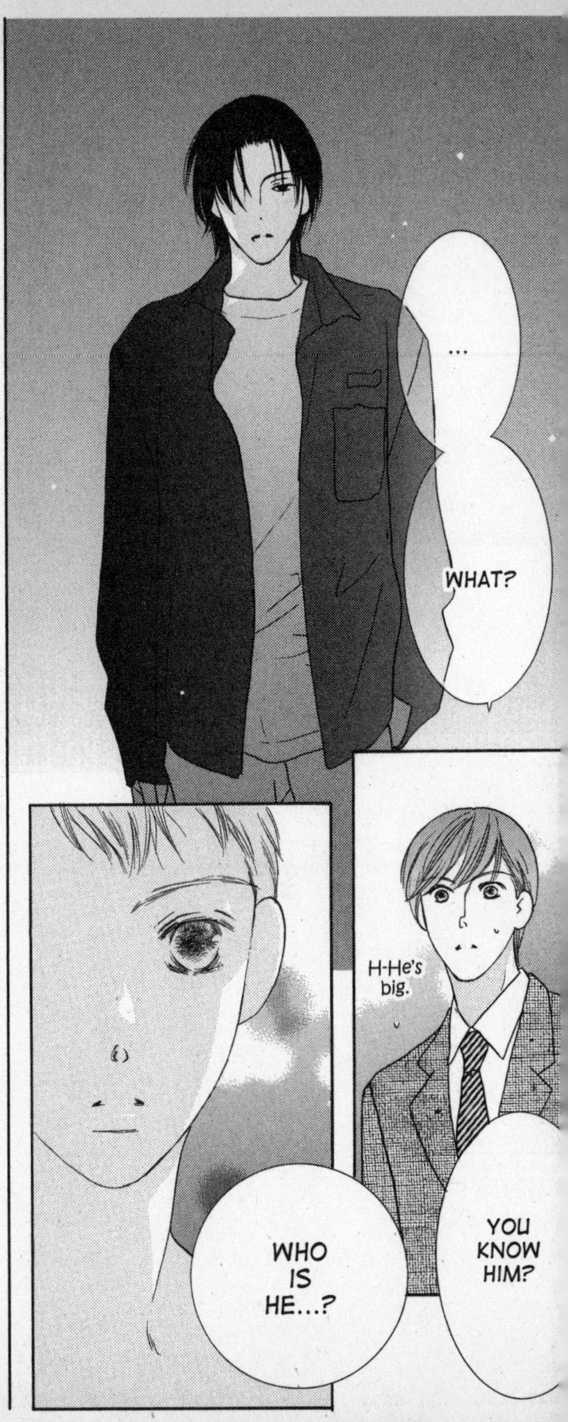
...
WHAT?
H-He's big.
YOU KNOW HIM?
WHO IS HE...?

5

So, when I go shopping when I haven't had a chance for a long time, I go with the spirit that I'm going to hit a gold mine. Sometimes, however, weird things catch my attention. Like things I have no use for...The other day, it was a carved wooden bird (do you call it a mobile? the one you hang from the ceiling). As soon as I saw it, I thought "AAH!!! When you pull the string, the wings flap!! Even if you have it, it'd be a nuisance...where are you going to put it...but I've never seen anything like it..." and on and on. I went into a mental maze in front of the bird. I think the store clerks must've been so afraid of me...they looked like they were really hesitant to talk to me...I gave up getting it (since I'm already an adult...) but that was close...

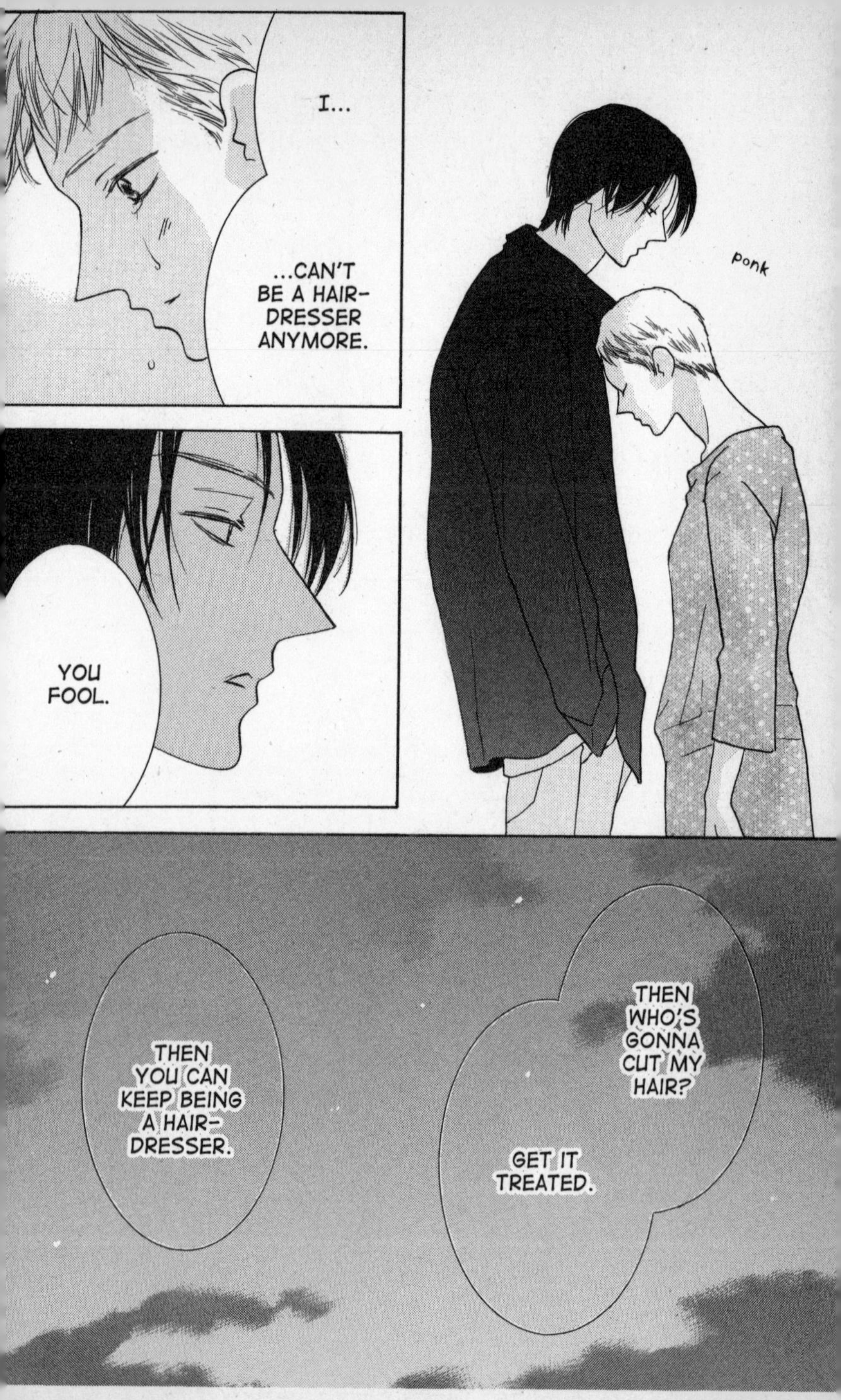
ponk
I...
...CAN'T BE A HAIR-DRESSER ANYMORE.
YOU FOOL.
THEN WHO'S GONNA CUT MY HAIR?
GET IT TREATED.
THEN YOU CAN KEEP BEING A HAIR-DRESSER.

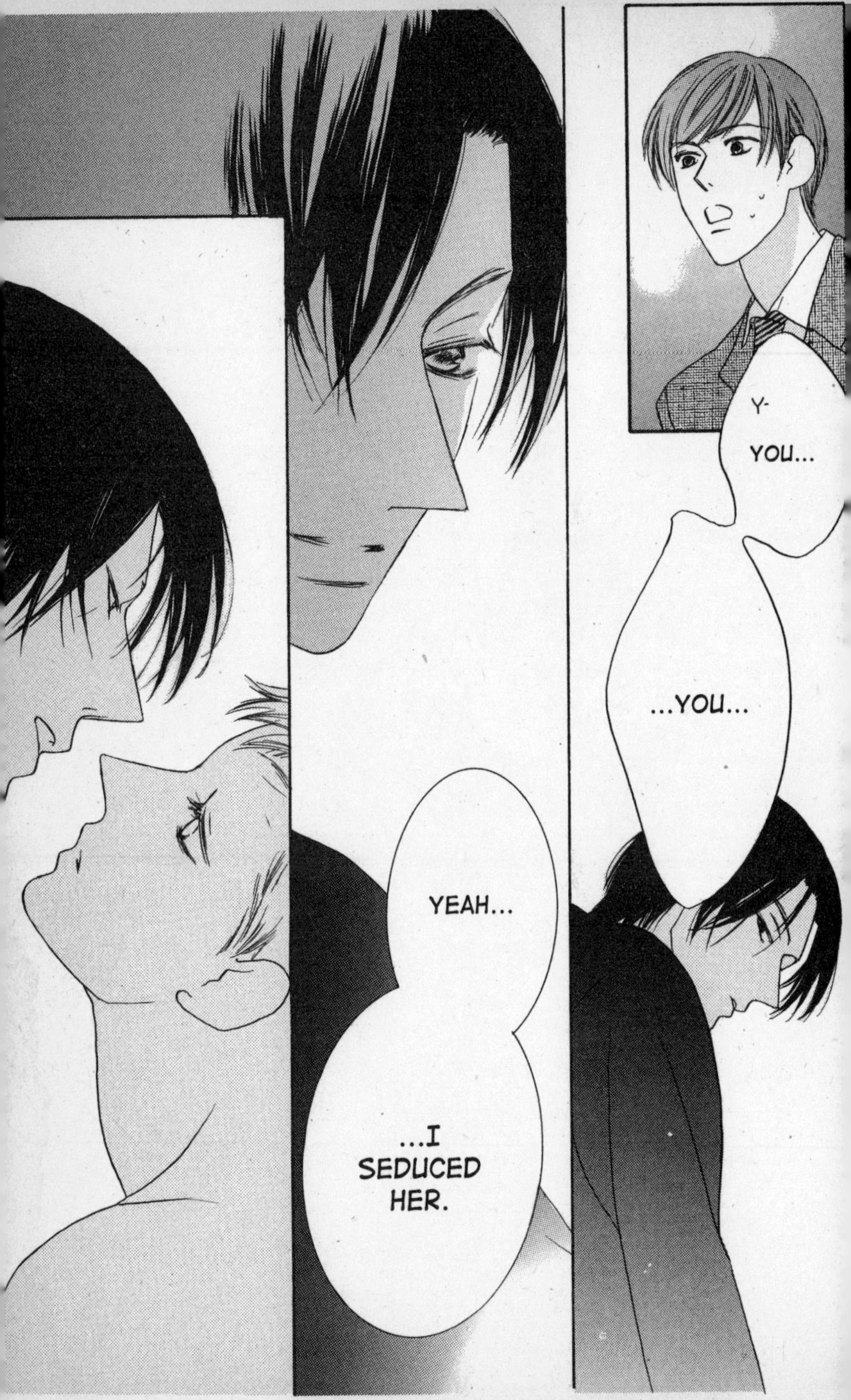
Y- YOU...
...YOU...
YEAH...
...I SEDUCED HER.

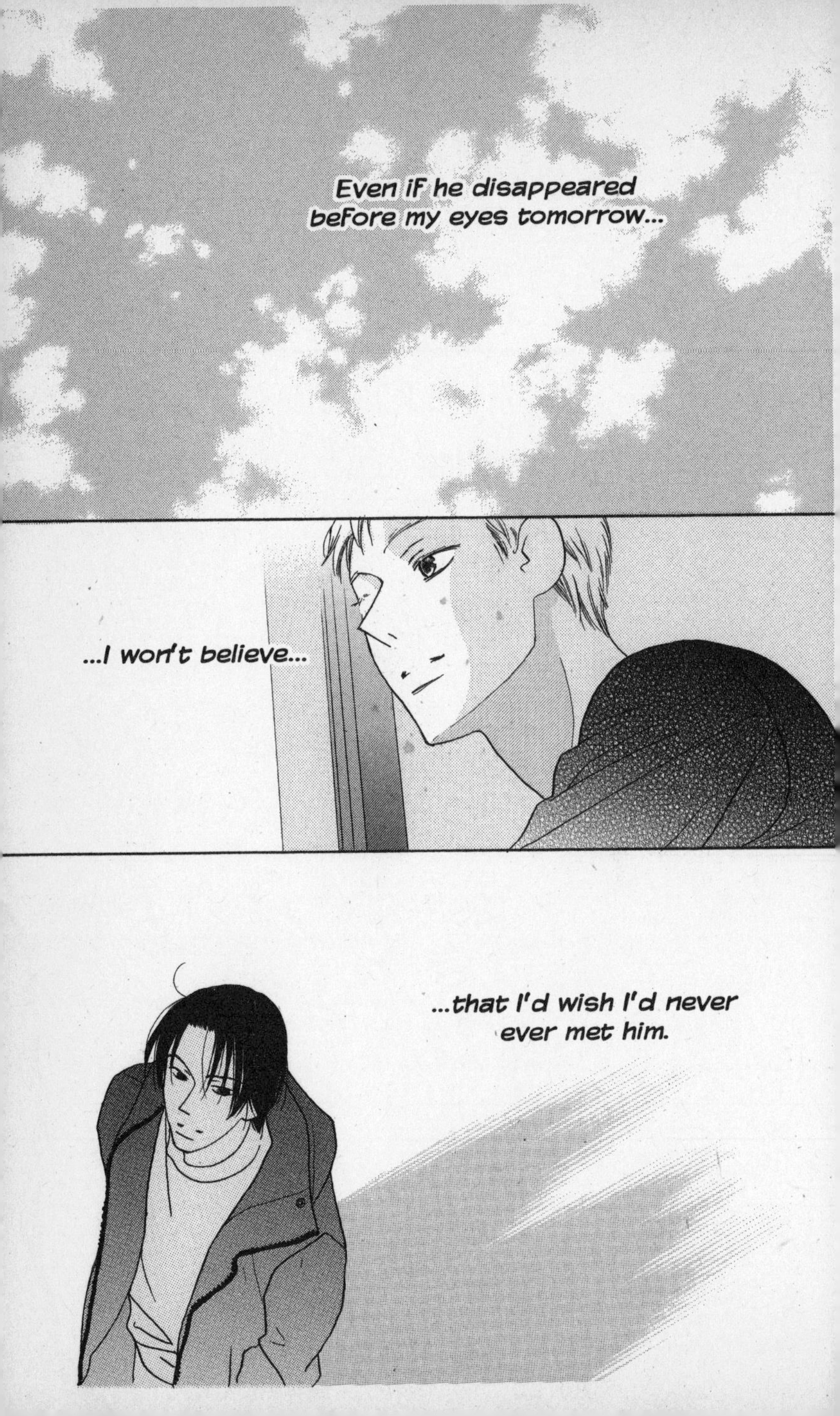
Even if he disappeared before my eyes tomorrow...
...I won't believe...
...that I'd wish I'd never ever met him.

You make me feel like a natural woman.

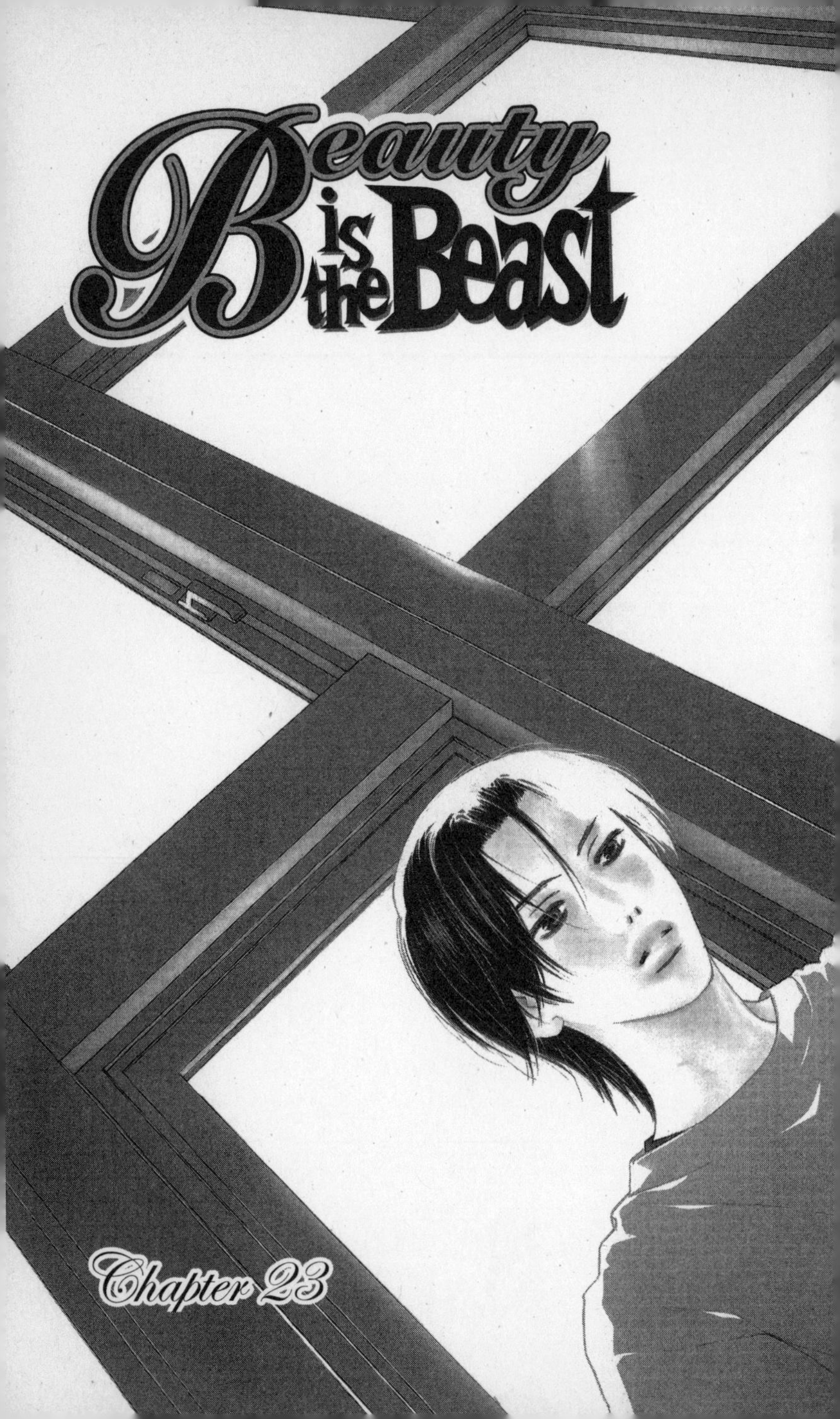
Beauty is the Beast
Chapter 23

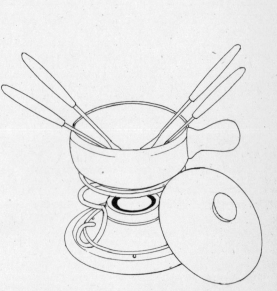

BEAUTY *IS* THE BEAST

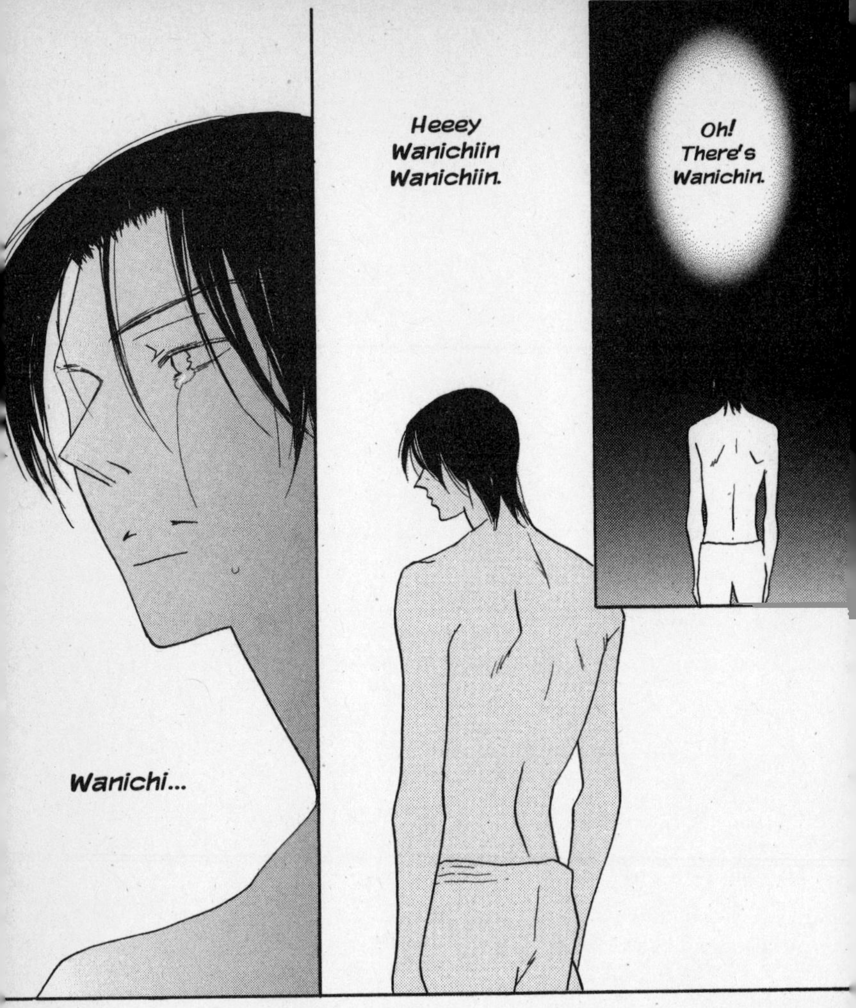
Oh! There's Wanichin.
Heeey Wanichiin Wanichiin.
Wanichi...

When I get stuck doing the storyboards or the pages, I try out pro-wrestling tricks on my dog. The dog's flustered expression is so cute... Hee hee...
Nowadays, he gets away before I can do a move on him. The dog...has improved...
Beauty Is the Beast is entering the climax in the magazine — the next volume will be the last. I hope you read it until the end.
As always, I thank my editor, all my staff, and all my readers from the bottom of my heart.

See You! Tomo Matsumoto

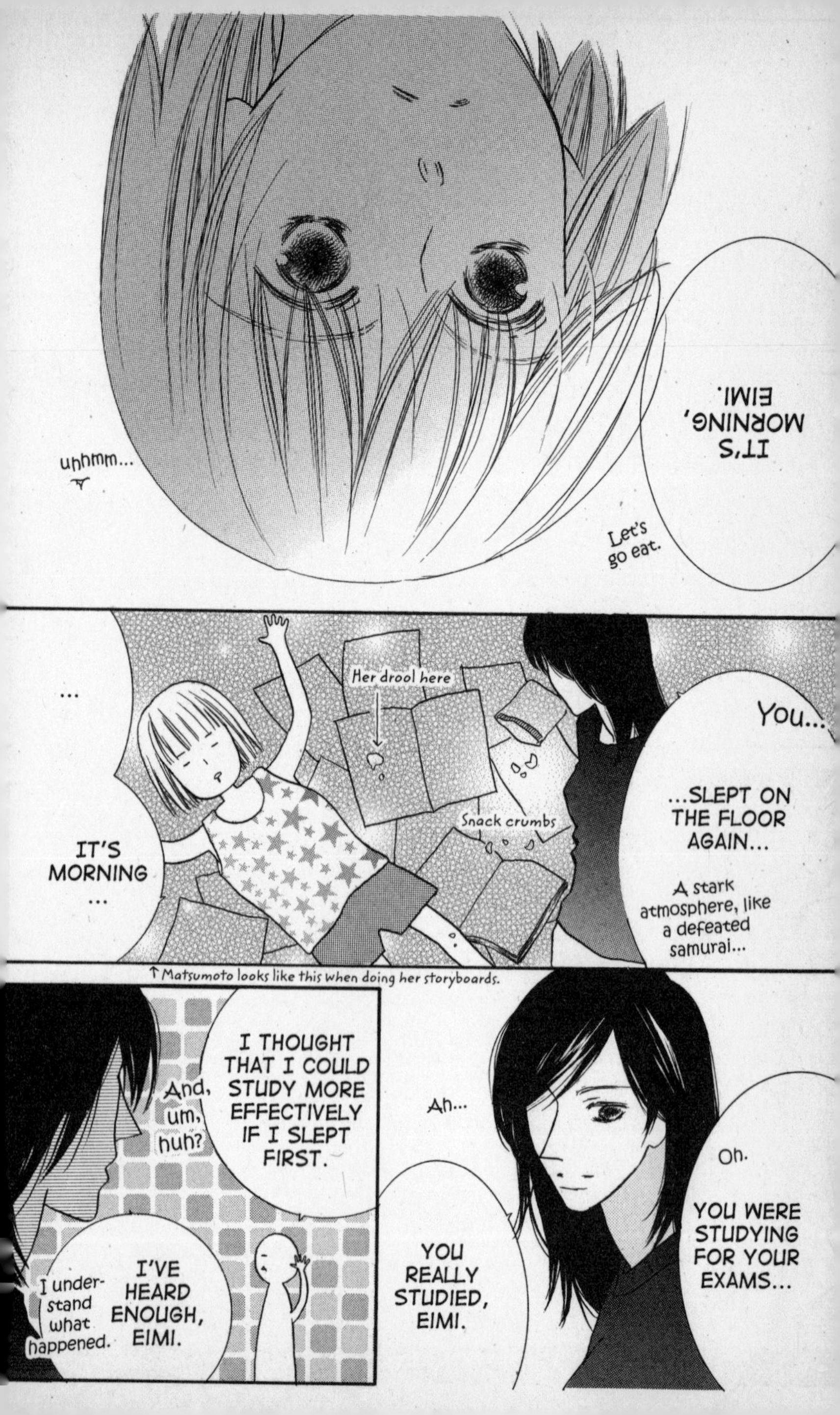
IT'S MORNING, EIMI.
Let's go eat.
uhhmm...
You...
...SLEPT ON THE FLOOR AGAIN...
A stark atmosphere, like a defeated samurai...
Snack crumbs
Her drool here
IT'S MORNING ...
...
↑Matsumoto looks like this when doing her storyboards.
Oh.
YOU WERE STUDYING FOR YOUR EXAMS...
Ah...
YOU REALLY STUDIED, EIMI.
I THOUGHT THAT I COULD STUDY MORE EFFECTIVELY IF I SLEPT FIRST.
And, um, huh?
I'VE HEARD ENOUGH, EIMI.
I under-stand what happened.

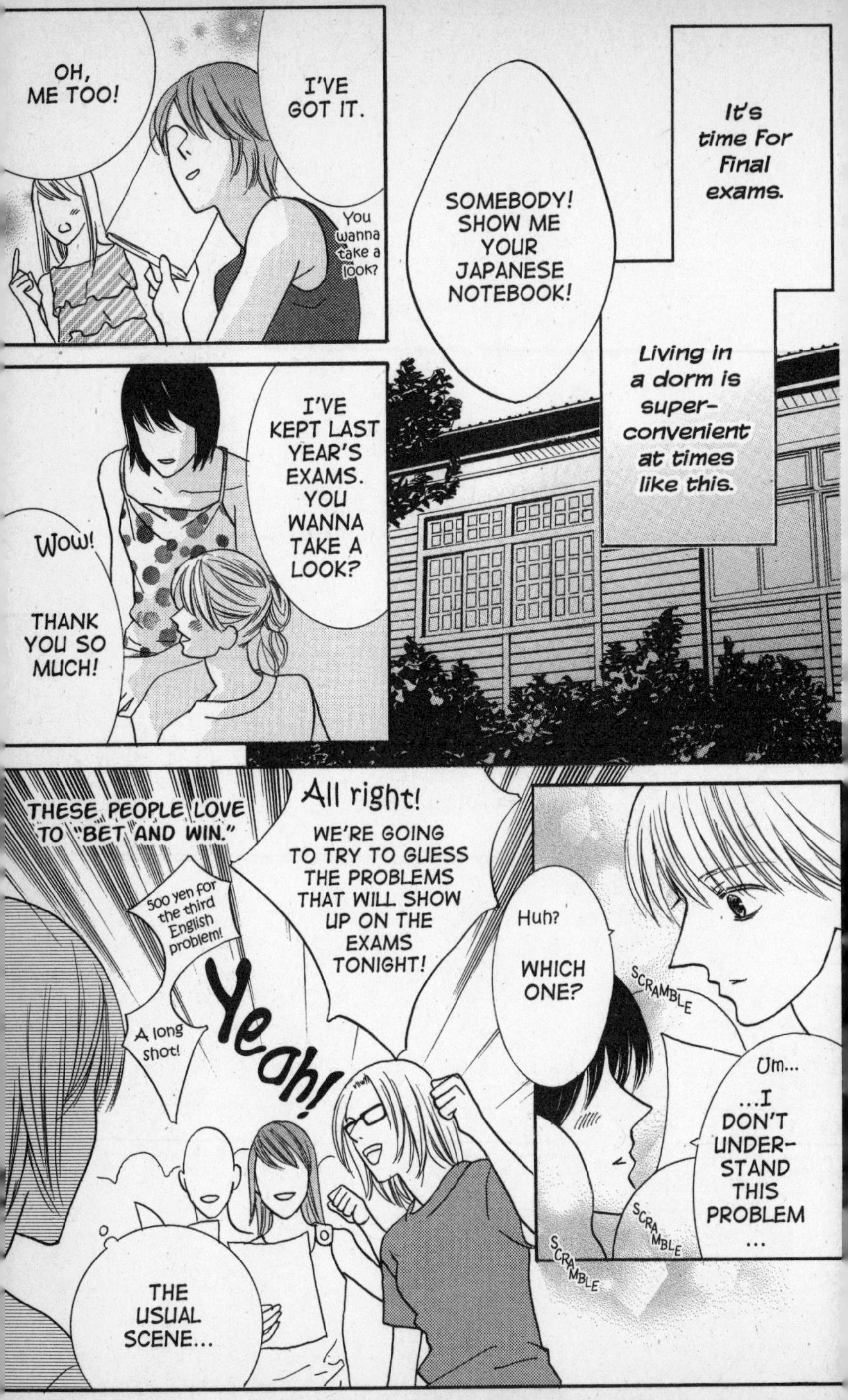
It's time For Final exams.
SOMEBODY! SHOW ME YOUR JAPANESE NOTEBOOK!
Living in a dorm is super-convenient at times like this.
I'VE GOT IT.
OH, ME TOO!
You wanna take a look?
I'VE KEPT LAST YEAR'S EXAMS. YOU WANNA TAKE A LOOK?
Wow!
THANK YOU SO MUCH!
Huh?
WHICH ONE?
SCRAMBLE
Um...
...I DON'T UNDER-STAND THIS PROBLEM...
SCRAMBLE
SCRAMBLE
All right!
WE'RE GOING TO TRY TO GUESS THE PROBLEMS THAT WILL SHOW UP ON THE EXAMS TONIGHT!
THESE PEOPLE LOVE TO "BET AND WIN."
500 yen for the third English problem!
Yeah!
A long shot!
THE USUAL SCENE...

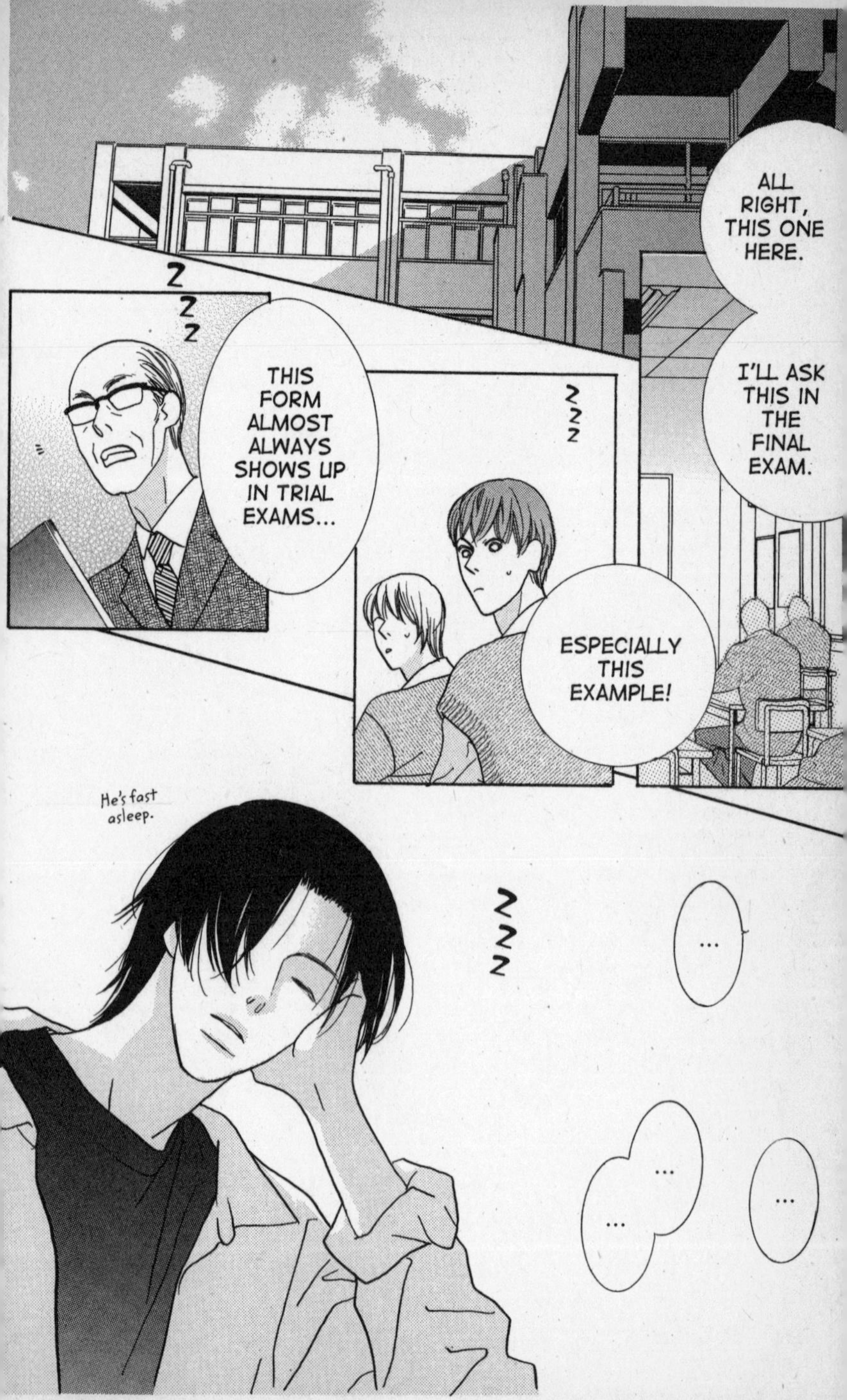
ALL RIGHT, THIS ONE HERE.
I'LL ASK THIS IN THE FINAL EXAM.
ZZZ
ESPECIALLY THIS EXAMPLE!
ZZZ
THIS FORM ALMOST ALWAYS SHOWS UP IN TRIAL EXAMS...
ZZZ
...
...
...
...
He's fast asleep.

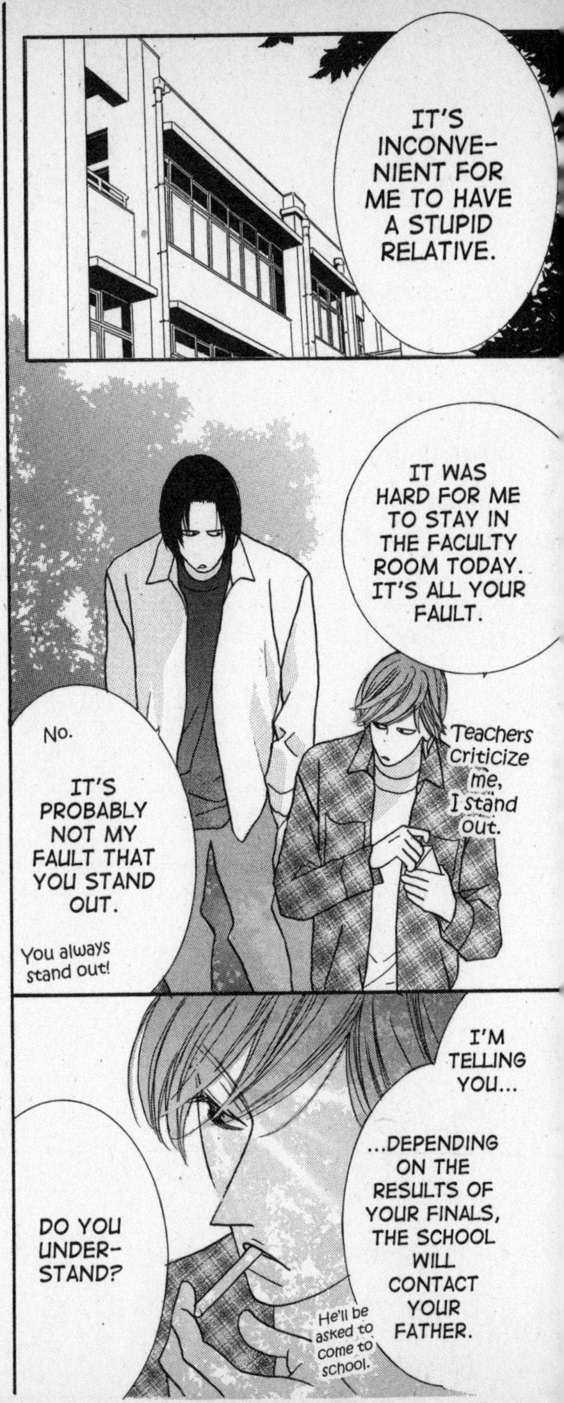
IT'S INCONVENIENT FOR ME TO HAVE A STUPID RELATIVE.
IT WAS HARD FOR ME TO STAY IN THE FACULTY ROOM TODAY. IT'S ALL YOUR FAULT.
Teachers criticize me, I stand out.
No.
IT'S PROBABLY NOT MY FAULT THAT YOU STAND OUT.
You always stand out!
I'M TELLING YOU...
...DEPENDING ON THE RESULTS OF YOUR FINALS, THE SCHOOL WILL CONTACT YOUR FATHER.
He'll be asked to come to school.
DO YOU UNDERSTAND?

6

My honest opinion is that having divorced parents doesn't necessarily mean you're unhappy. I grew up in a similar environment.
Often in a drama or something, when a child with divorced parents appears, and is portrayed as an unfortunate child with a complicated upbringing, I think "wait a minute!" (☺) Of course, for a child, it is a serious incident, but I don't think it's a misfortune or a tragedy. It's not you, it's the parents' problem. Even if your parents break up, you're you. I wonder about the belief that you shouldn't get divorced because the children would suffer too. It's more difficult living with parents who don't get along.
So to kids whose parents are divorced, I don't want you to think "poor me," no matter what.

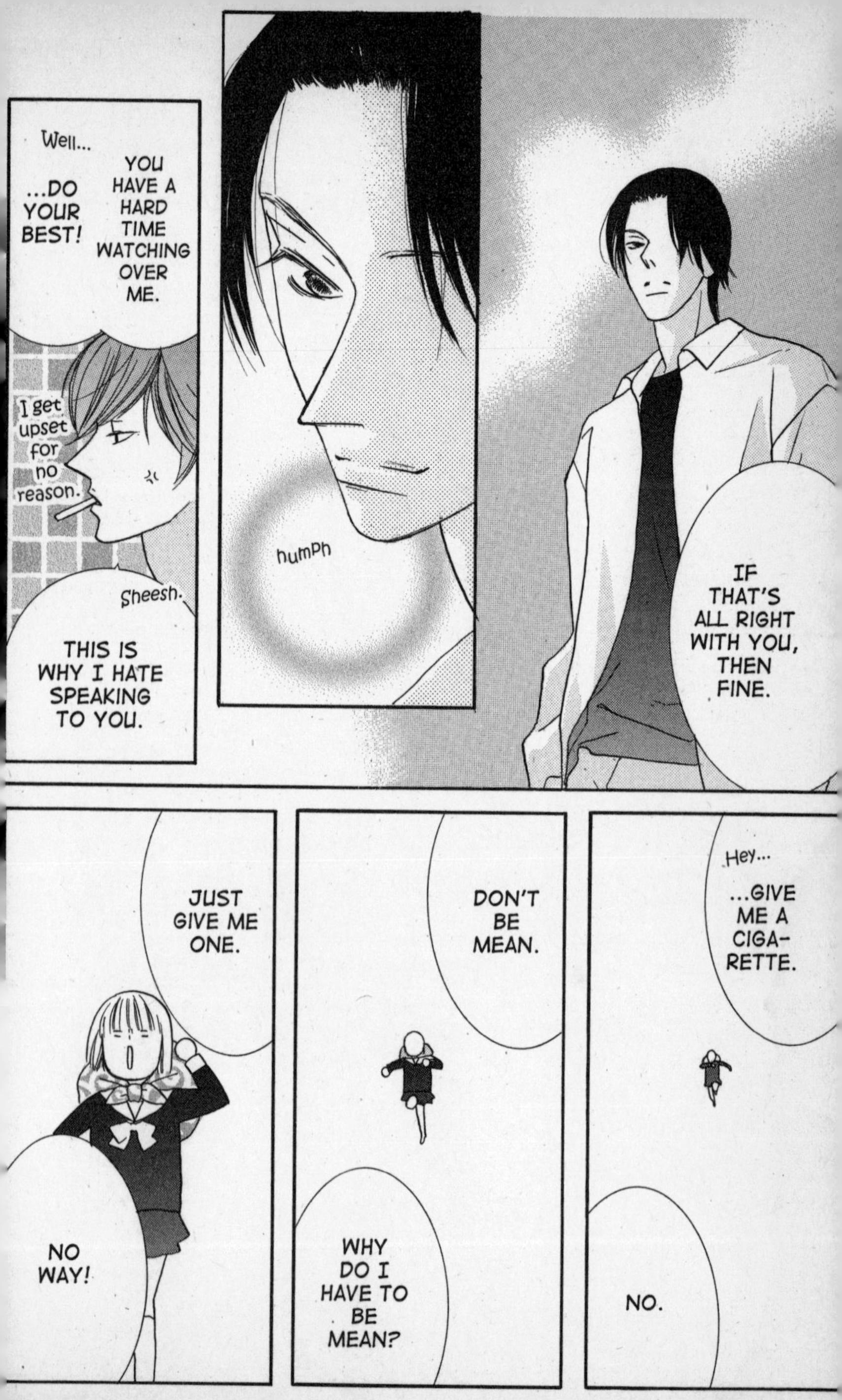
IF THAT'S ALL RIGHT WITH YOU, THEN FINE.
humph
YOU HAVE A HARD TIME WATCHING OVER ME.
Well... ...DO YOUR BEST!
I get upset for no reason.
Sheesh.
THIS IS WHY I HATE SPEAKING TO YOU.
Hey... ...GIVE ME A CIGA-RETTE.
NO.
DON'T BE MEAN.
WHY DO I HAVE TO BE MEAN?
JUST GIVE ME ONE.
NO WAY!

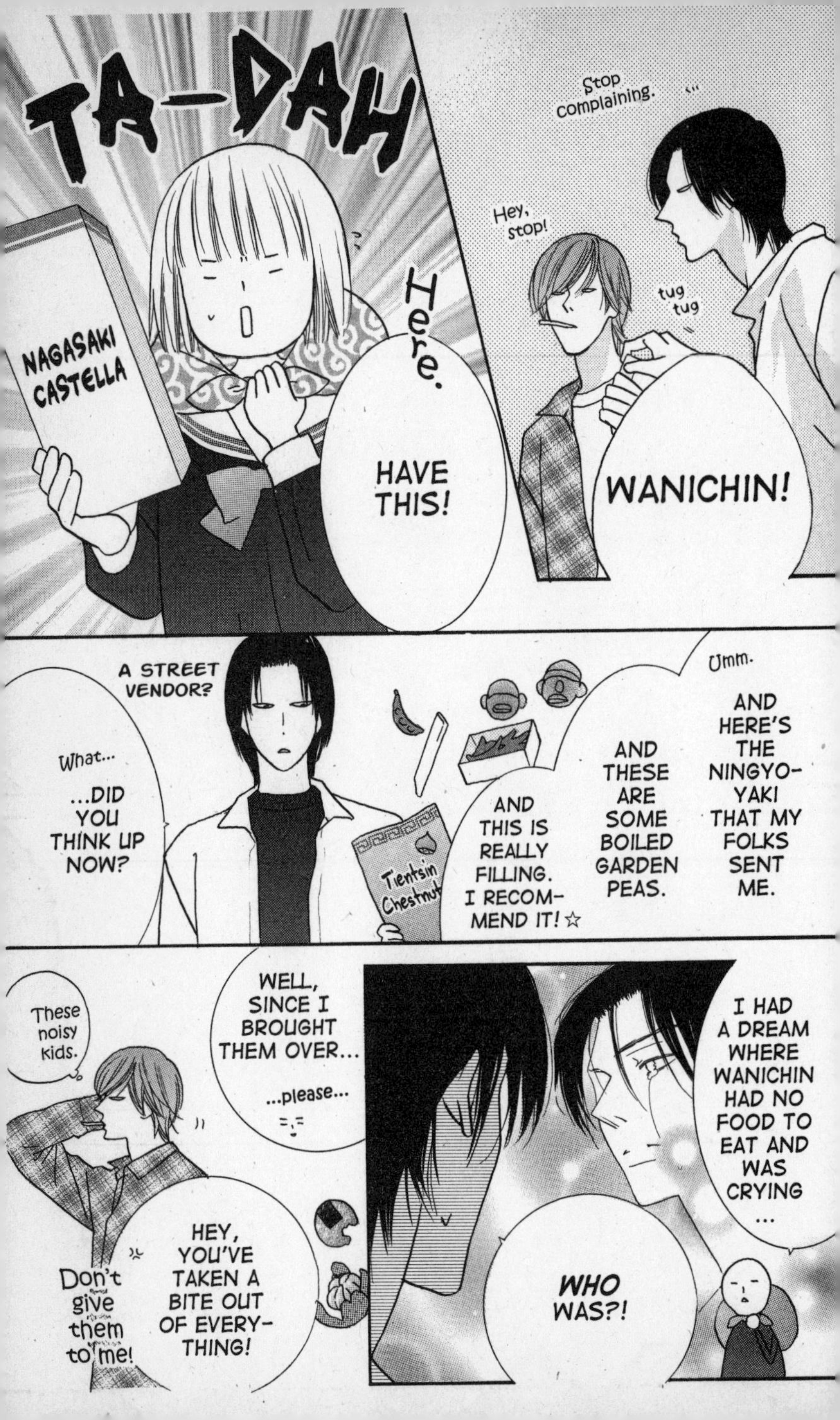
Stop complaining.
Hey, stop!
tug tug
WANICHIN!
TA-DAH
NAGASAKI CASTELLA
Here.
HAVE THIS!
Umm.
AND HERE'S THE NINGYO-YAKI THAT MY FOLKS SENT ME.
AND THESE ARE SOME BOILED GARDEN PEAS.
AND THIS IS REALLY FILLING. I RECOMMEND IT! ☆
Tientsin Chestnut
A STREET VENDOR?
What...
...DID YOU THINK UP NOW?
I HAD A DREAM WHERE WANICHIN HAD NO FOOD TO EAT AND WAS CRYING ...
WHO WAS?!
WELL, SINCE I BROUGHT THEM OVER...
...please...
These noisy kids.
HEY, YOU'VE TAKEN A BITE OUT OF EVERYTHING!
Don't give them to me!

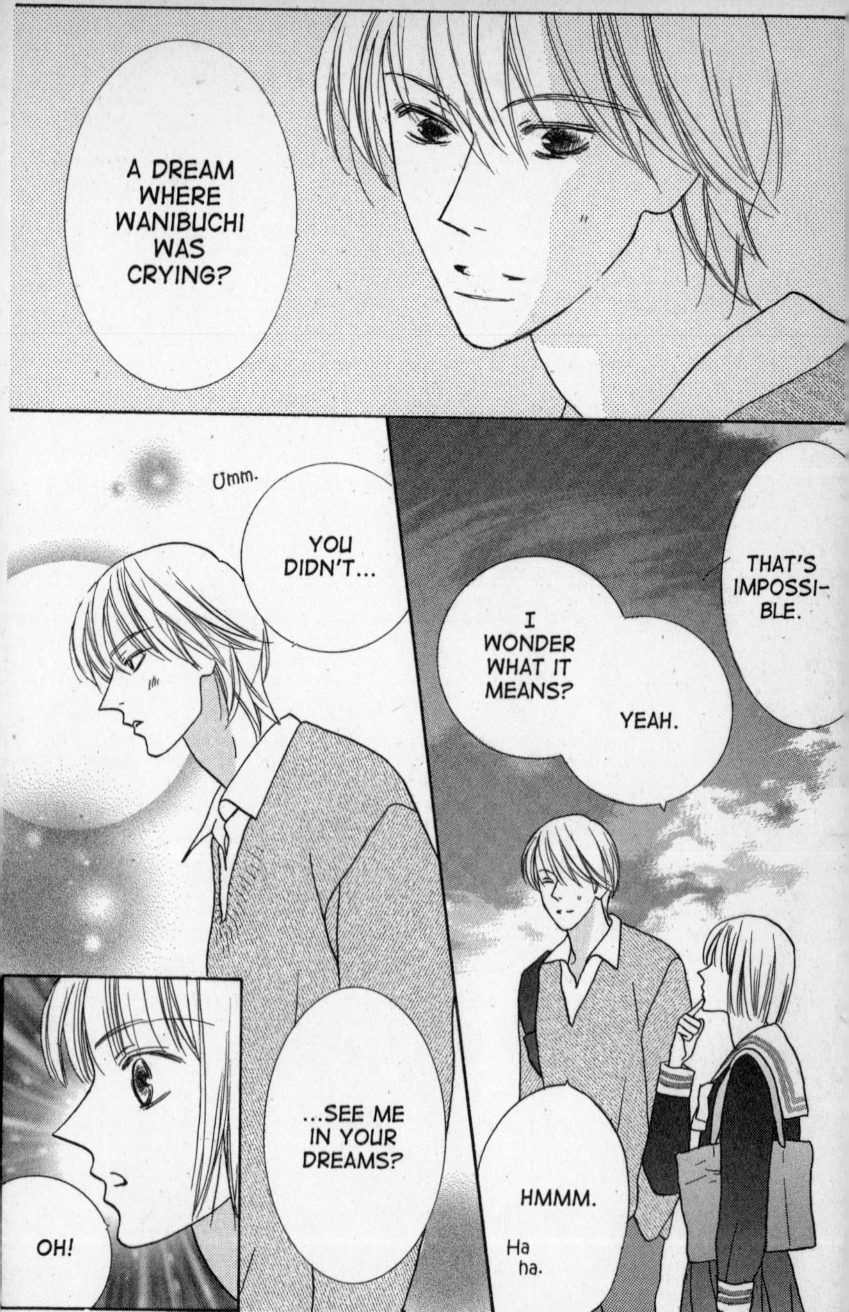
A DREAM WHERE WANIBUCHI WAS CRYING?
THAT'S IMPOSSIBLE.
I WONDER WHAT IT MEANS?
YEAH.
HMMM.
Ha ha.
Umm.
YOU DIDN'T...
...SEE ME IN YOUR DREAMS?
OH!

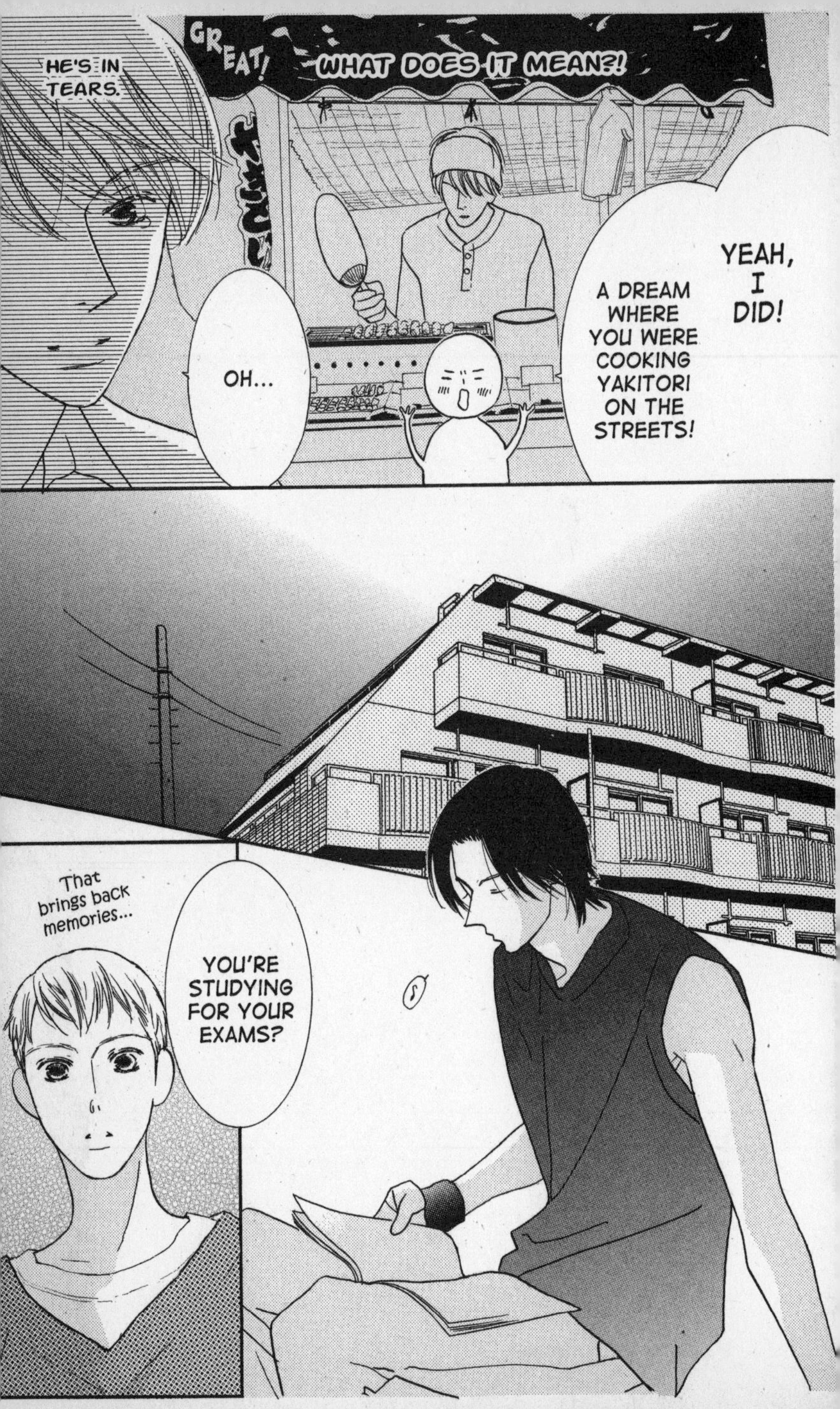
YEAH, I DID!
A DREAM WHERE YOU WERE COOKING YAKITORI ON THE STREETS!
WHAT DOES IT MEAN?!
GREAT!
OH...
HE'S IN TEARS.
YOU'RE STUDYING FOR YOUR EXAMS?
That brings back memories...

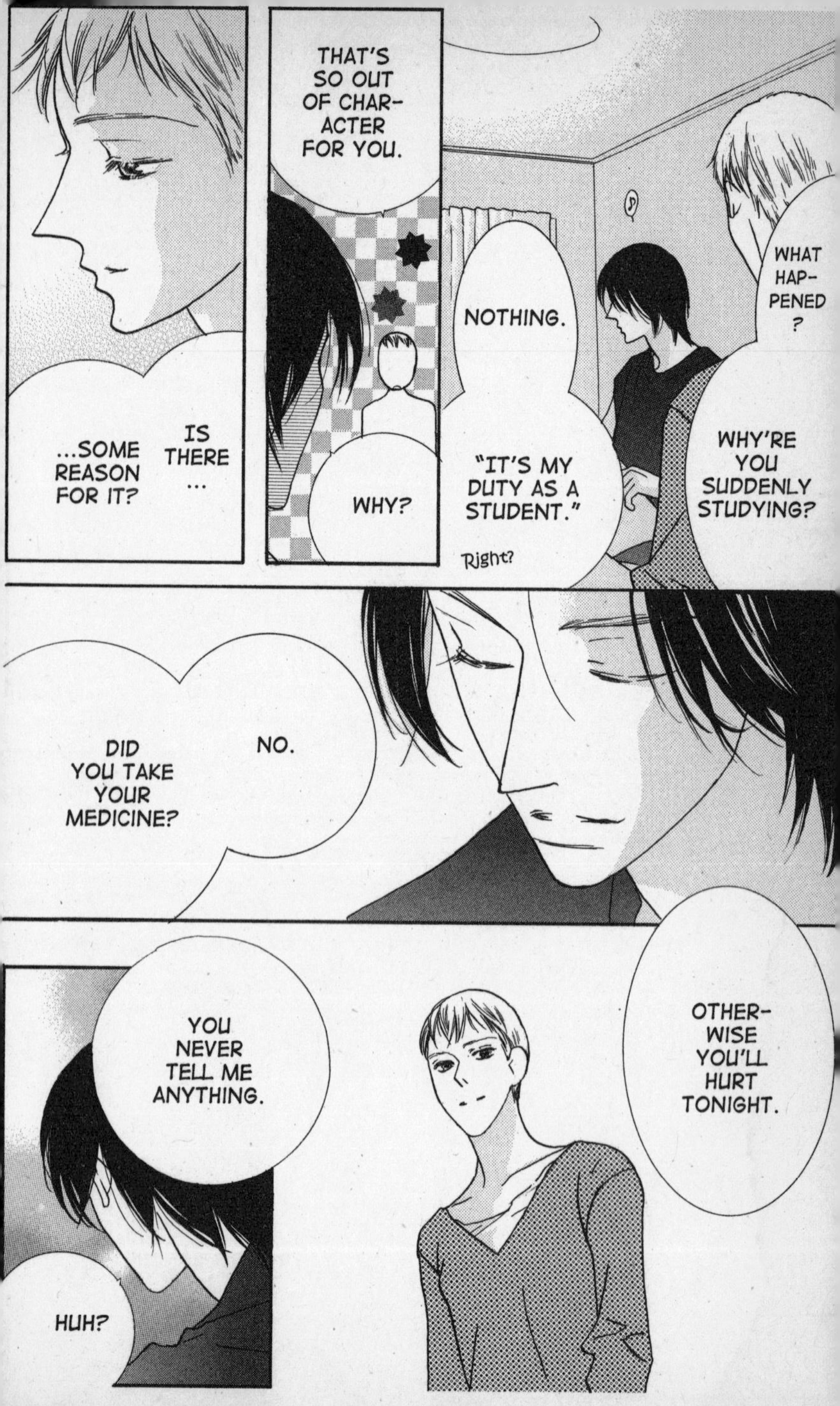
WHAT HAPPENED?
WHY'RE YOU SUDDENLY STUDYING?
NOTHING.
"IT'S MY DUTY AS A STUDENT."
Right?
THAT'S SO OUT OF CHARACTER FOR YOU.
WHY?
IS THERE ...
...SOME REASON FOR IT?
NO.
DID YOU TAKE YOUR MEDICINE?
OTHERWISE YOU'LL HURT TONIGHT.
YOU NEVER TELL ME ANYTHING.
HUH?

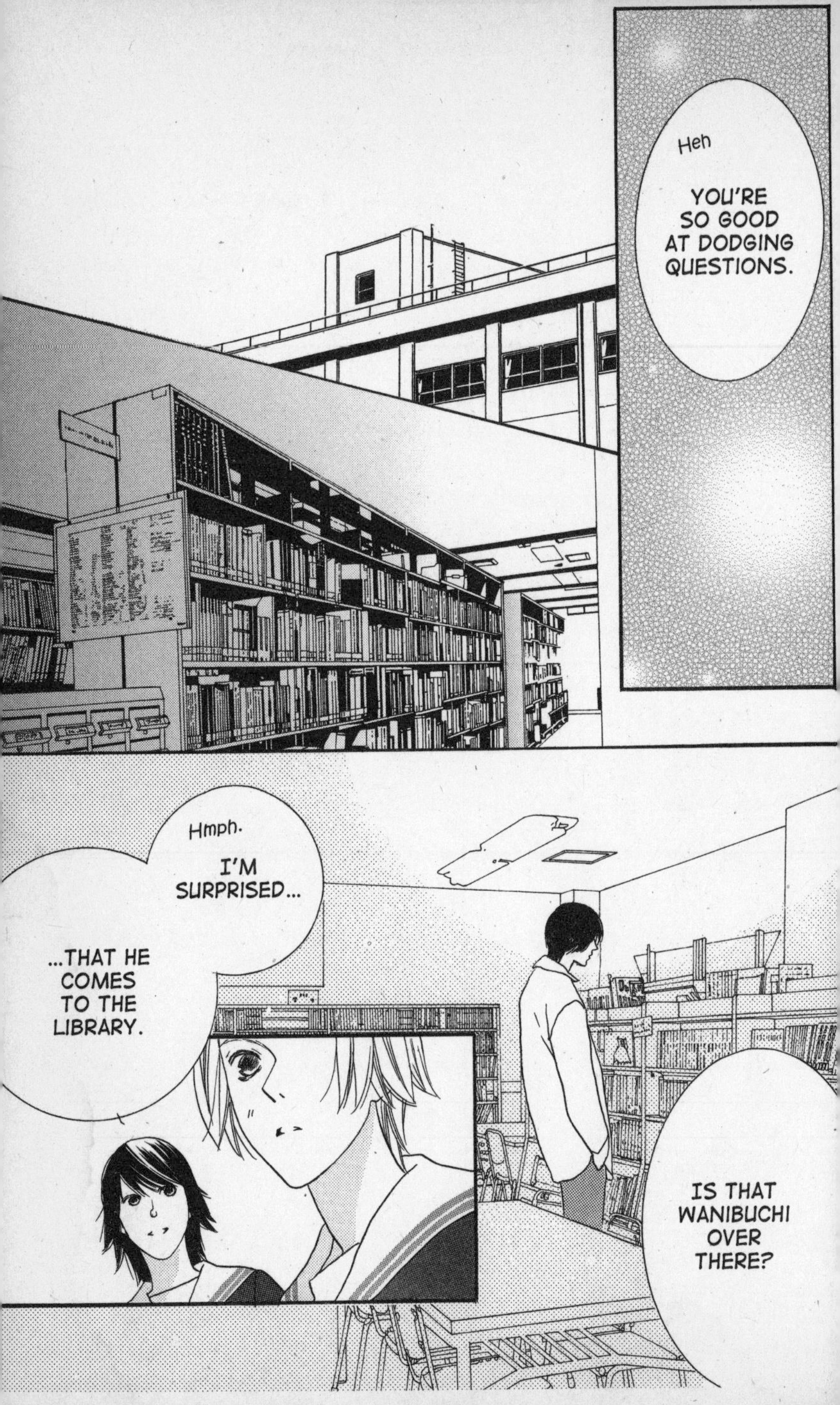
Heh
YOU'RE SO GOOD AT DODGING QUESTIONS.
IS THAT WANIBUCHI OVER THERE?
Hmph.
I'M SURPRISED...
...THAT HE COMES TO THE LIBRARY.

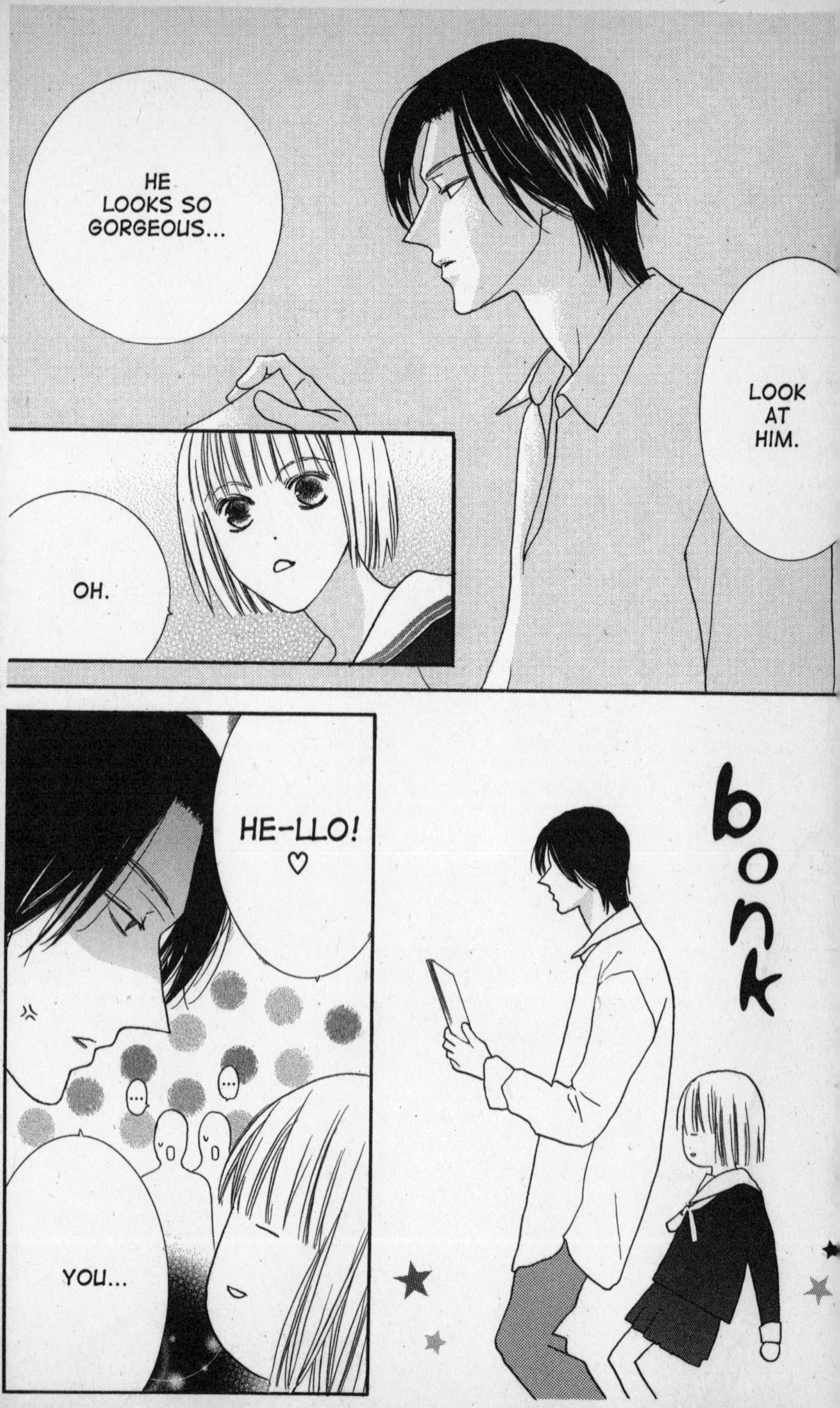
LOOK AT HIM.
HE LOOKS SO GORGEOUS...
OH.
bonk
HE-LLO! ♡
...
...
YOU...

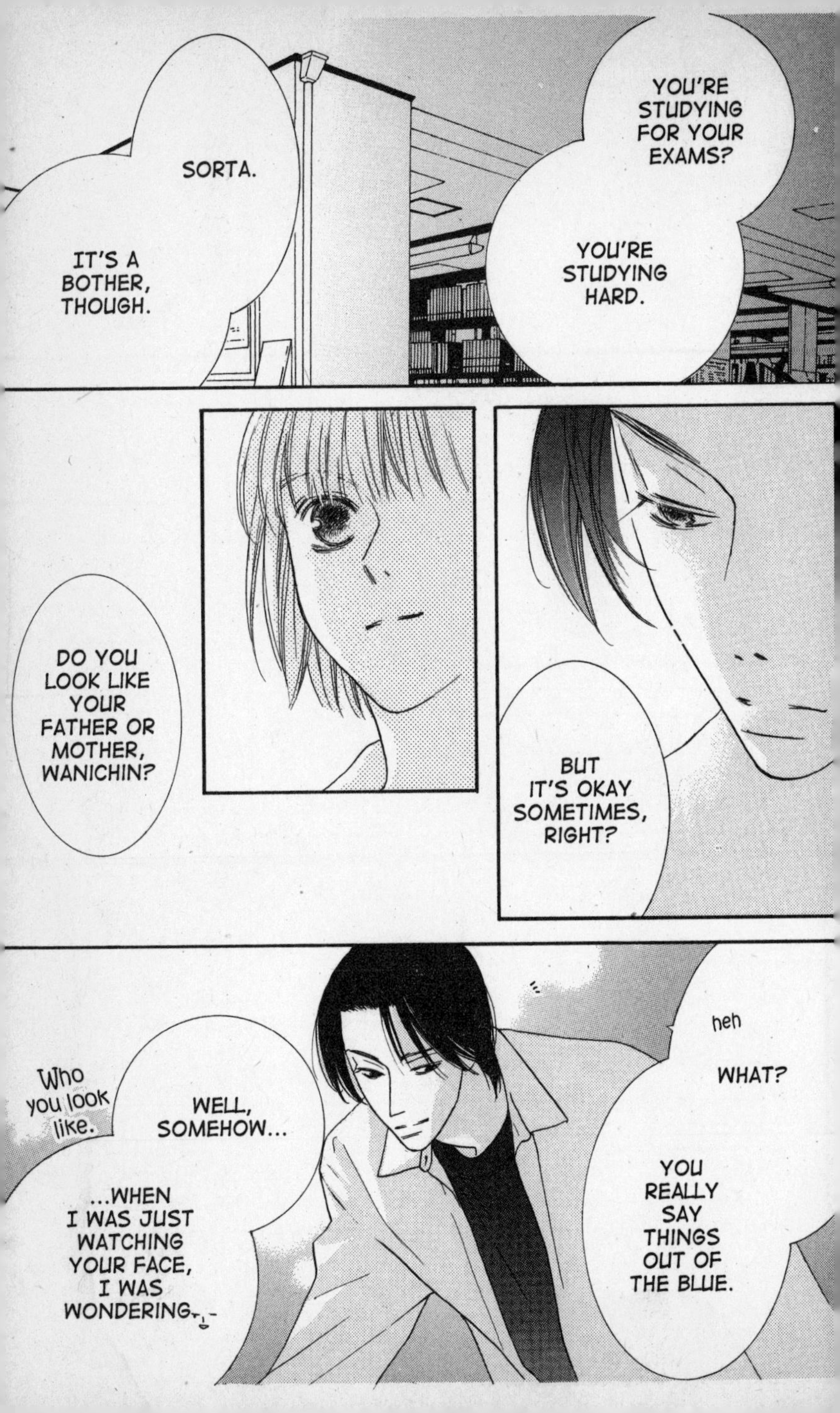
YOU'RE STUDYING FOR YOUR EXAMS?
YOU'RE STUDYING HARD.
SORTA.
IT'S A BOTHER, THOUGH.
BUT IT'S OKAY SOMETIMES, RIGHT?
DO YOU LOOK LIKE YOUR FATHER OR MOTHER, WANICHIN?
heh
WHAT?
YOU REALLY SAY THINGS OUT OF THE BLUE.
WELL, SOMEHOW...
...WHEN I WAS JUST WATCHING YOUR FACE, I WAS WONDERING...
Who you look like.

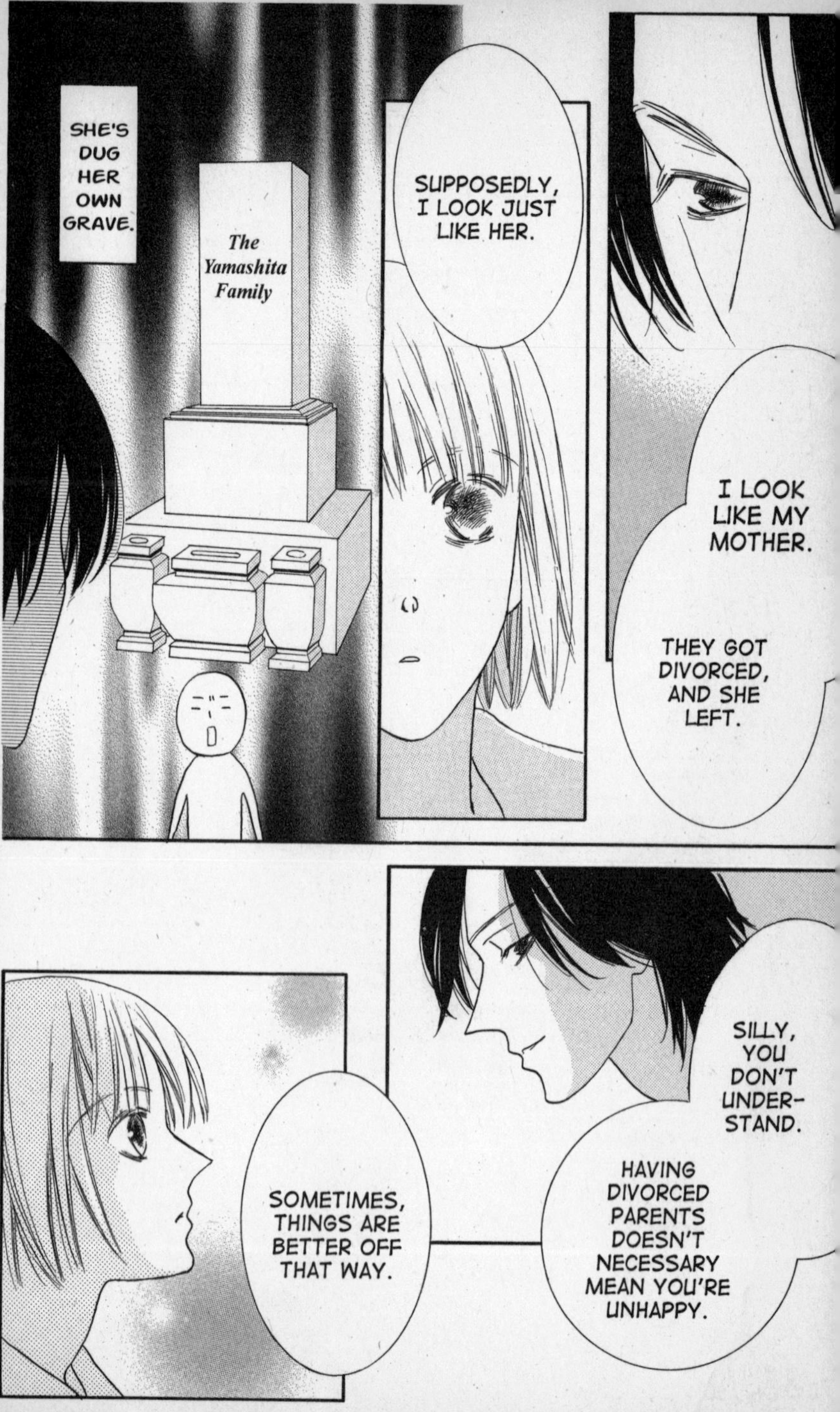
I LOOK LIKE MY MOTHER.
THEY GOT DIVORCED, AND SHE LEFT.
SUPPOSEDLY, I LOOK JUST LIKE HER.
SHE'S DUG HER OWN GRAVE.
The Yamashita Family
SILLY, YOU DON'T UNDER-STAND.
HAVING DIVORCED PARENTS DOESN'T NECESSARY MEAN YOU'RE UNHAPPY.
SOMETIMES, THINGS ARE BETTER OFF THAT WAY.

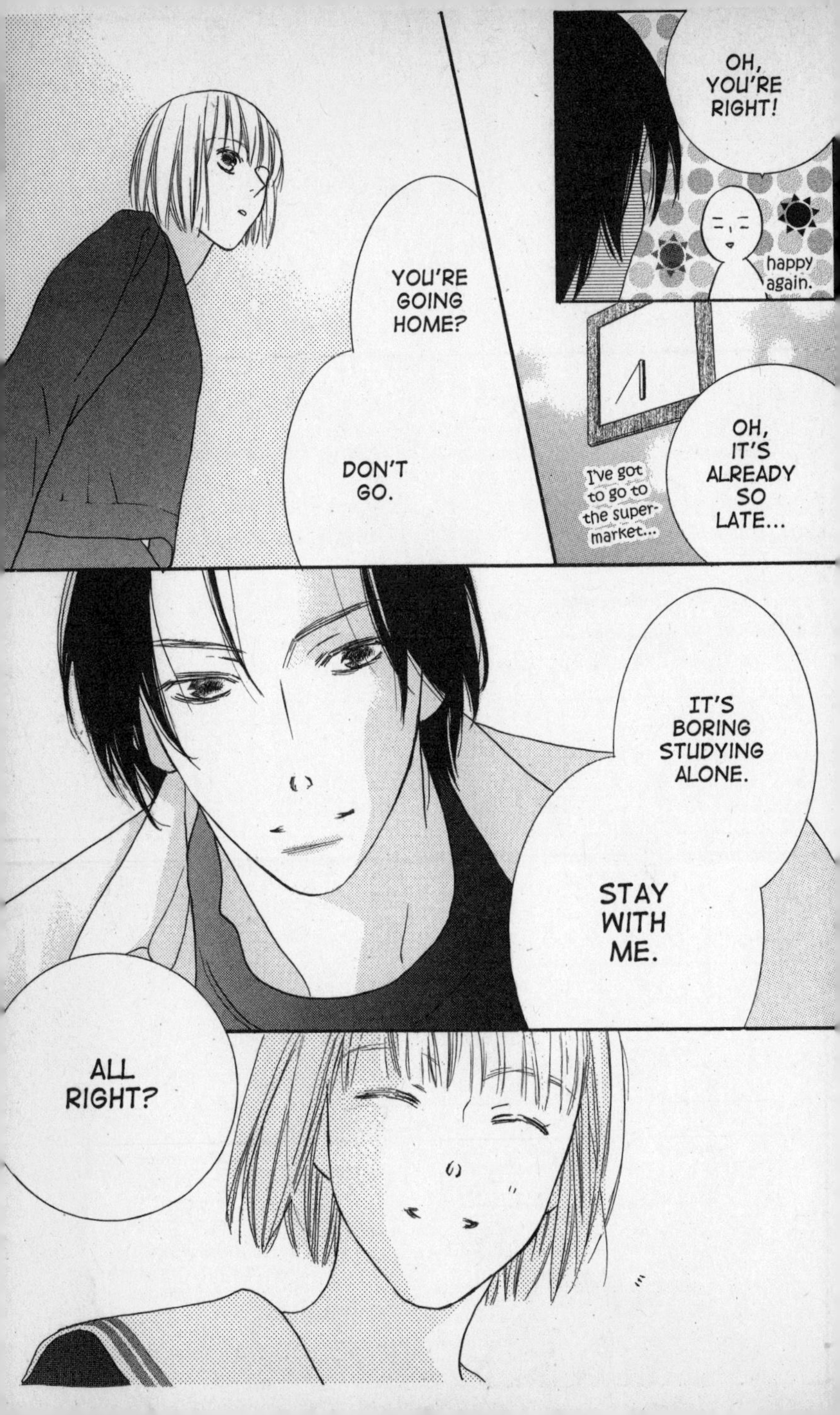
OH, YOU'RE RIGHT!
happy again.
OH, IT'S ALREADY SO LATE...
I've got to go to the supermarket...
YOU'RE GOING HOME?
DON'T GO.
IT'S BORING STUDYING ALONE.
STAY WITH ME.
ALL RIGHT?

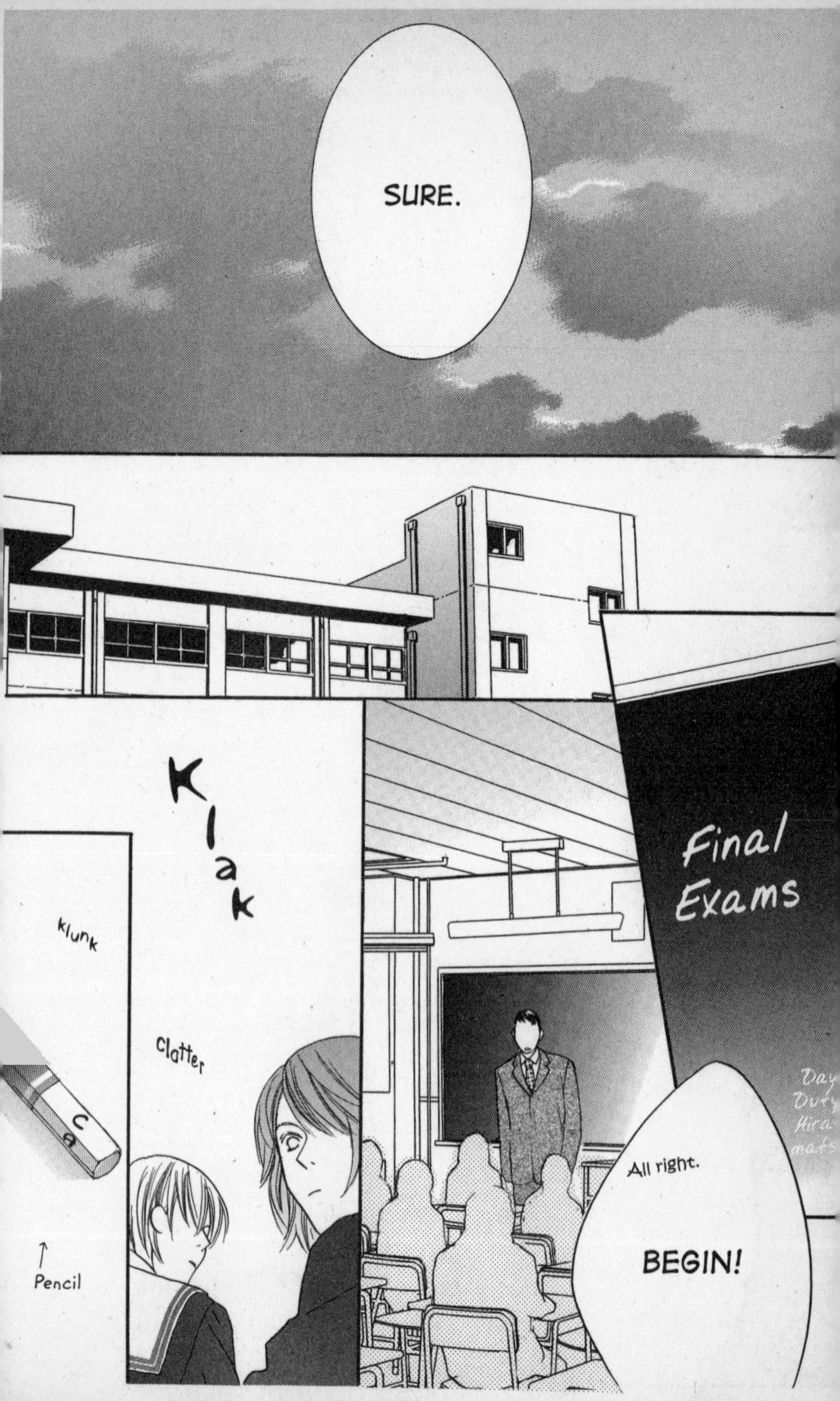
SURE.
Final Exams
All right.
BEGIN!
Klak
Clatter
klunk
Pencil

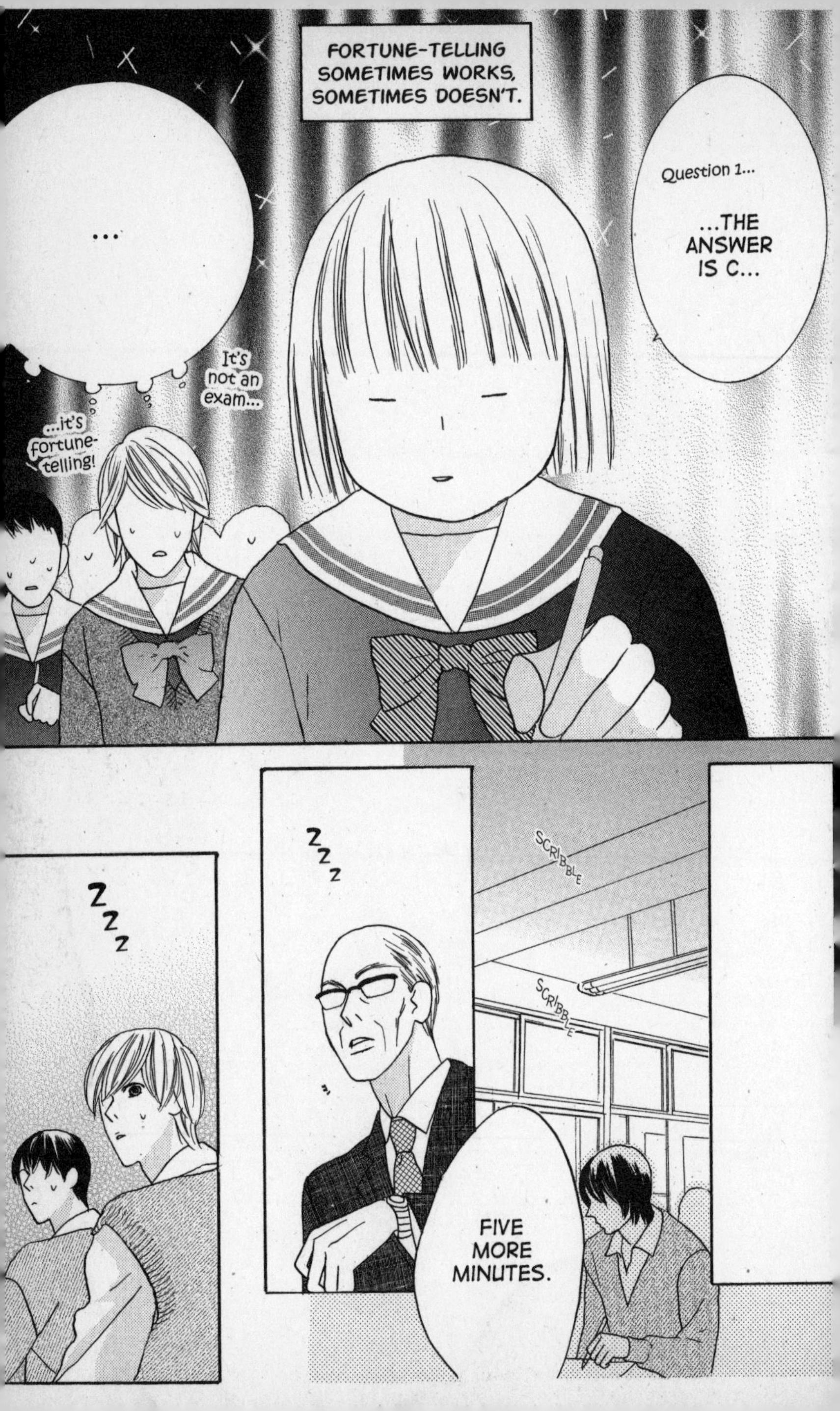
FORTUNE-TELLING SOMETIMES WORKS, SOMETIMES DOESN'T.
Question 1...
...THE ANSWER IS C...
...
It's not an exam...
...it's fortune-telling!
SCRIBBLE
SCRIBBLE
ZZZ
FIVE MORE MINUTES.
ZZZ

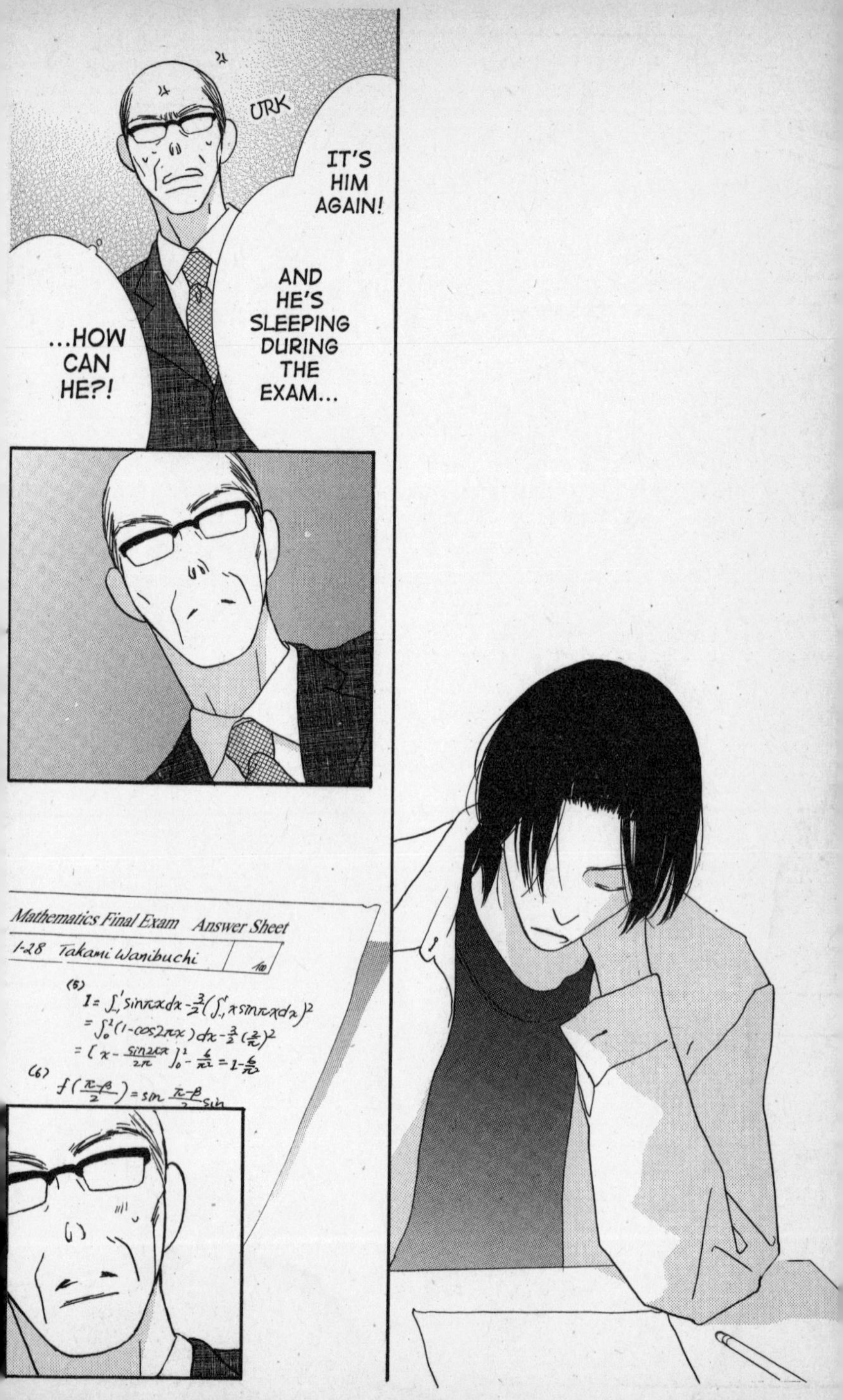
URK
IT'S HIM AGAIN!
AND HE'S SLEEPING DURING THE EXAM...
...HOW CAN HE?!
Mathematics Final Exam Answer Sheet
1-28 Takami Wanibuchi
100

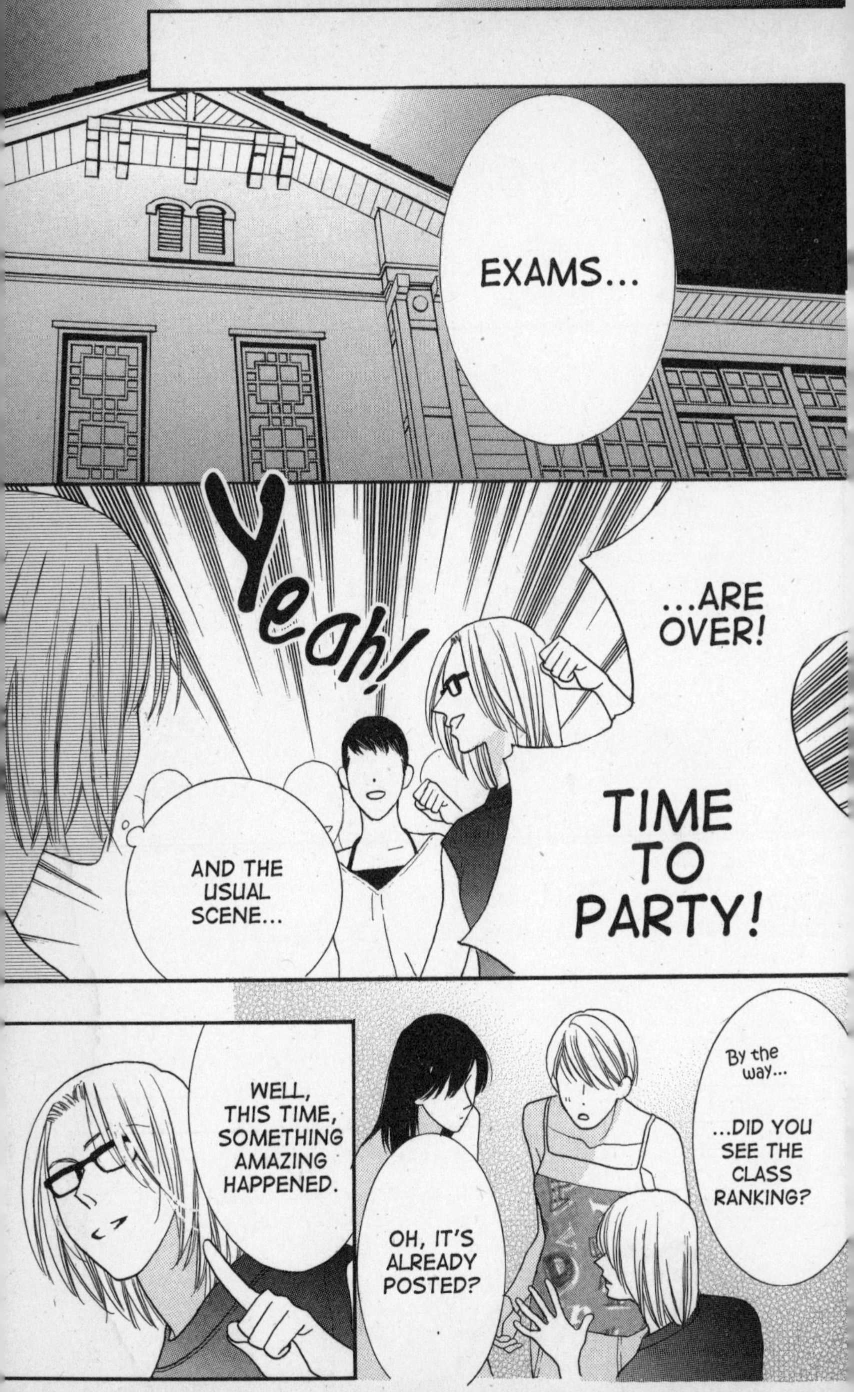
EXAMS...
...ARE OVER!
TIME TO PARTY!
Yeah!
AND THE USUAL SCENE...
By the way...
...DID YOU SEE THE CLASS RANKING?
OH, IT'S ALREADY POSTED?
WELL, THIS TIME, SOMETHING AMAZING HAPPENED.

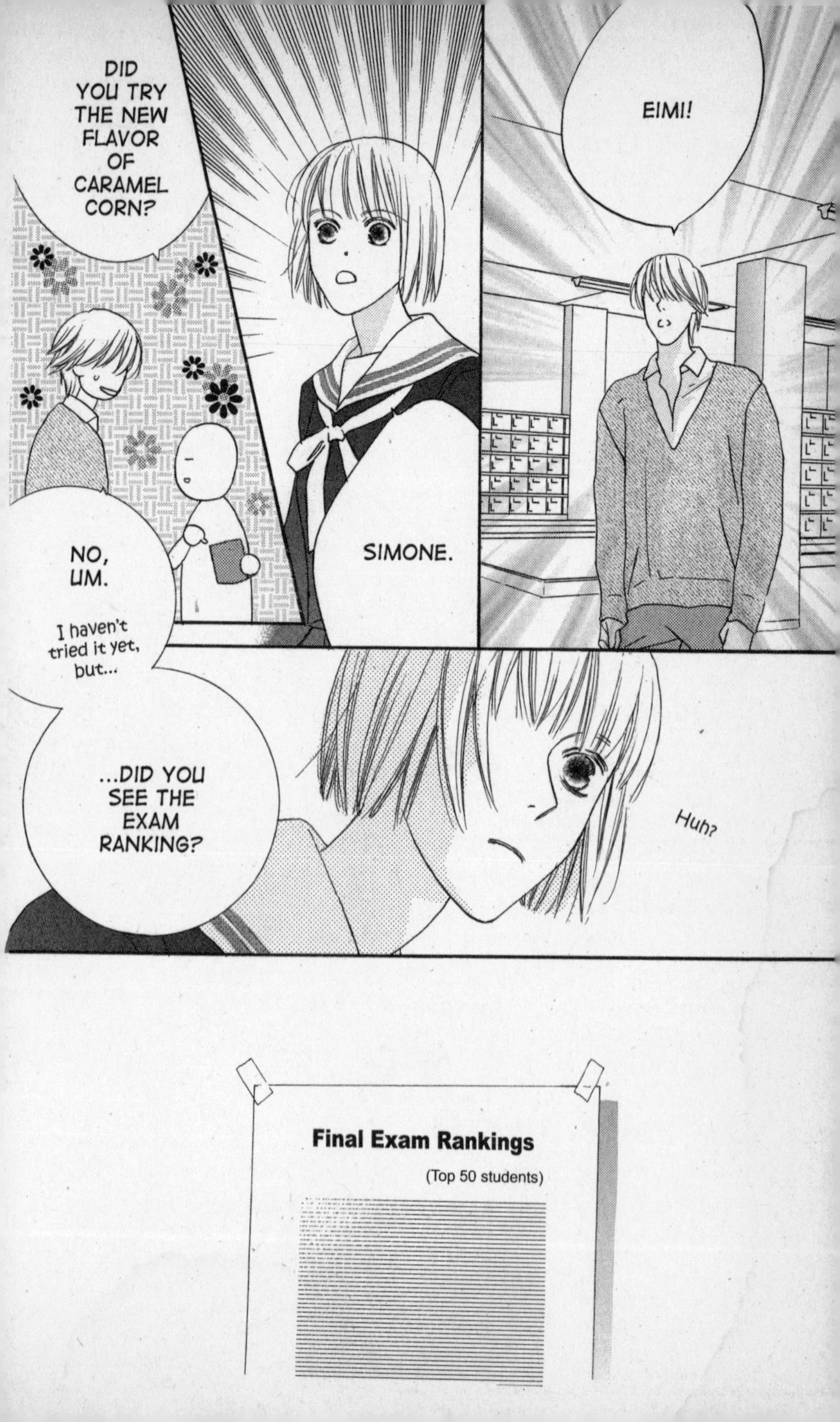
EIMI!
SIMONE.
DID YOU TRY THE NEW FLAVOR OF CARAMEL CORN?
NO, UM.
I haven't tried it yet, but...
...DID YOU SEE THE EXAM RANKING?
Huh?
Final Exam Rankings
(Top 50 students)

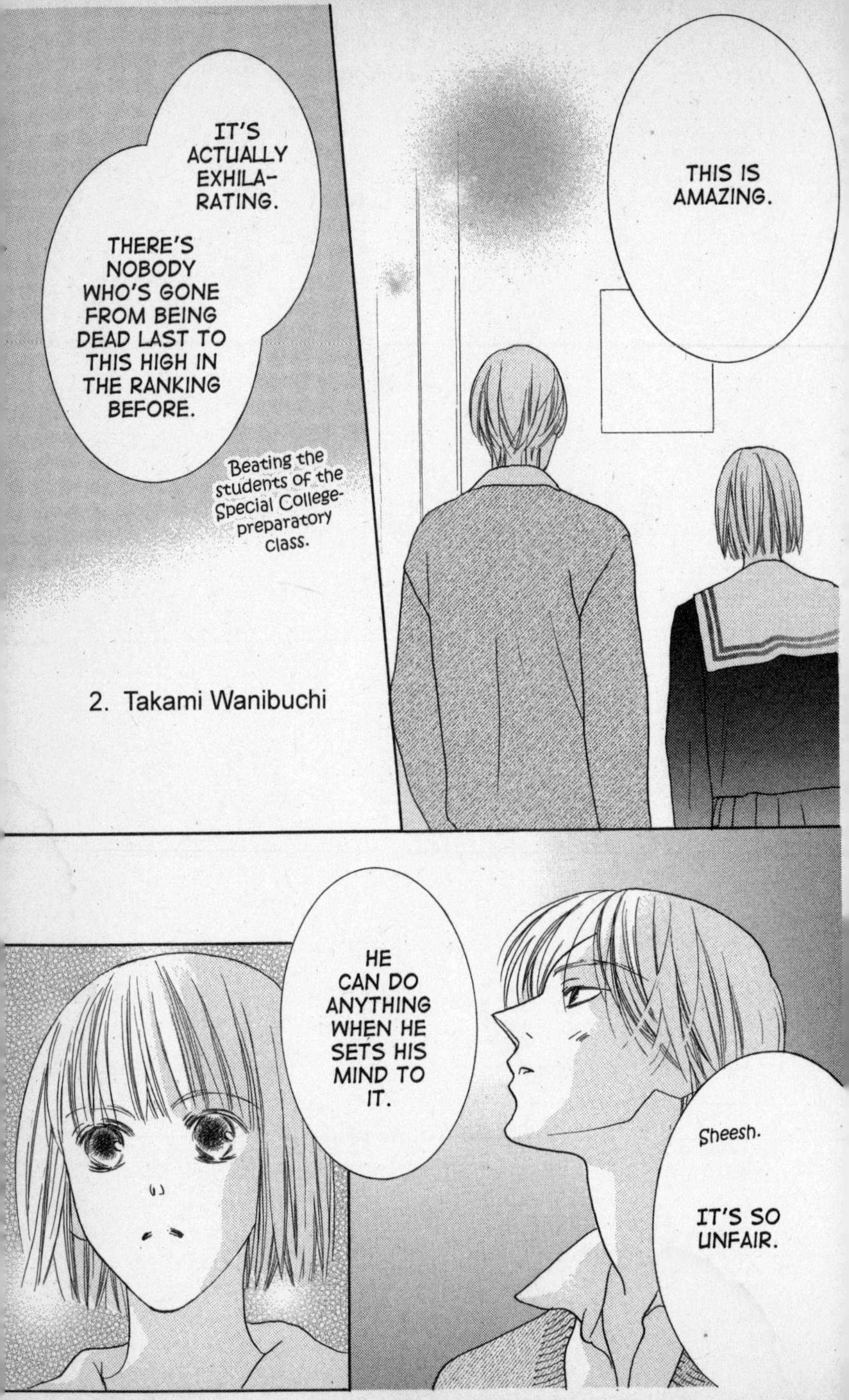

THIS IS AMAZING.
IT'S ACTUALLY EXHILA-RATING.
THERE'S NOBODY WHO'S GONE FROM BEING DEAD LAST TO THIS HIGH IN THE RANKING BEFORE.
Beating the students of the Special College-preparatory class.
2. Takami Wanibuchi
HE CAN DO ANYTHING WHEN HE SETS HIS MIND TO IT.
Sheesh.
IT'S SO UNFAIR.

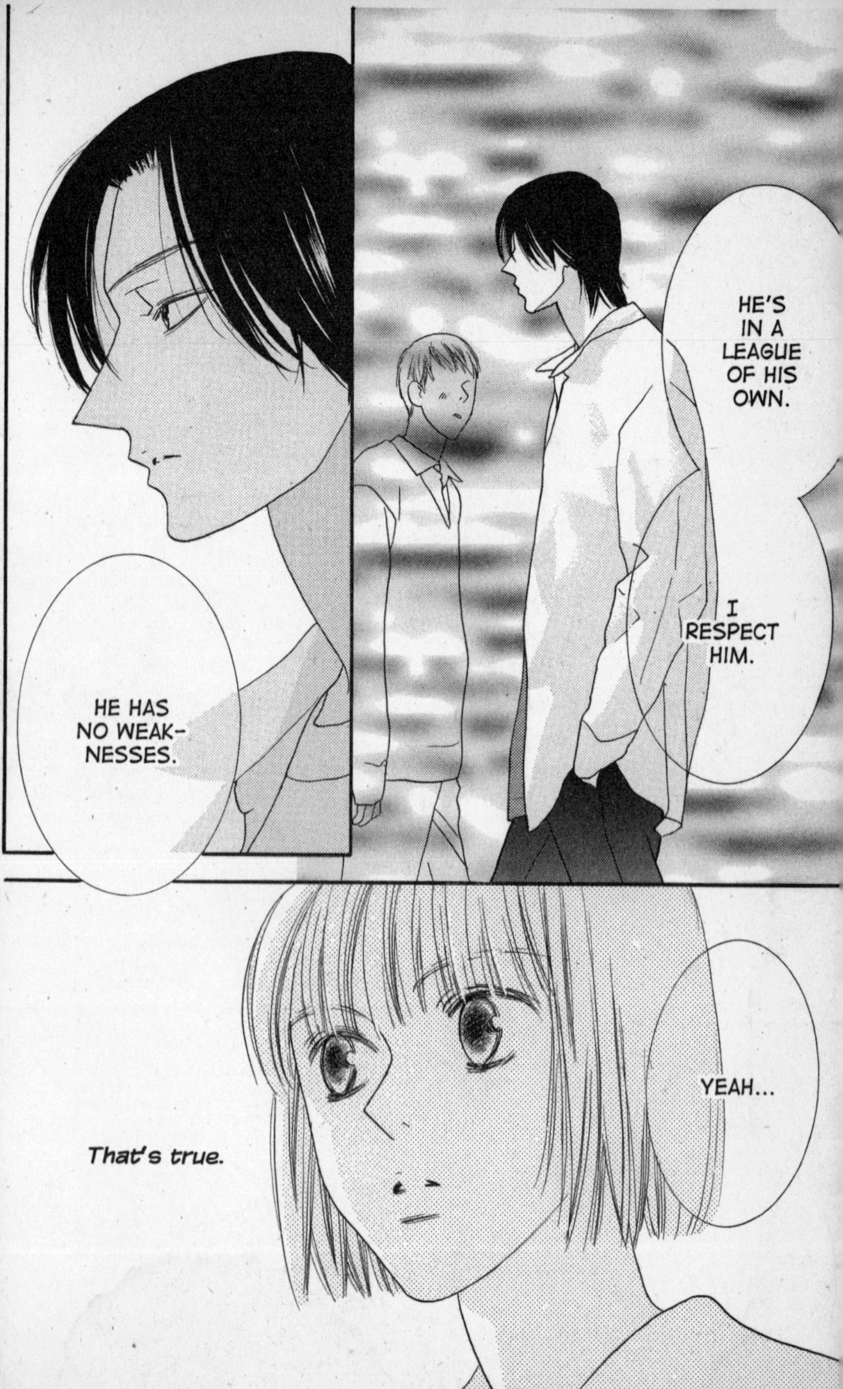
HE'S IN A LEAGUE OF HIS OWN.
I RESPECT HIM.
HE HAS NO WEAK-NESSES.
YEAH...
That's true.

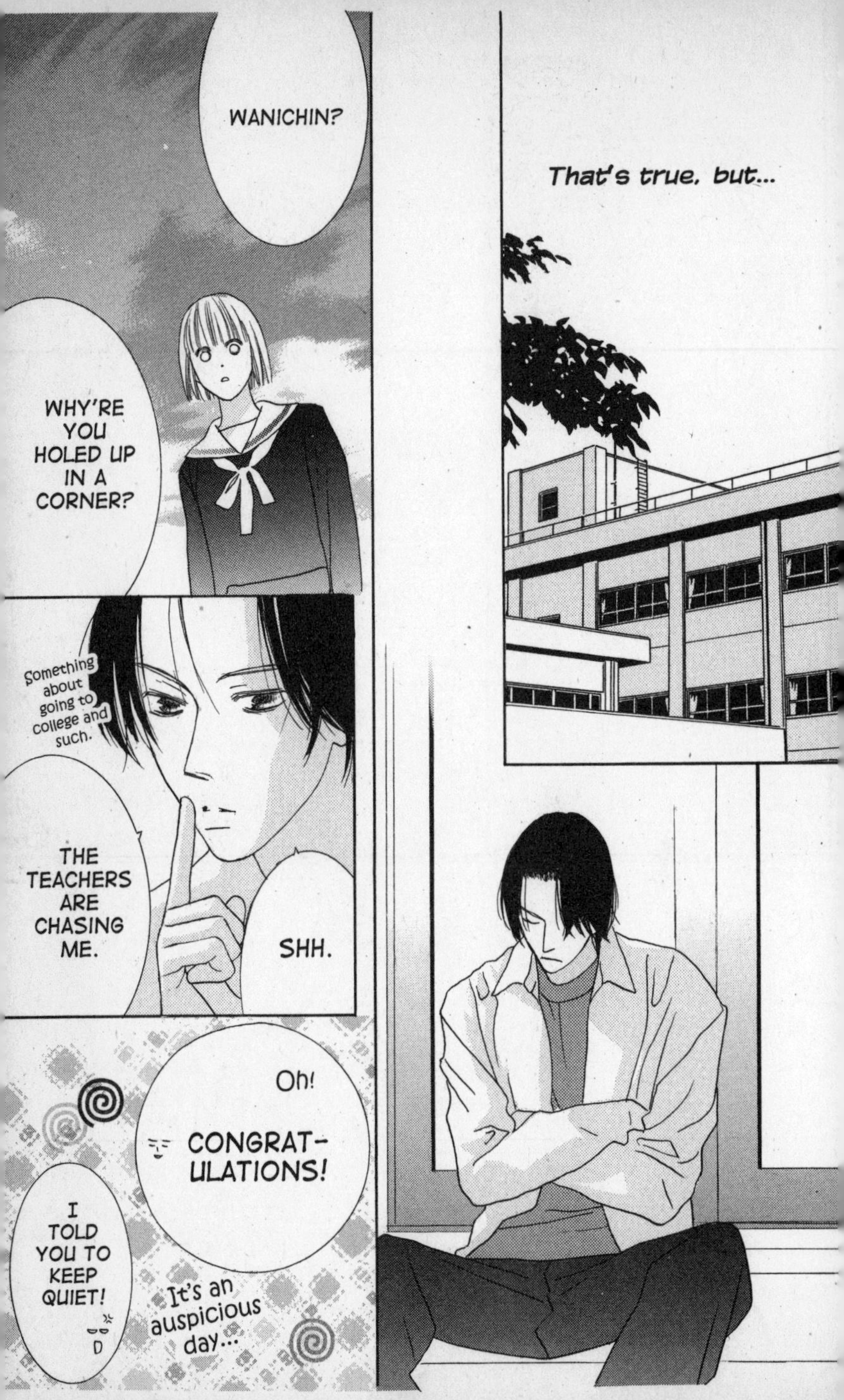

That's true, but...
WANICHIN?
WHY'RE YOU HOLED UP IN A CORNER?
SHH.
THE TEACHERS ARE CHASING ME.
Something about going to college and such.
Oh!
CONGRAT-ULATIONS!
I TOLD YOU TO KEEP QUIET!
It's an auspicious day...

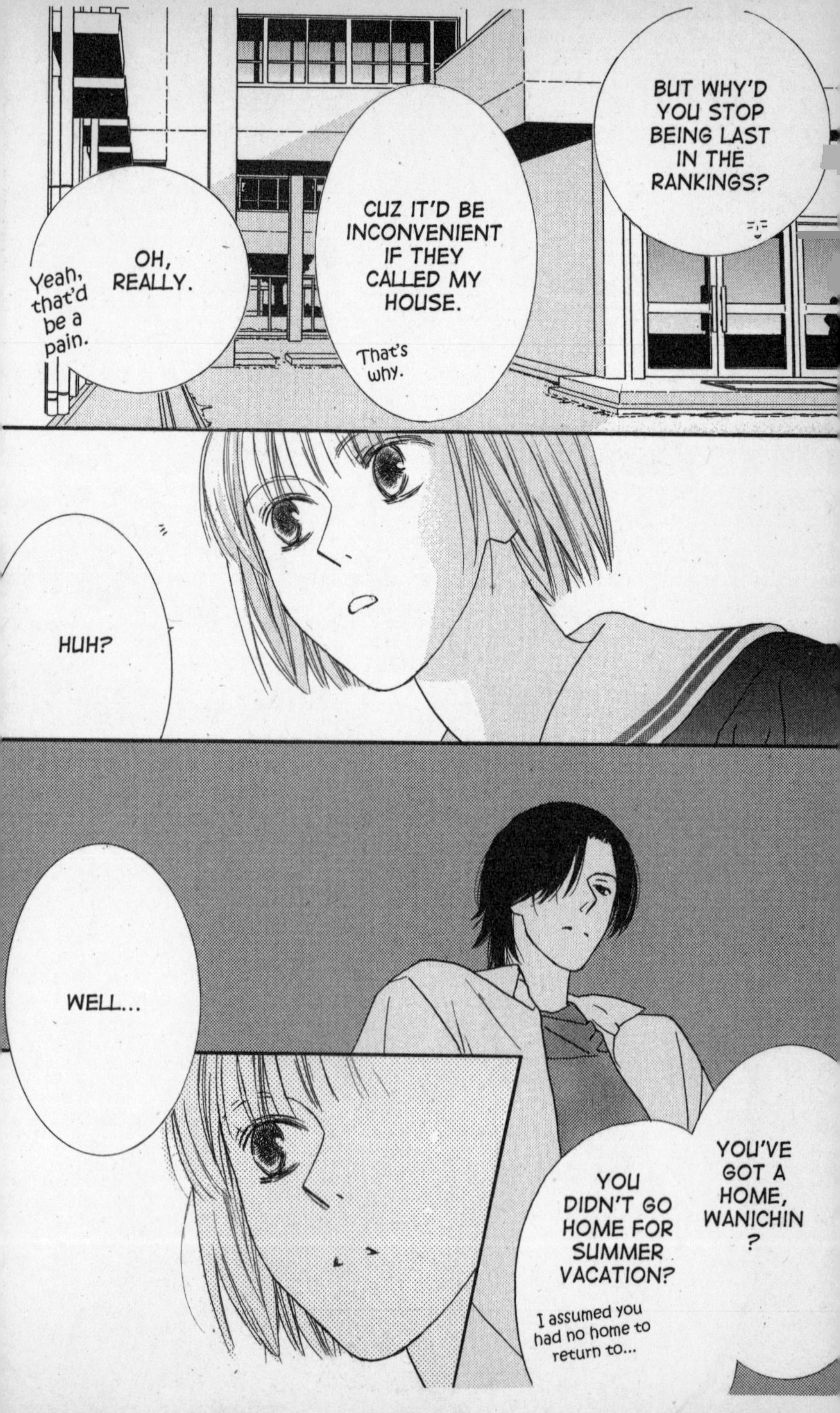
BUT WHY'D YOU STOP BEING LAST IN THE RANKINGS?
CUZ IT'D BE INCONVENIENT IF THEY CALLED MY HOUSE.
That's why.
OH, REALLY.
Yeah, that'd be a pain.
HUH?
WELL...
YOU'VE GOT A HOME, WANICHIN?
YOU DIDN'T GO HOME FOR SUMMER VACATION?
I assumed you had no home to return to...

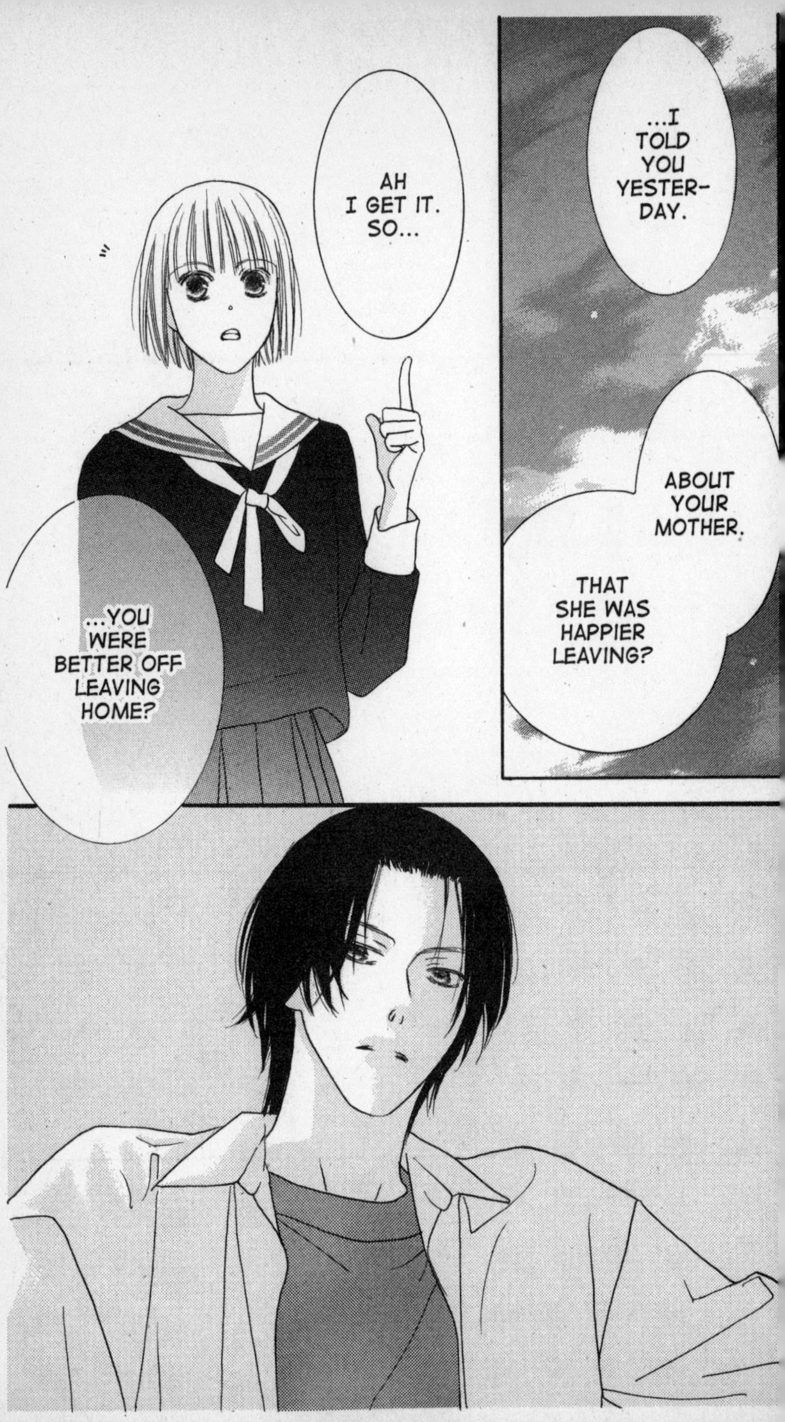
...I TOLD YOU YESTER-DAY.
ABOUT YOUR MOTHER.
THAT SHE WAS HAPPIER LEAVING?
AH I GET IT. SO...
...YOU WERE BETTER OFF LEAVING HOME?

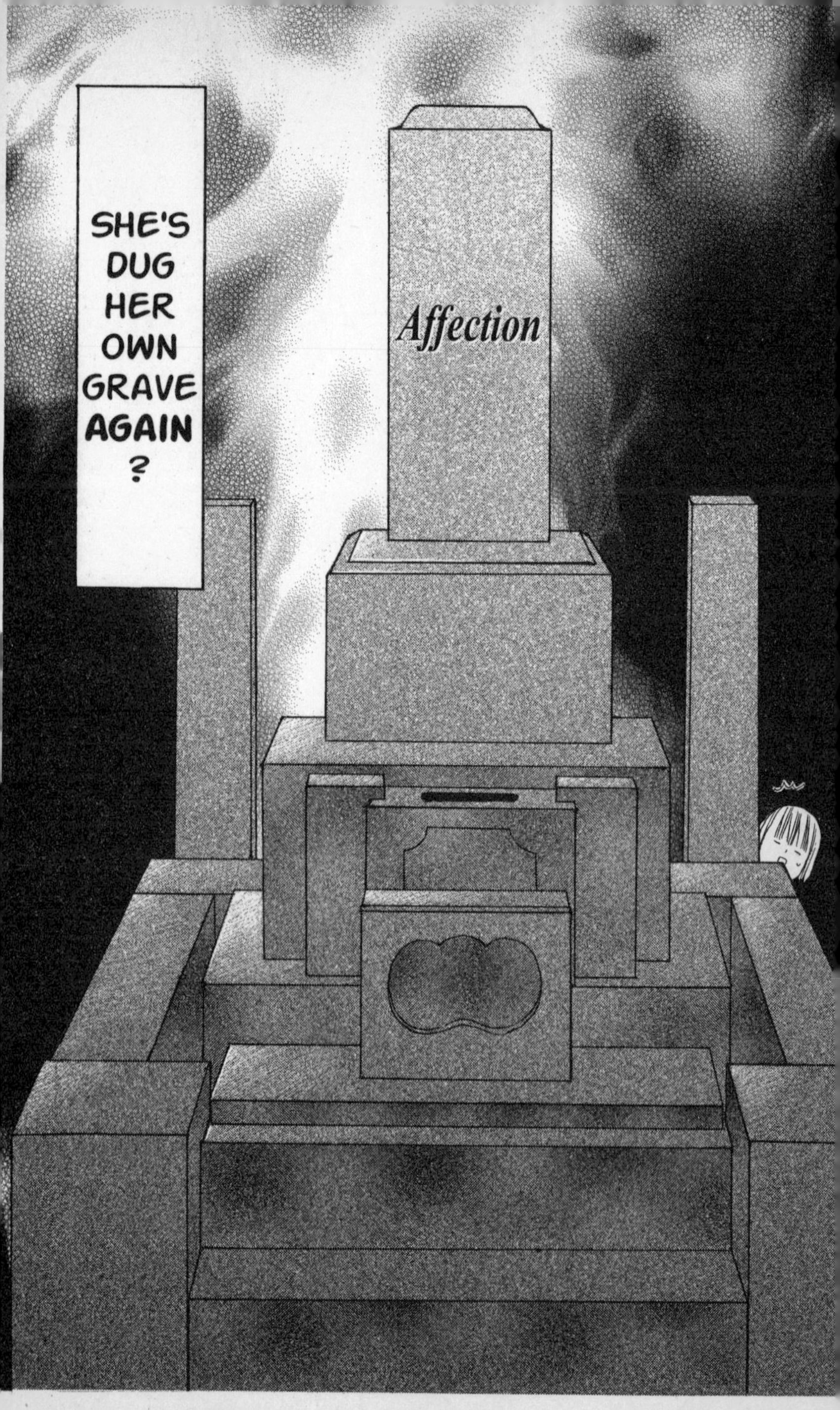
SHE'S DUG HER OWN GRAVE AGAIN?
Affection

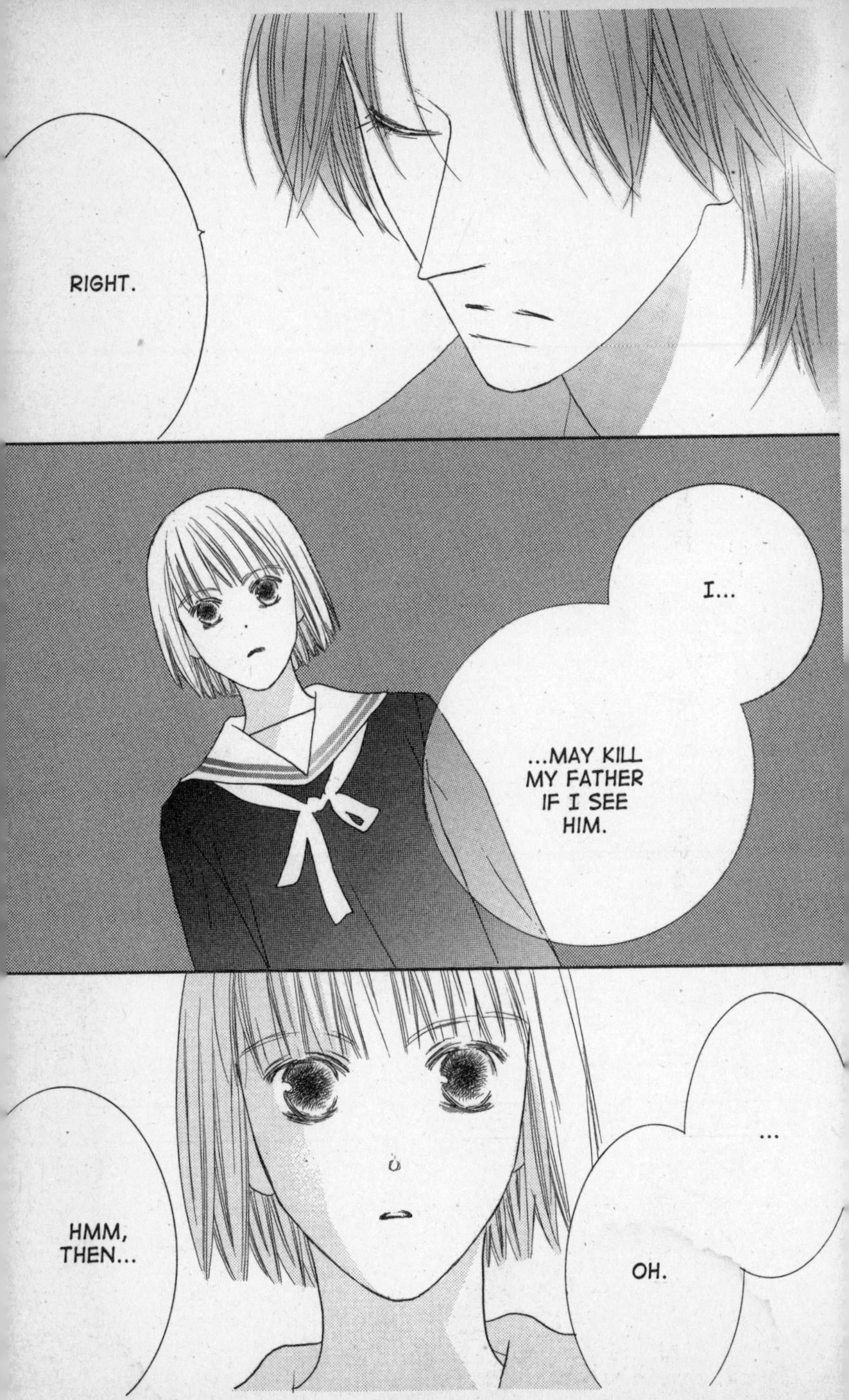
RIGHT.
I...
...MAY KILL MY FATHER IF I SEE HIM.
...
OH.
HMM, THEN...

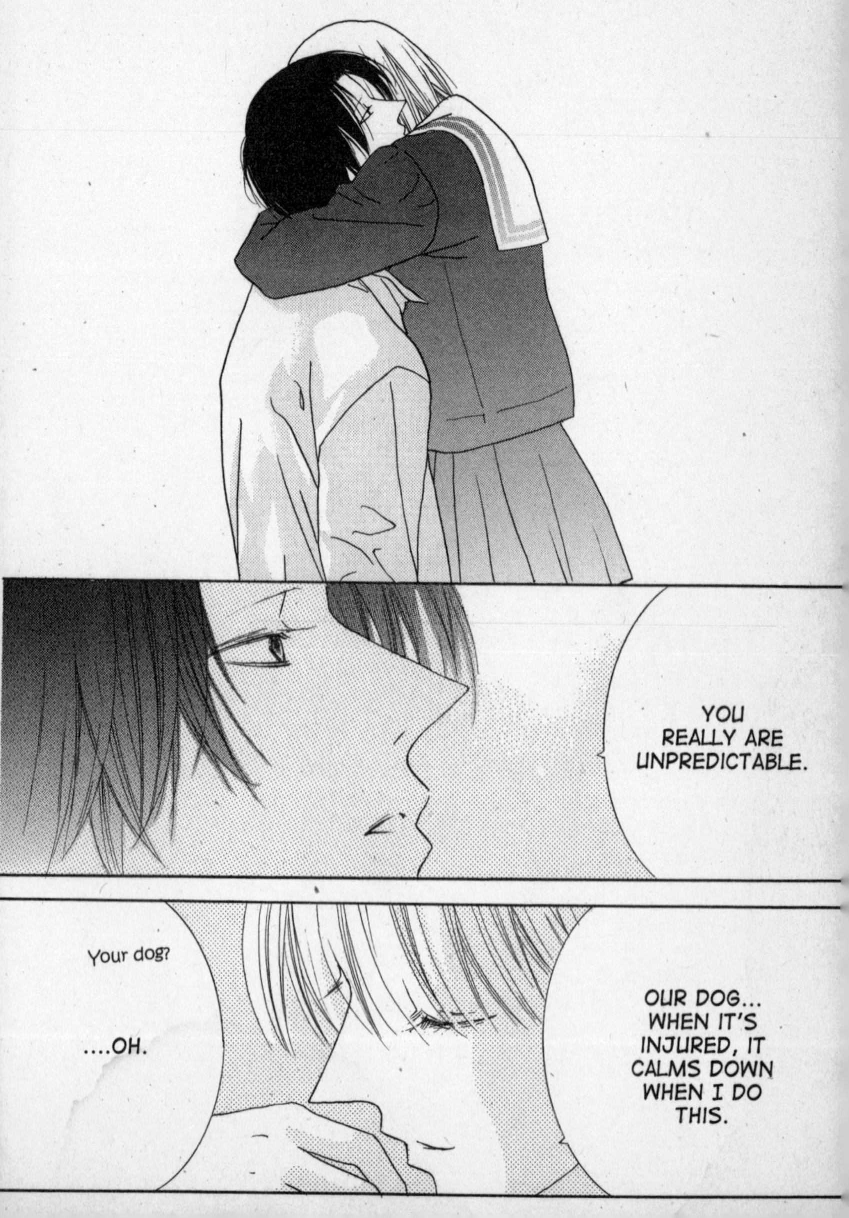
YOU REALLY ARE UNPREDICTABLE.
OUR DOG... WHEN IT'S INJURED, IT CALMS DOWN WHEN I DO THIS.
Your dog?
....OH.

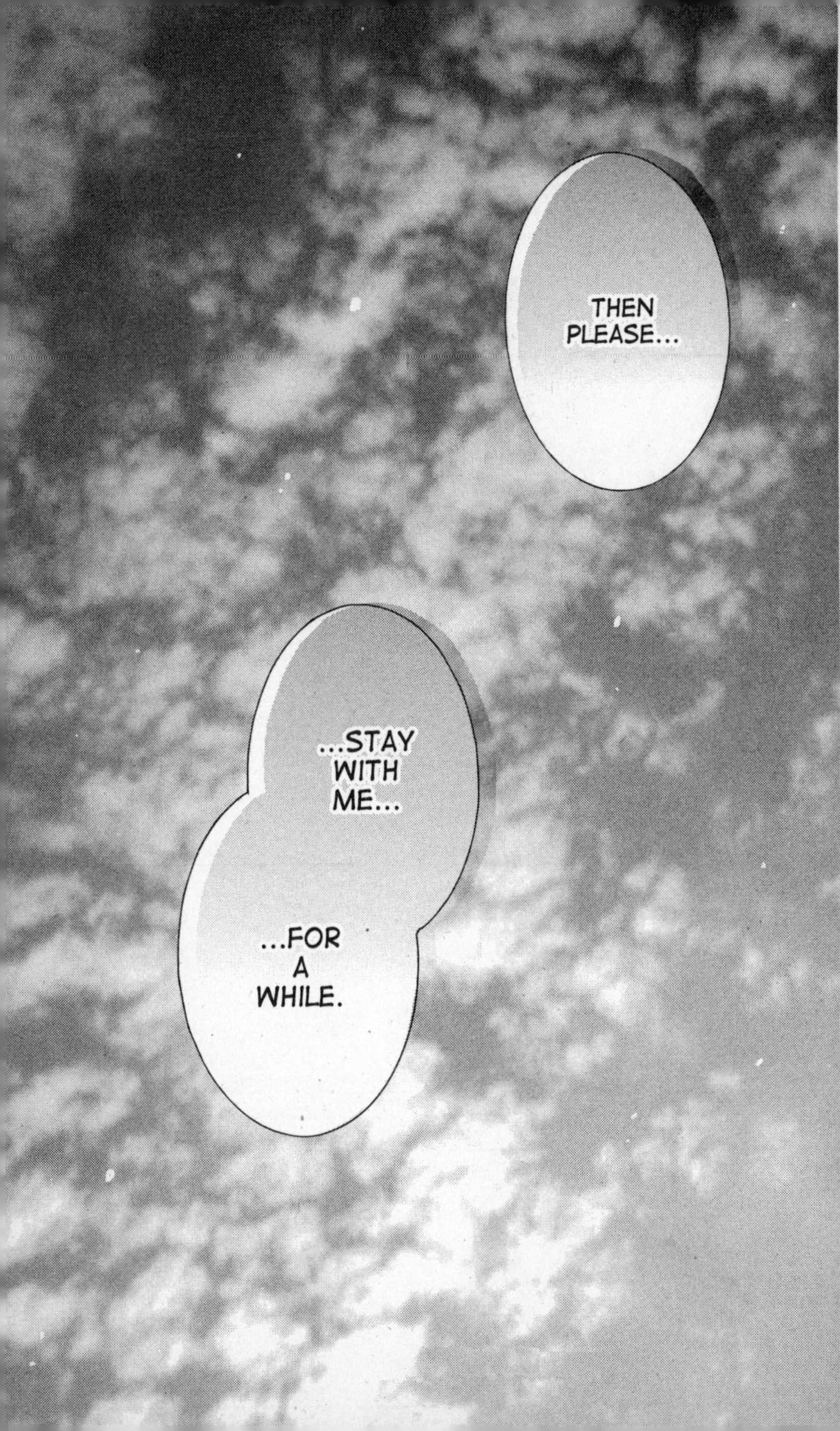
THEN PLEASE...
...STAY WITH ME...
...FOR A WHILE.

Seikei Academy Uniform

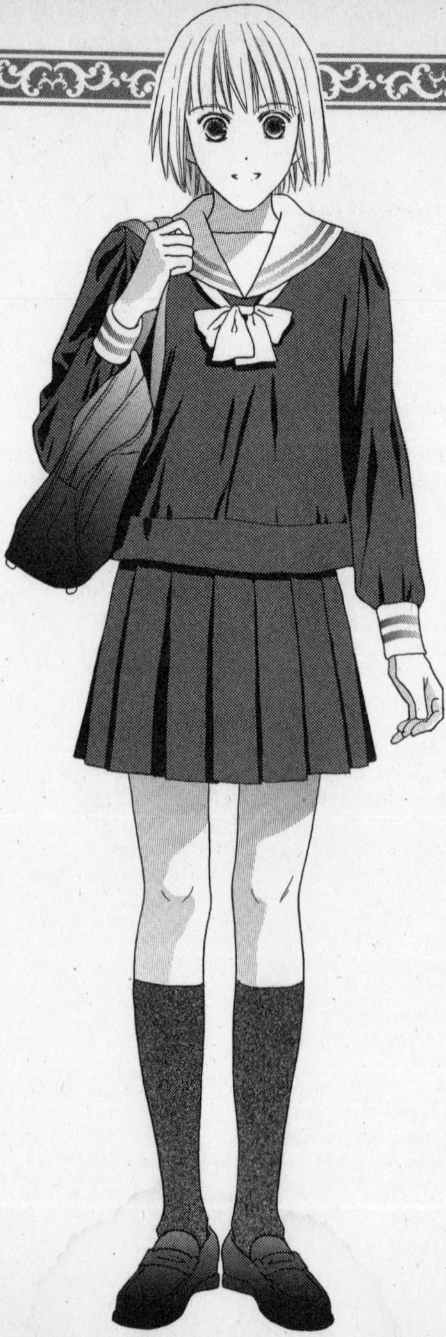

Navy Sailor

I wanted to make the uniform like those of a private academy (it's to my taste, too), so I made the uniforms this way. But nowadays, most schools have blazers instead, and I was aghast that there were very few photo materials available. (I should've realized earlier.)

Two Lines

There has to be two lines on the collar.

But it takes time to cut the screen tone, so we use a tone of two lines with the same space between, and paste them. It's one of the procedures that my assistants hate.

Ribbon

White, red, striped, bow-tie. There are many different kinds of ribbons. But, when drawing the combination of sailor + tied ribbon, it was fairly (!!) difficult to keep a good balance, and I regretted it. (Too late.)

Skirt

You can choose a box pleated skirt or a pleated skirt. You can fully see the mangaka's capriciousness in this!!

Socks

There are school-certified navy knee socks. When loose socks were really popular, I liked knee socks, but I like loose socks now, too.

Glossary

Some high school experiences are universal. Others need a little more explanation. In these notes you will find interesting information to enhance your *Beauty Is the Beast* reading enjoyment.

Page 7, panel 2: Hokkaido Stew
TV commercials for "Hokkaido Stew" soup mix air during the winter. The mix is probably referenced because Eimi and Misao are speaking in Hokkaido dialect.

Page 8, panel 3: Kurume
Kurume is a city in Fukuoka prefecture, in northern Kyushu. Kurume is famous for its Tonkotsu ramen.

Page 9, panel 1: Hanten
Hanten are short, padded coats worn indoors. They aren't the coolest fashion statement for high school girls, but sometimes comfort takes priority.

Page 11, author note: Showa and Heisei era
The Showa era was 1926-1988 and the Heisei era is the current era, which began in 1989.

Page 15, panel 2: Yakuza
Japanese mafia. There are three types of yakuza—tekiya (street peddlers), bakuto (gamblers), and gurentai (hoodlums). Wanibuchi would probably fall into the gurentai category, which is modeled after American gangsters like Al Capone.

Page 20, panel 3: Intense like a potter
Potters stare intently into the kiln where their goods are baking, much like Eimi is staring at her sweet potato.

Page 22, panel 1: *Kita no Kuni kara*
This drama was about a divorced father and his two young children who relocate to Hokkaido, and their everyday experiences. The title means "Secret from the Northern Country." The show aired in 1998, and was 2 episodes long.

Page 47, author note: Sadako
The evil girl in the Japanese movie *Ringu*. In the English adaptation, *The Ring*, the character's name is Samara.

Page 76, panel 3: Earpicks
Like Q-tips, but usually made of bamboo and not thrown out with every use. Some earpicks are decorated with good luck charms and other figures.

Page 104, panel 4: Kusudama
Kusudama are origami paper balls used for festivities, decoration, good luck, and protection against illness. The larger versions are broken open to start off a celebration, while the smaller ones are given as gifts and worn as jewelry on holidays. The word Kusudama means "medicine ball," and they are sometimes filled with aromatic and medicinal herbs.

Page 115, panel 1: Negi
Negi are Japanese green onions, similar to leeks found in American stores, but the white part of the stalk is longer and the green leaves are not as tough.

Page 122, panel 4: Nosebleed
Simone might have hit his nose in the fall, but in manga nosebleeds have special meaning, signifying that the character is in the grip of a powerful lust.

Page 150, panel 3: Tenosynovitis
The swelling of the tendons and tendon sheath, which can be caused by repetitive stress. Carpal Tunnel Syndrome is a type of tenosynovitis. Other causes include rheumatism and infection.

Page 167, panel 2: Nagasaki Castella
Castella is a type of cake introduced to Japan by the Portuguese in the 16th century. Originally, it was made with equal parts flour, sugar, and eggs, but over the years other ingredients have been introduced. Nagasaki is famous for its Castella.

Page 167, panel 3: Ningyoyaki
These cakes are baked in molds of various shapes, including faces and animals, and filled with sweet red bean paste.

Page 196, panel 1: Yakitori
Grilled chicken on skewers. A popular street vendor food.

Page 166, panel 3: Hiroyuki Otaka
A beauty expert who writes articles about make-up for women's magazines in Japan.

Page 172, panel 3: BONK
In Japanese, bonking someone behind the knees with your knees to make them buckle is called hiza kakkun. Hiza means "knees" and kakkun is the noise their crumpling knees make.

Page 174, panel 3: Yamashita gravestone
In Japan, families are typically interred in individual urns under the same gravestone.

Page 182, panel 5: An auspicious day
In Japan, this is said when congratulating someone on a special event such as a wedding or birth.

Tomo Matsumoto was born
on January 8th in Osaka
and made the switch from
nurse to mangaka with her
debut story *"Nemuru Hime"*
(Sleeping Princess) in *Lunatic
LaLa* magazine in 1995.
Her other works include
Kiss, a series about piano
lessons and love, *23:00*, a
book about street dancing,
and *Eikaiwa School Wars*
(English School Wars), which
is currently serialized in
LaLa Monthly magazine. Ms.
Matsumoto loves dancing
and taking English lessons.

BEAUTY IS THE BEAST
Vol. 4
The Shojo Beat Manga Edition

STORY & ART BY
TOMO MATSUMOTO

English Translation & Adaptation/Tomo Kimura
Touch-up & Lettering/Inori Fukuda Trant
Graphics & Cover Design/Yukiko Whitley
Editor/Pancha Diaz

Managing Editor/Megan Bates
Director of Production/Noboru Watanabe
Vice President of Publishing/Alvin Lu
Vice President & Editor in Chief/Yumi Hoashi
Sr. Director of Acquisitions/Rika Inouye
Vice President of Sales & Marketing/Liza Coppola
Publisher/Hyoe Narita

Bijo ga Yaju by Tomo Matsumoto © Tomo Matsumoto 2004. All rights reserved.
First published in Japan in 2004 by HAKUSENSHA, Inc., Tokyo. English language
translation rights in America and Canada arranged with HAKUSENSHA, Inc.,
Tokyo. The BEAUTY IS THE BEAST logo is a trademark of VIZ Media, LLC. The
stories, characters and incidents mentioned in this publication are entirely fictional.

No portion of this book may be reproduced or transmitted in any form or by any
means without written permission from the copyright holders.

Printed in Canada

Published by VIZ Media, LLC
P.O. Box 77010
San Francisco, CA 94107

Shojo Beat Manga Edition
10 9 8 7 6 5 4 3 2 1
First printing, August 2006

PARENTAL ADVISORY
BEAUTY IS THE BEAST is rated T for Teen
and is recommended for ages 13 and up.
It contains mature situations.

store.viz.com

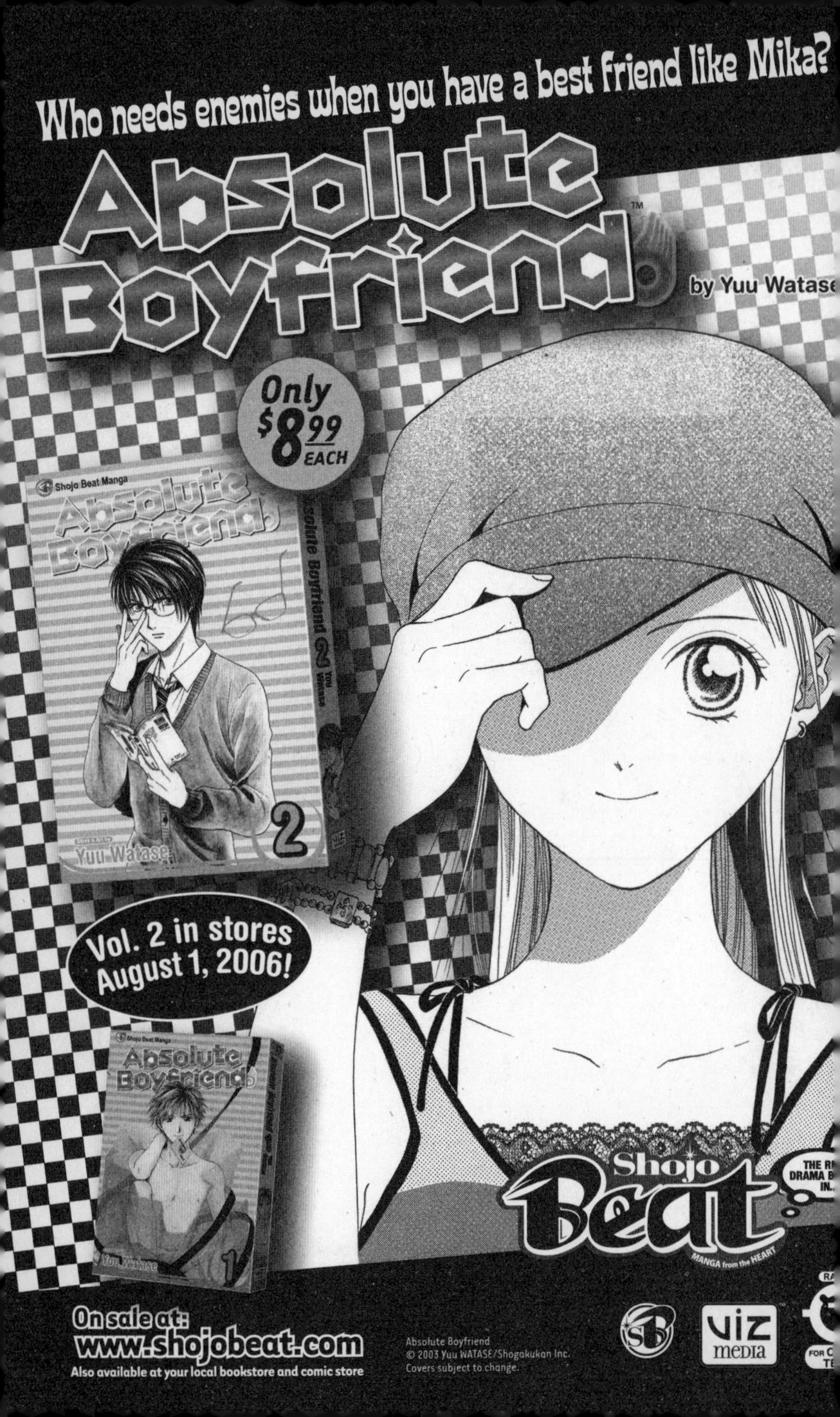

Who needs enemies when you have a best friend like Mika?
Absolute Boyfriend™
by Yuu Watase
Only $8.99 EACH
Shojo Beat Manga
Absolute Boyfriend
Absolute Boyfriend 2 Yuu Watase
2
Yuu Watase
Vol. 2 in stores August 1, 2006!
Shojo Beat Manga
Absolute Boyfriend
Yuu Watase
1
Shojo Beat
MANGA from the HEART
On sale at:
www.shojobeat.com
Also available at your local bookstore and comic store
Absolute Boyfriend
© 2003 Yuu WATASE/Shogakukan Inc.
Covers subject to change.
VIZ media

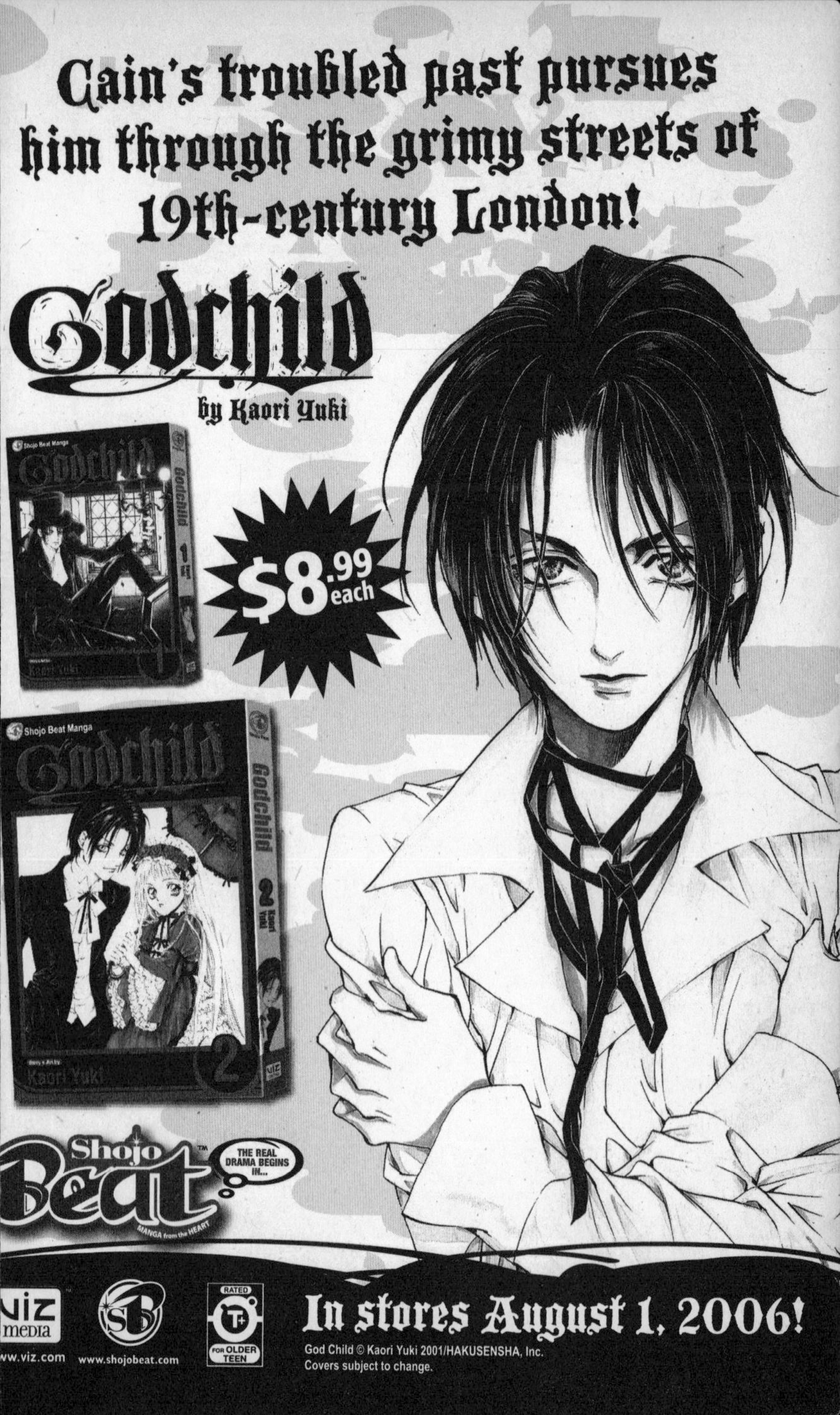
Cain's troubled past pursues him through the grimy streets of 19th-century London!
Godchild
by Kaori Yuki
Shojo Beat Manga
Godchild
1
Kaori Yuki
$8.99 each
Shojo Beat Manga
Godchild
2
Story & Art by
Kaori Yuki
Shojo Beat
THE REAL DRAMA BEGINS IN...
MANGA from the HEART
VIZ media
www.viz.com
www.shojobeat.com
RATED T+ FOR OLDER TEEN
In stores August 1, 2006!
God Child © Kaori Yuki 2001/HAKUSENSHA, Inc.
Covers subject to change.

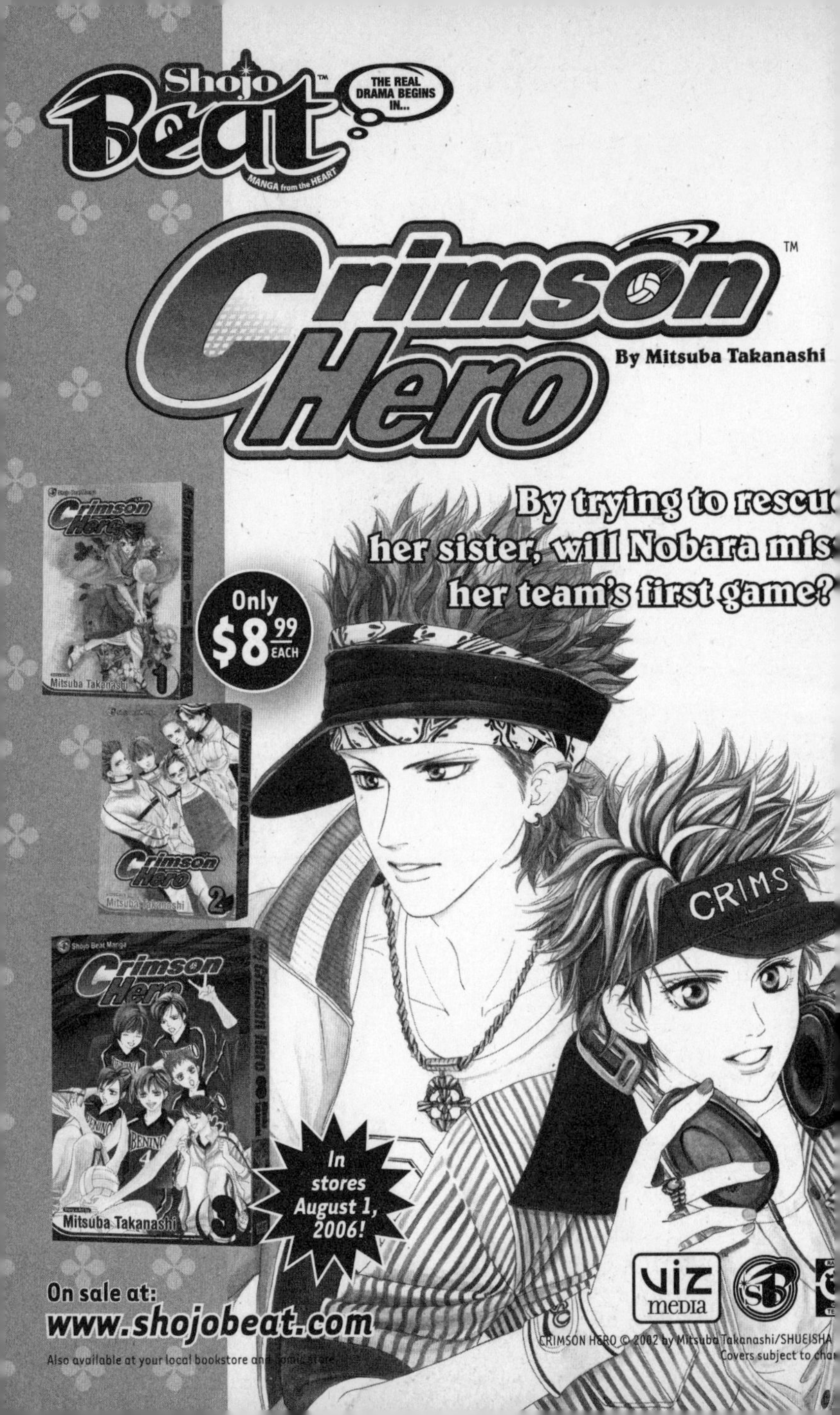
Shojo Beat™
THE REAL DRAMA BEGINS IN...
MANGA from the HEART
Crimson Hero™
By Mitsuba Takanashi
By trying to rescu
her sister, will Nobara mis
her team's first game?
Only $8.99 EACH
Crimson Hero
Mitsuba Takanashi
1
Crimson Hero
Mitsuba Takanashi
2
Shojo Beat Manga
Crimson Hero
Mitsuba Takanashi
3
In stores August 1, 2006!
CRIMS
On sale at:
www.shojobeat.com
Also available at your local bookstore and comic store.
viz media
CRIMSON HERO © 2002 by Mitsuba Takanashi/SHUEISHA
Covers subject to cha

SB

Tell us what you think about Shojo Beat Manga!

Our survey is now available online. Go to:

shojobeat.com/mangasurvey

Help us make our product offerings better!

viz media

Shojo **Beat**

THE REAL DRAMA BEGINS IN...

MANGA from the HEART

FULL MOON WO SAGASHITE © 2001 by Arina Tanemura/SHUEISHA Inc.
Fushigi Yûgi: Genbu Kaiden © 2004 Yuu WATASE/Shogakukan Inc.
Ouran Koko Host Club © Bisco Hatori 2002/HAKUSENSHA, Inc.

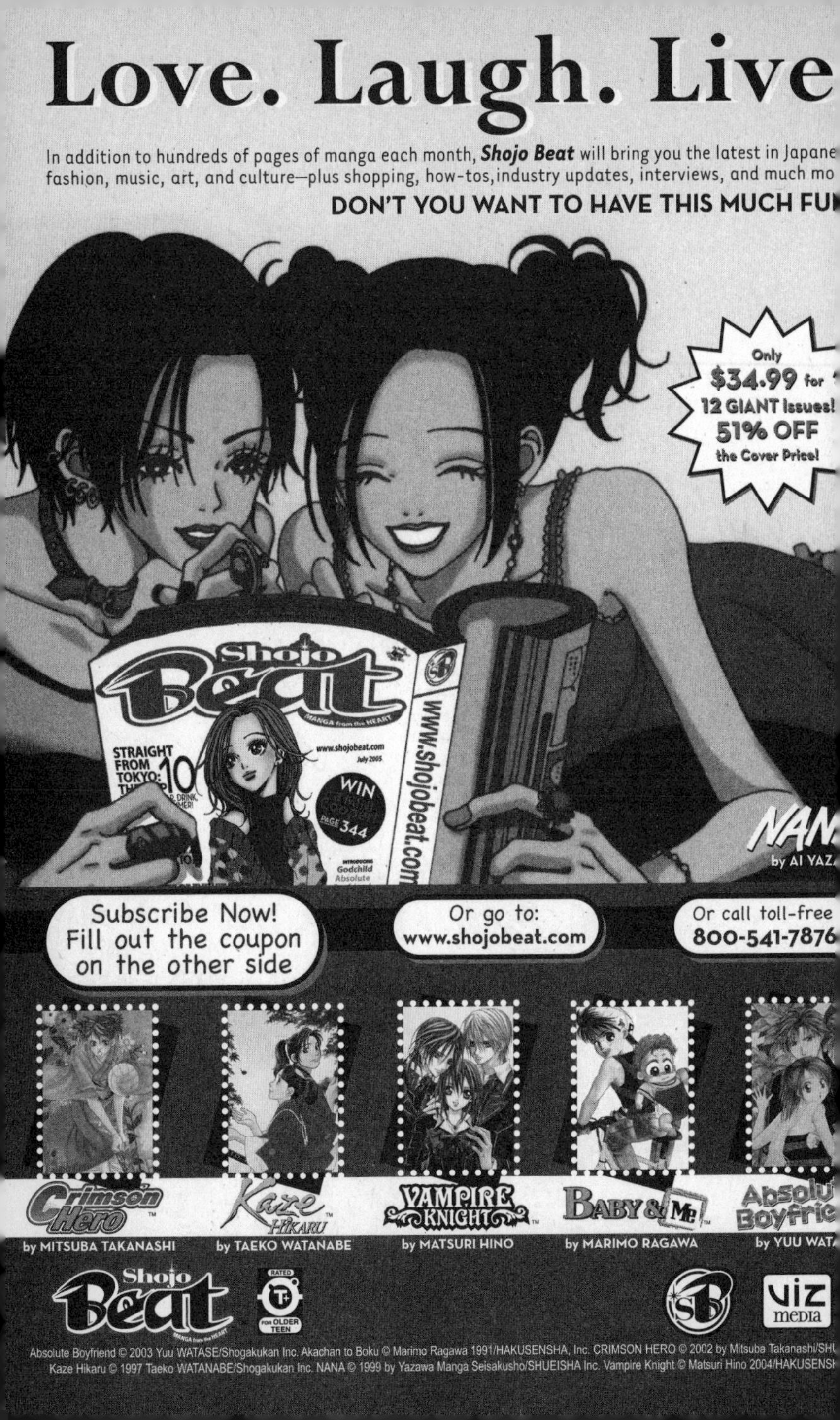
Love. Laugh. Live
In addition to hundreds of pages of manga each month, Shojo Beat will bring you the latest in Japane
fashion, music, art, and culture—plus shopping, how-tos, industry updates, interviews, and much mo
DON'T YOU WANT TO HAVE THIS MUCH FU
Only $34.99 for 12 GIANT Issues! 51% OFF the Cover Price!
Shojo Beat
MANGA from the HEART
www.shojobeat.com
July 2005
STRAIGHT FROM TOKYO: 10
WIN
PAGE 344
Godchild
Absolute
www.shojobeat.com
NANA
by AI YAZ
Subscribe Now! Fill out the coupon on the other side
Or go to: www.shojobeat.com
Or call toll-free 800-541-7876
Crimson Hero
by MITSUBA TAKANASHI
Kaze Hikaru
by TAEKO WATANABE
VAMPIRE KNIGHT
by MATSURI HINO
BABY & Me
by MARIMO RAGAWA
Absolu Boyfrie
by YUU WAT
Shojo Beat
MANGA from the HEART
RATED T+ FOR OLDER TEEN
viz media
Absolute Boyfriend © 2003 Yuu WATASE/Shogakukan Inc. Akachan to Boku © Marimo Ragawa 1991/HAKUSENSHA, Inc. CRIMSON HERO © 2002 by Mitsuba Takanashi/SHU
Kaze Hikaru © 1997 Taeko WATANABE/Shogakukan Inc. NANA © 1999 by Yazawa Manga Seisakusho/SHUEISHA Inc. Vampire Knight © Matsuri Hino 2004/HAKUSENSH

Save OVER 50% OFF the cover price!

Six of the most addictive Shojo Manga from Japan: Nana, Baby & Me, Absolute Boyfriend (by superstar creator Yuu Watase!!), and more! Plus the latest on what's happening in Japanese fashion, music, and culture!

Save 51% OFF the cover price PLUS enjoy all the benefits of the 🅢 Sub Club with your paid subscription - your issues delivered first, exclusive access to ShojoBeat.com, and gifts mailed with some issues.

only
$34⁹⁹
for 12 HUGE issues!

☑ **YES!** Please enter my 1-year subscription (12 GIANT issues) to *Shojo Beat* at the special subscription rate of only $34.99 and sign me up for the 🅢 Sub Club.

NAME

ADDRESS

CITY   **STATE**   **ZIP**

E-MAIL ADDRESS   **P5GN03**

☐ **MY CHECK, PAYABLE TO SHOJO BEAT, IS ENCLOSED**

CREDIT CARD: ☐ **VISA**   ☐ **MASTERCARD**

RATED
T+
FOR OLDER TEEN

ACCOUNT #   **EXP. DATE**

SIGNATURE

☐ **BILL ME LATER PLEASE**

CLIP AND MAIL TO ➤
SHOJO BEAT
Subscriptions Service Dept.
P.O. Box 438
Mount Morris, IL 61054-0438

Canada add $12 US. No foreign orders. Allow 6-8 weeks for delivery.